Emanuel Schreiber

Reformed Judaism and Its Pioneers

A contribution to its history

Emanuel Schreiber

Reformed Judaism and Its Pioneers
A contribution to its history

ISBN/EAN: 9783337295905

Printed in Europe, USA, Canada, Australia, Japan

Cover: Foto ©ninafisch / pixelio.de

More available books at **www.hansebooks.com**

Dr. ABRAHAM GEIGER.

Born May 24th, 1810, at Frankfort-on-the-Main.
Died October 23d, 1874, at Berlin.

REFORMED JUDAISM

AND

ITS PIONEERS.

A Contribution to Its History.

BY

DR. EMANUEL SCHREIBER,
Rabbi, Congregation Emann El, Spokane, Washington.

———

"Irrevocable as is the victory of the liberty and civilization of the Jews, is the Reform." (Zunz: Gottesdienstliche Vortraege. p. 481.)

———

SPOKANE, WASHINGTON,
SPOKANE PRINTING COMPANY,
1892.

TO THE

MEMORY OF MY THREE TEACHERS,

MY DEAR FATHER,

HERMAN SCHREIBER,

MY GRANDFATHER,

LEVI SCHREIBER,

OF

LEIPNIK MAEHREN,

AND

REV. DR. ABRAHAM GEIGER,

WHOSE NOBLE TEACHINGS HAVE INFLUENCED MY WAY

OF THINKING, IN DEEP APPRECIATION AND

GRATITUDE THIS VOLUME IS LOV-

INGLY DEDICATED,

BY THE AUTHOR.

PREFACE.

I present this book to the public in general and to the American Jews—the name Jew is our only historically justifiable name—in particular.

It is a fact that the public at large knows little or nothing concerning "Reform-Judaism." As to the Jews themselves, the majority have a most superficial knowledge of the subject-matter. Some know of it only from the slanderous attacks heaped upon it by the orthodox press. Others have the notion that a disregard for effete religious ceremonies and a denial of exploded dogmas is all that Reform-Judaism stands for. The fact, however, is that Reform-Judaism is not merely destructive, but also constructive, as readers of this book will find.

The idea to write such a work occupied my mind already fifteen years ago while Rabbi in Germany. My sense of justice was aroused whenever I had occasion to read the eleventh volume of Graetz' "History of the Jews." The way the Jewish Reform movement and its representatives are treated there is so contemptible, that a man who loves truth and hates falsehood must throw away with disgust and loathing such a miserable apology of "history." The whole volume is a tissue of falsehood, slander and petty invectives against the ablest and best Jewish men of this century. The pen which wrote the eleventh volume of Graetz' "History" was not prompted by love of justice and truth, but by jealousy, envy and intentional meanness. That volume is not history, but a falsification of history, a pasquinade, through which its author has forfeited the name of a historian. I have proven this by incontrovertible evidence in my book: "Graetz' Geschichtsbauerei"

(Berlin, 1881, Wilhelm Issleib). In 108 pages I have demonstrated by copious extracts from Graetz' "History," that *not religious motives*, but *personal spite* and jealousy were the ruling powers of Graetz' unjustifiable and mean attacks against the Jewish Reform-movement and its pioneers. I have asserted and proven that "die Tendenz des elften Bandes der Graetz-schen Geschichte der Tendenz des ersten und zweiten Bandes derselben Geschichte diametral entgegengesetzt ist." (The tendency of the eleventh volume of Graetz' history is diametrically opposed to the tendency of the first and second volumes of the same history. See page 108 of my "Graetz' Geschichtsbauerei.") In the first two volumes Graetz denies the belief in revelation, miracles, and treats the patriarchs, Joseph, etc., as legendary heroes. In the eleventh volume he condemns the most innocent Reforms like the "organ" in the Synagogue, confirmation, in a manner worthy of the Rabbi Jacob Joseph, of the Russian Congregations in New York.—I said then what I repeat now. "Ich seh euch zweierlei Gesichter zeigen, eins darunter ist nothwendig falsch." (I see you, sir, bearing two faces, one of which is necessarily false.)

I challenged Graetz or his disciples to refute my arguments, *if they could*, adding however, that such a thing would be hardly possible considering the fact that I quoted Graetz' own words for the purpose of strengthening my evidence.* Instead of proofs and arguments, however, they answered with mean invectives and personal abuse, which since time immemorial was the only weapon of cowardice. My book has ever since been extensively quoted and referred to by writers on Jewish history, who agreed with my views.

Some people may think that I had a personal grudge against Graetz, and that my views on his "historiography" are prejudiced and not shared by authori-

---

* "Wer mit Gruenden widerlegen kann der thue es. Ob diess im vorliegenden Falle ueberhaupt moeglich ist, nachdem wir immer Graetz' eigene Worte als Beweis zitirten, wird abzuwarten sein" (ibidem).

ties. I therefore feel impelled to declare, that I never met Graetz, never wrote to him, in fact never had the least personal reason to attack him. Love of truth, justice and fair play alone are the motives of my criticism.

Now it would make no difference at all, whether other renowned scientists and historians agree or disagree with me on the subject. For *truth and one are a majority*. In fact majorities are not often found on the side of truth, as falsehood and hypocrisy pay better.

Still, for the sake of those who have no confidence in their own sound judgment, I quote some authorities.

Abraham Geiger has the following to say on "Graetz' History of the Jews:" "To my regret I must confess, that the work is by no means entitled to the pretense of being the product of genuine historiography and research. For I would greet with true joy a really good work on Jewish history. The work contains histories, which are loosely connected, but no history. We miss the development and the moving force. While I dislike an artificial pragmatism, I cannot favor a history utterly devoid of ideas. Now, Graetz' history has no beginning, how can it rest on a foundation? It is a peculiar proceeding, indeed, to begin a history with the fourth volume, to have it followed by the third, then the fifth. And what do we hear concerning the character of the Talmud, the Mishnah, the Boraithas, the Gemarahs? A mass of names, which are, after all, entirely indifferent to us. The religious conception of the epoch in its totality, the legal-religious character, the development of these periods are hardly touched upon. Thus the whole history of the later time remains incomprehensible. We notice painfully the absence of the dignity of historical treatment, of that consecration, which lifts up the historian when about to present a grand picture of humanity."—(See Geiger's Zeitschrift, IV, p. 146-150, VI, pp. 220, 221, 222, 291). "Graetz is utterly wanting in historical intuition and intellect which can master the material."

(Posthumous Works, V, pp. 293-294) "is a charlatan
of the first water" (ibid. 257).   "Heine and Boerne
are treated in the eleventh volume worthy of Graetz"
(ibid. 329). Mommsen, the greatest living German historian calls Graetz' "Talmudistic" historiography "a literary corner."   Prof. Bresslau compares him with
Onno Klopp.   Dr. Bamberger calls him the "Stoecker
of the Synagogue."   Dr. Oppenheim, Prof. Cohen,
Marburg, Claude Montefiore, Emil Lehman, Prof. Neubauer, Dr. Felsenthal, Chicago, Prof. Ewald, Goettingen, Dr. Kohler, New York, Prof. Ludwig Geiger, Dr.
Leopold Loew, Szegedin, Prof. Lazarus, in Berlin, and
numerous other Jewish scholars have expressed similar
views on Graetz' historiography.   The Rev. Dr. Gut-
heim had the following to say on Graetz' eleventh volume of his history: "It is a source of general regret,
that the learned author descended from his exalted
standpoint, by passing judgment on events and persons
that are within the memory of men still living, in the
spirit of bitter partisanship."   (Translation of the
fourth volume of Graetz' "History of the Jews," New
York, 1873.)

But the wrong inflicted on the leaders of our Reform-movement by Graetz' misleading statements can
only be corrected by an unbiased historiography.   The
following nine chapters are an earnest attempt to set
aright before the people the men who were partly slandered, partly ignored, or belittled by Graetz.

"Unschuldig Verurtheilten zu ihren Rechte
verhelfen ist die groesste Mizvah, die man ueben
kann." †

I originally intended to publish the work in German, but having removed from Bonn to this country I
concluded to write it in English, the more so, as no
work of this kind exists in the English language. *

---

* To set aright before the eyes of the world those men who were
innocently condemned, is one of the noblest acts.   (See my Graetz'
Geschichtsbauerei, p. IV, preface).

† H. S. Morais' "Eminent Israelites of the Nineteenth Century"
has a few pages on Holdheim and Geiger.

My special thanks are due to Dr. Immanuel Ritter, Phoebus Philippsohn, and Leopold Loew. Their writings on Friedlaender, Salomon, Chorin and Holdhave greatly assisted me, although I had not seldom occasion to disagree with them on important points.

Prof. Ludwig Geiger, Prof. M. Lazarus, in Berlin, and Dr. Immanuel Loew in Szegedin encouraged me in different ways, and considered the idea of publishing a work of this kind a most happy one.

Should God grant me health and strength I shall publish several more volumes of this kind, and conclude the work with a complete "History of the Jewish Reform-movement to the Present Day."

Those who are afraid that the great influx of Jews from Russia and Poland will retard the progress of the Reform-movement in this country, I refer to chapter VII of this book. There they will learn that "Holdheim," one of the greatest of Reform-Rabbis, hailed from Kempen, which is even to-day a hot-bed of Polish orthodoxy. Let us trust in the power of the spirit. It will conquer in the end.

I have consistently refrained from writing the biographies of men who still live, labor and help to make history. While opinions may differ on the subject, and the remark of a friend, that a little "taffy" during lifetime is preferable to a large dose of "epitaphy," may contain more truth than poetry, yet I consider my principle good. As long as men's lives are not concluded, we cannot pass a final judgment on them. Men and circumstances are too much subject to change. Biographies of living men, particularly when they are influential, are as a rule eulogies, hence worthless. Bissmarck, for instance, in the last few years, after his fall, has shown traits of character which were utterly unknown to his biographers of former years.

My special thanks are due and cheerfully offered to the following men, who have taken special pains to further the publication of this book: Hon. Jacob Schiff, New York, Hon. Julius Rosenthal, Attorney-at-Law, Chicago, Rabbis M. Samfield, of Memphis, Bien, of

Vicksburg, Bogen and Goldschmidt, of Greenville, Leucht, of New Orleans, Cohen, of Mobile, Berkowitz, of Kansas City, Grechter, of Milwaukee, Felsenthal and Isaac Moses, of Chicago, Bloch, of Portland, Freudenthal, of Trinidad, Charles Weil, Pres. Congregation, Pine Bluff, B. Wolf, of Fort Smith and Congregations of Denver, Los Angeles, Little Rock and Spokane.

I also acknowledge with pleasure, that Messrs. Ansell & Reeves, of the Spokane Printing Company, have from beginning to end, in every possible way assisted me in the publication of this work. I can conscientiously recommend them to my friends.

In thus giving the history of this publication, I must also add an information, without which this history would not be complete. It might be asked, and not a few of my friends have asked the question, why I had not given this book to the "Jewish Publication Society of America," the apparent purpose of which, in accord with its Constitution, is to encourage American-Jewish writers. In my own justification I must make a statement. On June 1st, 1889, I proposed to send my manuscript to the "J. P. S." But no answer came. I waited patiently several months, but no answer came. I addressed at last, in December of the same year, a personal letter to the President of the Society, Mr. Morris Newburger, politely requesting him to see to it, that my letter is answered and my manuscript is asked for. He, like an honest, straightforward man, who knows no duplicity, replied at once, and the Secretary of the Society requested me to send the manuscript, which I did. This was in January, 1890, at a time when not yet one book of the Society was published. Again no answer came. In June of the same year a Convention of the Society was held. Not even mention of my manuscript was made there. Dr. Felsenthal, *a member of the Publication Committee*, told me in July in Chicago, that not only has he not been informed during all this time, of the existence of my manuscript, but even while in Philadelphia at the Convention, no intimation was made to him about it.

And yet, as a member of the Publication Committee, the manuscript, or part of it, ought to have been sent to him. At the Convention in June it was carried, in the face of a strong opposition, that the J. P. S. should reprint Graetz's "History," while not even mention was made of my manuscript, notwithstanding the fact, that I had offered it twelve months before the Convention met. Although disgusted, I addressed once more a letter to the President, Mr. Newburger, telling him in plain language my candid opinion about the business methods of the Publication Committee.* I intimated that it was controled by satellites of Graetz, who would like to suppress the publication of my book, because I dared to criticise a historiography, which an authority like *Mommsen* designated as a "literary corner;" because I showed up in his true light a so-called historian, whom Geiger styled as "a charlatan and swindler of the first water" (Geiger, Nachgel-Schriften, Vol. V, p. 257). How right I was in my supposition is proven by the following answer of Mr. Newburger:

Philadelphia, July 21st, 1890.

Dr. E. Schreiber,

Little Rock, Ark.

"My dear Doctor :—Pressure of business and absence from the city must serve as my excuse for not answering your favor of the 15th ult. sooner.

I have carefully read your letter and will keep it before me. Just now, when Graetz's first volume is under consideration, the time for urging your book is unpropitious. —Dr. Felsenthal, of Chicago, stands very high with his

---

* I repeat again that I have no fault whatever to find with the President, Mr. Newburger. He acted from beginning to end like a MAN. It is the Committee I blame, which, lacking the courage to say openly that it would not publish Reform literature, made use of the unmanly weapon of disgusting procrastination. The fact is, the Publishing Committee of the J. P. S. is controled by two or three men who are enemies of Reform, while the J. P. S. is supported financially by people, 95 per cent. of whom are Reformers. Such a state of affairs is, to say the least, ridiculous in the extreme.

colleagues in the committee, and it may be well for you
to correspond with him on the subject.   In the meantime why not organize a local committee   *   * and
add as many as possible to the membership of the J. P.
S. ?   I am sure that a good effort on your part in *that
direction* would be appreciated by all. If you are willing
to accept the post, I shall be very glad to appoint you
Chairman of the Committee for your District.

I remain,

Yours sincerely,

MORRIS NEWBURGER."

This letter is indeed instructive.   It tells in so
many words that a Society, started ostensibly for the
purpose of encouraging home talent, would not publish
a book which *criticises falsifications of our history.* The
fact that I entered into correspondence with the Society
a year before Graetz's English reprint was under consideration, is of course of no consequence whatever
with a committee which is controled by open and secret
enemies of Reform-Judaism, who would, if they could,
suppress every free word.   Of course, at a time when
Graetz' publication is under consideration, it would not
be "propitious" to urge the publication of a book
which demonstrates beyond the shadow of a doubt
the fact that Graetz's historiography *is unreliable,
utterly wanting in historical intuition, and influenced by
personal spite and bitter partisanship.*   The President of
the J. P. S. deserves the credit of being candid in ex-
posing the policy governing the Society, which
CLAIMS to encourage American authors.

That the honorable President meant well, is further proven by his advice to correspond with Dr. Felsenthal, "who stands very high with his colleagues" in
the committee.   It shows how high he stands, when he
was not considered worth while to be informed of what
was going on in the Society.   But this passage is interesting for another reason.   Hear ye then.   It is not

the ability and worth of a publication which recommends it. The author must try and influence the members of the committee. I think if Dr. Felsenthal had been shown my manuscript he would not have objected to its publication. When in Chicago he recommended my work on the strength of his knowledge of my literary activity, and personally induced his Chicago friends to subscribe for my book. Twelve years ago, in a review in the "Zeitgeist" of my "Selbstkritik der Juden," * Felsenthal among other things said: "Dr. Schreiber, the author, is Rabbi in Bonn, and belongs to the few German Rabbis of the present who do not consider it as their whole life's work to indulge in archaeological, philological and literary historical studies, but who express honestly their convictions and who do not covertly keep it back and hypocritically deny it or turn it into the contrary. He is one of those who are active for the progress of Jewish life, and for its purification." †

No doubt just for this very reason, that the opponents of Reform in the Committee knew of Felsenthal's opinions about me, his honest, outspoken views on Reform-Judaism, and his hatred of hypocrisy, underhanded work and duplicity, they shrewdly concealed from him everything relating to my manuscript. For they know full well that Felsenthal is on record as holding the same views on Graetz's disgraceful historiography as are held by Geiger and other honest historians of renown.

I can give names of other members of the Publication Committee who live nearer Philadelphia, and yet were never informed of the existence of my manuscript. Shame on such business methods !

---

* Berlin, 1880 Carl Duncker, 160 pages. This is one of the very few Jewish books which made after nine years a second edition necessary. It was republished in Leipzig, 1889, by F. Wilhelm Friedrich, Hofbuchdrucker. This book was quoted copiously in the German "Reichstag" by Professor Haenel, one of the leaders of the "Fortschrittspartei."

† Dr. Felsenthal of Chicago, on Dr. Schreiber's "Selbstkritik der Juden," Zeitgeist of August 5th, 1880, page 253.

But the most interesting part of the letter is the end. For there a distant hope is held out, that an effort to get a number of subscribers might possibly induce the Committee to publish my book.*

It is needless to say that after this letter I peremptorily demanded back my manuscript.   But my book is published, and may the unbiased reader judge for himself whether it deserved such treatment at the hands of the J. P. S.   Let those who have read the publications of the J. P. S. impartially compare my book with those, and I am not afraid of their honest verdict.   I call for their unbiased judgment, because I have greater confidence in the *vox populi* than in a Publication Committee which is apparently controled by people who have personal axes to grind, who are influenced by partisanship, bigotry, and that petty spirit of inquisition which has created in Rome an "*Index librorum prohibitorum.*"   There are men in the Committee of the so-called Jewish Publication Society of *America*† who would to-day suppress a reformatory publication, just as was done by that hypocrite S. A. Tiktin in Breslau, who, like a censor of the Inquisition, prohibited the Jewish printer Sulzbach from publishing M. Brueck's "Rabbinical Ceremonies" (1836), because cant and hypocrisy *were unmasked in that book.*   But Brueck's book was published after all in Breslau,‡ and was the indirect cause of breaking Tiktin's influence. Hypocrisy and Jesuitism are, thank God, rapidly losing ground in America, and its main representatives are being shelved by their own Congregations.

---

* Such a principle might be excusable in political organizations, where the "workers" for the party are rewarded with offices. A Publication Society ought to reward ability and ideal work, and nothing else.

† Lucus a non lucendo.   For in reality it suppresses American Jewish literature, and goes begging to England for rehashing of old matter. Just because the "Society" published Graetz's history, the Committee ought to have given the other side a chance to express its views.   This would have been fair play, truly American.   As it is, the "Society" is un-American, an English branch.

‡ See page 290 of this book.

And so go out into the cold world, thou, my beloved book! Many a sleepless night and many a troublesome day thou hast caused me. * Being a child of truth thou hast met, like thy mother, with many enemies, even before thy birth. Many are they who wanted to strangle thee before thy birth. For eight gloomy weeks I mourned thee as dead,* and with the prophet of old I cried: "So have I then labored in vain, and for years wasted my strength for nothing." But, thank God, thou wast found again. Thou goest on a great journey, on thy own merits. Thou art not backed by the name of a leading publisher. This, my dear child, requires money in this great country. A Society, which ought to have taken pleasure in introducing thee has neglected this duty. "The watchmen, instead of caring for thee smote thee and took away thy veil." And why? Because as the child of truth thou didst not learn to flatter, to cringe, "LO JADAATI ACHANEF," and because thou didst not learn to call "good evil and evil good, sweet bitter and bitter sweet." Thou wilt have a rocky road to travel on this account. For only the good people love truth, and they are, alas, in the minority. And yet, thy mission is enviable. For " truth is the seal of God " *Chothmo Shel Hakadosh Boruch Hoo Emess.* Thy purpose is noble. Thou metest out justice to those grand men in modern Israel, who were innocently persecuted, because they struggled in the cause of truth and light. "Happy then art thou, how pleasant is thy lot, how beautiful thy inheritance." The time will come when thy work will be recognized and appreciated.

SCHREIBER.

SPOKANE, WASH., February 25, 1892.

---

* The manuscript was lost, and by mere accident it was found again.

CONTENTS.

CONTENTS OF CHAPTERS.

CHAPTER I.

MOSES MENDELSSOHN.

Mendelssohn, though claimed by the Reformers and by the Conservatives, was neither a Reformer nor was he orthodox. He was a philosopher of the rationalistic type, but had no understanding for historical criticism. Hence the conflict in his teachings. Judaism for him was legalism. His translation of the Pentateuch into German causes a profound revolution in the Jewish religion. It opened to the Jews the treasure-house of modern thought, weakened the influence of Talmudism, and emancipated Judaism in Germany from the baneful control of Polish Rabbis. Mendelssohn's disciples, the "School of Biurists" demolish mountains of legal observances and usher in the new era.

CHAPTER II.

DAVID FRIEDLAENDER.

Reared under exceptionally favorable circumstances, he enjoys a happy youth. A better education of the Jews is his ideal. His intimacy with Mendelssohn. The "Salon," a literary center of Berlin's aristocracy, breaks through the social restraints that obstructed the intercourse of Jews and Gentiles. The "Free-school" (Freischule), non sectarian. Its influence in Germany and Austria. Friedlaender's first translation of the Hebrew Prayer-book into German caused a storm. His struggle for the emancipation of the Jews. He is no Jewish chauvinist. We are Jews, not by race, but by religion. Lazarus Bendavid, forerunner of radical Reform-Judaism. Graetz's falsification of modern Jewish history. Friedlaender's sensational letter to Teller. Other literary work. Friedlaender and Israel Jacobsohn. The Jacobsohn-Temple and the first German sermons in Berlin. The orthodox party alarmed at the great success of Reform in Berlin, denounces the Reformers to the Prussian government as innovators. Friedrich Wilhelm III. justly afraid lest a more attractive mode of worship among the Jews might diminish the number of Jewish converts to Christianity, pleases the orthodox Jews by closing the Reform-Temple. Wholesale apostasy of the better class of Jews in Berlin and other Prussian cities the consequence. "Society for Culture of the Jews" (Culturverein). Leopold Zunz. Political reaction and Judenhetze. Friedlaender honored.

CHAPTER III.

ISRAEL JACOBSOHN.

Jacobsohn, a self-made man. No scholar, but highly practical. A successful merchant and enthusiastic philanthropist. He begins the Reform with the school children. The "Jacobsohn School" and "Jacobsohn Temple" in Seesen erected by Jacobsohn at at cost of one hundred thousand dollars. First organ in a Jewish house of worship. Ritual Reforms. The German sermon in the Synagogue strongly opposed by orthodox Rabbis. Pijutim. The German sermon in America. The Hebrew language in the Synagogue. Dedication of the Temple in Seesen. Jacobsohn as a preacher. His energy. The Sanhedrin at Paris convoked by Napoleon, 1806, proves a farcical show, utterly void of principle, and hurtful to the cause of Judaism in France. The Central Jewish Consistory of France, as the result of the Sanhedrin, moulded on the pattern of the secular power, tinged with a semblance of Catholic hierarchy, is the cause of the religious stagnation of Judaism in France. French Jews atheistic, and at best indifferent the whole year, but orthodox on the Day of Atonement, i. e., Jewish Catholics or Catholic Jews. In the science and Reform of Judaism France is an unknown quantity. The little there is was done by German scholars. England, under the sway of Chief-Rabbis, offers the same spectacle. Wherever the Church is the subservient vassal of the State, hypocrisy and servility flourish and liberty of conscience is curtailed. Consistory in Cassel. First Confirmation of boys and girls in the Synagogue. Jacobsohn in Berlin. The closing by the police of his Temple breaks his heart. The centennial of Jacobsohn's birthday fittingly celebrated in Berlin, Halberstadt, Braunschweig and Seesen.   pp. 45-59.

— —

CHAPTER IV.

ARON CHORIN.

The Earldom of Maehren, a most prolific contributor to the science and history of modern Judaism. Moses Brueck, a forgotten radical Reformer. Chorin's youth. Unsuccessful in business. His preparation for the Rabbinate. Rabbi in Arad. His salary four florins weekly. His "jeshibah" (Rabbinical school). His eloquence as a preacher. His correspondence with the leaders of Judaism in Austria and Hungary. Mordechai Benet, the Moravian Land-Rabbi, calls him the "light and pillar of Israel." Chorin as a Reformer. He permits in his Congregation to eat of the sturgeon (fish). Other Rabbis declare it an "unclean fish." Ezechiel Landau on Chorin's side. Mordechai Benet turns against his former favorite Chorin. The literature on the sturgeon burnt. Chorin victor, but exposed to the enmity of unscrupulous fanatics. The Pressburg clique persecutes him. His book: "Reconciliation of Faith with Practical Life" (1803), advocates Reform, the study of philosophy, and attacks superstitious customs. Mordechai Benet insists on the burning of the heretical book, but Chorin is upheld by his Congregation. Disturbances in the Synagogue on the Sabbath of Penitence, when Chorin is cursed by an influential member of his Congregation (1804). Cho-

---

CHAPTER V.

GOTTHOLD SALOMON.

arbitrary measures. Salomon's twenty-fifth jubilee as a preacher.
Salomon the pioneer of German Jewish Homiletics. He frees the
Jewish sermon from the imitation of Christian preachers. His extensive travels. Salomon and the Rabbinical Conferences in Braunschweig, Frankfort and Breslau (1844-1846), in the interest of Reform. Abraham Geiger as instigator of those Conferences. Salomon as a member of the liturgical commission advocates strongly
the use of the vernacular in the main prayers. His seventieth birthday. His published sermons form a library. His farewell sermon
in 1857. His death in 1859. He was one of the last "Biurists." His
German translation of the Bible. Geiger speaks of him as "the first
and most eminent Jewish preacher," who has "made the Jewish sermon a power" which "now takes the first rank among the means of
religious edification."   pp. 94-163.

CHAPTER VI.

ABRAHAM KOHN.

His youth. He studies the Talmud in jeshibahs, and devoted
secretly his time to so-called profane studies. For two years he sleeps
only four hours a night. He lives on dry bread as a student in
Prague. In 1830 he dedicates the Synagogue in Pisek, Bohemia. In
1833 he is called as Rabbi to Hohenems, Tirol. As an enthusiastic
Reformer he contributes to Geiger's "Zeitschrift," comes out in
favor of the Hamburg Temple, and takes Geiger's part against Tiktin in Breslau. His success as a preacher and teacher. In 1844 his
misfortune calles him as "preacher and teacher" to the very large
Congregation in Lemberg. His school there is a most phenomenal
success. His missionary work as a Reformer in Galicia. The new
Temple (1846). The oppressive and disgraceful special taxation of
the Jews in Galicia. After hard and weary labors, Kohn succeedes
in abolishing the taxes on meat, candles, fish, a. s. f., although Jews
opposes the abolition from selfish motives, because they have a lease
on the taxes. Out of revenge they try to hurt Kohn in every possible way. Failing, however, in checking his growing popularity,
they make use of the despicable weapon of murder, by poisoning the
noble and good man. He dies the death of a martyr, in the cause of
Reform Judaism.   pp. 164-178.

CHAPTER VII.

SAMUEL HOLDHEIM.

In Holdheim can be seen the evolution from the lowest type of
orthodoxy to the extreme wing of radical Reform. This development is gradual. Graetz utterly fails to understand this, and hence
describes him as a "hypocrite" and "enemy of Judaism." When a
boy he is recognized as a Talmudical luminary. In Prague, as a
man in years, he sits down on a bench with young students in the
lecture room. As Rabbi in Frankfort, on the Oder he labors for
the recognition of Judaism by the Prussian government. He blames

form-Judaism. Holdheim's death. Dr. Sachs' contemptible fanaticism, as compared with old Rabbi Oettinger's tolerance relative to Holdheim's interment. Geiger is called to officiate at the funeral.

CHAPTER VIII.

LEOPOLD LOEW.

Born in Moravia of poor parents. Life in the Jeshibah. Hard study in all branches of knowledge. Immigration to Hungary. Rabbi of Nagy Kanizsa. Reform-Programme. Sermons in the Magyar tongue. Rabbi in Papa, 1846. Great troubles and struggles against fanaticism. Fair means and foul are used to make his stay there impossible. Loew's "Ben Chananja," a valuable monthly in the interest of Judaism. Loew takes prominent part in the Hungarian Revolution against the government. His revolutionary sermons masterpieces of pulpit oratory. He and his father-in-law, Rabbi Schwab, are imprisoned for weeks, and the only two prisoners who are not shot, and freed for "want of proofs." Loew for years under police surveillance. Red-tape in Austria and stupidity of government officials. The Hungarian Jewish school fund. The orthodoxy in Papa disappointed, that their Rabbi was not shot, attempt to supply the government with the "wanting proofs" and work for his re-arrest, but fail. Loew called as Rabbi of Szegedin, 1850. His Reform-programme. He enjoys peace and declines positions in Lemberg, Bruenn, Bucharest, Buda-Pesth and Berlin. Extensive literary labors in the field of Jewish archaeology. At loggerheads with the Austrian government, he is nevertheless "persona grata." Geiger on the "Ben Chananja." Delitzsch on Loew's "Lebensalter." Loew's absence from the Jewish Congress in Hungary due to principle. He is a prominent member of the Synods in Leipzig and Augsburg, (1869-1871). He belongs to the "historical" school.

CHAPTER IX.

ABRAHAM GEIGER.

Berthold Auerbach places Geiger's work in the nineteenth century in the same category with Moses Mendelssohn's work in the eighteenth century. Einhorn calls Geiger "the most prominent teacher of Judaism in our generation." Geiger descends from a family of scholars. At the age of six he reads the Bible and Talmud, Hebrew and German. Disgusted with the "Cheder," he is besieged with doubts concerning the divine origin of the books of Moses. In 1829 he enters the Heidelberg University, and meets there with such specimens of Jewish candidates for the Rabbinical profession that he is disgusted with Jewish theology. He goes to Bonn, with the intention to study oriental languages. There he meets with a better class of Jewish students, and resolves to devote his talents to the Reformation of Judaism. S. R. Hirsch, Gruenebaum, Frensdorff, S. Scheyer, Dernbourg and Ullman. He forms a Society for the purpose of preaching. He pleads for the establishment of a Jewish theological faculty. He wins the prize by his essay: "What has Mohammed taken from Judaism?" He starts a "Society for the Furtherance of Culture." Geiger becomes Rabbi in Wiesbaden (1832), introduces weekly sermons and an "Order of the Synagogue." Geiger's "Zeitschrift fuer Juedische Theologie" (1835). Zunz, Rappoport, Stein, Dernbourg and other contributors. The historical critical School, Reform-Rabbinism and a scientific Jewish theology inaugurated by Geiger. First Rabbinical Assembly in Wiesbaden (1837), convoked by Geiger, is attended by fifteen Rabbis. Geiger is called to Breslau (1838), where under Tiktin orthodoxy has full sway. Hot contests. The Prussian government is urged by the orthodox party not to naturalize Geiger, i. e., to annul his election. His enemies use the foul means of political denunciation, but fail. Eight foolish charges against Geiger. Tiktin's followers excited by his speech at a funeral want to throw Geiger into a grave. They urge the government to depose Geiger. Geiger insists upon the name of "Rabbi" instead of "Preacher," as a question of vital principle for the growth of Reform-Judaism. Geiger sacrifices his "Zeitschrift" as a peace-offering. Eight Rabbis of Silesia and Posen declare Geiger unfit to be a witness in a court of justice. Seventeen of the most prominent Rabbis of Germany and Austria break a lance for Geiger and free research. The "Rabbinical Opinions on the Compatibility of Free Research with the Office of Rabbi." The Reformer Philippsohn, though requested by the Breslau Congregation to give an opinion on the subject, does not answer, out of personal animosity against Geiger. These "Rabbinical Opinions" belong to the most interesting literature of responses in Jewish history. Friedlaender's, Chorin's, Holdheim's, Wechsler's, A. Kohn's, Herxheimer's, Einhorn's, Hess', Guttman's, Wassermann's, Levy's, Aub's, Maier's, Cahn's, L. Adler's, Stein's and Gruenebaum's "opinions." Dr. Aub calls Geiger "the first representative of the scientific theology of Judaism." Resolutions, signed by the members of the Breslau Congregation, expressing their admiration for Geiger, are presented to him (1842). Tiktin dies (1843), but no peace restored. Geiger's salary increased, and Tiktin's son elected Rabbi of the orthodox party, but paid by the Congregation. Geiger favors a split, which has to come sooner or later in every large Congregation. Geiger declines a call to St. Petersburg, tendered him through Dr. Lilienthal, of Riga, later Cincinnati. Geiger's Prayerbook, 1854. His opinion on "Sunday service." His pamphlet on the "Hamburg Prayer-book," which he criticises as too conservative. "Merely outward embellishments of the service might prove to be luxuriant death-chambers of our religion." His criticism of the Frankfort Reform-Society. "Revolution is not Reform." Reform of the entire community preferable. "Reform should emanate from Rabbis and Congregations." Geiger the organizer of the Rabbinical Conferences of 1844-1846. He is the President of the Breslau Conference, 1846. Geiger's labors for the emancipation of the Jews in

Prussia. His extensive literary work. His "Leo Da Modena,"
most interesting. His contributions to the "Zeitschrift der Deutsch-
Morgenlaendischen Gesellschaft." Geiger the "highest living authority on Samaritan literature." His lectures before the candidates
of Jewish theology. They are discontinued after the establishment
of the Rabbinical Seminary in Breslau. Although the institution
owed its existence to Geiger, he was cheated out of the position as
its Director, in violation of the desire of the founder of the Seminary, Jonas Fraenkel. The institution becomes a hot-bed of Jesuitism, standing for no principle, consistent only in its inconsistency.
Geiger's "Urschrift," 1857, is next to Zunz's "Gottesdienstliche
Vortraege," the most epochal Jewish publication of this century. It
revolutionized the study of Bible and Talmud, of the ideas on the
origin of Christianity, on Sadducees and Pharisees, and its results,
are gaining ground among leaders of Christian theology. The
twenty-fifth anniversary of Geiger's Rabbinical career grandly celebrated (1857). Death of Geiger's wife Emilie (1860). Geiger on the
"Talmud." His sensational letter to Zunz against circumcision and
dietary laws. He resumes the "Zeitschrift," which he published
uninterruptedly until his death. The greatest literati of Europe,
Jews and Christians, among its contributors. Dr. Stein's resignation, and Geiger's acceptance of the position in Frankfort-on-the-
Main. Causes of this important step. Farewell demonstrations.
Geiger in Frankfort. He is disappointed on account of his failure to
establish a theological faculty in Frankfort, which hope is the
main reason of his departure from Breslau. "Society for Jewish Affairs." Literary activity. Geiger on the Jews in Roumania. His
views are applicable to the Jews in Russia. He opposes "political
missionary activity." "Civilization cannot be imported." "The
sources of the evil. Ignorance, fanaticism, hostility to culture
must be stopped. Out of the midst of the land itself must emanate
the forces of civilization and regeneration. Who has ever assisted
the Jews in Germany? Did they ever ask the mediation of France,
England and America?" Geiger in favor of the "resurrecting Rabbinical Conference." The Conference in Cassel, 1868. The Synod
in Leipzig, 1869. Geiger compares it with the Philadelphia Conference
of the same year. The comparison is most favorable to American
Reform-Judaism. "Here we meet with flesh of our flesh, spirit of
our spirit." Indecision one of the great defects of the
Leipzig Synod. Philippsohn's bombastic "resolution" devoid
of principle, betrays the desire to make a sensation and to cause an
effect outside of Judaism. Geiger's "Prayer-book, second edition,"
1870. His "Judaism and its History" in three volumes, is most popular. Geiger's poetical genius. Call to Berlin. The assurance that
he would find opportunity to teach Jewish theological students induces him to go to Berlin. Geiger in Berlin (1870). The Synod at
Augsburg. Geiger more in harmony with the assembly, as more
radical resolutions are passed there. The "retarding elements are
absent", and a fresh, courageous spirit pervaded the Synod." His
activity in the "Hochschule fuer die Wissenschaft des Judenthum's"
is most straining for him, but he looks upon it as the happiest period
of his life. A "band of brave, enthusiastic students" constitutes
his audience. He is troubled about the hostility of the majority of
young Rabbis to progress and Reform. "Where is the after-growth
which will replace us?" "People want a man, who, however, should

INTRODUCTION.

This book does not claim to be a complete history of Reform-Judaism. The time for such a work has not arrived yet. As a contribution to such a history, however, the author flatters himself to have rendered some service to the future historian.

The history of Reform-Judaism may be divided into three distinct periods.

1st. The Humanistic period.

2nd. The Aesthetical-Homiletical period.

3rd. The Historical-Critical period.

Mendelssohn, Friedlaender, Isaac Euchel, Lazarus Bendavid, Herz Homberg, Hartwig Wessely, Peter Beer, the men of the "*first stage,*" as Geiger designates them,* hold a similar relation to the Jewish Reform-movement that the Humanists Reuchlin, Erasmus of Rotterdam, Melanchthon and Ulrich von Hutten held to the Christian Reformation.

Israel Jacobsohn, Aron Chorin, Joseph Perl,† David Fraenkel, editor of the "Sulamith," J. Heineman, editor of the "Jedidjah," Wolf Heidenheim, grammarian and translator of the prayer-book, the Hamburg preachers and the teachers of schools and authors of catechisms, Johlson, and to a certain extent I. N. Mannheimer were the men of the "*second stage.*" Their main work and object was to make the character of the Jewish worship less repulsive to the

---

* Posthumous Works, II, p. 260.

† Joseph Perl, born Tarnopol, 1773, died there 1839. He established (1813) a school at a great sacrifice of time and money, and boldly attacked the Chassidim in his "Mgalleh Tmirin," a Hebrew imitation of the "epistolae obscurorum virorum" (1819). He entertained a lively correspondence with the representatives of Jewish culture in Germany, and was appointed honorary member of the Berlin "Cultureverein" (Society for the Dissemination of Culture among the Jews). See I. N. Mannheimer's eulogy, and his biography in Bush's Jahrbuch, 1846-47, by N. Horowitz and Kerem Chemed, V, p. 163, by Sal. Rappoport

young, to the more educated classes of Jews and to Christians, who happened occasionally to visit a synagogue.

Questions of decorum and order in the service, sermons in the vernacular, the introduction of German hymns and prayers, music and liturgical changes were the sharp end of the wedge. But useful and necessary as these changes were, inasmuch as their impulse sprang from a purely æsthetic want, they were not born of the true spirit of Reform.* This spirit is based on inward principle and not on a mere outward æsthetic want. The political reaction in Prussia after the overthrow of the Corsican Titan made the civil and political condition of the Jews most deplorable. The better educated Jew had to face the painful alternative, either to forego all hope of honorably devoting his talents to the government or to forswear the religion of his fathers. Many also were too weak to resist the temptation, and sold their birthright for a mess of pottage. While we cannot excuse such apostasy, it cannot be denied that Judaism in the official form in which it presented itself, was not of a character to inspire with enthusiam the new generation, bred under the most refining influences of classical Hellas and Rome, so as to make them prefer the glory of martyrdom to the crown of civic honors.

The contrast between cosmopolitan rationalism and belief in tradition, the conflict between the philosopher Mendelssohn, † and the orthodox Jew Mendelssohn, ‡ were too glaring to be smoothed by a sentimental piety, of which the new generation knew very little. The generation, reared under the influence of Mendelssohn's legalism, refused to lead a double life. If reason is free, they claimed the right to be free. If Judaism is

---

* See Geiger's criticism of the Hamburg-Temple in his pamphlet: "Der Hamburger Tempelstreit eine Zeitfrage." See page 336 of this book.

† As a philosopher Mendelssohn believed in natural religion, denied revelation, miracles, and condemned soulless ceremonialism.

‡ As a Jew Mendelssohn insisted on the eternal validity of every Mosaic Rabbinical law.

less than reason, then it was a stranger in the world of
modern thought. Indeed, Mendelssohn's own children
and thousands with them, who cared more for a heart-
appearing, soul-stirring religion than for a Jewish Commonwealth and its Palestinian national laws left
the storm-beaten, flag, inscribed with the immortal
truth: "Hear, oh Israel, the Eternal is One." Do
we not find analogous cases to-day? Do we not see,
how, under the very eyes of orthodox parents, their
Jewish sons and daughters are swelling the ranks of
Ingersoll and his partisans?* The few liturgical Reforms, which were introduced in some Synagogues in
obedience to asthetic wants failed signally to cure a
disease, which was eating into the very heart of
Judaism. To this must be added that the better element was disgusted with the aping of Protestantism
lack of substance and vitality, the shallow moralizing
tone of the new preachers, the superficial views of
Judaism, which not a a few of them scattered among
the multitude. It may indeed be asked, how could
better things have been expected at that time? The
great facts of *Jewish History* were not yet clearly known,
the philosophy of Judaism was proportionately vague
and uncertain. No Jewish author of consequence had
undertaken to write the annals of his coreligionists;
chaotic confusion reigned in their chronicles. To know
what Judaism is, it is of the utmost necessity to ascer-
tain in the first instance, what it had been. The past
would prove the index of the future.†

This was one of the most critical epochs in the
checkered history of Israel. Was then Judaism doomed
to death? Was it preserved during the prosecutions
of centuries at the price of the precious blood of so many
martyrs and heroes, in order to die now of inanition?
Could it only thrive and flourish in the darkness of the

*All those Russian Jewish Nihilists, who disgrace yearly American
Judaism by celebrating wild orgies on the Day of Atonement are
sons of ultra-orthodox parents.

† See a very graphic description of this period in Jost, "Das Judenthum und seine Sekten," III, pp. 333, 334 and especially 335.

ghetto, but not bear the refreshing and emancipating
influence of the Nineteenth Century? No, a hundred
times no. When the night is at its darkest the sun's
reviving light is nearest. In those trying days the
science of Judaism, was born. It became the Savior,
who consoled weeping Judaism in the words of the
prophet to the mourning Rachel, "Cease crying,
for there is a reward for thy work, and thy children
will return unto thee."

Two men arose, Leopold Zunz and Abraham Geiger. The former was the founder of a Science of Judaism,
the latter was the founder of a Scientific Theology of
Judaism, and laid the basis of the Reform on the
adamantine rock of science.

With Geiger's "Zeitschrift fuer Juedische Theologie," the *third stage* of Reform Judaism, *i.e.*, *the historical, critical period* was inaugurated and conquered in
its victorious march, one citadel of orthodoxy after the
other. The triumph of Reform-Judaism in America is
due to the labors of this historical-critical school, to
which the author of this book has the honor to belong.
To this school belongs the future. The frantic efforts
which are made from one side to set Romanticism on
its throne, and from another to supersede it by shallow
sensationalism, coupled with arrogance and ignorance,
will be impotent to hurt it for any length of time. As
soon as the charm of novelty will be over, the reaction
is sure to follow.

Applying this method of treating the history of
Reform-Judaism to this book the first "humanistic-
period" includes Mendelssohn and Friedlaender. The
second "aesthetical-homiletical-period" includes Jacobsohn, Chorin, Salomon and Kohn. The representatives
of the third "historical-critical-period" are Geiger,
Holdheim, Loew. It must however be conceded, that
Holdheim cannot be fully counted to this last period.
It was only towards the end of his life, especially in his
book "*Maamar Haishuth*" that he succeeded in applying the methods of the historical-critical School of Reform-Rabbinism.

CHAPTER I.

MOSES MENDELSSOHN.

Moses Mendelssohn is generally termed the "Father of Reformed Judaism." On the other hand the so-called "Liberal Conservatives" or, as Leopold Loew in his caustic style called them, the "Neuorthodoxen Romantiker" claim Mendelssohn as their champion. The fact, however, is, that Mendelssohn was neither a reformer nor was he orthodox. By dint of his philosophical and aesthetical writings, he was the first to break through the social restraints that obstructed the intercourse of Jews and Christians. He had, however, neither the aggressive temper nor the bold self-confidence that stamp the leader of parties. Practically, he was most sincerely devoted to the orthodox form of Judaism and complied with the most rigid injunctions of the "Shulchan Aruch." Mendelssohn was a philosopher of the Eighteenth Century, somewhat tinged with rationalism, but not a historian or a critic. His was the contemplative spirit which instinctively shrinks from rude contact with reality. Judaism was for him law and nothing but law, immutable, and eternal. Religion, he claimed, is natural to all men; Judaism, however, is a revealed legislation. As such it is binding upon all Jews, and for all times; its ceremonies and symbols are the bond of union of the scattered sons of Jacob. These ideas are clearly and unmistakably expressed in his Polemical book "Jerusalem," concerning blind obedience. He says: "Indeed I cannot see, how those born in the House of Jacob can in any shape or manner, emancipate themselves from the law. We are, to be sure, permitted to think about the law, to search occasionally into its spirit, and where the lawgiver has not given a reason for the same, to conjecture a reason. The reason for the law was perhaps determined by time, place and circumstances. Hence the law could possibly be changed in accordance with time, place and circumstances—provided it would please the Almighty, to make known to us His will concerning the same, just as loud, as publicly, and beyond every possibility of doubt as He did, when giving the law. As long as this does not come to pass, as long as we cannot show such an authentical immunity from the law, our subtle reasoning cannot release us from the rigid obedience, which we owe to the law."* This is not the language of a reformer. For according to this uncompromising point of view not the least reform, no matter how insignificant and innocent, is justifiable. This standpoint ignores entirely the historical development in Judaism, for which, I repeat again, Mendelssohn, had no appreciation and no understanding. Mendelssohn, himself plainly says with respect to Lessing's Religio-Philosophical conception, "I for my part, have no comprehension of this education of the human race, to which my late friend Lessing has been persuaded. There is only such a thing as progress for the individual man. But that mankind as a whole should steadily advance and perfect itself in the course of time, is, it seems to me, not the intention of providence."†

According to this theory Hillel, Rabbi Jochanan Ben Saccay, Rabbi Jehuda Hannassi, Simon Ben Shetach, Shmaja, Abtalion, Johannes Hyrkan and other prominent teachers of the Talmud, who have changed and abolished laws of Moses, ‡ have com-

---

* Mendelssohn: Jerusalem III, 356.

†Gesammelte Schriften III, 317-318, letter to Hennings v, p. 598. He himself tries to explain or to justify this lack of historical understanding with the fact, that the Jews of that time were "people without a fatherland." (Letter to Abbt v, p. 368.)

‡ See my "The Talmud," p. 36-40. Denver, 1884.

mitted sins. But aside from this, Mendelssohn himself has expressed views, which are not at all consistent with this conception, in fact utterly incompatible with the exigencies and wants of Judaism of the
Nineteenth Century. As I do not propose to say more
about Mendelssohn than is absolutely necessary for the
better appreciation of the spirit of that time, †
I have to confine myself to a few quotations from
his writings. Speaking of the Rabbinical interpretations of the Mosaic Laws, he is compelled to concede
"that the folly of men has through misunderstanding
and misleading transformed the good into evil,
the useful into the harmful" (III, 350;) and again:
"The climate and the times make the observance of the religious ceremonies, in many respects more burdensome than they are." In his correspondence with Lavater he uses the following language:
"I will not deny that I have noticed in my religion
human additions, abuses and excrescences which, alas,
only obscure its splendor."

A Geiger, Holdheim and Einhorn could not have
put it much stronger, considering the time these words
were uttered, and considering the fact that Mendeissohn
had to be cautious in view of his numerous suspicious
opponents, who saw in him an Apostate and Heretic,
because he had translated the Pentateuch into German.

Those who understand how to read between the
lines will notice that whenever Mendelssohn speaks of
Socrates and the "Sophists" in his "Phaedon" he
means himself and the Polish Rabbis. Just read the
following: "At that time, as in all times, the mob of
Greece paid the highest respect to those scholars,
whose principal purpose and object has been to favor

† More on this subject see my "Mendelssohn's Verdienste um
die Deutsche Nation (Zuerich, 1880) translated into English in
the American Israelite, Cincinnati, 1880.

deep-rooted prejudices and old superstitions, and to fortify them by all sorts of seeming reasons, sham arguments and cunning subtleties." ‡

These words fit better the Rabbis of Mendelssohn's time than the Sophists of the Age of Socrates. And again: "We all who seek the truth recognize this poisonous breath of hypocrisy and superstition, and we wish to be able to wipe it off without doing harm to the true and the good." *

But Mendelssohn had entirely forgotten or perhaps, intentionally omitted, to point out to his contemporaries these "human additions, abuses" and "superstitions," which may be "wiped off" without harm to the Essence of Judaism. He wisely left this by no means easy task to his Disciples and to the reform Rabbis of a later period. But no unbiased admirer of Moses Mendelssohn can gainsay that his last passage is, to say the least, utterly at variance with the above quoted declaration that "nobody born in the House of Jacob, can in any shape, manner or form whatsoever, emancipate himself from the yoke of the law," no matter how much circumstances might change the life of the Jew, except it be that God Almighty Himself has solemnly, released him of the same. In other words the alternative is placed before the Jews, either strictly to observe every ceremonial law—and Mendelssohn does not except the Talmudic-Rabbinical laws—or to forego his right to be a Jew. No wonder, that such a conception forced, as it were, the Jew, who could not believe in the obligation of every ceremony, and who yet shrunk from joining the ranks of Atheism, to embrace christianity which teaches through the Apostle Paul, that a second dispensation or covenant has done away with the first.

We see from these quotations, that Mendelssohn cannot well be claimed by the reformers, and still less

‡ Mendelssohn: Gesammelte Schriften, von G. B. Mendelssohn, II. p. 72.

*Ibidem.

by the conservatives. But he became by his very appearance on the scene a silent reformer, unconsciously, perhaps even against his will. Especially by his translation of the Pentateuch and the Psalms into German, a work, originally undertaken by him in the interest of his own sons, for their private use, he became the author of a profound revolution in the Jewish religion, the scope of which the "Sage of Dessau" hardly dreamt.

For the Jew of Germany in those days was German in geographical location only. In speech and habit he was a foreigner in the land which he inhabited. It would lead me too far to explain here the reasons of this sad state of affairs. Suffice it to say, the Jew of that period was the product of centuries of the most outrageous persecutions, and entrenched behind the cyclopean walls of Talmudic sophistry and idle argumentation he became indifferent to the world outside of his ghetto. Especially in Prussia the Jews were treated most shamefully. They had to pay a toll like animals, and when a Jew wanted to enter the enlightened city of Berlin he could do so through one gate only, the so-called "Rosenthaler Thor." But a limited number of Jews were permitted to marry, and had to pay dearly for this privilege. The great infidel and friend of Voltaire the "Philosopher of Sanssouci," I mean King Frederic the Great, who is credited with the noble saying, "Jeder Kann Nach Seiner Facon Selig Werden." (Everybody can carve out his salvation according to his own way) did not live up to his own preaching, at least so far as the Jews were concerned. I will only mention his shameful ordinance that all Jewish young men contemplating matrimony had to buy goods from the Royal Porcelain factory of Berlin for a considerable amount. And what kind of goods? Not useful crockery of some benefit to a household. Oh no. They were compelled to buy those wares which nobody else wanted—the unsaleable goods. Thus our good Mendelssohn had to buy twenty life-sized monkeys manufactured of porcelain, which can be seen this very day among the relics of the Mendelssohn family. *

But the oppression from without is nothing as compared to the persecution from within.

The baneful influence of Poland was holding full sway over the Jews in Germany. Polish Rabbis relentlessly controlled the synagogue. Polish "teachers" held their tyrannical scepter over the school and succeeded in shutting out from it every ray of light and air. Their language was a terrible "Kauderwelsch," a hybrid Jargon of Hebrew, German, Slavonic and God knows what. The Rabbis did not tolerate the reading of a German book. One day Moses Mendelssohn sent a boy whom he had befriended for a book. The poor boy thinking of no evil, book in hand, was harshly accosted by an officer of Jewish charities with the question: "What have you here? I hope it is not a German book." But as soon as the fanatic, heartless and cruel "man of charity" had found his suspicion verified, he dragged the unfortunate lad to the bailiff, and not even Mendelssohn's interference could save the innocent boy from expulsion from Berlin. This was done in the capital city of Prussia in the year 1746. †

Moses Mendelssohn's German translation of the Pentateuch sounded the first bugle call by which the fortresses of Mediaevalism crumbled into dust. This work was an event and holds the like relation to the Jewish reform movement that Luther's translation held to the great protestant reformation. The influence of this translation was manifold. In the first place it facilitated a more correct understanding of the doctrine, the literature and language of the Bible.

Secondly—and this is of the greatest importance, —it served the purpose of a text-book of the German

* Hensel: Die Familie Mendelssohn I, p. 2.

† Kaiserling: Moses Mendelssohn, Sein Leben, 1862, p. 12.

for the great mass of the Jews, who were at that time unable to read a book written in the Vernacular. *

Most likely for this very reason the German of Mendelssohn's translation was written in Hebrew letters. Thus it opened to the Jews the treasure house of modern thought. Last but not least, this translation was the means of weakening the preponderating influence of the Talmud, which not only engrossed the attention of the Jewish youth to the utter exclusion of secular knowledge, but even perverted the exegesis of the Bible and caused the study of the scripture to be comparatively neglected. ‡

The Talmud says: "The Thora had fallen into oblivion; then came Ezra of Babylon and established it anew, and once more it was forgotten and Hillel arrived from Babylon and established it anew." We are fully justified in saying, the Thora was forgotten, but Moses Mendelssohn came from Dessau and by presenting its teachings in the garb of a modern tongue, he rendered its true meaning apparent to every reflecting mind and gave back to the Thora its proper place in the education of the young.

The refining influence of this translation soon became evident among the contemporaries, friends, followers and immediate disciples of Mendelssohn, the so-called "Mendelssohnians" or "Mendelssohn-school," which in a wider sense comprises the vast circle of all those noble men, who, in different parts of Europe, zealously labored and worked for the better education of the Jewish masses. A wide field of knowledge, embracing the rich results of modern science, philosophy and art, was thus laid open to their industry. Eagerly they availed themselves of the proffered opportunity. Schools were established in every important city of Ger-

---

* The Y. M. H. A. In New York instructs Jewish-Russian immigrants in English. They do for these people almost as noble a work as Mendelssohn did for the Jews in Germany by means of his translation of the Pentateuch. The U. Y. M. H. A., proposes to do this work in all larger cities of the Union.

‡ Felix Adler: Creed and deed, page 220.

many and Austria, (Berlin, Koenigsberg, Frankfort,
Wien, Prag, Breslau, Wolfenbuettel, Seesen (and other
cities, in which the elements of liberal culture were
imparted to the young. Ere long we find a new
generation of Jews engaged in honorable competition
with their christian brethren for the prize of learning
and the reward of literary distinction. A new vital
energy was coursing through the veins of the Jews.

The following men may be considered as "Mendelssohnians:"

Salomo Dubno, born 1737, Died 1819; Hartwig
Wessely, born 1725, died 1805, famous for his brave
struggle in the cause of school education in Austria;
Herz Homberg, born 1749, died 1841, superintendent
of all German schools in Galicia. These men were
Mendelssohn's co-laborers on the commentary to his
translation, and formed the "School of Biurists," who
undertook to read the Pentateuch with an eye to
grammar, taste and sound logic. This work proved a
death-blow to the subtle play of dialectics and idle
argumentation of the Talmud, and perhaps without
even intending it, demolished mountains of legal
Rabbinical observances. To the same circle must be
counted Isaac Euchel, born 1756, who translated the
Jewish Prayer-Book into good German. This was,
if I am not mistaken, the first attempt of this kind;
Aron Wolfssohn, (1756-1835) teacher of the Wilhelms-
school in Breslau; Lazarus Bendavid, (1762-1832);
Dr. Herz Salomon Maimon, (1753-1800);* Isaac Satnow,
(1733-1803,) who published several books "Immanuel,"
"Meor Enajim," and others; Joel Loewe, (1790-1803,)
the grammarian; Jehuda Loeb Ben Seeb, (1764-1811,)
author of a Hebrew grammar which was quite popalur
in those days; J. Heiman, (1778-1855,) publisher of
the German periodical "Jedidjah;" David Fraenkel,
publisher of "Sulamith," a Jewish monthly; Wolf
Heidenheimer, (1754-1832,) editor of the Prayer-Book

---

* See Salomon Maimon's Autobiography translated into English
by Murray. (Boston, 1888, Cupples and Hurd.)

and translator of the Machsor, quite a scholar; Joel
Bril, Peter Beer, (1758-1838,) philosopically inclined;
and most prominent of all David Friedlaender. While
these men, most of whom were contributors to the
Hebrew Periodical "Hameassef" the "Gatherer," and
therefore called "Meassefim," one and all have done
their duty towards bringing about a better state of
culture among the Jews of that period, it is only the
last named man who is entitled to a place among the
Pioneers of Reform-Judaism. I will therefore proceed
to a biography of David Friedlaender, and I do it with
special pleasure, as he is most unjustly dealt with by
Prof. Graetz in his "History of the Jews," Vol. XI.[*]
Before proceeding to the biography of David
Friedlaender it will not be superfluous to show
his estimate of the work of the "Measseph." I do
this from two reasons: In the first place, because he,
as an untiring contributor to the periodical was fully
competent to speak on the subject impartially.
Secondly, because these words give the best insight
into the state of Judaism in those days and explain the
true inwardness of Friedlaender's utter disgust with
it, and his consequent famous letter to Probst Teller,
which gave rise to so much sensation and comment
and produced such a tremendous commotion in the
camp of Israel. In a letter to Aron Wolfson, he said
almost despairingly: "I consider the nation, [†] as it is,
in spite of all show of culture, taste and intelligence,
incorrigibly bad, and I deem useless the work of enlightenment as carried on by the "Meassefim," and in
a vein of the most bitter sarcasm he continues: "Nobody reads our books written in Hebrew—for whom
do we write them?" Somebody proposed indeed to
have placed the following sign before the Jewish

---

[*] See my "Graetz' Geschichts bauerei," Berlin, 1881.

[†] Mendelssohn always applied the expression "nation" when
speaking of the Jews. But, as we have ceased to be a "nation" after
the destruction of Jerusalem, this term is erroneous. See my
Mendelssohn's Verdieuste um das and Judenthum Bonn, 1880.

printing establishment: "Here books are printed which are never read. This is, I think, true in the fullest sense of the word." Still more melancholy and gloomily he expresses himself in a letter to the same friend in the year 1805, saying: "The cause of Judaism is done for; utterly done for."

CHAPTER II.

DAVID FRIEDLAENDER.

David Friedlaender was born in Koenigsberg in 1740 and died in Berlin in 1834. He was reared under the most favorable circumstances, as his father, Joachim Moses Friedlaender, was well to do, intelligent and respected for his integrity and charity, and his mother, Henriette, born Fisheles, a noble, pious and most benevolent woman of whom Hartwig Wessely spoke as a "mother to the poor." His parents took great care in securing for him the opportunities of a good education. He spent his pocket money in the pleasure of dispensing charity, and to practice virtue was his beau-ideal. He could not imagine even in the halcyon days of his youth, that such a thing as doing wrong is in the least possible. He was greatly worried on account of the impracticable education of the Jewish youth of those days, which was due to the unfortunate social, civil and political position of the Jews in Prussia. In the "Reglement" of September 29, 1730, the King of Prussia openly and unmistakably expressed his intention to make the laws concerning the Jews outside of Berlin of such a character that they would become extinct. In Koenigsberg, however, the Jews were protected by the more liberal administration of the Province, and in consequence they felt keener the necessity for a better education of the young. Thus more practicable disciplines were taught and less time was given to the study of the Talmud and Hebrew, at least among the well-to-do classes. Friedlaender,

endowed with great talents, took advantage of the opportunities offered him to secure a good education.

In 1771 Friedlaender, then twenty-one years old,
moved to Berlin, where in 1772 he married the
daughter of Daniel Itzig, one of the wealthiest and
most charitable Jews of Berlin. But his wealth and
influential connections did not, as is alas too often the
case nowadays, dampen his idealism and enthusiasm
for Judaism and Jewish knowledge. On the contrary,
they induced him to devote more time to study and
learning, to widen his sphere of activity, to broaden
his intellectual horizon and to labor untiringly for the
enlightenment, elevation and amelioration of mankind,
but more particularly of his politically and spiritually
enslaved co-religionists. It was in fact his thirst after
knowledge and his burning desire to do something for
his down-trodden brethren that caused him to leave
Koenigsberg and go to Berlin, the home of Mendelssohn, whose social intercourse he enjoyed daily for fifteen years.*

Every evening, and especially on Sabbaths and
Holidays, Jewish young men came to Mendelssohn's
house with the purpose to learn and improve intellectually. Pedagogics, religion, education and Bible
formed the topics of conversation. Friedlaender,
Euchel, Lindau, Wolfssohn, Bendavid, belonged to
the most regular visitors. No wonder then, that these
and many others became in time the most enthusiastic
Apostles or Disciples of the "Sage of Dessau," or the
"Plato of the Jews" as Mendelssohn was popularly
called. But David Friedlaender was not content with
these daily conversations in the house of the philosopher. He was to Mendelssohn what Mendelssohn was
to Lessing, an intimate friend, a faithful follower and
admirer, a most ardent Disciple and Apostle, and last
but not least, his confidant, to whom he revealed his
innermost thoughts and ideas on the progress and

* Moses Mendelssohn, Fragmente von ihm und neber ihn von
David Friedlaender, Berlin, 1819, p. 21.

future of Judaism and on the most delicate questions
of religion. *

It is with him, that Mendelssohn minutely discusses the plans concerning the amelioration and education of the young among the Jews, and other important subjects. To him the master confides his
ideas as to the measures to be taken against fanaticism
from without as well as from within.

No wonder that through the high esteem in which
Friedlaender was held by Mendelssohn the Jews in
Berlin commenced to respect and to love him. His
good humor, wit, eloquence, and kindness were qualities which could not fail to make him popular. It was
to a great extent his merit to have brought about a
certain social intercourse between the more cultured
Jews and Christians. This was accomplished through
the literary circle which met weekly in the "salon" of
Dorothea Veit, daughter of Mendelssohn, and Henriette
(De Lemos) Herz, wife of Dr. Markus Herz. This
woman who possessed a face in which the features of
Hellenic and oriental beauty were blended in exquisite
harmony, had acquired, under the guidance of competent masters, considerable proficiency in the ancient and
modern languages, and to her great talent and mind,
stored with various knowledge, was added the charm
of a very sweet disposition. Attracted by her fame
and captivated by her genius the most eminent men of
the day sought the privilege of her society. The art
of conversation, in which the French were the masters,
and which until then had received but little attention in
the Prussian capital, was for the first time cultivated
in the "Salon" of the "Tragic Muse." For thus they
called Henriette Herz. Sparkling wit and profound
philosophy were alike encouraged. Statesmen,
princes, men of science and artists considered it an
honor to be permitted to attend these gatherings.
Nicolai, Engel, Ramler, Schleiermacher, Teller,
Zoellner, Knuth, Alexander and Wilhelm Von Hum-

---

* "Unterhaltungen" in the quoted "Fragmente" p. 38-62.

boldt, Count Alexander von Dohna-Schlobitten,
Gentz, Friedrich Von Schlegel, Mirabeau, Dorothea
and Rahel Levin, afterwards Varnhagen Von Ense,
were among the intimates of her circle. At the same
time by Fanny Itzig, sister-in-law of Friedlaender
there was opened a similar Salon in the capital of
Austria. This salon was the center of the world of
literature, art, diplomacy and nobility of birth. Such
circles contributed considerably towards breaking
through the social restraints that obstructed the intercourse of Jews and Christians. Among the most intimate friends of Friedlaender were Knuth, the tutor of
the two Humboldts, and later Wilhelm and Alexander
Humboldt themselves. But Friedlaender was not a
man of mere theory. He therefore founded, in company with his friends Mendelssohn, Euchel, Daniel
Itzig and Wessely, the Jewish free school "Freischule,"
at Berlin in 1778, which was opened to pupils in 1781.
The building was given by Daniel Itzig while his son
Isaac and his son-in-law, David Friedlaender, worked
out the plan of education. In connection with the
school an oriental printing establishment and book
store were established. It deserves mention that the
Prussian government favored these institutions and
granted them freedom from taxation. In 1786 the
"Freischule" had already eighty pupils, half of whom
were instructed free of charge. David Friedlaender
and Isaac Daniel Itzig were the directors of the school.
The teachers were part Jews and part Christians. The
following were the branches taught. Penmanship,
mathematics, bookkeeping, drawing, geography,
Hebrew, German and French. Every year
a public examination was held. Within ten
years no less than six hundred pupils were
educated in the "Freischule." But unfavorable
political circumstances, jealous rivalry and orthodoxy
did not a little to impede the progress of that institution.
In 1805 Lazarus Bendavid was chosen superintendent
of the school. He devoted in the most unselfish manner, and with untiring zeal, his labors to this school

until December 29, 1825, when it was closed, as its pupils were transferred to the Jewish "Gemeinde-schule," of Berlin, which was opened in the year 1826. It was characteristic of the "Freischule," that it was non-sectarian, opening its doors alike to Jewish and Christian pupils. But on September 15, 1819, owing to the spirit of re-action in Prussia, the law prohibited Christian children from attending the school.

The influence of the "Freischule" was by no means merely local. For the light kindled sent forth its rays throughout Germany and Austria. Similar "Freischulen" were founded in Breslau, Frankfort, Dessau, Wolfenbuettel, which had the honor to number among its pupils Dr. Marcus Jost and Dr. Leopold Zunz, Seesen and others. But especially for Austria the example of the Berlin "Freischule" was of the utmost importance. In consequence of the "Toleranz Edict of the Emperor Joseph II, Herz Homberg was appointed Royal Superintendent of all the German schools of the Jews in Galicia and Lodomeria. In this quality and later as "Schulrath" (counsellor of the schools) in Prague he faithfully labored in the spirit of Mendelssohn and Friedlaender, by making the schools of those countries nurseries of German culture and by introducing appropriate text-books on Judaism and its ethics. These schools became excellent levers of progress and paved the way for the great work of religious Reform of Judaism. Inasmuch as all those schools were non-sectarian in character their influence in those days can hardly be overrated. In this connection it is but proper to mention Friedlaender's first attempt at literature, undertaken in the interest of the "Frei-schule." I mean the little "Reader for Jewish children," for the benefit of the Jewish Freischule, (Berlin, 1780,) which contains the German, Latin and Hebrew alphabet, the articles of the Jewish creed according to Maimonides, and some moral stories from the Talmud.

Friedlaender translated two German idyls of Gessner into Hebrew. They are published in the "Meassef," the one treating of "charity" the other of "prayer." In 1785 he wrote two essays on the ethics of commerce for Zoellner's "Reader for all classes.

After Mendelssohn's death, January 4, 1786, the eyes of the world were naturally directed towards David Friedlaender, who more than any other of Mendelssohn's disciples was expected to carry on the work so auspiciously begun by his venerated master; and he did not disappoint those hopes. Aside from his attempts to translate into German passages from Isaiah and Job,* he published "prayers of the Jews for the whole year, translated and explained by David Friedlaender, Berlin, 1786." This work was done mainly for the benefit of the women.‡ In his "Open letter to the German Jews" he complained greatly of the neglect of woman in matters of Judaism. The "Berliner Monatsschrift" in reviewing this translation said, among other things: "It is indeed an important step towards the furtherance of enlightenment among the Jews."

This translation of the Hebrew prayers, however, met with the same storm of opposition on the side of the German-Polish Rabbis, who were at that time entrusted with the guardianship over the spiritual welfare of the German Jews, as did the introduction of Moses Mendelssohn's German translation of the Pentateuch and Psalms and their introduction into the schools and homes, and as did the establishment of schools for the young, where other things besides Talmud were taught. Even "Dikduk" (Hebrew Grammar) and Bible-reading in the original text were regarded by those Rabbis, at least as a waste of time, even if not sinful. A certain Eleasar Fleckeles in Prague in a pamphlet" "Olath Zibbur" declared in all earnestness the translation of Hebrew into German "the greatest of all sins," which is followed by the most horrible curse. In answer to this Friedlaender published his

---

*Jedidjah, vol. VI, p. 3.

‡ Every attempt at Reform in Judaism started with the emancipation of woman.

"open letter to the German Jews," (Berlin, 1788.) In
this little pamphlet he treated Rabbi Landau and his
Satellite Fleckeles without gloves. He said, among
other things, that they did not care for the "Holiness
of the teachings, the enlightenment of the spirit of the
holy scriptures, but for the dead letter of scripture
only. If I do not understand one word of the prayer
which I prattle, as long as it is in Hebrew, it will—
according to the ideas of these men—produce devotion,
knowledge of God's benevolence and resignation to the
divine will. If I do not know what the prophets and
the teachers of the law have said and taught, as long
as I repeat often mechanically their words, it will make
me better, wiser and more rational." He also tells
them in as many words that their opposition to German translations is not so much based on zeal for religion as on their fear of losing their authority and prestige.

In 1788 David Friedlaender published mainly for
pedogogic reasons, "Koheleth" (Ecclesiastics) into
German. In connection with this appeared an essay on
"the best of the Holy Scriptures, from a pedagogic
point of view," in which he pointed out the necessity
for a compendium of the Jewish religion and ethics
(catechism.) This, he said, must be based on a
thorough understanding of the Biblical literature, and
must be more than a mere slavish imitation of similar
products in another religion. His earnest admonitions
in this respect did not fall upon barren ground, as he
lived to see men forthcoming, who have done noble
work in this direction.

In 1787 Friedlaender published in Hebrew "Hane-
fesh" (the soul,) for the use of pupils in the higher
classes of Jewish schools. In this he comprehensively
summarized the proofs of the immortality of the soul as
laid down in Moses Mendelssohn's "Phaedon.',

As this present work is in the main devoted to
the history of the Jewish Reformation we can only
incidentally dwell on the great struggle for political
and civil emancipation of the German Jews, in which

Friedlaender had taken so prominent a part. In this connection must be mentioned his "Outspoken thoughts of a Jew about the proposition, that the Jews abolish the Purim Festival.*" It had been claimed by a Christian writer that the Purim fosters hatred against the Christians among the Jews, which statement Friedlaender strongly refuted.‡ Another publication of the same character, is his "Answer of the Jews in the Province of Lorraine to the petition offered to the National convention by all the communities of the city of Strassburg," translated from the French into German by Friedlaender, October, 1791. The communities of Strassburg were opposed to the grant of equal rights to the Jews.

In 1793 Friedlaender published "Documents concerning the reform of the Jewish colonies in the Prussian states." He succeeded in setting aside many burdensome and disgraceful laws, to which the Jews in Prussia were subjected. To his untiring labors is in the main due the famous edict of 1812, granting to the Jews equality of right with other citizens.

In this document he said to the state: "Do not wait with the grant of the emancipation to the Jews until they are all cultivated and reformed. No. On the other hand he urgently admonished the Jews, not to delay the reformation until they should have gained their emancipation; for the reformation is in itself the noblest and best part of the emancipation, while the emancipation is the most effective means to make useful citizens of those Jews, who were by legislation deprived of the privilege and the opportunity to serve their country. This is, by the way, the best refutation of the trite argument brought forth by the enemies of reform in Judaism, that the Jewish reform movement owed its existence and origin wholly to the

---

*Berlinische Monatsschrift, June, 1790.

‡ The book "Esther" gave rise to this accusation. It is a novel composed during Maccabean era, and naturally reflects the sentiments of those years of religious persecution and irreligious apostasy.

desire of the German Jews for emancipation. This shameful argument which is even to-day used by the "new orthodox romantics," as represented by Dr. Hildesheimer, and others, against reform, finds a most crushing refutation in the powerful Jewish reform movement in Free America, where, thank God, a struggle for emancipation of the Jews was never necessary.

Another merit of Friedlaender's "documents" is the unbiased and impartial spirit pervading them. He did not belong to the Jewish Chauvinists, who always sing loud praises in favor of their race, and never tire of reiterating the myth of the superiority of the Jewish talent. All he conceded was, that in consequence of long oppression in certain branches of business, from which he was not debarred by law, the Jew developed greater shrewdness. This may be a hint to some of our "great orators" in "Bnai Brith" conventions and even in the pulpits, to indulge a little less in their spread-eagle speeches about the superiority of our race and to pay more attention to the actual needs of Judaism. It is not the race but the religion of which we ought to feel proud. D'Israeli's declamations about our race have been paraded too often to be effective, even if they were true. Let us not delude ourselves. When we look more critically, and less enthusiastically, upon those passages of Lord Beaconsfield's work, where the mental superiority of our race is so eloquently described, we will find that they are full of inaccuracies. Just look at that "grand passage" in "Coningsby" in the dialogue between Coningsby and Sidonia, on which our Jewish newspapers still harp with great relish. How incorrect: How far remote from historical truth; it is not true, that the prime ministers and leading diplomats of Europe have been at any time in this century composed of Jews. Such unfounded statements instead of doing good, create envy, jealousy, ridiculous overrating of the power of the Jews and produce in its wake Antisemitism: Neither can it be historically proven, that artists like Rossini and others were Jews. But granted they were descendents of the Hebrew race, they manifested no interest in the cause of Judaism. On the contrary, instead of glorifying them we ought to reproach and denounce them, that they, endowed with great talent and genius, have, like Esau, sold their birthright for a mess of pottage; have deserted our stormbeaten, but never surrendered flag; have gone over to the enemy and thus set the bad example of apostasy and treachery to their contemporaries and to the youth. It is high time, that our orators and journalists should cease to laud to the skies men who were, or are, successful in the domain of art, science and politics, simply because they were accidentally born of a Jewish mother, although they have never shown the least interest in our cause. If you are afraid to denounce them or to remind them of their duty as Israelities, to struggle in the cause of God, be it so and ignore them, but cease to lionize them. Suppose Lord Beaconsfield, Gambetta, Sarah Bernhardt and other eminent persons were Jews or of Jewish descent? What of it? One Riesser, Zunz, Geiger, Cremieux, Jacobsohn, Friedlaender or Kosch has done more for Judaism than all those great politicians, artists, millionaires and professors combined.

A worthy ally of Friedlaender was Lazarus Bendavid, who in his pamphlet, "Something on the Characteristics of the Jews," urged upon his coreligionists in Austria not to be idle in accomplishing their own emancipation, and in proving that their real faults originated from their oppression. This pamphlet created so great a sensation that Bendavid was summoned before Cardinal Migazzi on a charge of assailing Christianity. ⸸

Bendavid proved that he did not attack Christianity, as his traducers asserted. But he spoke his mind very plainly on the Jewish ceremonial law in a manner

---

⸸ It is greatly to be regretted, that the attention of the Cardinal was called to Bendavid's so-called onslaughts on the Christian religion by men, who claimed to be orthodox Jews. But history repeats itself. Maimonides underwent a similar experience.

which reminds one of the modern reformers. He said among other things: "If in Austria an excellent prince (Emperor Joseph II) has committed the error of commanding† the enlightenment of the Jews as a duty of the state; * * * If the outward change is to have a salutary effect, the Jews themselves must create the reform from within. They must learn to understand, that their ceremonial laws have become inapplicable and senseless for the present time, and they must have a purer religion, more worthy of the common Father of all mankind." He complains that there are four classes of Jews: Those who observe strictly every ceremonial law; those who neglect the ceremonial law out of mere convenience and frivolity, and are the cause of the antipathy against enlightenment on the side of the first class; those who, while in favor of progress, practice the old ceremonies out of mere weakness; and those who, while they do not practice the old observances, are God-fearing, highly moral and virtuous, but are placed in the same category with the second class. "Oh!" exclaims Bendavid, who belonged to this last mentioned class, "do away with the senseless ceremonial law; tell your children that it was once placed as a useful hedge around the garden, but that what has served for the slavish sense of past centuries, for the sake of saving and preserving the inner kernel, has to be given up as inappropriate to-day. Then they will recognize and understand, that it only depends upon this inner kernel. Guard you then this inner kernel by bettering and ennobling the character of man. Show yourselves to be believers in the one, eternal, benign Being who has created all men, preserves all, has endowed all with the feeling to acklowledge Him, and has laid upon this beautiful world the charm which impels us to adore Him."

These were remarkable words spoken almost one

---

† Bendavid apparently means, that mental, moral and spiritual progress cannot be enforced, and is a result of slow preparation and gradual development, as Isaiah said: "Can a whole nation be regenerated with one stroke?"

hundred years ago. They were words in the wilderness, and yet germs planted into the soil of history, buried for a time only, destined, however, to bear ripe fruits in later years. But let us never forget that it was Lazarus Bendavid, a disciple of Mendelssohn, who dared to speak thus in 1790 at Vienna. He deserves a prominent place in the history of reform-Judaism, although Graetz deems it necessary to state: "Auf den gang der Juedischen Geschichte in der Neuzeit hat Bendavid nur unmerklich eingewirkt."[*] It cannot be too often and too strongly urged that it was a great moral movement which lay at the bottom of the Jewish reform movement. While Bendavid's words might not immediately have exerted their deserved influence, they surely became the general conviction of all enlightened Israelites. Like all great leaders in the world of thought, who exerted seemingly but little influence upon their own generations, Lazarus Bendavid's prophetic words were addressed to generations yet unborn, and have been taken up and woven into the accepted teachings and opinions of our own days. Many a great reformer, who was decried and misjudged by the masses of his time, is remembered and honored to-day, while his traducers, who condemned him or belittled his just merits, are forgotten, or looked upon as narrow, small-minded and bigoted people. As the mists of superstition and error disappear, the heretics and infidels of ages gone by are coming to be appreciated. Time is a better judge than a partial and biased historian. It plays havoc with many a great name, and it likewise brings us to a true appreciation of the services rendered to mankind by men long ignored and disparaged. "They who make up the final verdict are not the partial and noisy men of the hour, but a court of angels. A public not to be bribed, not to be entreated and not to be overawed, decides

---

[*] "Bendavid's influence upon the development of Jewish history in modern times was hardly noticeable." Hist. of the Jews XI, 152. Not noticeable to—Graetz! How true are the words of the Psalmist, "some people have eyes and do not see, have ears and do not hear!" (Ps. 105, 5-6.)

upon every man's title to fame." While these tru-
isms are of general interest under all circumstances,
they apply with special force to the unjust way in which
men like Bendavid, Friedlaender, Zunz, Geiger, Holdheim and the great galaxy of Israel's noblest leaders
of the nineteenth century are dealt with in the last volume of Graetz's "History of the Jews" for no other
reason than that they had the misfortune to father
and foster what was then very unpopular in Germany, the Jewish-reform movement. In this connection I call attention to my book where I criticised
Graetz's unjust historiography.*

I come now to a very serious crisis in Judaism, to
a struggle of despair within the camp of modern Israel
in general and of the Jewish community of Berlin in
particular. A tidal wave of apostasy hurled itself
upon Judaism in Germany. The reasons for this sad
state of affairs were manifold. In the first place young
men eager for advancement in life found their Jewish
creed an insuperable obstacle in their way. The professions, the army, the offices of the government were
closed against them. On the threshold of every higher
career the Jew was placed before the painful alternative, either to forego all hope of honorably devoting
his talents to his country, or to forswear the religion
of his forefathers. In the second place, Judaism of
those days, with its network of legal trivialities, with
its "Beth-Hamidrash,‡" "Cheder" and 'Schul,†' with
a worship utterly incompatible with the culture and
civilization of the age and repulsive to the aesthetical
requirements of the rising generation, had no charm or
interest for the youth raised under the refining influence of the classic thought of Hellas and Rome.

Let us further place ourselves in the position of

*Graetz's Geschichtsbauerei von Dr. E. Schreiber, Rabbiner in
Bonn. (Berlin, 1881, Wilhelm Issleib.)

‡ So-called higher Academy for the purpose of studying the
Talmud.

† Literally "school." It is however, used as a term for house of
worship" (Synagogue.)

those intelligent Jews, who, in their conversations with enlightened Christians have found more points of agreement than of disagreement; and yet they were oppressed and repelled as members of the same country, although knowing and feeling themselves belonging to it with every fibre of their heart.

Add to this that rationalism stripped the positive religion of much of its substance and individuality. Schleiermacher, the same preacher, who delivered the famous "discourses on religion for the educated infidels," (reden ueber die religion an die gebildeten unter ihren veraechtern,) although the author of the protestant revival in Germany, spoke the language of Pantheistic teachings. Theological dogmas, according to him are not true in the sense of scientific propositions, but approach the truth only so far as they typify emotions of the most noble and exalted character. His ardent sermons full of depth, and appealing fervently to feeling, sentiment and emotion, could not fail to greatly impress those Jews who never had heard a stirring Jewish sermon. Take all these causes combined and the example set by Moses Mendelssohn's offspring, His daughter, Dorothea Veit, embraced Catholicism, left husband and children and married the immoral Friedrich von Schlegel.

It occasions but little surprise, that intelligent Jews, allowing Christianity to be what its expounders have defined it to be, found it not very difficult, to assume the name of Christian, without adopting the creed of Christianity. That fidelity to the faith of their forefathers which had so long marked the conduct of the Jews, began seriously to waver, and in many instances gave way. Many were led to the baptismal font by ambitious parents, who prized the crown of civic honors more highly than the glory of martyrdom. Many of the most illustrious names of contemporaneous German history were thus lost to Judaism. The Jewish communities of Berlin, Breslau,

*Author of a frivolous novel, "Lucinde."

and Koenigsberg suffered most by these wholesale conversions. The Apostates were as a rule wealthy people,
and well educated. Not indeed, that the new converts
became true and loyal Christians. On the contrary,
they considered the rite of baptism a mere hollow form,
and left it to the state, which had insisted upon their
conformity to justify the deep disgrace that was thus
brought upon the Christian sacraments. Those who
left the old, the storm-beaten flag of Judaism from
mercenary motives deserve, of course, much more blame
and reproach than those who have surrendered it, because Judaism failed to satisfy their innermost cravings
and longings. The great mistake of the latter class—
and they were in the majority—was two-fold: In the
first place they were lacking the historical sense which
teaches that great movements can only take place
gradually after a long and very slow preparation, that
history does not jump and that the parents have to do
hard, very hard work, before their children, and not
seldom their grand-children, are permitted to reap the
fruits of their untiring labors. Secondly, they did not
understand the idea of a progressive development and
hence did not believe in nor appreciate the possibility
of a Reform of Judaism.

But need I reiterate here that Mendelssohn himself, in fact the whole generation, labored under this
same want of understanding of a historical progress
and development? Was not this wild haste, this impatience, this restless tearing down of all and everything that centuries had built up, characteristic of the
era of Rationalism of the epoch of the French Revolution, which like a hurricane swept over France, and
with bloody hands tore down not only the ancient
bulwarks of superstition, but destroyed the fortress
of every religion and society. The inert masses, who
did not want to follow their rapidly advancing leaders,
who in their enthusiasm had lost their due appreciation for those who could not follow them, must bear
the responsibility for the deplorable conversion craze of
that period. Then it was, that David Friedlaender

created a sensation by publishing an "Open letter of Jewish fathers to Councillor Teller of the consistory."* In this letter in behalf of himself and some co-religionists he offered to accept Christianity in case they might be permitted to omit the observance of the Christian Festivals, to reject the doctrine of Trinity of the Divinity of Jesus and whatsoever is commonly regarded as essentially and specifically Christian. In fact he wanted a Christianity with Christianity left out. Judaism, Friedlaender claims, recognizes three eternally true principles: The Unity of God; the immortality of the soul; and the mission of man to strive after moral perfection and happiness. The ceremonial laws are perishable, and while they conveyed at one time moral lessons, they are valueless now. The belief in a Messiah, as contained in the prophets, has been misunderstood and misrepresented in the Talmud. We do not hope or wish to return to Jerusalem and to establish there a Jewish kingdom. Teller's answer was as could not otherwise have been expected, discouraging in the extreme. Some Christians saw in the "Sendschreiben" an attempt of the Jews, allied with Christian rationalists, to destroy positive Christianity and to introduce in its stead the religion of reason. § Schleiermacher looked at it in the light of a satire on intolerant Christianity, which excluded the Jews from the enjoyment of their rights of citizenship. While Friedlaender doubtless made a serious mistake in publishing the "Sendshreiben," his intentions were good. As he himself puts it, in said letter, he was afraid that the younger generation would fall a prey to orthodox Christianity, and therefore he wanted to save what could be saved on the principle that half a loaf is better than no bread at all. It was an act of despair and the fact that it has proved a failure, is the best that can be said of it. We

*Sendschreiben einiger Juedischen Hausvaeter an den Probst Teller, 1799.

§ J. A. De Luc "Lettre aux Auteurs Juifs d'un memoire addresse a Monsieur Teller," Berlin, 1799.

fully endorse Geiger's opinions on this subject: "He (Friedlaender) entertained to the end of his life the deepest aversion to the acceptance of Christianity. But it cannot surprise us in the least, that he became downhearted at times and was prepared to make certain concessions, which, while in full accord with his conscience and honesty, he ought not to have made. But this extravagance is only a characteristic of that restless self consuming epoch,"* Graetz, however, in his "impartial" history accuses Friedlaender in connection with this "letter" of impure motives, cowardice, selfishness" and "ambition." It is with due appreciation of such epithets, that Geiger says: "Whosoever is impudent enough to attack the venerable Friedlaender on account of some expressions of impatience and disgust sins against the noblest aspirations of Judaism."§ Friedlaender labored untiringly for fifty-five years in the cause of Judaism. Such a man cannot help making mistakes. The literature on the "Sendschreiben" was quite extensive. The following phamphlets appeared in rapid succession: "An Einige Hausvaeter Juedischer Religion, by a preacher in Berlin," Beantwortung des an Herrn Probst Teller erlassenen Sendschreibens, nicht von Teller;" "Beantwortung des Sendschreibens" by Teller himself; "Moses and Christus," by a protestant pastor; "Lettre aux Auteurs Juifs," by J. A. De Luc; "Briefe Bei Gelegenheit der politisch—theologishen Aufgabe und des Sendschreibens Juedischer Hausvaeter." though published anonymously is conceded to have been written by Schleiermacher; "Gespraech Ueber Das Sendschreiben." Beitrag zu den Ueberzeugungen einiger Hausvaeter Juedischer Religion, by Dr. Kochen. (Jena, 1800.)

On March 11, 1812, was published the famous edict according to which the Jews were declared citizens of the Prussian state. The Jews naturally

*Geiger: Wissensch. Zeitschrift, vol. IX. p. 248.
§Ibidem.

felt happy. They were anxious to show their gratitude and patriotism. When the Corsican Titan, the
heir of the revolution, marched with iron heel over the
writhing bodies of downcast Royal Absolutism, sweeping away the frail cobwebs of Autocratic presumption
and humiliating Prussia in particular, the people rose
in arms against him, and among the fighters for German independence was the flower of the Jewish youth
of the Fatherland. Their blood irrigated the battle-
fields; their graves opened by the side of the tomb
which sheltered the mangled corpses of their Christian
comrades. Had not the King appealed to their
patriotism? They equipped a volunteer regiment at
their own expense and in a letter to Count Von
Grote, dated January 4, 1815, the Prussian Minister,
Prince Von Hardenberg, says among other things:
"The history of our late war against France has proven
that the Jews have by faithful adherence become
worthy of the state which had made them citizens.
The young men of the Jewish faith have been the comrades of their Christian fellow citizens and we have
among them examples of true heroism, of the most
praiseworthy contempt for the dangers of war; and the
Jewish inhabitants, especially the ladies, have vied
with the Christians in sacrifices of all kinds."* Friedlaender recognizing that the outward emancipation
without the inward reorganization of the Jews would
prove a failure, and be accompanied by the most dire-
ful results, commenced seriously, his untiring work
in the cause of Jewish reform, the more so as the edict
of 1812 was the outcome of his indefatigable labors
during thirty years. He published a phamphlet entitled "A word at the right time," on the necessary
reformation (umbildung) of the service in the synagogue and the educational system of the Jews. (Berlin,
1812.) Although he did not sign his name, everybody
knew that Friedlaender was the author. The follow-

*See my Prinzipien des Judenthum's, verglichen mit denen
des Christenthum's Leipzig, Baumgaertner, 1877, p. 60.

ing passage in this pamphlet was not only the right
word for that time but has not lost its force in our
days, seventy years later: "Concerning the cult every
religious Israelite must say to himself that many
things in the prayers are incompatible with the wishes
of his heart, and that they are therefore an 'abomination of the Lord,' as Scripture puts it. Here I stand
before God, I pray for my King, for my fellow-citizens,
for myself and mine, not for return to Jerusalem, not
for the restoration of the old Temple and Sacrifices. My
heart has nothing to do with these wishes, their
realization would not make me happy, my mouth shall
not utter them." Friedlaender appeals then to all who
value truth and conviction, to unite in creating a
rational divine service in a language intelligible to all.
He further claims that too much time is devoted in
the Jewish elementary schools to the study of Hebrew
at the expense of other more important and more
practicable disciplines. But he most urgently pleads
for the publication of suitable text-books of the Jewish
religion, in accordance with a scientific spirit.* Strange
to say, notwithstanding the thousand and one text-
books which have been published in the German, English, French and Italian languages since that time, this
desideratum is still a pious wish. Our Sabbath-schools
are still without a good text-book. It was also Friedlaender, who pleaded for a thorough religious instruction of the girls. At that time he found an ally in his
work in Israel Jacobsohn, of whom more shall be said in
the following chapter. Although Jacobsohn was more
conservative, less thorough and capable than Friedlender, they worked harmoniously together on various
occasions. The prayer-book of the Jacobsohn-Temple
and the "Sermons devoted to the edification of educated
Israelites," edited by Friedlaender,§ are the fruits of
this co-operation.

These sermons were not delivered by Friedlaender

*I read a paper on this very subject in the Cleveland Rabbinical
Conference of 1890. (See Conference papers, etc., Cincinnati, 1891.)
§Berlin, 1815, first series.

himself, but by younger men, who often used them as
a basis for their discourses. The following passage of
a sermon on "religion and reason" is not yet antiquated.
Starting with a sentence of the philosopher Ibn Ezra,
"reason is the angel which mediates between God and
man," he continues, "Reason and religion can never
contradict each other; religion teaches us our relation
to the creator and our duties toward him, while reason
enables us to discriminate between the good and the
evil, between the true and the false—The contempt of
reason has produced religious cranks on the one side
and scoffers on the other, both because people laid
greater stress upon the letter than upon the spirit. He
who judges the life of the present by the letter of the
scripture, is a dreamer and visionary; he who judges
the letter of the Bible by the measure of his own days,
by the standard of his age, becomes a scoffer. Both
do not enter into the spirit of the Allegorical expression
of the Bible; they do not know how to discriminate.
Therefore the blind believer does an injustice to the
present, while the scoffer wrongs the past."

Alas! Friedlaender's last years were embittered
by the shameful way in which his co-religionists were
duped by the Prussian Government. Kings are slow
to learn the lesson of history, but quick to forget their
promises when exacted under the dire necessity of dark
hours. Hardly had the last sound of the musketry
rattled along the lines, hardly had the last cannon peal
died away among the echoes of blood-reeking mountains, when, once more, the Jew was told that to him
the state owed no debt of gratitude and was under no
obligation. The doctrine of the "Imperium in Im-
perio" once more raised its hydra-head, and was promulgated even by the philosophers' cringing sycophants
who occupied the chairs at the universities.* The
victories of Waterloo and Leipzig completely upset the
feelings of the Germans. The novel sense of power
intoxicated them; their mind lost its poise; romanticism

*Emil G. Hirsch. The basis of reform, a discourse. 1880, p. 5.

flourished; the violence of the middle ages was mistaken for manhood and held up to the emulation of the present generation. Whatever was not German was not considered good; whatever was foreign was despised, or, at best ignored,* and the Jews were made to feel the sharp sting of this feverish vanity.

The hints which Friedlaender pointed out in his pamphlet, entitled "A word at the right time concerning reforms in the Jewish worship," were most severely criticised by the orthodox Jews in Berlin, who were at that time in the majority. The King of Prussia intended to send a "cabinets order" to Friedlaender, couched in language by no means amiable, in which he would have given him to understand his opposition to reform. Minister Hardenberg, however, prevented this message. In the meantime Jacob Hertz Beer, the rich father of the highly talented Michael and Meyer Beer, had established in his house a private synagogue with a service in accord with the plans mapped out in Friedlaender's brochure. So did Israel Jacobson, who had moved from Cassel to Berlin. Jacobsohn confirmed ‡ his son and delivered German sermons and oomilies. The following enthusiastic young men: Isaac Auerbach, Edward Kley, K. F. Guensburg and Leopold Zunz, officiated as preachers in the Jacobson-Temple.† But the Prussian Government in its "parental care" for its Jewish subjects closed this Synagogue in 1817. The same fate would have befallen the Beer-Temple, had it not been for the accident, that the old Synagogue of Berlin had proved too small for the increasing membership and needed repairing badly, so that the Temple of Beer was used as an Interim-Synagogue by the congregation. Thus the

"*Deutsch Christlich ist mein Streben, und wer nicht Deutsche Roecke traegt ist nicht vaterlaendisch." See my Principien des Judenthums, 1877, p. 56. The same causes are at the root of modern German Antisemitism.

‡ This was, the first Jewish confirmation in Berlin.

† Isaac Noah Manheimer, later a power in Vienna, was added to the number of preachers.

congregation was compelled to accept the Temple as
it was with its preachers, its German sermons, its
prayers, and songs, accompanied by the stirring peals
of the organ. Now, while the progressive party and
the rising generation were happy over this state of affairs, the old conservatives, assisted in their opposition
by the Rabbi Meyer Simon Weyl, strongly denounced
this kind of worship. As both parties insisted on
their right, the matter came before a Governmental
Commission. The proposition to have on the Sabbaths
and Holidays first the Hebrew old fashioned service
and then the German prayers, songs and sermons,
which was sustained by the ministers of the Government, was also opposed by the intolerant zealots.
They brought their grievance before the narrow-
minded king, who, disregarding the just claims of the
reformers, ordered the private synagogues to be closed,
prohibited the erection of a new Temple and interdicted most severely innovations in the mode of worship, especially in the language and form of prayers.
(1823.) It is claimed by competent authority that
Frtedrich Wilhelm III was afraid lest a more attractive mode of worship among the Jews would diminish
the number of Jewish converts to Christianity.
Strange agreement between Jewish fanatics and
Christian bigots. It reminds one of the time when
Jewish zealots requested the Dominicans in France to
burn the writings of Maimonides, which was done at
Paris and Montpellier in 1242. Thus stagnation and
stability were sanctioned, and the police made an end
to a reform movement which had promised so much.

In 1814 Friedlaender was entrusted with the work
of a new edition of Mendelssohn's "Phaedon," to
which he wrote the introduction. In 1816 he was requested by the Bishop of Warschau to make to the
government "Propositions concerning the reform of the
Israelites in Poland," which he cheerfully did. These
plans are published with introductory remarks in a
pamphlet, "On the Amelioration of the Israelites in the
Kingdom of Poland." (Berlin, 1819.) Friedlaender laid

much stress on the discrimination between the Ethical and Ceremonial laws and said among other things: Ceremonies and customs are only temporary, capable of change, demanding abolition as soon as the welfare of society renders it imperative. When symbols and religious observances fail to influence the sentiment and actions of the people, then religion and reason demand that they be publicly declared void of authority. He then decries in the strongest terms the baneful influence of Rabbinism in Poland, and treats the Polish Rabbis without gloves. He describes their ignorance in all things but the Talmud, and shows how by means of their great civil authority, with which they were vested by the government they hindered the enlightenment of the Polish Jews. So long as their sanction of reforms is necessary nothing can be expected, as it is to their interest to shut out every ray of light from their dominion. They have nothing to do with the worship in the Synagogue. Twice a year, on the Sabbath before Passover, (Sabbath Haggadol,) and the Sabbath before the Day of Atonement. (Shabbath Shubah,) they deliver a kind of a discourse, such as it is.

These Rabbis do not propose to give moral instruction and to produce religious elevation, but they display their art of sophistry and of idle disputations even at the expense of logic. In fact, the only practicable labor of those Rabbis is their advice in matters concerning the dietary laws. They are naturally staunch opponents of every reform, fearing the loss of their authority. While they are good, moral men, they are utterly incapable of raising and elevating their co-religionists in the least to a higher standard. Friedlaender proposed, as indispensable towards bringing about better results, the introduction of the language of the country in the daily conversation; the abolition of the jurisdiction of the Rabbis and of the Jewish laws concerning money matters. All those who favor a modern mode of worship must have the right to establish it.   Good schools, educated teachers and able preachers would do the rest.

While these publications were a source of joy to Friedlaender, he was not a little mortified to be compelled to write in defense of his co-religionists against the literary crusade which was inaugurated against them from all sides, a subject of which I have spoken before.   Thus appeared his "Open letter" to an old friend of his, Von Der Recke, "Contribution to the history of the persecution of the Jews by Literati in the Nineteenth Century." † As an answer, Prof. Voigt published a pamphlet, "Open letter to Mr. David Friedlaender," which is full of mean invectives against the venerable Septuagenary.

Another fruit of the "reaction" was the "Society for the promotion of Christianity among the Jews," whose appeal was the cause of Friedlaender's last work: "To the admirers, friends and disciples of Jerusalem, Spalding, Teller, Herder, Loeffler, Leipzig, 1823." * Prof. Krug, the philosopher of Leipzig, wrote the preface to the book.   Krug laid bare the inconsistency of which Protestantism makes itself guilty by an attempt to convert the Jews. Friedlaender thought that the "society" would only serve as a spur and inducement to the Jews to study better their own religion and to continue the reforms in school and synagogue, so auspic ously commenced by them.   He said among other things, "that again t the theory of supernaturalism, which bluntly declares the acts closed, Judaism cannot enter into a struggle, as it is merely a question of dogma and blind belief with the supernaturalists; as to the advocates of Rationalism, they themselves agree with the Jews, that the so-called Prophecies in the Hebrew Bible contain not the least allusion to the founder of Christianity.   And as the only disagreement between Rationalists and Jews is

---

† Beitrag zur Geschichte der Verfolgunag der Juden im Neunzehnten Jahrhundert, durch Schriftsteller, 1820.

*An die Verehrer, Freunde und Schueler Jerusalem's, u. s. w.

to be found in the "means" and "method" towards attaining happiness, what is the use to quarrel about forms and ceremonies? He was sorry to hear, even from Rationalists, bitter words against Jews and Judaism. He conceded that Judaism too, like other religions, had its periods of decline. "It is for this very reason, that the new age is working with might and main for a restoration; hence the attempt to banish all abuses which, like the rust, cover the gold of the eternal truths, from synagogue, school and home."

In spite of old age, Friedlaender's warmest interest in the cause of Judaism never faltered. When the "Freischule" was merged in the "Gemeindeschule," of Berlin, he was entrusted with the working out of the plan of instruction. When the "Society for culture and science of the Jews," (Culturverein,) was started by Zunz, Gans, Moser and others, and a "Magazine for the science of Judaism," (Zeitschrift fuer die Wissenschaft des Judenthums, Dr. Zunz, editor) was published, Friedlaender was one of the contributors. He published three "Letters on the reading of the sacred scriptures" and a "Translation of the sixth and seventh chapters of Micah," where he shows the relation of religious reforms to the Bible.

Although Friedlaender was strongly denounced by the Rabbis, he never attacked them personally. He simply criticised the system of Rabbinism which was then in opposition to every religious progress. Had he lived to see the time when Rabbis, headed by Geiger, have become themselves leaders of the reform movement, he would doubtless have modified his judgment on Rabbinism.

Thus Friedlaender towers among the great and noble galaxy of Mendelssohn's disciples and friends as a bold, courageous reformer, consistent from beginning to end. He died, December 25, 1834, highly honored and respected by all who knew him. He died at the age of eighty-five, two years after the appearance of a work which marks an epoch in the history of Reform-

Judaism, I mean Zunz's "Monumentum aere perennium," "Die Gottesdienstlichen Vortraege der Juden."* The Jewish congregation of Berlin passed resolutions, highly appreciative of Friedlaender's works. Among other things, his zealous labor as elder of the congregation in the cause of the emancipation of the Jews in Prussia, his charity, humanity, inflexible honesty and his literary efforts, are greatly appreciated.

He could lay down his head to rest, fully satisfied that the future of Judaism was safe as long as men like Leopold Zunz labored in its cause.

---

*Liturgical lessons of the Jews (Berlin, 1832.) I do not claim, that this translation of the title of Zunz's Magnum Opus is fortunate. Not even the German title conveys an edequate idea of the work.

CHAPTER III.

ISRAEL JACOBSOHN.

Israel Jacobsohn was born at Halberstadt, October 17, 1768; died at Berlin, September 13, 1828. Although, by no means the equal of David Friedlaender as a philosopher and scholar, Israel Jacobsohn exerted a most decisive influence in the direction of Reform Judaism.

The zeal of the cultivated and educated class of Israelites during the period of transition, manifested itself in two different directions:

First: Emancipation from the bondage of restrictive laws against them.

Second: Emancipation from the thralldom of mediaevalism and Talmudism.

The first aim was easier to accomplish, the more so, because a great many Jewish men made their mark in science, art and industry, particularly so in Holland and France, where they found considerable encouragement from all sides. But not so easy a task was the internal enfranchisement from the yoke of Talmudical authority and Rabbinism. Here a struggle became necessary, a hot and hard fight indeed, which is not yet ended. The governments in Germany did not encourage Jewish Reform, knowing too well that it would stem the tide of apostasy in the ranks of Israel, and that it would awaken and strengthen the spirit of progress and liberalism, not only in religion, but in politics, and thus weaken despotism and monarchical absolutism. It therefore required great minds and strong manhood to accomplish this object. A man possessed of those valuable qualities was Israel Jacobsohn, a merchant, not belonging to the literary profession. He was from his nineteenth year the son-in-law of the strictly orthodox Rabbi in Braunschweig. By no means a scientist or scholar, he replaced this want more or less by his practical talent, his good common sense, his bold spirit of enterprise and energy, by a natural versatility in social intercourse, inexhaustible kindness and self-denial, glowing fantasy, swift activity, a pleasant imposing and prepossessing appearance. He read a great deal, studied hard, and thus became finally a thorough, I might almost say, American self-made man.

He was of the conviction that the service and mode of divine worship in the Synagogue of his days was of a character to displease even the strictest adherents of the Jewish traditions. He did not like at all the cold, philosophical naturalism, the negative rationalism and sovereign criticism characterizing the so-called Jewish aristocracy of Berlin at that time. He was a true hearted Jew in the noblest sense of the word. But, alas! he lacked scholarship and that deep knowledge and understanding so necessary for a successful Reform, the right and justification of which even the most pious could no longer deny.

Therefore he at first began the work with the youth, the school children; and he lavishly spent his time and wealth for that purpose. It is superfluous to mention that he used his influence to alleviate his co-religionists socially by abolishing a great many restrictive laws and statutes. He erected at his own expense in 1801 a Boarding School (Bildungsanstalt) for poor boys in Seesen (Braunschweig,) and, what is indeed remarkable for that time, this institution, which is to-day considered one of the best in Germany, has never been sectarian. From the very start Christian pupils were received, and to-day the school has an attendance of more than three hundred pupils, half of whom are

Christians. Jacobsohn spent more than 100,000 thalers for this school which is called the "Jacobsohn-Schule." In 1810, July 17th, he dedicated in the town of Seesen a Temple, which he had erected at his own expense. He introduced certain modifications, innovations or reforms into the service, which was the first attempt at Synagogical reform in Germany.

He introduced regular weekly sermons in the German language, which had not previously been customary, prayers in the vernacular by the side of the Hebrew, a choir singing with organ accompaniment, and a Confirmation as a fitting close of the school career of the boys and girls. In order to make room for the sermon, the ritual, encumbered by the weeds of Synagogical poetry, (mystical Pijutim,) most of which was couched in a barbaric language, were abbreviated.

Other measures to correct abuses of long standing followed, so that little by little the outward appearance of divine worship assumed a more dignified character. Israel Jacobsohn, always mindful of the welfare of his co-religionists, transplanted in 1815 the reforms of worship to Berlin. He erected there at his own expense a Temple, (Jacobsohn Temple,) and in 1818 assisted in founding the Temple at Hamburg, which soon became a leading stronghold of Reform in Germany.

Let me state right here, that it was by no means an easy task to introduce sermons delivered in the pure German language into the Synagogue. This reform was opposed by all the Rabbis at that time, who held public lectures twice a year, wherein they, for the benefit of the learned, explained some difficult passages of the Talmud, and then for the general public gave expositions of some Haggada. ‡ They spoke the language of the Ghetto, "Juedisch Deutsch," and considered the use of the pure German as a profanation. I am of the opinion that they would not have

---

‡ "Haggada" comprises the ethics and poetry of the Talmud.

opposed it, if they themselves had been able to deliver sermons in a correct language. We have analogies in this country, where, although at least three-quarters of the Jewish population were born in Germany, or in countries where German is spoken, Jewish preachers can be found strongly opposing German lectures. But strange as it may seem, it is a fact, that not one of the opponents of German is able to deliver an acceptable German lecture. There are no less than eight hundred German Christian preachers in this country, in whose churches no other word than German is heard either in prayer and song, or in sermon and lecture. Are they therefore not good American citizens? From the moment we oppose the use of the German language in the Synagogue on the ground, that it is not the language of the country, we are bound to take the next step and abolish the Hebrew language also; not only on this ground, but on another more important one, that the majority of all the Jewish worshippers and attendants of divine service throughout the United States do not understand, yes, I accentuate this sentence, do not understand the Hebrew prayers, no matter to which congregation they may belong, whether Portuguese, English, Orthodox, Reform or Polish.

In every congregation of this vast country there are, with the exception of a very few Portuguese-English congregations, more worshippers who do not understand Hebrew than who do not understand German. The German language is especially important for Reform Judaism, because Jewish Reform originated in Germany; all its great men were and are Germans; the vast literature on the subject is German, and even in this country the leaders are born Germans. It is a notable fact, however, that a praiseworthy reaction is setting in, in this respect, in America, inasmuch as German sermons are still required in most of the congregations and the most favored preachers are those, who are able to preach in both the English and German languages.

In this connection it deserves to be mentioned, that the first German sermons were written by Moses Mendelssohn, two on the occasion of the battles at Rossbach and Leuthen, one in celebration of the peace of Hubertsburg. The first ones were delivered by the chief Rabbi Aaron Moses in the Synagogue of Berlin. German sermons were a horror in the eyes of the majority of the Jews at that time, and were looked upon as a sinful innovation, and almost as a desecration. The first German Jewish preacher was Joseph Wolf in Dessau, a disciple and admirer of Mendelssohn. In 1806 he founded, in company with David Fraenkel, the German monthly "Sulamith." In 1808 he delivered his first German sermon in compliance with the wish of the Jewish Congregation of Dessau on the occasion of the Fiftieth Jubilee of the Count Leopold of Dessau. The embarrassed man became sick on account of the great excitement, but his sermon delivered in the presence of the Count, the officials of the government, of the city, and of a large assembly of Christians and Jews proved a success; so much so, that the congregation engaged him to preach on important Sabbath- and Holidays and actually paid him one and a half thaler, a little over a dollar, for each sermon. Later he was appointed as preacher and secretary of the Congregation, with a fixed salary of ten thaler, (not quite eight dollars,) monthly. And the good man gave the full value for the money received. These first six sermons, translated into Hebrew, were in 1812 published at Dessau.

The first sermon delivered on the feast of weeks contains no less than twenty-seven printed pages. Our American Jewish Congregations pay larger salaries to their Rabbis, and are fully satisfied with a sermon which takes twenty minutes to deliver.

Jacobsohn delivered a sermon in honor of the dedication of his School and Temple at Seesen in 1810. He adopted the costume of a Protestant pastor and all the bells of the town were ringing during the ceremony. His sermon elicited great applause; and a Princess of

Brunswick, a sister of Count Karl Ferdinand surprised him with a wreath of oak, wound by herself, and a highly flattering poem which was recited by the daughter of a Protestant minister.

Like Friedlaender, Jacobsohn was convinced, that only the rising generation was susceptible for the better. He said in this sermon among other things:

"Nur aus einem anfangenden und aufbluehenden, nicht aus einem verbluehten Menschenalter kann eine dauernde Umwaelzung des Geistes hervorgehen."*

Israel Jacobsohn's reforms implied a revolution in the character of Jewish worship. The purely devotional element acquired a prominence which was never before heard of. The very word employed to designate the purpose of Temple service. "Erbauung," (edification,) was something strange to the vocabulary of the Jews. Thus Jacobsohn became an important factor in the history of Reform Judaism. He accomplished much by correcting the abuses which had been allowed to grow up unrestrained in the gloomy period of mediaeval persecution. He won back to Judaism those whose affections had been estranged by the barbarous form in which it appeared.

Israel Jacobsohn was a man of wonderful energy, restless activity and a great flow of language. With his natural eloquence he now touched his audience to tears, and now moved them to the highest pitch of enthusiasm. Had his knowledge kept pace with his fertile imagination, he would have become a great preacher.

The Jews of Braunschweig, Lueneburg and Baden are indebted to him and to Wolf Breidenbach for the abolition of the disgraceful "Leibzoll," a tax exacted from their bodies which placed them on an equal footing with animals. (April 23, 1803.) In a letter to

---

*"A lasting spiritual revolution can arise only from a blooming, and not from a decaying generation." (Sermon delivered at the dedication of the Jacobsohn-Temple at Seesen, July 17, 1810. See Sulamith" III, I, 303).

Napoleon, Israel Jacobsohn proposed the appointment of a council for the Jews in Europe with a Patriarch at its head. Romantic as this idea appeared, it perhaps influenced Napoleon to convoke the Sanhedrin at Paris. The great Corsican convened in 1806, a Parliament of Jewish Notables at Paris, in order definitely to settle the relation of the French Israelites to the state. Soon after an imperial decree convoked the Grand Sanhedrin for the purpose of ratifying the decisions of the Notables.

The glories of Jerusalem of old were to be renewed in the modern Babylon on the Seine. On February 9, 1807, the Sanhedrin met in the Hotel de Ville. Great care was taken to invest its sittings with all the pomp, solemnity and outward show so necessary for a performance utterly devoid of truth, sincerity and inmost conviction. The seats of the members were arranged in crescent shape about the platform of the presiding officers, as had been customary at Jerusalem. The president was saluted with the title of Nassi (Prince) as in olden times. The ancient titles and forms were copied with scrupulous exactness. The first meeting took place on a Sabbath and most of the members came ostentatiously in carriages and did not abstain from writing on that day. This, as was the whole proceeding, was done to please Napoleon. The servility manifested in the speeches was disgusting in the extreme.

Bonaparte was simply deified. Twelve questions were laid before the Sanhedrin, and the answers were nothing but shrewd evasions or downright falsehoods. Especially must this be said of the affirmative reply to the question : Is a divorce according to the French law valid without a religious divorce ?

The answer to the question, whether Judaism permitted inter-marriage between Jews and Christians, was a tissue of untruth and hypocrisy. Just think of a gathering of 110 Jews in 1807, two-thirds of them Rabbis, encouraging intermarriage of Jews and Christians. For this is just what the declaration amounted to. They declared that only marriages be-

tween Jews and idolaters were forbidden, that the
European nations, (Christians and Mohammedans)
were not regarded as idolaters, not even by the
Talmudists. Hence, there can be no prohibition against
intermarriage from the standpoint of the Talmud.
Nevertheless, they (the Rabbis) could not solemize
such a marriage on account of the ceremony on such
occasions. But this would not matter much, as the
civil marriage is valid any way, because the state
recognizes its validity. Even the Rabbis cannot help
recognizing a Jew or a Jewess, who has married a
Christian, as full members of Judaism in every respect.
I ask every unbiased reader, whether such an answer
is worthy of a Jewish representative body? No
wonder, that although the opening of the Sanhedrin
attracted universal attention in Europe, its proceedings
were void of interest and beneficial results. Parturiunt
montes, nascitur ridiculus mus.—David Friedlaender
and his friends were right in calling the Sanhedrin a
"farcical show,", given by Napoleon to his sensation-
loving Parisians.* Dr. Geiger in his "Allgemeine
Einleitung in die Wissenschaft des Judenthums,"
(General introduction into the science of Judaism,)
speaking of the Sanhedrin says:

"The whole thing was a great lie, at least a show,
the questions were premature, the answers merely
shrewd serpentine curves altogether without consequences."†

"The only fruit of the great show in Paris was the
creation of a new constitution for the French Synagogue,
elaborated by the joint efforts of the Imperial Com-
missioners and the Notables. The form of government adopted was moulded on the pattern of the
secular power, tinged with a semblance of Catholic
hierarchy.

*David Friedlaender: Ueber d. Verbesserung der Israelitea in
Koenigreiche Polen, introduction, p. 32.

†Nachegelassene Schriften, volume II, Berlin, 1875, Louis
Gerschel, p. 239.

A system of consistories was organized throughout France, culminating in a Central consistory at Paris with a Grand Rabbi at the head, who appears in the Synagogue—in the attire of a Catholic Bishop.

This Central consistory watched over the consistories, Rabbis, Synagogues and Congregations. They in turn were to form a sort of police for the individual Jews who watched and saw that the resolutions of the Sanhedrin were carried out, that the practice of usury was prohibited, and furnished to the French government every year the number of Jewish young men, old enough to do military service. What a disgrace for the Rabbis to play the part of spies and detectives, and what an insult to the young Frenchmen of Jewish persuasion, even to insinuate their intention of evading their patriotic duty of serving their country, and to suspect them of cowardice. The introduction into Judaism of a species of graded hierarchy dependent upon temporal rulers for its support was, as could not have been otherwise expected, fraught in its wake with consequences fruitful of evil results. If it is true that the supremacy of the church over the state has proven since times immemorial the disturbing element of the peace of nations and has endangered the very existence of governments, it is equally certain that no religion can long continue to maintain its purity when the church becomes the subservient vassal of the state. Hypocrisy and servility flourish, liberty of conscience is curtailed, and a spirit of petty, base time-serving eventually prepares the downfall of institutions whose perfect safety is consistent only with perfect freedom.

The French Synagogue with its consistorial system presents a case in point. During the past eighty years, just in that period, when a refreshing and quickening spirit enlivened Judaism in Germany, it has stagnated. No single ray lights up its dreary record, no single luminous thought, no single whole-souled effort to appropriate the larger truth of our progressive age dignifies its annals. Hence, the majority of the Jews in Paris are atheistic the whole year, but strictly orthodox on Rosh Hashana and Yomkippur. As a rule the French Jewish press make a great ado over the fact that the Rothschilds and other millionaires and dignitaries of the army, attired in their military suits, their breasts decorated with medals and crosses, have paid a visit to Jehovah once a year.* The young generation is worldly and estranged from Judaism. The following extract from a letter of the famous Parisian banker, L. R. Bischoffsheim, to Dr. Abraham Geiger, dated September 7, 1872, fully corroborates the above: "I have been for a long time a faithful reader of your periodical and am in full accord and sympathy with the views you express on the mission and future of Judaism. It however, seems to me, that the time has arrived, when the word should become action.

The majority of the forty thousand Jews of Paris have severed almost every link connecting them with Judaism ritually, so that virtually they are Jews in name only. Many of the best and wealthiest families attend no more the Synagogue—very likely, because the service is too orthodox for them, and what is still worse, permit their daughters to marry Christians. And while these daughters do not embrace Christianity, which means here Catholicism, their children are with but few exceptions, raised as Catholics. The education of the children, so far as religion is concerned, is almost zero, and when religious instruction is given, it is in such glaring contradiction to the life and practice of their parents at home, that the inconsistency cannot remain hidden from the sight of the children."†

---

*If Isaiah would live to-day, he would tell such gentry: "When you come to be seen by me who asks this of your hands, who cares for it, whether you enter my courts? Cease to offer unto me an offering of falsehood and hypocrisy, it is an incense of abomination unto me" (Isaiah, chapter I.) Your new moons and holidays are hateful unto me, I am tired of them. And though ye may fold your hands in prayer, I turn away my eyes from you, and no matter how much you pray, I do not listen to you." (Ibidem.)

†Geiger, Nachgelassene Schriften, vol. V, p. 345-46, and my Abraham Geiger als Reformator des Judenthums Loebau, 1879, p. 147-148.

In the science and literature of Judaism, French Judaism is an unknown quantity. Whatever has been done in this respect was done by German scholars there, by Frank Dernburg, Darmstaedter, Munk and others.

If Paris offers such a sad spectacle, what can be expected of the small congregations in the interior? In the history of the Jewish Reform movement France merits no mention. The same, if not a worse state of affairs, we find in England where, under the sway of a fanatic Chief Rabbi every attempt towards a progressive development of Judaism in Great Britain and the Dominions was and still is most relentlessly stifled and checked. Germany and America,* offer the only oasis in the desert.

After this necessary digression let us return to Jacobsohn.

After the humiliation of Prussia, **Napoleon** created the "Kingdom of Westphalia" under his brother Jerome, who, in an edict of January 12, 1808, declared all the Jews of the kingdom without exception, citizens and the equals of his Christian subjects. He abolished the so-called Jew-tax, and granted to foreign Jews the right to settle in his land under the privileges enjoyed by Christians. The capital of the Kingdom of Westphalia was Cassel.

King Hieronymus (Jerome) made Israel Jacobsohn his "Geheimen Finanzrath" (Secret counsellor of finances.) Jacobsohn had held the same position under Count Karl Ferdinand. In memory of the day of emancipation of the Jews of the Kingdom of Westphalia, Jacobsohn ordered a golden medal to be made emblematical of the Union of the two so long hostile creeds upon which the following words were coined in Latin:

"To God and the Fatherly King united in the Kingdom of Westphalia."†

---

*American Reform Judaism is nothing original, but the offspring of German Reform.

† The work was done by a Jewish artist, named Abramson, of Berlin. See Spicker: 'The position of the Jews in Germany," page 287.

Jacobsohn urged the King to convoke twenty-two notables at Cassel and to organize the Jews of Westphalia after the manner of those in France, which was done. Jacobsohn was elected President of the Commission and entrusted with the working out of a plan for a Jewish consistory in the Kingdom of Westphalia. The seat of the consistory was Cassel, Jacobsohn its President, while Loeb Meyer Berliner, the old Rabbi of Cassel, later Grand Rabbi of Westphalia, Mendel Steinhardt, Simon Kalker, and the two laymen David Fraenkel of Dessau and Jerome Heinemann were members of the consistory.

While the consistory in France has done next to nothing for the cause of a progressive development of Judaism, the consistory of Westphalia, inspired by the ever active and energetic Israel Jacobsohn, has better understood and practically carried out its mission. It has accomplished much in giving indirectly to the Jews of Germany a service in the Synagogue more in keeping with the wants of the nineteenth century, although what was called "Reform" then, is considered almost orthodox to-day; at least in this free progressive country of ours. Graetz himself, who treats Jacobsohn no better than he does Friedlaender, and who insinuates, that whatever Jacobsohn has done was actuated by the motive of vanity, conceit, and a desire for notoriety, is compelled to make the following concessions:

" Jacobsohn's impetuosity was necessary, in order to do away successfully with the rubbish and trash, which had accumulated in such gigantic proportions, especially in the smaller congregations. It would have been of no avail to handle it with delicate fingers.[*]

Among other things the Rabbis had to preach in German, and to perform the ceremony of Confirmation of the young.

This ceremony took its origin in the Jacobsohn-school of Seesen, and Jacobsohn was one of the first, if

---

[*] Graetz: Geschichte der Juden, XI, p. 310.

not the first, to confirm his son in 1814 or 1815 in Jacobsohn's Betsaal, (private Synagogue) in Berlin.

This ceremony is one of the institutions introduced by the Reformers, which, in spite of great and long opposition, has strongly seized upon the popular heart and is to-day, at least in America, generally accepted even by the orthodox Jews.

This reform is the best refutation of the frequent reproaches against the Reformers, that they destroy and abolish without creating anew. Indeed it is only fit and proper at the age when children's character begins to assume definite outlines, when reason unfolds and temptations of life approach nearer, that we utilize the impressiveness of a great public gathering, the sympathetic presence of parents and friends and the earnest monitions of a wise and reverend teacher, in order to confirm them in the virtuous endeavor to strive after moral perfection and assist them to the best of their ability in building the kingdom of righteousness. The Confirmation *per se* is not a theatrical show, as Graetz and others style it, as long as it is not made so by the folly of some parents who outvie each other in exhibiting their daughters laden with jewelry, in an attire more adapted for the ballroom than for the house of worship. Another great mistake is made by ignorant preachers, who, in imitation of the Catholic or Episcopalian Confirmation, exact formal vows, sometimes even in the form of an oath, from children at the age of thirteen years, who cannot reasonably be expected to answer for their convictions fifteen or thirty years later. The great desideratum in this respect is that the Confirmation should take place at the age from fifteen to seventeen years when the confirmants are better able to comprehend the fundamental questions of religion.

David Friedlaender was a great assistance to Jacobsohn as an adviser, but Jacobsohn himself had to be very careful about reforms, as King Jerome like all sovereigns sided with orthodoxy.

One day he reproached Jacobsohn on account of his "Sectirerei" without giving him a chance for explanation. *

The closing by the Prussian Government of his Temple was a terrible blow for the good man and enthusiastic Jew. Dr. Herzfeld, Land Rabbi of Braunschweig, says this on this deplorable subject:

"The Temple in Berlin was closed, the "pious ones" (die Frommen) did not rest with their calumnies in honor of God. This not only broke the heart of the noble Jacobsohn, but drove hosts of Jews out of the pale of Judaism, so that the Rabbi of Berlin on his death-bed said: "I wish this had never happened. It is far better to proclaim Shma Jissrael in German than not to recite it at all." † It goes without saying that Jacobsohn might have lived longer, had his hope in this regard not been so mercilessly blasted.

Jost, a personal friend of Jacobsohn, said of him: „He breathed new life into the form of the dead; without language he acquired the gift of oratory; without music he created melodies conducive of devotion." ‡

The centennial of Jacobsohn's birthday was solemnly celebrated in the Temples of Berlin, Halberstadt, Braunschweig, and especially in Seesen where the director of the Jacobsohn school, Dr. Arnheim delivered a touching eulogy of which we excerpt the following passage:

"Jacobsohn never wavered, never was despondent, though his eye could not behold the fruits of his labor. The belief in God furnished him with the belief in himself, and he felt himself amply rewarded that he was permitted to see the dawn of the coming day, to direct his eyes from the top of the mountain to the promised land. He knew no difference of person. The needy man stood near to him, no matter what his

---

* Jost: Das Judenthum und seine Sekten, III, p. 326, note.

† Herzfeld: sermon on the religious Reform delivered in Nordhausen, September 13, 1845. (Nordhausen, 1845.)

‡ Jost: Israelitische Annalen, 1839, p. 235.

social standing. He preferred to practice charity in secret, hidden from the eyes of man, but whenever his example would induce others to emulation, he did not shun publicity. Small and mean people only cannot appreciate, in their narrowmindedness, true goodness.''

Following are the names of those who were present as delegates at the celebration in Seesen: Professor Dr. Steinthal, representing the Jewish congregation of Berlin; Dr. Ehrenberg, representing the Samson School in Wolfenbuettel; Dr. Baerwald, representing the Congregation and Philanthropin School in Frankfort on the Main; Rector Horwitz, representing the Boys' School in Berlin, and Assessor Kruse of Gandersheim, representing the State of Braunschweig. The five sons of Jacobsohn sent in memory of the day 500 Thaler to the Jewish Congregations of Berlin, Halberstadt and Braunschweig, to be distributed among the poor irrespective of creed. Services in honor of the centenary of Jacobsohn's birth were held by Grand Rabbi, Dr. L. Herzfeld in Braunschweig, and by Dr. Joseph Aub, Rabbi of Berlin. The latter said on that occasion, that the most fitting way for the Jews of Berlin to honor Jacobsohn, would be the establishment in Berlin of an institution for the education of Rabbis, who favor progress and Reform in Judaism. Such an institution was opened in Berlin, May 6, 1872, under the name of ''Hochschule fuer die Wissenschaft des Judenthums,'' * in which Dr. Geiger was the leading spirit. Dr. Immanuel Loew, Rabbi in Szegedin, the author of this book, and Professor Felix Adler, New York, were the first three students, matriculated in May, 1872, in this seat of learning.

Jacobsohn died in Berlin, September 13, 1828.

---

* The institution was founded by Prof. M. Lazarus and other generous Jews. Since May 7th, 1883, the name of ''Hochschule'' had to be changed to ''Lehranstalt'' (institution of learning.)

CHAPTER IV.

ARON CHORIN.

Born in Weisskirchen, Maehren, August 3, 1766, died on the 27th of August, 1844, in Arad, Hungary. Chorin as a pioneer of Reform-Judaism deserves greater consideration than the men, of whom I have so far spoken, from the fact that he was the first Rabbi, who, more than half a century ago, in his capacity of Rabbi, was in favor of Reform. For a Rabbi to do so in those days demanded not a little courage.

Friedlaender and Jacobsohn were wealthy and independent merchants. Chorin, however, was a poor man, with a large family dependent on his small salary.

As I do not suppose that Aron Chorin is so well known as the other pioneers of Reform-Judaism, from the fact, that he had not the good fortune to live and labor in Germany, where his work would have been better appreciated, I will begin at the end and introduce this fearless champion of Reform with an extract from one of the four funeral sermons delivered at his burial. In these words, spoken by Rabbi Daniel Pillitz, of Szegedin, we find verified the maxim of the Talmud. "The way that a man is spoken of after death is the best criterion of his life." ‡ It is as follows:

"Chorin taught as he believed and acted as he taught. While his teachings were ahead of his generation and his contemporaries were not ripe for

---

‡ "Mehesspado shel Adam Nikkar Shahoo Adam Japhai."

his doctrines, he had the courage to stand for his convictions, to fight for them at a time, when he stood yet entirely alone and in opposition to a world which was bitterly opposed to him. He was not afraid of the difficult struggle; he came forward and manfully endured the hot day's work."

The "Markgrafschaft (Earldom) of Maehren (Moravia)" small though it is, has contributed largely to the history of modern Judaism. Some of the most celebrated Rabbis, authors, and preachers of Europe were born, or have labored in Maehren. Jonathan Eibeschuetz was born in Eibeschuetz, Maehren, where his father, Nathan Natia, was Rabbi. Rabbi Elieser Trietsch (a town in Maehren) was considered a great authority.*

The most renowned Jeshibahs (Rabbinical schools) of the last and even of this century were located in Leipnik, Nickolsburg and Boskowitz. In the first mentioned town, where the author of this book was born, men like Rabbi Baruch Fraenkel, called "Baruch Taam" on account of his work bearing this name, had sometimes as many as two hundred disciples, ("Bachurim,") † ranging from the age of fifteen to forty years. After his death men like Rabbi Shlome Quetsch and Rabbi Moses Bloch, shed lustre upon Judaism. Rabbi Moses Bloch, my teacher, is Professor of Talmudic and Rabbinical disciplines, also President of the "Landes-Rabbiner-Anstalt" (Rabbinical Seminary) in Budapesth, the capital of Hungary, and author of several important works on Rabbinical literature. Mordechai Benet (Marcus Benedict), whose name will be mentioned in connection with the subject of this biography, was Chief Rabbi of Maehren and had a large Jeshibah in Nickolsburg. He and three others, Akiba Eger (Posen), Jacob Lissa and Moses Szofer

---

*See his decision on the Hamburg Prayer-book, of which I speak later on.

†"Bachur," the singular form of "Bachurim" means "young man." It is however used to designate "young students of the Talmud in a Jeshiba." (Talmudical school.)

(Pressburg) succeeded in gathering around them a large
number of "Bachurim," at a time when the Jeshibahs in
Germany (Fuerth) Frankfurt A. M., Halberstadt,
Altona-Hamburg, Metz and others), were dying of inanition.   Samson Raphael Hirsch, the leader of modern
orthodoxy, the originator of the school, which Leopold
Loew so fittingly characterized as the "New-orthodox
romantic," was also Chief-Rabbi of Maehren.   But it
must be stated, that he did not feel at home among the
great Talmudists of Nickolsburg, because he could not
cope with them as an equal in Rabbinical lore.   Aside
from this all these Moravian "Lamdonim" (Scholars)
were, notwithstanding their piety and zeal for the
preservation of Judaism, not at all pleased with that
small, petty orthodoxy which makes a fetich of the
"Schulchan Aruch," and whose only knowledge of
Judaism consists in knowing by heart the "Beer heteb,"
(a compendium of Jewish ceremonies.)   For an
orthodoxy of the Hirsch-Lehman-Hildesheimer stamp
Maehren was already too far advanced sixty years ago.
Hirsch therefore preferred to accept the call tendered
him by the then very small Congregation in Frankfurt
on the Main, * where he hoped to, and in fact, did find
the proper field for his ultra-orthodox notions.   That
he accepted this call is the best proof of our statement
concerning Maehren.   Of prominent men in modern
Jewish history as authors, preachers and reformers I
will only mention a few:

Dr. Leopold Schwab, Rabbi of Prossnitz, Maehren,
later Chief-Rabbi of Pesth; Rabbi Fassel, of Prossnitz,
later Rabbi of Gross-Kanissa, Hungary, a great
scholar, profound Talmudist, an important writer on
Jewish law and a reformer; Professor Dr. Moritz
Steinschneider, of Prossnitz, one of the greatest Jewish
bibliographers living; Dr. Leopold Loew, Rabbi
of Papa and Szegedin, justly called "The Hungarian
Geiger," one of the greatest and most interesting

---

*The congregation consisted then of only eleven members. It
must, however, be borne in mind, that one of the Rothschilds and
other very wealthy men were among the number.

Rabbis of this century, and very prolific as an author of Jewish literature, especially on archaeology. In this connection I must mention another Moravian who was very little appreciated in his life-time and who deserves an honorable page in the history of Reform-Judaism. I mean Moses Brueck. * He was born in 1812 in Prerau, Maehren, one mile from Leipnik, studied in Prague, traveled through Germany and emigrated to Hungary. In 1848, he took part in the Jewish Reform movement at Gross-Becskerek. He died in 1849, as an officer of the Hungarian army, and was buried with military honors in the Jewish cemetery at Hold-Mezo Basarhely. He was radical in his Reform ideas, and published the following works: "Rabbinishe Ceremonialgebraeuche," "Pharisaeishe Volkssitten" and "Reform of Judaism," in one hundred theses, commented on and explained. He says on page 76: "This book was commenced and completed in one month, but contains the material collected in twenty years." He says more in one page than a great many others say in fifty pages.

These one hundred theses deserve more than passing notice. An appeal to the Jews precedes them, of which we excerpt the following:

Reform is the motto of the glorious year 1848. For eighteen hundred years the better class of Israel demanded Reform from their Rabbis, but we see still the same Babylonian monster. The masses of the people were therefore compelled to do this work themselves, and the consequence is that Judaism is reduced to the attendance of the Synagogue once a year. * * * * * Now is the most favorable moment for a thorough Reform in Judaism; the better class of Jews favor a conciliation of religion with the demands of life. Do not wait for the results of some Rabbinical Synod, from which at best, some insignificant concessions but no salvation can be expected. Manifest your will, and the yoke which for two thousand years

* See my article in the "American Israelite," August, 1889.

almost oppressed us with its burden, the fetters which
were forged in the centuries of spiritual slavery will fall.
The sanctuary of Israel, which was laid in a grave as
a mummy, will resurrect; the domestic and public worship, now dead, will again be revived. They all will
awake, who by fanaticism were intimidated in their
struggle for light and truth; they all will awake, who
so far have fought in vain for the right of Israel, and
in legions our brethren will rally around the unfurled
banner of religious Reform, and the sound will be
heard: Israel is redeemed.

Of the one hundred interesting theses I mention
the following most striking ones:

7.   All prayers, with the exception of the Shma,
are recited in the vernacular.

9.   Male worshippers have to uncover their heads.

12.   The reading of the Thora can take place out
of a neatly-bound Bible.

13.   After the reading in Hebrew follows the
reading and explanation in the vernacular.

14.   Nobody is called to the Sefer Thora.

15.   Three years' cycle and no Haphtarah.

29.   The Kaddish prayer is abolished, memorial
services (haskarath neshamoth) being sufficient.

22.   On New Year, during the Mussaph prayer,
cornets are blown, and the blowing of the Shofar is
dispensed with also after the Neila prayer on the day
of Atonement.

26.   The Lulab on Succoth is done away with.

39.   The week begins with Monday, and the
weekly day of rest is celebrated on Sunday.

The dietary laws are abolished (51-59.)

60.   Only on the eve of Passover the eating of un-
leavened bread is required.

Very elaborate explanations concerning the justification of those radical reforms are given.

See Fuerst's favorable criticism in the Allgemeine

Zeitung des Judenthum's 1837, I, page 324, and
Geiger's Wiss. Ztsch, III, 426."

The recognized authority on Cabbalah and Jewish
religious philosophy, the pioneer and pathfinder in the
field of Modern Jewish Homiletics, the great master in
the treatment of the Talmud and Midrash in the pulpit,
the eloquent orator, in short, the man who justly enjoys the reputation of being the best Jewish preacher
in the German tongue, namely, Dr. Adolf Jellinek, in
Wien, was born in Ungarisch-Brod, Maehren. The
philosopher and physician, Dr. Gideon Brecher, hails
from Prossnitz. Rabbi Bruell, who published a
splendid book on the Talmud, scientific and critical,
hails from Kojetein. So do his sons; Dr. Nehemias
Bruell, the successor of Dr. Geiger in Frankfurt on the
Main. He was editor of the "Juedische Jahrbuecher,"
devoted to Jewish history and literature, and one of
the very few honest Rabbis and outspoken Reformers
in Germany. ‡ His brother, Dr. Adolph Bruell, editor
of the "Wissenschaftliche Monatsblaetter," is well
versed in oriental, especially Samaritan, literature; the
late Rabbi, Dr. Ph. Frankel, an eminent scholar and
writer, preacher in Berlin; Leopold Dukes, Dr. David
Kauffman, an able writer on Jewish philosophy in the
middle ages and Professor of the Rabbinical Seminary
in Buda Pesth; Professor Wolf, the Historian, Vienna;
Dr. Porges, Rabbi of Leipzig; Dr. Gustav Karpeles,
the well known author, and a great galaxy of able
younger scholars, writers, physicians and lawyers,
especially in Vienna, they all hail from the little Earldom of Maehren.

Aron Chorin was born in Weisskirchen, about a
mile distant from Leipnik, so that I have the right,
and I feel proud of this privilege, to call him almost
my townsman. His father, Kalman, though making
a scanty living only, saved no expense to secure the

‡ He died February 5, 1891. See my obituary of Bruell in the
"Reform Advocate," of March 20, 1891, also Dr. Emil Hirsch's edi-
torial in the same number.

best teachers of the small place for his son Aron. According to the custom of those days, Talmud, Thora, Rashi and some Hebrew Grammar, taught in the most unscientific manner, composed the curriculum. In 1780 the parents of Chorin moved to Deutsch-Kreuz, Hungary. But as the opportunities for the study of the Talmud in that place were limited, the boy, then fourteen years old, was sent to the neighboring town of Mattersdorf, where a "Jeshiba" was flourishing under the supervision of Rabbi Jeremias, a Talmudist of great renown, who was honored with the title "Gaon." § During the two years of his sojourn in Mattersdorf, the boy studied so faithfully and zealously, that he was able to prepare himself, without the assistance of a teacher, for the Talmudical lectures of the great Rabbi, Ezechiel Landau, of Prague, whither in 1782 our ambitious Aron had directed his steps. In the classical capital of Bohemia he first commenced to study Hebrew Grammar and German. It is claimed that he lived in Prague in a family suspected of Sabbataism, ‖ and that there is to be traced the germ of his reformatory ideas. After three year's sojourn in Prague, Aron, then nineteen years old, went home in order to marry, (1785.) According to the rules of Orthodox Judaism, a man ought to marry at the age of eighteen years. That modern orthodoxy sets aside this law is one of its inconsistencies. The name of Chorin's wife was Rebecca and this marriage was blessed with seven children, three sons and four daughters. Chorin embarked in business, but, like the true scholar he could not make a success of it, because he was not designed to be a business man. He accepted the call extended to him by the Congregation of Arad. So we meet him as Rabbi in Arad, where he went in

---

§ Literally "pride," but in this connection a title for exceptional scholarship in Rabbinical lore.

‖ Sabbathai Zebi, (born 1625, died 1677,) a Kabbalist who claimed in 1655 at Jerusalem, to be a Messia. He adopted in Abrianopel, in 1665, Islamism and died in 1677. He was the founder of the great sect of the Sabbathians.

the spring of 1789, the year of the French revolution.
His salary was four Rhenish Gulden a week, free
rent and the customary perquisites, but in the months
of Nissan, Sivan and Tishri the salary was doubled.
A year later his salary was raised to five Gulden
weekly I mention this fact without fear that the
American Jewish Congregations of 1892 will try to fix
the salaries of their Rabbis according to the standard
of Hungary, one hundred years ago. But small as
Chorin's Congregation was, they felt so proud of its spiritual guide, that they were willing to keep a "Jeshibah"
for him, which meant quite a sacrifice for a small
Congregation, where the burden of supporting the
students naturally fell upon a few members. It was
the rule, that the "Bachurim," (students) took their
meals in the houses of the wealthier members of the
Congregation. The poorer classes had a "Bachur"
for the Sabbath, once every month or six weeks.
Chorin was painstaking both as a teacher of "Bachurim"
and in his own studies. The Talmud, Bible, Hebrew
Grammar, the Philosophers of the middle ages, Sohar
and Midrash engaged his special attention. He was
an eloquent preacher (Maggid) and won soon golden
opinions, not only from his own Congregation, but
from the Jewish merchants, who came to Arad on
business. His teachers, R. Jeremias, and Moses
Muentz, of Altofen, corresponded with him on Talmudical topics. Mordechai Benet, Chief Rabbi, of Machren of
whom I have previously spoken, called him "a great and
prominent Rabbi, the light of Israel, a pillar." I
mention this intentionally, because Prof. Graetz, true
to his method of belittling every man connected with
the Jewish Reform-movement, speaks of Aron Chorin
as "an equivocal character and tedious prattler, of
varnished education, and mediocre Talmudical
scholarship. He favored the new movement without
having a clear judgment." ‡ Graetz's judgment of

‡ History of the Jews, vol. XI, p. 421. He calls him "Choriner,"
not Chorin.

Chorin is, to say the least, dimmed by partisanship and prejudice, from which a historian must emancipate himself. The fact that Chorin favored the new movement, so antipathetic to Graetz, is no justifiable reason for disparaging his merits. As Graetz raises to the skies the Chief Rabbi, Mordechai Benet, of Nickolsburg, (Ibid., page 419,) on account of his profound scholarship in the Talmud and his noble character, we are surely entitled to believe more in Mordechai Benet's opinion of Chorin than in Graetz's. We come now to Chorin's struggles in the cause of progress and Reform in Judaism.

In 1792 Rabbi Hirsch, of Temesvar, inquired of his former teacher, Rabbi Ezechiel Landau, of Prague, whether the sturgeon, a species of fish called "sterlet, storchlein," belonged to the clean fish which were permitted to be eaten by the Jews. The Jews in the Orient were in the habit of eating these fish and the Sphardish members of Hirsch's Congregation wanted to do the same. Rabbi Hirsch sent two samples of the fish to Prague and Rabbi Ezechiel declared them "kosher," i. e., fit to be eaten by the Israelites, (Levit. XI, 9.) Thus the affair seemed to be settled and from that time on the Jews of Temesvar gave the sturgeon a place in their bill of fare. Chorin, on hearing of it, permitted his Congregation the same luxury, not, however, before he had seen the declaration of the renowned Rabbi of Prague. This incensed the Rabbi Isac Krieshaber, Krakau, (Galicia,) who was in charge of the Congregation at Paks (Hungaria) and who was a bigot and fanatic of the worst type. He became in later years the cause of great trouble to Chorin. At first he directed a polite epistle to the Rabbi of Arad, requesting him to retract his declaration concerning the sturgeon, (1798.) Chorin flatly refused to do so. Krieshaber then called a number of Rabbis to his assistance and tried to induce them to declare the sturgeon an "unclean fish" on the strength of a fine distinction made by Nachmanides in his commentary to the Thora (In the year 1266,) as to what constitutes the elements of "scales." His main objection was, however, the trite argument of orthodoxy in all ages and climes, that old custom prohibits the use of sturgeon at the table of Jews. He called the Oriental Jews, who were in the habit of eating the fish, "frivolous Sabbathaians." This Rabbi Krieshaber went, however, further in order to carry his point. Knowing only too well that the generally esteemed Ezechiel Landau, of Prague, who was considered authority. had also decided in favor of the sturgeon, he wrote to Chorin, that Rabbi Ezechiel had in the meantime recanted his decision. This was a downright falsehood, invented by the "pious" Rabbi, who, like a good many of his stamp, lay greater stress upon the religion of the pot and kettle than upon the lessons of ethics, truth and righteousness. However, this untruth did not help his case, as the Rabbis of Prague, Michael Bachrach, Eleazar Fleckeles and Samuel Landau were not slow in giving the lie to Krieshaber's false statement with respect to Ezechiel Landau's recantation of the decision.

In the meantime the Chief Rabbi of Maehren, Mordechai Benet, took sides against Chorin in the question of the sturgeon, prevented the publication in Vienna, of a polemic treatise written by Chorin, and warned the Congregation of Arad not to eat the fish in question. On the other hand the Rabbi of Altofen, Hungary, sided with Chorin and declared that Krieshaber was guilty of a falsehood. This document was signed by the Rabbi, Moses Muenz, Wolf Rappoport, Samuel Kann, Jacob Benet, Michael Rechnitz and Samuel Rausnitz. The Rabbis of Prague came forth again with a similar declaration. It must be borne in mind that it was not a question of a Rabbinical, but of a Mosaic law, which created this controversy. According to the decision of the Chief Rabbi of Maehren, he who would eat of the sturgeon was unfit to render testimony in a court or to take an oath. In a pamphlet published by Krieshaber this Rabbi of Paks thanks God that he never de-

voted himself to such studies as Chorin was engaged.
The literature on this question was to a great extent
destroyed by the enemies of both parties.

In 1798 appeared the first pamphlet of Chorin in
Prague under the title: "Imre Noam." (Pleasant
words.) In 1799 the same author published a
brochure entitled "Sirjon Kaskassim," (The scaled
coat of mail,) doubtless alluding to the scaled fish.
(Levit. 11, 9.) This pamphlet is a reply to the
"Markkel Noam" (Pleasant Rod) of Rabbi Krieshaber,
of Paks, and contains, among other things in its sixty
pages, the vehement declaration of the Rabbis of
Prague against Krieshaber. The latter however felt
by no means discouraged, but tried to place R.
Eleazar Flekeles of Prague on the defensive, demanding of him a recantation of his decision, and threatening in all earnestness that all those permitting the
sturgeon to be eaten by the Jews will not enjoy the
great privilege of partaking of the banquet which God
Almighty will give to his thirty-six chosen and pious
ones in the world to come, where the fabulous
Leviathan † will constitute the main and most favored
dish in the bill of fare. But the Rabbi of Prague rejoined him saying:

"You make yourself ridiculous indeed; it would be
far better if you would cease to indulge in such useless
and sophistical disquisitions in order to invent new
burdens. Did not the old Palestinian, Rabbi Isac,
declare: Be satisified with the prohibitions of the
Thora, and do not lay upon yourself new limitations,
of which the Thora knows nothing?"

The controversy concerning the fish came to an
end, but Chorin, though coming out a victor, had con-
jured up the enmity and bitter hostility of the great

---

† Leviathan is a monster of the sea, which drinks daily all the
water of the ocean, which God replaces. This fish can converse in
seventy languages, and had been salted by God on the first day of
creation for said banquet. It is needless to state that this legend
is one of the numerous Talmudical hyperboles which contains more
poetry than truth.

majority of his colleagues. Chorin and the noble galaxy of the outspoken, honest and courageous Reform-Rabbis of the nineteenth century, learned to their sorrow what this means. For the Krieshhabers type of Rabbis are not dead yet; they are still stubbornly fighting against the cause of a progressive development in Judaism, and what is deplorable in the extreme, they are to this very day not at all particular in their methods. To-day, as a hundred years ago, they do not care whether the means to be employed in the work of checking the Reform-movement, are fair or foul. The opportunity to be revenged on Chorin was soon offered his enemies.

Several merchants of standing, who were in the habit of visiting Arad, strongly encouraged Chorin to go to the Somogy, where they thought he would be elected Rabbi of the entire district. He went there in the spring of 1802, and received from all sides definite assurances of his election. On his way home he preached in Gross-Kanizsa, where his manners and lectures found such great favor that the President of the Congregation, Moses Lackenbacher, a man of great wealth and influence in Hungary, not only offered him his hospitality for three weeks, but promised to secure his election as Rabbi of the district of the Somogy, which was an important and influential position. But, alas! the words of the Psalmist proved once more to be true: "Do not put your trust in nobles, in the son of man, in whom there is no salvation." (Ps. 14: 63.) The friend turned a foe. After Chorin's departure, Lackenbacher went on a business trip to Pressburg, where the hatred against progress and reform was fierce, and the leaders of Judaism there succeeded in influencing him against Chorin to such an extent, that, instead of working in the Somogy in favor of Chorin, he did all in his power against him, in consequence of which Chorin failed to be elected. But greater troubles were in store for our Reformer.

In the year 1803 he published another book at Prague under the title, "Emek Ha-Schaveh," which

Fuerst translates, "Reconciliation of Faith with Practical Life," a philosophical treatise. It is divided into three parts, "Rash Amana; Neshama Chajah; Dirath Aron."* In this book Chorin accuses the Rabbis who prolong the service in the Synagogue by their loud recitation of a large part of the prayer "Shema," of making the service tedious to the people. He shows in the work his acquaintance with the rudiments of astronomy, geography, physics, grammar, things which were a terra incognita at that time to the Rabbis in Hungaria. Chorin's opinion on the principle of the "oral law" (Thora She-bal-peh) of tradition, in the third part of this book, is very important. He gives as a reason why the old teachers and scribes did not write down the "oral law," the fact that by doing so they would have prevented the teachers and Rabbis of later times and coming ages from making new laws or establishing changes and innovations in accord with the exigencies and wants of new epochs. This conception is a full justification of the introduction of reforms, and, coming as it did, from a Rabbi in Hungary, eighty-six years ago, is remarkable indeed. He tried also to prove in the same work that the study of philosophy is by no means incompatible with the Talmud, and that often the noblest lessons were conveyed in, apparently, very insignificant passages of the Talmud. He tried also to interpret philosophically the Kabbala. Theoretically not opposed to the Kabbala, he most emphatically denounces "the mob, who believe that there are men who, by means of senseless combinations of spoken or written letters, are capable of forcing the laws of nature to be changed from their regular course. It is, however," he continues, "clear that this belief is incompatible with sound reason; for 'shall the axe boast over him, that heweth therewith?" (Isaiah 10.15.) The fact that the Talmud speaks of the efficacy of amulets (Sabbath,

---

‡ "Principle of faith, living soul, dwelling of" Aron are literal translations of these titles.

61) does not influence Chorin in the least. He thinks that such efficacy is only imaginary and should be ascribed to the phantasy of the patient.

This book, which, as will be seen, caused Chorin annoyances and persecution, is well recommended by Rabbi Moses Muenz, of Altofen, and by Moses Kunitzer, Rabbi of Ofen, who praised Chorin in a Hebrew poem and encouraged him to continue unterrified in his good course. It is probably on account of this and because of Kunitzer's decision in favor of the reformed Prayerbook of the Temple in Hamburg, (1819) that Graetz represents Kunitzer as a "queer fellow" and a "fool."[‡]

Chorin had intended to publish a second edition of the book, augmented, revised and enlarged, but the orthodox party succeeded in preventing its publication. The copy, prepared as it was for the printer, is now in the possession of Dr. Immanuel Loew, Rabbi and successor of his father, Leopold Loew, in Szegedin.

I mentioned before, that since the controversy on the sturgeon Mordechai Benet, the Chief Rabbi of Maehren, had changed his friendly attitude toward Chorin. But after the appearance of the "Rosh Amana," he took the part of an open enemy. In a letter to Chorin's Congregation in Arad he said that the book contained heresies and must be burnt. The Congregation of Arad, however, supported their Rabbi, and demanded of the Rabbi of Nickolsburg proof of the heretical character of the book in question. But Mordechai Benet's letter sufficed to create a faction in the Congregation opposed to Chorin. One fanatic, a very rich and influential member of the Congregation, became the leader of the opposition party and went so far in his bitterness that on the Sabbath "Shubah" (Sabbath of Penitence) of 1804, he demonstrated his feelings of penitence and contrition by uttering the most insolent curses against the Rabbi during his sermon in the Synagogue. Several members of the

---

‡ History of the Jews, XI p. 421.

Congregation, incensed at such unprecedented impudence, commenced to murmur and were ready to avenge the insults offered to their beloved Rabbi and punish the desecration of the Synagogue. But Chorin, hearing the murmuring and seeing the threatening storm, ordered the Synagogue to be closed from within and, like a true priest of peace, pacified his Congregation with the words of the Psalmist: "May our enemies curse, thou, O God, wilt bless," (Psalm 109:28) and continued his sermon.

Such occurrences were quite frequent in the history of the Jewish-Reform movement. In 1871 I was present at the Heidenreuter Synagogue in Berlin when a man by the name of Lachman loudly cursed my late revered teacher, Dr. Abraham Geiger, during the delivery of his sermon. On April 3, 1842, when Geiger was about to deliver his funeral sermon at the grave of Heyman Oppenheim in Breslau, the orthodox mob, incited against Geiger by the funeral sermon of the "pious" Rabbi Tiktin, who preceded Geiger, screamed and yelled and were about to throw Geiger into the grave. He, however, like a true follower of Aron, mindful of the word of the wise Hillel, "Love, peace and further peace," did not insist upon the right to speak, but concluded his hardly begun eulogy with the words: "I do not want to disturb the rest of the dead. Go in peace." ‡

All attempts at conciliation failed until the leader of the opposition declared that the testimony of the Rabbi of Altofen, relative to Chorin's book would satisfy him. On August 8, 1805, the Rabbi of Altofen gave his opinion to the effect that, while the author of the "Rosh Amana" had written some things which must appear strange to the mob and concerning which disputes had arisen in centuries gone by, he is unable to find heresies in the book and holds, that the Congregation of Arad is in duty bound to honor and

‡ See my "Abraham Geiger als Reformator des Judenthum's," p. 71, Loebau, 1879.

respect their Rabbi. But this document, though made out by Rabbi Moses Muentz, was not signed by him. While kindly disposed towards Chorin, he was so much belabored by Chorin's enemies, that he wanted if possibly to remain neutral. The orthodox party insisted on his condemnation of the book and the infliction of an exemplary punishment upon the author. He then invited two fanatic Rabbis of Assod and Zsambek to come to Altofen on September 1, 1805, in order to sit in council over Chorin, who was also summoned. The opposition party in Arad was represented by three members. The Rabbi of Altofen did not appear at the meeting. The narrow-minded Rabbi Samuel Butschowitz, of Assod, announced to Chorin, who was received in the yard of the Synagogue with insults, that unless he recanted his heresies set forth in his book, his beard would be cut off. In vain Chorin asked, that the passages, upon which the charge of heresy was based, be pointed out. Disgusted he signed the following words:

"Having been informed that my book, 'Emek Ha-Shave' has created an excitement among some Rabbis, I declare, that I submit my opinions to the judgment of the sages of the present time. Altofen, September 2, 1805. Aron Chorin."

It was a great mistake on his part that he went to Altofen at all, as he must have known the character of his self-constituted orthodox tribunal. Every recantation is an error.

After leaving his inquisitors he was received by a volley of stones from the promising youth of the Jewish community of Altofen. His wise judges usurped also the right to reduce his salary, although the Congregation of Arad, paid it. I mention this in order to show the mean, contemptible and vindictive spirit which animated those watch-dogs of Zion, who, not content with his recantation, tried to starve a poor colleague, who had to support on a small salary a family of seven children. But they did not succeed in their nefarious scheme. The Congregation of Arad indignantly refused the verdict, and bitterly reproached the Rabbi of Altofen on account of his duplicity. Chorin at last did the right thing by appealing to the Hungarian Government, (Statthalterei,) and requesting the same to annul the verdict of the Rabbinical tribunal, in which appeal he was successful. Not only did the Government cancel the decision of the Rabbis, (June 24, 1805), but sentenced the ringleaders of Chorin's opponents to pay the cost of the law suit. Chorin pardoned his enemy and declined to accept the payment of expenses. But it was no victory for Chorin, as the sentiment of the Hungarian Jews was against him, and his opponents in Arad were by no means conciliated. In order to be free from annoyances and in deference to his aged father, Chorin's pen rested for about ten years.

It rested but it rusted not. For on October 18, 1818, the famous Temple in Hamburg was dedicated and a reformed ritual with German prayers and hymns accompanied by the organ, and sermons was introduced. The prayers concerning the coming of a personal Messiah were partly omitted, partly modified in accord with the requirements of the new age. This induced the Rabbinical College of Hamburg, composed of the Rabbis Baruch Meyer, Moses Jacob Jafe and Michael Speier, not only to publish an interdict against the new ritual on account of its innovations, but to prevail on the Senate of Hamburg to close the Temple. The consequence was, that the different Rabbinical authorities of Europe were asked by the officers of the new Temple in Hamburg, to give their opinions on the justification of these Reforms. Chorin, in spite of his sad experiences a decade ago, had the courage to endorse most of those Reforms. (April 7, 1818.) Moses Kunitzer, of Ofen, and two Italian Rabbis, Shem-Tob Samun, of Livorno, and Jacob Vita Recanati also expressed themselves in favor of the Reforms. These opinions were published by Elieser Liberman, of Austria, who added them to his own arguments, under the name "Nogah Zedek" and "Or Nogah." (Dessau,

1818.) In consequence of this the Rabbis of Hamburg asked the opinions of other Rabbis and these were published under the name "Eleh Dibre Habrith," (Altona, 1819;) and translated in a German extract by Shalom Kohen, who himself was a Reformer. The opponents of Reform had no men in their own ranks capable of translating those Rabbinical opinions into German. Following are the names of the Rabbis who condemned the Reforms of the "Hamburg Temple:"

Salomon Cohen, of Fuerth, Hertz Schoyer, of Mainz; Moses Szopher, of Pressburg; Mordechai Benet, Chief Rabbi of Machren; (Nickolsburg;) Rabbis of Prague, (Elieser Flekeles, Samuel Landau, Levin Melisch;) Rabbi Elieser, of Trietsch, Rabbi Abraham, of Bresslau; R. Elieser Levi, of Triest; Akiba Eger, of Posen; Aron Joschany, of Ravitsch; Rabbi Maseltob, of Modena, Italy; the Rabbis of Padua (Mnachem Asaria Castelnuovo, Jacob Ascher Luzzatto, Israel Mordechai Cunion,) Moses Ahage, Rabbi of Mantua; Rabbi Samuel, of Amsterdam; the Rabbis of Livorno, (Salomo David, Chajim Malach and ten more signatures.)‡ Rabbi Moses Tobias, of Hanau; Rabbi Jacob, of Lissa; Rabbi Hirsch Katzenellenbogen, of Winzenheim, a member of the consistory in Ober-Elsass. Moses Szopher, Elieser of Trietsch and Mordechai Benet sent each two letters. The language used by these Rabbis is not very polite. Cohn, of Fuerth accuses the Reformers of arrogance and atheism and applies to them the words of Isaiah; "When ye make many prayers I shall not hear," (I, 19,) which that prophet applies to murderers only, "whose hands are full of blood." The fact that the Temple people had no services on week days was sufficient for the Rabbi of Fuerth to advise them not to have any service at all. In the same strain continues Moses Szopher: "Oh that they would abstain from all worship." He calls the Reformers "infidels," "small

‡ It must, however, be remarked, that not all the signers were Rabbis. Many of them were "Dajanim." (Assessors.)

foxes which destroy the vineyards." His objection to an organ or other musical instrument is based on the fact that on account of our mourning over the destruction of the Temple in Jerusalem, music, as expressive of joy and pleasure, must be excluded from the Synagogue. But from this point of view R. Moses ought to have objected to music at home and in concerts. His argument for the retention of the Hebrew language in the Synagogue to the exclusion of any other language is amusing. "In court," he says, "when appearing before the king we have to converse according to etiquette in the language of the king, not in our own, though the king might understand it. Now God's language is Hebrew, hence Hebrew must be the language of prayer." The good Rabbi had only forgotten to prove that Hebrew is God's language. We would have expected a better argument from the President of the largest Rabbinical school of his age. The Chief Rabbi of Maehren brings forth a remarkable "historical" fact, which if true, would furnish new material to the modern anti-Semites. He claims that the Jews had been expelled from Spain and Portugal on account of their Reformatory inclinations. How religious fanaticism can dim the judgment of men is best proven by his harsh and unjust words against Aron Chorin. At the conclusion of his "opinion," he said, "as to the approbation of the Rabbi of Arad, Rabbi Aron Chorin, who spoke favorably of the Hamburg Reforms, far be it from us to accept from him any teachings concerning religious matters, as this man possesses only a very moderate knowledge of Talmud and Rabbinism and devotes his time to worldly sciences only." This was written December 31, 1818. But the same Rabbi, Mordechai Benet, in a letter of March 23, 1793, twenty-five years before this time, bestowed upon Chorin the epithets, "a great and prominent Rabbi;" the "light of Israel," the "right pillar." But so it was at all times, that "Ssineah Mkalkeleth Hashurah," (Hatred clouds the judgment.) R. Mordechai Benet's argument against the use of German or the vernacular in the prayer-book is, to say the least, very peculiar. "The psalms," he argues, "must be recited in Hebrew, because the sense of some verses can be explained in different ways while the translation admits of but one sense only." * He also claims that the use of music during divine service is inadmissible because it disturbs the worship.

The Rabbis of Prague decided that the Hamburg Temple people "were neither Jews nor Christians, but individuals without faith, whose prayers were sinful and whose only purpose in introducing Reforms was to make themselves liked among the Christians." (January 1, 1819.) A quarter of a century later, in 1844, no less a personage than the celebrated Rabbi, Salomon Jehuda Rapoport, of Prague, was not afraid to give officially the following decision:

"Those Reformers who pray in German and abandon the Hebrew language are our brethren, inasmuch as in doing so they have, as is well known, not violated the precepts, which are contained in the Mishna and in the casuists." † E. Elieser, of Trietsch, calls the Temple people "apostates' and 'Chorin a man who intends to tear down entirely the barriers and bounds of the ancient teachers." Sarcastically he alludes to the fact that the Reformers had to go to Hungary and Italy for the sake of getting approbation and with respect to them he applies the rather strong passage of the Talmud, "Harozeh Leshaker Jarchik Edatho," (He who intends to lie looks for witnesses from a far distance.) He also advises the Hamburg Rabbis to prevail upon the Senate of Hamburg to close the Temple of the Reformers, and—I use his own expression—"to paralyze the arm of the evil-doers." He says, he will pray, that God may overthrow those blasphemers, who threaten to shake the pillars of our holy religion. (January 10, 1819.) In his second

---

* See: Weil "Aron Chorin," page 59.

† Rabbinische Gutachten ueber die Beschneidung, Frankfurt, 1844, page 120.

letter he is much exasperated on account of a pamphlet
by Lazar Riesser of Altona, the son-in-law of Raphael
Kohn, and father of the famous lawyer Gabriel Riesser.
This pamphlet was published in the form of an "Open
letter to my co-religionists in Hamburg." † It not
only defends the Reforms but deals harshly with the
Hamburg Rabbis, who oppose them. They are called
"hypocrites and tartuffes" who "sow discord in Israel,
and bar the way to the sons of those who are anxious
to return to the grace of the father." Riesser compares
the devotion, order and decorum reigning supreme in
the Hamburg Temple with the disorder and noise in
the Synagogues. Such words spoken in elegant German by a man whose scholarship was recognized, and
whose family connections were imposing to both parties,
could not fail to create a sentiment in favor of the new
movement, the more so, as truth was on his side. Rabbi
Elieser, of Trietsch was especially incensed, because in
order to give his pamphlet a larger circulation, Riesser
published it in German. Here again we find proof of
the partiality pervading Graetz's "History." He declares that Riesser's motive in publishing his pamphlet
was revenge against the Rabbis of Hamburg. ‡ Why,
is it so unlikely that Riesser spoke as he did from conviction? Suppose somebody should say that all the
Rabbis who opposed the Hamburg Temple Reforms
were actuated by personal motives? Would that be
unbiased history? No! it would be "Tendenz-
Geschichte." (Partisan History.)

Aside from this, it is next to impossible for the
historian to trace men's motive of a fact. It is wrong-
ing the dead, who have no chance to defend themselves,
for a historian to speak with certainty of their motives.
The wrong is greater, when as in the present case, the
motive is represented as bad. Or does Joshua Ben
Prachia's maxim "Judge every man charitably, kindly
and favorably," (Abot I, 6,) not apply to the historian?

† An meine Glaubensgenossen in Hamburg, 1819.

‡ Hist. of the Jews vol. XI, p. 423.

I dwelt at some length on the "decisions" of the recognised European authorities of those days concerning the Hamburg prayer-book, in order to demonstrate to the Jews of America, that the so-called conservative Congregations and Rabbis of this country are to some extent included in those bulls and excommunications. For the Reforms of the Hamburg Temple of 1818 have been introduced in almost every conservative Synagogue of this country. The prayer-book of Dr. Jastrow and Dr. Szold, which is considered conservative in America, goes further in its expression of the principles of Reform-Judaism than the old prayer-book of the Temple in Hamburg. This proves that "hersey" is in the main a question of chronology and of geography. The heretics of fifty years ago are the saints of to-day, and those who are considered conservatives Jews in this country are numbered among the radicals by the conservatives of the Samson Raphael Hirsch, Hildesheimer and Lehman type in Germany. Whenever controversies are necessary, let us therefore be more tolerant and less bitter. Fortiter in re, suaviter in modo.

After this digression let us return to Chorin. No sooner was it known that his "decision" favored the Reforms of Hamburg, when Rabbi Muenz of Altofen directed a strong missive to Chorin, in which he placed the alternative before him, either to recant his opinion or to lose his position as Rabbi. Chorin was poor, the father of a large family, and well aware of the fact, that he could not expect under the circumstances to get another position. He would not permit his family to starve on account of his advanced ideas, and—recanted in February, 1819. Who will condemn him? Has Prof. Graetz a right to call him on this account "an insincere character?" * And what did recantations ever amount to? Ask the annals of history. Galileo may recant, but his lips nevertheless drown the clanking of the chains, however faintly they

* History of the Jews, XI, p. 421.

quiver, "e pur si muove." (and still she moves.) Indeed but a year later, Chorin reaffirmed his views in
the "approbation" on the Hamburg Temple Reforms, in a book entitled, "A Word at the Right
Time." * This book is divided into two parts: Gate
of the doctrine, containing the duties to our fellow-
men, no matter whether Jews or Gentiles; gate of worship, in which Chorin advocates a Reform of the
divine service, on the basis of his "decision" in the
matter of the Hamburg Temple-Reform. He is the
first Rabbi who attempts to justify Reforms by citing
Talmudical passages, and the utterances of Rabbinical
authorities. This method which has been, and is to a
great extent still followed by progressive Rabbis, attacks the Talmud with the Talmud, and wages war
against orthodoxy with its own weapons; thus, on the
one hand sustaining the claims of modern Judaism by
arguments from the armory of the Talmud, but on the
other pre-supposing the authority of the Talmud. It is
rather poor policy for Reform-Judaism to play the part
of the beggar of alms from orthodoxy. Geiger was
the first to see this and to place Reform-Judaism on an
independent footing, on the basis of science and historical criticism.

Chorin closes his pamphlet with an appeal to the
Rabbis (pages 55-61), urging upon them to be tolerant,
warning them most impressively against persecution,
and imploring them to further agriculture and trade
among the Jews. M. L. Biederman, of Pressburg, became Chorin's friend and admirer, and the progressive
party among the Jews in Pressburg and Vienna were
urged by their friends in Germany to further Chorin's
interests in every respect. The consequence was, that
the Censor, Loeb Hatzfeld, of Vienna, translated
Chorin's "Word at the Right Time," into German
and had it printed. Had it not been for the political
state of affairs in Hungary, Chorin would have been
elected preacher in Vienna. Rabbi Mordechai Benet

---

*Dabar Beitto, Vienna, 1820.

had prevented the introduction of the Hamburg Temple Ritual into Vienna. Chorin's suggestions had no little influence towards establishing the present "Wiener Cultus," which, while not based on the principles or Reform-Judaism, is a great improvement on the orthodox style and is now introduced in hundreds of Jewish Congregations in Austraia, Hungary. The decision of the Vienna Congregation to have marriage ceremonies performed by the preacher, was also Chorin's work.

Chorin's "Word at the Right Time," shared the fate of the prophet who is the more appreciated abroad, the less he is recognized at home. While in Hungary the pamphlet would have been excommunicated had it not been for Michael Lazar Biederman's influence, it created a sensation in Germany from the fact that its author was a Rabbi. The advocacy of "Reform" by merchants, (Friedlaender, Jacobsohn,) teachers and preachers, (Zunz, Salomon, Kley, Wolf. Guensburg, Auerbach, Bendavid,) was a matter of daily occurence, but to see "Reform" defended with Rabbinical weapons was unheard of before, and it was a great and pleasant surprise to all the friends of "Reform." Israel Jacobsohn sent Chorin a tabatiere as a token of appreciation, and assured him of his esteem and friendship. The Government of Baden asked for the opinion of Chorin "as to what belonged to the duties of a Rabbi and what has been done in Austria towards an improvement of the Jewish cult?"

In June 23, 1820, the new Temple in Karlsruhe was dedicated and therefore the Government, which favored a Reform movement among the Israelites, but wanted to do full justice to all its Jewish subjects, ordered Banker Haber, the agent of the Government, and President of the Congregation, to communicate with Chorin.

Chorin requested his friend Hatzteld in Vienna to answer the second question, while he tried to give a satisfactory reply to the first in a pamphlet "Iggereth

Elassaf."‡ The drift of his answer is, that the laws
of the Thora can be temporarily suspended by a
religious body. The so-called customs and usages,
however, can be abolished even by the Government,
provided Jewish experts and scholars favor such aboli-
tions. It was a good thing that the small Governments of Germany, (Baden, Anhalt, Braunschweig,
Hessen, Oldenburg, Schwaben, Thueringen, Hessen-
Darmstadt,) have, as a rule, taken kindly to the introduction of Reforms in Judaism. For without this support the success would have been questionable because the movement was in its infancy. To-day the
Reformers would be the first to oppose even the most
favorable interference of the Government. Wherever
ideal aims are at stake, the words of the psalmist must
hold good: "In the sweat of thy brow shalt thou eat
thy bread;" through struggles, and not seldom hotly
contested ones, we should gain to victory. What we
conquer inch by inch will be a lasting gain. This has
been proven in the wonderful success and astonishing
achievements of the Jewish-Reform movement in
America. Nowadays it is in Germany and Austria the
orthodox party that finds favor with the Governments,
and it is not slow in using its influence with the
Government towards checking Reform, wherever there
is a chance to do so. It is better so than *vice versa.*
For, "not by physical force, not by material power,
but by my spirit says God." (Zach., 4-6.)

Chorin was strongly in favor of a "synod" with
power to decide questions concerning the Jewish religion and its relation to the exigencies of the new age.
He said among other things that a synod could permit
writing or travel on the Sabbath.† In 1837 Chorin
published a pamph'et "Hillel," which is divided into
three parts, to-wit: Humanity and love of self; laws of
Moses concerning our duties to our fellow men, irrespective of creed; comments on the thirteen articles of

* Prag, 1826, M. I. Landau, pages 28-46.
† Zir Noam, Prag 1831, M. I. Landau.

creed. His ideas on, or rather against, fasting are remarkable indeed. (pp. 46-47.) On page 90 he says, "that according to the Talmudical principle, all those, who believe in God and His Revelation, will share the blessings of eternal salvation.* On pages 160 and 161 he invests every Sanhedrin with the right to change or to institute ceremonies in accord with the requirements of time and circumstances. (Deut. 17, 11.) The first Synod in Leipzig, (1869,) and the second in Augsburg, (1871,) would have, it seems to me, fully come up to Chorin's ideal. Chorin was in favor of riding in railroads on Sabbath- and Holidays, of a Jew playing the organ on Sabbath, of shortening the time of mourning for the dead, and of permitting the head to be uncovered during divine service in the Synagogue which while customary in almost every Reform Congregation in America, is even to this very day, considered an unheard of heresy in Europe. I know of only one Jewish Temple in Europe where the male worshipers remove their hats during divine service. This is in the Reform Temple of Berlin in the Johannisgasse, where Dr. Holdheim was Rabbi, and where the Sabbath was transferred to Sunday. Chorin was, like all idealists and enthusiastic Reformers, an optimist, and the first Rabbi who called attention to the necessity of elevating the Hungarian Jewish Congregations. He deserves the same recognition on account of his labors in the cause of the emancipation of the Jews of Hungary. The Pressburg clique, did not even desire a thorough and total emancipation, as Moses Szopher was afraid lest such a consummation might deal a deadly blow to the rule of uncompromising, fanatic orthodoxy, whose representative he was. We find analogous cases in Jewish history in France in 1789, and long before that time in Holland. Owing to Chorin's influence, Arad could boast in December, 1832, of no less than fifty-nine Jewish handicraftsmen,

* Sanhedrin 105. see Zunz: Zur Gaschichte und Literatur, page 385.

representing almost every trade. This Congregation
possesses to-day one of the best Jewish schools in
Hungary. Chorin had to undergo great and fierce
struggles in promoting this school. At that time only
three large Congregations, Pressburg, Altofen and
Pesth supported schools. Chorin could not, however,
succeed in introducing his strongly advocated Reforms in his own Synagogue. His advice was sought
for from outside by men like Moses Israel Landau and
Peter Beer of Prague. The former was the editor of
the periodical "Bikkure Ittim," (first ripe fruits of the
times,) published in Vienna. These two men had
formed a "Society for the elevation and improvement
of the worship in Prague." Chorin recommended the
introduction of the organ. In a letter of June 16, 1835,
he writes:

"I hear good news from Prague. In September the
new Temple will be opened and the celebrated Dr.
Zunz, of Berlin, is appointed as preacher. I hope this
Temple will tend towards the true glorification of the
worship. In Vienna they have only beautified, not
essentially improved the divine service. If, as I hope,
they will carry out in Prague my suggestions, their
Temple will become the pattern for less wealthy Congregations that cannot afford to imitate the glittering
pomp of Vienna."

In 1803 Chorin composed "Selichoth," (prayers
of penitence,)and became the only composer of Selichoth
in Hungary. They were printed at Ofen, in 1819.
Chorin also introduced the performance of the marriage-
ceremony in the Synagogue. Marriage-ceremonies
were performed according to old orthodox custom in
the yard of the Synagogue or on the street. In 1868,
I saw my former teacher, Dr. Israel Hildesheimer, the
present leader of the new orthodoxy in Berlin, per-
forming a marriage-ceremony on the street in Eisenstadt Hungary. In 1827, Chorin delivered the
prayer for the emperor and country in the German
language. In 1839 Chorin advocated Congregational
singing and the use of the organ. In 1840, he had

after all these struggles the great satisfaction of hearing the stirring peals of the organ resounding every Sabbath in his Synagogue.

The introduction of the organ into the Synagogue of Arad in 1840 must be looked upon as a very important step towards Reform. Some readers of this book may not feel inclined to think so, from the fact that the organ is introduced into a number of orthodox Synagogues of America. But America in 1892 is not what Europe was in 1840. The following facts will prove my assertion. In Vienna, with a Jewish community of 100,000 souls there is even to-day not one Jewish house of worship in which there is an organ. Dr. Guedeman, preacher of the Vienna Temple in the "Leopoldstadt," in 1871 denounced an organ in the Synagogue "as the worst kind of idolatry," and compared it with Simri's act of the most shameful licentiousness. * Professor Graetz, who denies the supernatural origin of the Pentateuch in the first two volumes of his "History of the Jews," strongly opposes an organ in a Synagogue."† Dr. Israel Hildesheimer, a leader of orthodoxy in Germany, publicly revoked a few years ago his Rabbinical certificate given to his disciple, Dr. Goldschmidt, because the latter favored an organ in the Synagogue. Indeed an organ in the Synagogue is regarded even this day as the "Shibbolet" of the orthodox and Reform-parties in Germany.

The "Hirsch-Lehman-Hildesheimer" school declares a Synagogue in which there is an organ—"Anti-Jewish." Wherever in Germany in the last two decades an organ has been introduced into a Synagogue, it was the signal for a split in the Congregation and for the establishment of a new orthodox Congregation. In the Temple of Prague the organ is permitted to be played on week days only at weddings and similar oc-

---

* See Guedeman's sermon: Jerusalem, Opfer und Orgel Wien, 1871, (Herzfeld und Baur.)

† See vol. XI of Graetz's "History" and my "Graetz's Geschichtsbauerei," Berlin, 1885, (Issleib.)

casions, not, however, on Sabbath- and Holidays.* In
other Congregations of Germany, they would not permit a Jew to play on the organ on the Sabbath- and
Holidays. They have therefore as a rule Christian
organists. These instances show the importance of
the introduction of an organ in 1840 by Chorin in
Arad. If I am not mistaken this was the first organ
introduced into a Synagogue of Austria-Hungary.
From a letter dated 1842 it can be seen how optimistic
Chorin was in the matter of the Reform of worship.
He said among other things: "I hope to introduce
(in Arad), the Hamburg cultus, which, however,
takes time, as we have not the prayer- and hymn
books."

It speaks well for Chorin that no less a man than
Dr. Leopold Zunz received his "Hattarath Horaah"
(diploma of Rabbi) from him. It was dated Arad,
November 18, 1834. It shows that Zunz, the recognized nestor and pioneer in the science of Judaism
entertained a higher estimate of Chorin than the prejudiced historian, Graetz. The following is a rendition
into German of this document, by the translator, Johann
Zimmerman, in Prague. "I offer my public thanks to
God for having fulfilled my cherished wish, that the
wise men in Israel should emulate our great Maimonides
in harmonizing the Mosaic law with philosophy and
thus fortifying and spreading more and more by this
means truth, peace, goodness and virtue. Praised be
God, who has shown me such a pure source of joy in
my beloved friend, the most erudite scholar and sage,
Morenu, Lippman Zunz, in whom are united thorough
knowledge of Israel's Thorah with other disciplines and
branches of science. Therefore I consecrate him to be
a Rabbi and bestow upon him the authority to act and
decide in accord with his wisdom and superior
knowledge of the Thorah in all matters relating to
what is permitted or prohibited, particularly considering marriage and divorce according to the laws of

*On account of the desecration of the Sabbath.

Moses. Aside from this he takes upon himself the duty to instruct and enlighten the Congregations of Israel, by means of sermons, in the fear of God and in the duties of men, in order that they may draw near to God and practice his teachings and commandments.

"May our Father in Heaven assist him and grant him strength in his office so that it may accrue to his own honor and to the honor of Israel at large.

Arad, November 18, 1834.

ARON CHORIN, Chief Rabbi."

It is a pity that Zunz did not stay in Prague longer than one year. He left because the Government had subordinated the preachers of the Reformed service to the so-called "Oberjurists," and Zunz was too independent to permit himself to be harassed by men whose superior he was in every respect.

In the pamphlet "Jeled Zekunim" (child of old age), which Chorin published when 74 years old, he gives a kind of autobiography. Once more, so he relates, in 1827, clouds threatened to obscure his clear sky. "A rabbi took it upon himself to incite a regular revolt against me. He came to Arad, December 18, 1827, armed with several letters from different Rabbis, who have hurled bulls of excommunication against me and against all who follow me. He succeeded in causing many scenes of trouble and disturbance, until the Congregation with the aid of the civil authorities put an end to them. The uncalled Rabbi had to leave the city and the ringleader of this scene, one of the members of the board of trustees, was suspended."

Chorin was the recipient of great honors in Vienna. On his way to Czernahora* (Maehren) he called on the Rabbi of Boskowitz, Abraham Placzek, who presided over a large "Jeshibah." (Rabbinical school.) Two Bachurim had the arrogance to

---

* The objects of his trip were to visit the grave of his grandfather Isaias Donat, and to see Moses Loew, the learned father of Dr. Leopold Loew.

insult grossly the venerable Chorin by suddenly invading the room where Chorin and his companion had just taken a seat, vociferously screaming: "Does the Rabbi intend to talk to this Apikores?" (Heretic, the original meaning is "Epicurean"). To the shame of the host be it said that he had not the manhood to reprimand his impudent disciples, but cowardly ran away. This scene created at the time a great sensation in Maehren, and, in justice to the Jews of Boskowitz, it must be stated, that very many of them most emphatically condemned such uncalled for fanaticism and tried their best to make Chorin forget this rude treatment from his colleague.

The Jewish married ladies of a little town, Mako, in the county of Csanada, Hungary, hold Chorin no doubt, in grateful rememberance. It was on the second day of Shabuoth, 1840, when the wise Rabbi, and still wiser board of trustees of the Jewish Congregation in Mako ordered several ladies who appeared in the Synagogue with their own hair instead of the "Scheitel" (perruque,) to leave the gallery. The ladies, or better their husbands, had the courage to seek recourse at the law against the perpetrators of this act of fanaticism. The learned Bishop of Csanada (named Lonovics), who had to decide the question, asked for Rabbi Chorin's opinion and, as can be imagined, it was given in favor of the women.*

In 1841 Chorin declared that rice and legumes are permitted to be eaten on Passover. † A similar decision had already been given January 18, 1810, by the consistory of Cassel in a circular to the Rabbis of the kingdom of Westphalen. Reference is made there to the fact, that already R. Zebi Ashkenassi and his son, Jacob Emden, the great opponent of Jonathan Eybeshuetz, had given this permission. Rabbi Isak

---

* See Leopold Loew. Der Juedische Congress in Ungarn, Pest, 1871, page 158.

† Orient, Literaturblatt, vol. II, page 33.

B. Schescheth (in the fourteenth century) and R. Saul, of Berlin, (eighteenth century) have done the same thing. The consistory of Westphalia circulated on the same day another letter permitting the use of sugar, syrup, candy, tea and tobbacco. These letters were signed by Israel Jacobsohn, Kalkar, Steinhardt, D. Fraenkel, of Dessau, editor of the "Sulamith" and Jerome Heineman. In 1841 Chorin gave a favorable opinion on the revised Hamburg prayer-book. In 1842 he was also called upon by the administration of the Jewish Congregation in Breslau, in order to give a decision on the question, whether free research is compatible with Jewish theology, and whether a Rabbi has the right to treat the Jewish theology, in a critical and scientific manner. The answer of Chorin, then seventy-seven years old, was in favor of Geiger and free research. More will be found on this important subject in the last chapter of this book on "Abraham Geiger." In a letter to a friend in Gross-Kanissa he said: "This labor was such a strain upon me, that I had to go to the mountains for a few days of recreation."

Chorin heard of the Rabbinical convention of Braunschweig in 1844, and saw in it the realization of his favorite idea concerning the synod. In August, 1844, he was invited to a Rabbinical convention in Paks, to which he sent an encouraging letter in the hope that it would be of benefit to the cause of Reform. But this convention was a perfect failure. Twelve days later, August 12, 1844, Aron Chorin breathed his last in the seventy-ninth year of his active and eventful life. The Congregation of Arad, in which he had labored fifty-six years, made known this fact to the most important Congregations in a letter written in the German and Hungarian languages. The funeral was very imposing, not only the Congregation, but the whole city of Arad attended the same. The news of his death was announced in all the churches on Sunday, August 25. Chorin lay down to his final rest on the Sabbath, after having conscientiously accomplished his work. During

the funeral the bells of all the churches were tolling.
Funeral sermons were delivered by Daniel Pillitz,
preacher of Szegedin, Lazar Skreinka, Rabbi of
Simand, and Chorin's intimate friend, Leo Jeiteles. A
Christian lawyer, Adam Viser, published a most touching eulogy in the Hungarian language. Memorial
services in the Synagogue of Arad were held twice, on
September 24th and October 21st, when orations were
delivered by Skreinka and Haskel Silbermann. Chorin's
name is always mentioned first during the "Haskarath
Nshamoth" (Memorial services for the dead) four times
a year, on the last day of Passover, on the feast of
Weeks, on "Shmini Azereth" and on the day of Atonement. On the anniversary of his death, (sixth day of
Ellul) a suitable memorial service is held. His Congregation still holds him in high respect. In 1850 it
was resolved, to place on the grave of Chorin his bust,
which was solemnly unveiled June 18, 1851. It was
well executed by a protege of Chorin, the sculptor
Jacob Guttman. Not only the whole Congregation,
but the civil, military, city and county authorities, and
delegates of neighboring Congregations honored
Chorin's memory by their presence on this occasion.
Chorin's successor, Dr. Jacob Steinhardt, delivered the
memorial address.

While in Hungary, especially in the large Synagogues, Chorin's death was ignored, he was, like all true
prophets, appreciated in other lands. The Jewish
Press of Germany, "Zeitung des Judenthum's" and
"Orient;" of France: "Archives Israelites;" and,
what is of greater importance, men like Jost, Geiger
and Zunz, appreciated Chorin's labors. In Jost's
"History of Judaism and its sects," (III, page 337);
in Zunz's immortal works, "Die Gottesdienstlichen
Vortraege der Juden," (Berlin, 1832, page 467-79,) and
"Zur Geschichte und Literatur," (Berlin, 1845, page
385); in Dr. Stern's "History of Judaism," page 225; in
Geiger's "Nachgelassene Schriften," (II, page 260);
in the "Bibliothek Juedischer Kanzelredner," by
Kaiserling (I Beilage, page 10-11); and by Leopold

Loew, whose biography of Chorin rendered me great services in this work, Chorin is most honorably mentioned and very highly spoken of. The silence of Hungarian Congregations and the detractions of Graetz could not belittle Chorin's established name as one of the pioneers of Reform-Judaism, who under the greatest difficulties, confronted by the most trying and provoking circumstances, and living isolated and removed from civilization, carried aloft single-handed the banner of progress boldly and courageously; who paved the way through howling deserts to the mountain of the Lord and brought us, the later generation, to the very border of the land of our promise, which, true enough, we ourselves have not fully conquered.

CHAPTER V.

GOTTHOLD SALOMON.

"As the living word will never cease to be the great lever of progress and civilization, the growing influence of the pulpit has been and is still the most potent factor in the history and development of Reform-Judaism—Be the lecturer called Rabbi, preacher, teacher, orator, if he understands how to find the true gold in the Bible and Haggadah, to spread and diffuse it, he surely will bring the right spirit and enthusiasm into the Temples. The spark once kindled will not be extinguished, persecutions will only fan it into a flame; for irrevocable as is the victory of freedom, of civilization, of equality of the rights of the Jews and of their scientific culture, is the triumph of the inspiring word, revealing the Reform. This word of the enthusiastic and inspired preacher and teacher of religion will console, enlighten, teach, elevate, edify, and thus become a blessing not only to emancipated Israel, but to all the inhabitants of Europe. * "When nations grow old and lose their liberty the prophets die out." † "I listened to the voices of the prophets and heard the whispered words of their successors, so few and far between, and from the ages of the past I let my eye wander back to those regions, where the scattered Congregations of Israel dwell in joy and in sorrow, and

* Zunz: Gottesdieustliche Vortraege der Juden, page 481, Berlin 1832.
† Zunz: Synagogale Poesie wachrend des Mittelerlters, Berlin, 1855, page 1.

might not the voice of enthusiasm, of love and piety, the voice of peace and knowledge which I had heard with delight, sound on and bring salvation to many!" *

Such words uttered by no less a man than Dr. Leopold Zunz suffice to prove, if proof were necessary, the great influence which the Jewish pulpit has exercised upon the development of Judaism. And indeed, the introduction of the German sermon into the Synagogue has proven to be the most important and the most effective step in the direction of Reform. The services which the first pioneer Jewish preachers have rendered to the cause of Reform-Judaism cannot be too highly appreciated. Such men are: Joseph Wolf, (1762-1826); Karl Siegfried Guensburg, (1788-1860); Isaac Levin Auerbach, (born 1785); Eduard Kley, (1789-1867); I. Wohlwill. (1799-1847); Naphtali Frankfurter, (1810-1866); Abraham Alexander Wolff, (born 1810, in Darmstadt, died Dec. 2, 1891, as Rabbi of Kopenhagen where he entered upon his position, May 16, 1829); Elias Willstaetter, (1796-1842); Samson Wolf Rosenfeld, (1780-1862). They, and a host of other men, who belong to the period of the transition of Judaism from the darkness of the ghetto to the light of the new age,† will always be considered by thoughtful and impartial men as able and noble generals in the army of modern Israel, who have rendered yoemen service in the cause of Reform-Judaism. Unbiased readers of Jewish history will not deplore with Graetz the "influence of the preachers."‡ As it is impossible to dwell at length in this book on the lives of all those men, I have selected the best known and most representative preacher of this epoch, namely, Gotthold Salomon, of Hamburg, because it was in the main his merit to have placed Jewish Homiletics upon an independent basis.

---

*Zunz: Vorrede zu seinen Predigten, Berlin, 1846, second edition, page 3.

†Geiger fittingly styles these pioneers "men of the second stage," (Nachgelassene Schriften, II, page 260.)

‡Geschichte der Juden, Vol. XI, page 417.

Gotthold Salomon was born November, 1, 1784, in Sandersleben, in the duchy of Anhalt-Dessau. Dessau is a well known name in Jewish history. Salomon's father was well versed in the Talmud; his mother was the daughter of Raphael Rothschild, the Rabbi of Bernburg. His parents wanted him to become a Rabbi, which position was at that time the beau-ideal of Jewish parents. He was educated in the strictest observance of the most minute precepts of the Schulchan Aruch. At the age of three, he commenced the study of Hebrew in the most unsystematic manner in the "Cheder;" at the age of seven, Salomon could fluently read whole portions of the Pentateuch and translate them into the Jewish-German Jargon. The transition to the study of Rashi, (commentary of R. Jarchi), and the Mishna was soon accomplished and at the age of ten the poor boy was tortured with the dialectic argumentations, and intricacies of the Talmud (Gmarah). At the age of twelve his teacher in the Talmud was forced to confess his inability to continue his instruction. Fortunately his uncle, Rabbi Joachim Heineman, took care of his further instruction and, unlike the Talmudists of those days, he devoted much time with his bright nephew to the study of the Bible, which greatly influenced Salomon's later mode of thinking. Four years he enjoyed the privilege of Heineman's tutorship and he emulated his almost ascetic piety. Salomon observed not only the prescribed fasts, (Tishea Beab, Zom Gedalia, 17th of Tamuz, 10th of Tebeth), but fasted on the so-called ten days of Penitence between the New Year and the Day of Atonement. (Shobebim). In the three weeks between the 17th day of Tamuz and the 9th day of Ab he recited nightly the lamentations over the destruction of Jerusalem. (Chazoth). Those ascetic exercises did not hurt Salomon. At the age of sixteen Salomon attended the elementary school of Caplan Bobbe.

But Salomon's thirst for knowledge could not be quenched in the little town of Sandersleben and, on being presented one day to his distant relative, the preacher Joseph Wolf, of Dessau, it was settled that he should go to Dessau, where a Jewish "Gymnasium"* existed. With eight Groschen in his pocket young Salomon started upon his journey.

The well known charity of the Jews, especially towards those who are engaged in the study of the Thorah, was also verified in the case of Salomon. In the "Beth-Hamidrash," presided over by Rabbi Sabel, he studied in company with other "Bachurim" the Talmud, but he did by no means neglect other disciplines. In a comparatively short time he acquired a commendable knowledge of history, geography, German literature and even of the German classics. He studied frequently all night. As he was compelled later on to make a living by giving lessons he acquired a pedagogic talent. In 1802 this talent secured him a position as teacher of German and Hebrew in the "Freischule" of Dessau. He composed a systematic catechism of the Jewish religion in the form of questions and answers. This method of teaching religion theoretically met with some opposition. He relates the following: A boy, stationed in the house of an orthodox Jew, made notes of his lessons in religion. Questioned by his host as to what he was doing and answering accordingly, the pious man quite shocked exclaimed: "What has a Jew to do with religion?" But in time even the most orthodox Jews gladly entrusted the religious education of their young to his care. As a reward of their ability Salomon delivered interesting little addresses to his pupils on Jewish subjects. These addresses were fully adapted to the child's comprehension. The children sometimes shed tears when listening to him. Here Salomon laid the foundation of his future fame.

---

*Gymnasium in Germany is a high-school or college, where the pupils study nine years, before they have a right to enter a University. After a rigid examination they receive the "testimonium maturitatis," which entitles them to call themselves students. There are very few American Universities, which can compare with a German "Gymnasium," so far as thorough studies are concerned.

In company with his colleagues and friends: David Fraenkel, Moses Philippson, Joseph Wolf, Riehter, Du Toit, Tillich, Olivier, and Spieker, he developed his thoughts and ideas on religion, education and Judaism. The annual examinations in the "Franz-Schule" afforded him the opportunity to speak in public. On May 30, 1806, he delivered his first public address in the presence of several Christian scholars. Professor Du Toit said: "The address deserves to be printed." * This was saying a great deal in Germany. For there it was not as here a matter of daily occurrence that every ignoramus who could get a place in a Congregation, called himself Rabbi, delivered stolen lectures, palmed them off as his own productions and, to crown the nefarious work, published them as original. In 1808, December 1, on the occasion of the school examination in the presence of the duke, Salomon delivered an address † on the "Aim of Education and the Reward of the Educators." Salomon said that the re-reward of educators, is in the main the inward reward. For their compensation is hardly sufficient to keep them from starvation. Their co-religionists, instead of showing them respect, look down upon them. This is done by two classes. In the first place by those who possess that "little knowledge," which is said to be "dangerous," and is so fittingly styled in German "Halbwisserei." To the second class belong the ignorant rich, who exert a tyrannaical and autocratic power over the poor "Meshubodim." ‡ The following words of his address contain some very wholesome food for reflection, in particular for a certain class of "Parnassim," § who, especially when rich, treat the salaried officers of their Congregations, the minister included, like mere employes of their stores. "The teacher of Judaism must renounce riches and con-

*See "Sulamith," Vol. I, page 64.
†Sulamith II, 1, 76.
‡"Meshubod" is a salaried officer of a Jewish Congregation.
§Literally "supporter," plural form of "parness." It is used as technical term for "president of a Jewish Congregation."

venience as rewards of his labors. He cannot count
upon honor and esteem except in a small circle of truly
educated men. He may have ears, but must not hear
the insults of the masses; he may have eyes, but he
must not see how disagreeably he is treated; he may
have a heart, but he must not feel the humiliations to
which he is subjected—Yet, the man of spirit and power
must not be deterred by all this, but confidently and
courageously go on in the work which he has begun
for the welfare of his brethren.

Salomon had another opportunity to influence the
rising generation by delivering every Saturday afternoon lectures before the "Society for the relief of poor
brides." Some of these addresses are published in the
"Sulamith."*

Pastor Demarees, of Dessau, assisted Salomon in
his studies, by furnishing him the homiletical works
of eminent Christian preachers, and by correcting his
sermons. Salomon attended once in a while the
services in the different churches, in order to hear the
sermons. There were no Jewish models of Homiletics
at that time. This accounts for the fact that not a few
of the first Jewish preachers in Germany have rather
overdone their excusable imitation of the Protestant
preachers. At any rate it had the advantage, that in
point of order and logical division of the material, the
Jewish sermons of the first three decades of this
century were models. The eminent Jewish preachers
of later periods, Geiger, Stein, Manheimer, Jellinek,
Joel, Sachs, Holdheim, S. Hirsch, Einhorn, Goldschmidt, L. Adler, Gruenebaum, Formstecher, Loew,
Bruell, etc., have succeeded in making the Jewish pulpit
independent of Christian Homiletics.

Salomon without the aid of a teacher mastered
sufficient Latin to understand the exegetic literature
written in that language. (Vulgata and others.)

---

*See Vol. III, 2, 327; IX, 1, 28, 2, 361. He lectured on "vanity
of vanities," in 1815 at the anniversary of the society. See his
Answahl von Predigten, Dessau, 1818.

In 1804 he was requested by Moses Philippson to take part in the new German translation with Hebrew letters and Hebrew commentary of the "Twelve minor prophets" (Trai Ossor). Salomon took the books of "Haggai and Sacharia." The whole work was entitled "Mincha Tehaurah" (Pure offering). The work was well received and re-published in Prague and Vienna.

In 1809, Salomon published the "Eight chapters of Moses Ben Maimon," which form the introduction to Maimonides' commentary on the Talmudical treatise "Aboth" (The fathers). Salomon offered a good translation with very valuable notes. Of his essays in the "Sulamith," the following deserve mention: "On Rationalism and Rationalists,"† where he explains religious enlightenment as "purifying our faith from the additions and excrescences of dangerous revery and foolish prejudices;" "Rabbi Moses Ben Maimon,"* an interesting historical essay on the life and works of this Reformer; "Review of Herz Homberg's Jewish Catechism." Salomon gives in this article a vivid characteristic of the old time. But he is not blind to the dark side of the picture. "Among the balmy plants in this garden of religion, the poison of superstition and disbelief was not wanting, of which the youth have partaken, and their effects were felt most painfully in maturer age, when they cursed the chains in which those tyrants had fettered them."

In 1810, Salomon married Rosette Cohn, a "pious maiden of a highly respected family of Dessau." As his income was limited, he established a boarding-school, (Pensionsanstalt), which in time was patronized by the sons and daughters of the first families from far and near.

---

*Sulamith, 1808, Vol. II, 1, 207.

† Sulamith, 1809, Vol. II. 2.

: The title of Homberg's book is "Imre Shafer," Wien, 1808. See Sulamith 1810. Vol. II.

In 1813 David Friedlaender, of Berlin, forwarded to Salomon his pamphlet; "On the Reform of the worship,"* and requested him to express his opinion on the subject. This was the first time that Salomon was drawn into the circle of the Jewish-Reform movement. Salomon expressed his views in a little pamphlet: "Light and truth, concerning the Reform of the Jewish cult, a correspondence between two friends of truth," Leipzig, 1813. Although Salomon did not sign his name, it is known that the letter of S—— to H—— meant Salomon. He dealt some hard blows to the "obscurants and blind adherents of the old—." They were, incensed against the author, and the Chief Rabbi, of Dessau, Michael Speyer, declared the pamphlet "heretic." He made a motion to the effect that the board of trustees of Dessau order the burning of the same near the entrance of the Synagogue, which was, however, not done. In 1814 Salomon published a "Biography of Moses Philippson, teacher of the free school at Dessau."

In 1815 Salomon, who never lost sight of his calling as a preacher, went to Berlin for the purpose of seeing what was going on in the "Jacobsohn-Temple." In consequence of his pamphlet on the "Reform of worship," he was well received by Friedlaender, Jacobsohn and other friends of Reform, and was invited to preach on the feast of conclusion in Beer's Temple. This was the first time of his preaching in a house of worship. The sermon was so well received, that Jacob Herz Beer, the father of Meyerbeer made Salomon a fine present, and sent him a letter of admiration. He also requested him to have this sermon printed. It is published among a "Selection of several sermons." (Dessau, 1818). This sermon, although by no means free from imperfections, gives a deep insight into the spirit, the religious conviction and the very innermost being of the man who has become one of the most eminent Jewish preachers of this century. The subject was:

*See page 36 of this book.

"What are the main sources of infidelity." Text
Isaias II, 3: "Come let us ascend the mountain of the
Lord and walk to the House of the God of Jacob."
"As at one time the law came from Zion and the word
of God from Jerusalem,—so shall instruction come to us
from this place devoted to the service of God. Certainly,
in a well and practically established divine service we
find the divine instrument to attain piety and virtue.

Yet while a well established service is liable to
lift a man up to his higher nature, to God and to
virtue, the worship as such will always remain only
the means to the great aim, but not the aim itself.
What is the advantage, if you fold your hands in
prayer towards Heaven and these hands are soiled with
the stain of vice; what is the profit, my brother, if
your heart is lifted up towards God when within it sin
yet dwells? What is the use, my sister, if your foot
hurries to the House of God, but your own house is
not managed in accord with order, morality and love;
what is the use if your steps are standing within the
sanctuary, but before entering and leaving it, they are
pursuing the paths of vice? What is the use if the
most pleasant sounds of gratitude towards the God of
truth emanate from your mouth, and yet ingratitude,
falsehood and malice dwell therein? Can it make you
better, my brother, if your eye, filled with tears, looks
to the Father of kindness and love, while the eye of the
poor, miserable brother sheds tears of sorrow and pain
on account of the wrong you have done him? Can we
then learn God's ways and walk in his paths? Can we
boast of our virtue when we carry the Lord merely on
our lips, and our hearts are far from Him?"

Speaking of the main sources of infidelity, and of prevailing indifference towards religion in general, and towards Judaism in particular, he continues his arguments, which hold good in every respect in our own progressive age and country, as follows: "In the first
place, it is one-sided Rationalism. I mean that
superficiality of thought and that inclination to reject
everything old, be it ever so good and venerable, and

to grasp anything new without choice and discrimination. I mean that recklessness, with which persons, who have gathered some knowledge from pamphlets and newspapers without earnest study, and without understanding or comprehending the sense of these things, sit in judgment over the sublimest matters of religion and ethics. I mean that licentiousness, with which, not only the religious ceremonies, but also the eternal truths of Judaism are trodden under foot.

Many of the children here and elsewhere will tell you about the history of ancient nations, which have long since passed away; but the history of their own people remains unknown to them."

These extracts from Salomon's first sermon show his bold, outspoken character, his courage of opinion, his forcible style, his sincerity and religious fervor, his strong convictions and purity of motives. It was no trifle for a young man, who had never preached before in a house of worship, to speak thus in his first sermon, to touch, and without gloves at that, the most vital questions of modern Judaism.

Salomon acted not like many young ministers of our days, both in Europe and here, whose only purpose seems to be, that their lectures please the Congregation; no, his principal object was to instruct, to enlighten, to elevate his hearers. We gladly miss in his first sermon that diplomatic reserve and politician-like shrewdness, that catering to the vanity of the audience and that careful overcautiousness, which, alas, characterize so many trial-sermons of young candidates for the office of minister in our days. Salomon spoke, as he felt, the truth, irrespective of what people thought of it, whether they liked or disliked it, and, like the prophets of old, he was not afraid, kept not back, but "proclaimed to the house of Israel their sins and transgressions." (Isaiah, LVIII, 1).

This was the great secret of his wonderful success in later years. For justly, our Sages say in the Talmud: "Only words that emanate from the heart will find entrance into the heart;" or, as Goethe puts it:

"What you don't feel, you'll never catch by
        hunting,
It must gush out spontaneous from the soul,
And with fresh delight enchanting,
    The hearts of all that hear control."[*]

In the preface to this sermon Salomon said: "The truth is of God and they who diffuse it are His servants. His servants, however, of the tribe of Levi, think more of the truth than even of their father or mother."[‡]

His sojourn in Berlin was a still greater incentive for Salomon to devote himself with might and main to the study of Homiletics. As he could not yet preach from the pulpit, he preached through his literary labors, especially through the publication "Selima's Stunden der Weihe," (Hours of devotion) a moral-religious treatise for the educated among the women (Leipzig, 1816). This book was a success, touching, as it did, familiar chords in the hearts of the mothers and daughters of Israel. The form of the book was most appropriate. A young lady, Selima, the daughter of a wealthy merchant, lays down in a diary her thoughts and sentiments on the most important religious truths, on the Jewish Holidays, and events in the family life. A spirit of pure, enlightened piety, far remote from romanticism and superstitious mysticism permeates every line of the little volume. It has contributed not a little towards diffusing a better appreciation of our religion among intelligent Jewish women, who, disgusted with the official Judaism of those days, were tempted to forsake the religion of their mothers. The best proof of the intrinsic value of this book is a venomous pamphlet in the Jewish German Jargon directed against it by a certain Meyer Elkan Fuerth

---

[*]"Wenn ihr's nicht fuehlt, ihr werdet's nicht erjagen,
    Wenn es nicht aus der Seele dringt,
Und mit urkraeftigem Behagen,
    Die Herzen aller Hoerer Zwingt."
                    Goethe Faust, I Theil.
[‡]Salomon apparently alludes to Deut., 33. 9.

under the title: "Makhsheboth Haleb, (Thoughts of the heart).

Salomon published, in conjunction with J. Wolf, a pamphlet; "Character of Judaism," (Leipzig, 1817). This publication was mainly polemical, and strongly and ably refuted the venomous accusations heaped upon the Jews by the *Hep-Hep* criers of Germany, particularly Professors Friedrich Ruchs, of Berlin, and I. F. Fries, of Heidelberg. Berthold Auerbach said that this book, "Character of Judaism," is not only defensive, but clearly and systematically lays down the positive foundation of Judaism. Through the arguments set forth and fortified by original sources, it has become a standard work. *

In 1818 Salomon published, together with Wolf, a Hebrew Reader, with a complete register of Hebrew and Chaldaic words, and, in conjunction with Maimon Fraenkel, a German anthology under the name "Teutonia." †

No wonder that Salomon's fame was spreading, and that, when the Temple in Hamburg was in search of a second preacher he was selected for this important position. Dr. Eduard Kley was the first preacher, but the new temple, which was dedicated October 18, 1818, made a second preacher necessary. Salomon's sermons, published in 1818 in Dessau and his knowledge of the Talmud, by means of which he could better disarm the opponents of Reform and fight them on their own ground, had not a little to do with his call to Hamburg. On the 7th of November, he delivered his inaugural sermon in Hamburg from the text: "My heart belongeth to the Legislators of Israel." (Judges, V, 9). This sermon produced a most favorable impression. His second sermon on Isaiah 64, 5-6: "We wither like a leaf, all of us, and our iniquities, like the wind, will bear us away," con-

---

*Gallerie der ausgezeichnetsten Israeliten aller Jahrhunderte, Stuttgart, 1831, vol. V, page 40-41.

†Leipzig, 1812, second edition 1815, third edition 1824.

tains the following beautiful closing passage "Now while the leaves fall from the trees, I take leave of you and return to my home; but when everything begins to bloom again, at spring-tide, which is full of song, I will return again if I myself will not then be withered like the grass."

In Dessau he published his "Sermons, delivered in the Temple of Hamburg," (1819). As usual his work was better appreciated in Dessau after his departure than during his stay. It was mainly his work, that the almost decaying Jewish free-school was transformed into the "Herzogliche Franzschule," and that an annual subsidy of several hundred Thaler and free fuel was given to the school by the duke. Salomon's reception in Hamburg, was very enthusiastic. His sermons created a furor among the Jews and Christians of Hamburg. The Temple was crowded with appreciative audiences. It was a matter of surprise in those days, to hear from a Jewish pulpit a rational conception of religion, expounded with great oratory and in classical language. Here the question may arise, why, in our days, especially in Germany, even the best preachers,—and there are some who surpass Salomon —cannot boast of a success similar to his. The answer is at hand. The age in which Salomon lived, at the beginning of his career, might be styled a "Homiletical era." The sudden, and unexpected downfall of Napoleon Bonaparte and the consequent redemption of Germany from foreign despotism and French rule tended to remind the Germans, who were always inclined towards religious laxity, of their gratitude to God, and revived their religious sentiment. True, this "reaction" soon took the form of romanticism, pietism, mysticism and bigotry among the Christians and often exhibited itself in fanaticism, hypocrisy, intolerance, and hatred against the Jews. But upon the Jews themselves the effect was by no means so disastrous. The orthodox Jews were not in the least disturbed about the *Hep-Hep* cries and the loss of the emancipation, as they considered oppression the

natural state during the "Galuth."* The more enlightened and educated Israelites, however, were bent
upon showing to the world the purity and sublimity
of their religion, thus refuting and annihilating the
false accusations heaped upon them by their enemies.
In this respect the spoken and printed sermons of the
"new" preachers and a reformed and better worship
have done invaluable service, as the non-Jewish world
could convince itself, that Judaism need only to be
understood, to be appreciated. No wonder the Jews
felt proud of their new preachers, who could vie with
the best Christian pulpiteers. Aside from this the
worship in the orthodox Synagogue naturally repelled
the new generation, bred under the refining influences of good schools, Gymnasiums and Universities.
It is therefore not surprising, that a great many Jews,
who hardly dreamt of entering a Synagogue on account of its uncultured Chazonim, † Shamossim, ‡ and
its tedious, incomprehensible Derashoth, (so-called
lectures on Talmudical topics) which were delivered
in a barbarous Jargon by Polish Rabbis, now flocked
to the Temple. There the stirring peals of the
organ, the songs of the choir, the prayers in the vernacular, the hymns, and the timely sermons appealed
to their hearts.

The number of Salomon's published sermons is a
library in itself. We select some extracts, which will
suffice to show that his main attention was directed to
touch the heart of his audience, and that he had the
courage "to call things by their true names." The
first sermon in his collection of "Sermons in the new
Israelitish Temple at Hamburg, First Series," (Hamburg, 1820,) on the text, "House of Jacob, come let
us walk in the light of the Lord," (Isaiah 2, 5,) was
delivered on the Feast of Weeks, 1819. It treats on

---

*"Galuth" means literally "exile." As a terminus technicus it
stands for "oppression of the Jews." According to orthodox doctrine
the "Galuth" will last until the Messiah will redeem Israel.

†"Chazan" means "Cantor" "perceutor," also "reader."

‡"Shammass" is "janitor," servant of the Congregation.

religious enlightenment. The following passages will always remain gems of Jewish pulpit-oratory: "Light is synonymous with reason. If, then, God calleth upon us to walk in his light, he calleth upon us to seek to know Him according to reason and truth. * * * We should correct false representations and opinions, we should oppose superstition and fanaticism, in order that there may be light within us and around us." * * Religious enlightenment consists in purifying our belief, in freeing it from the additions heaped upon it by pernicious fanaticism and silly prejudices, in forcing upon us the conviction that true religion is not a matter of memory, but a question of the heart." To those, however, who oppose enlightenment, because "skepticism, sensuality, folly follow in their train." he fittingly replies: "Is light then indeed pernicious because the unpracticed hand of the suckling knows not its use? Is truth injurious because it is misused by fools? Shall the sun not warm, the rain not refresh the earth, because the poisonous plant grows near the 'herb that is food for man?' Is enlightenment to be rejected because the frivolous understand not its aim and end? No, ye shall learn to distinguish by their characteristics, true and false enlightenment.   * *

Religious enlightenment makes the race of man more virtuous, more humane, more truth-loving, more moderate, more modest, more indulgent to the faults of others, more watchful over their own defects.   * *

How differently does false enlightenment manifest itself! Without inquiry they reject the old, be it ever so venerable, ever so sacred, and blindly seize on what is new, be it ever so pernicious and unholy, only because it glitters and dazzles. While heathenism and other religions teach asceticism, regard flight from the pleasures of existence in the light of piety, consider God as a malicious spirit, delighting in mischief, to whom the permanent happiness of man was repugnant, Judaism strongly repudiates such Puritanical teachings. God forbids us not, to partake of innocent joys.

He commands us not, to devote our days to gloom and sorrow."

Another sermon of Salomon, delivered in 1821, is considered a masterpiece, and is entitled: "Prophet-engeist und Prophetenwandel." (The Prophet's Spirit and the Prophet's Course.) The following are a few extracts which will surprise many of our younger readers, who are under the impression that Reform-Judaism is a matter of recent date only:

"In all times there have been narrow spirits who have considered it dangerous to instruct and enlighten the people on matters the most important to them. They held the selfish opinion—and many still hold it—that a troop of blind are more easily led than a body of clear-sighted men. The point on which the sages and philosophers of all nations have been, and are even now, still at variance, whether the moral and intellectual standard of the people should be raised, whether they should be enlightened, was decided thousands of years ago by thee, great teacher of man, noble instructor of the people. *'The people saw that the skin of thy face shone (Exod. 34, 33,) whilst thou gavest them in commandment all that the Lord had spoken.' A wise lesson for you, public instructors! To cause thy light to shine, such was thine aim, thine endeavor. All, all should be taught, enlightened; their powers of heart and head should be so raised that they should all learn to distinguish the true from the false, the eternal from the transitory; that they should glorify God, all become prophets of the Lord. *   *

Would you ask me whence the prophet obtained his strength, his courage? He derived them from the consciousness of having acted according to duty and righteousness. Because he was blameless, therefore was he fearless. This guileless, childlike, innocent heart was the armory, whence the hero drew weapons of defense in the conflicts of life. * * Reasonable and child-

*Salomon alludes to Moses' exclamation: "Would to God that all the people of Jehovah were prophets." (Number 11, 29).

like truth is the prophet's shield; the hope of brighter
hours, even in the darkest day, is the prophet's hel-
met; justice even towards those who injure him, the
prophet's coat of mail; unspotted innocence, the
prophet's breastplate; the love of God his standard and
watchword. * * To want little, to forego willingly, to be
moderate in his demands, modest in his wishes,
temperate in his enjoyment; such was the prophet's
wealth. * * Had those chosen of the Lord indulged in
many wants, in much outlay, in extravagant preten-
sions, they would have been false prophets, venal
servants of mammon, worshippers of the golden calf.
How could they chastise the rich and the powerful
with the breath of their lips, with the arrows of their
words, if they themselves had trembled and worshipped
before the same idols? How could they have dared to
approach the throne and to call aloud unto the
princes: Your thrones totter, and with them ye will
also be cast down, because the firmest supports,
justice, benevolence, virtue and truth, are wanting
alike to them and to you? He who would hold such
language must possess the strength of truth, must bear
treasures in his bosom, must require little, must be
rich in inward wealth. * * If all the people are to be
prophets unto the Lord, then must they all pursue
their course through life with a cheerful and contented
mind. I do not mean that love of pleasure, whose
followers live in one uninterrupted whirl, who prepare
the hall for a second festival ere the first is ended. But
it was forbidden to the high priest to indulge uselessly
in sorrow. Neither should prophets resign their hearts
wholly to sadness; always prepared for the service and
calls of his holy office, the prophet should preserve an
unclouded brow, a serene temper of mind, a cheerful
demeanor. * * Were the present ever so stormy, it
caused him not to tremble; in the haven, in which he
sought refuge, there was naught to fear. And the
future! To the prophets, from the greatest to the
smallest, it appeared radiant and bright as the
meridian sun. The prophets stood on high, waiting,

listening and watching; waiting, even though it tarried; listening, though but a whisper was heard;
watching, though it lay remote. * * Without this divine
spirit your learning cannot make you wise, your wealth
cannot make you rich, your strength cannot make you
powerful, your pleasures cannot make you glad. Why
does there exist among men, so much that is deformed
and feeble in their houses, in their institutions, in their
provinces, their nations, their governments? Because
a lying spirit rules among them, as among the
prophets of old; an idol and no God. They patch
together miserable rags and term them priest's garments, a heavenly mantle. But wherefore should I
speak in metaphor? They declare their own spirit to
be the spirit of God. What they desire not themselves
they forbid in the name of the Lord. * * The fool would
conceal his folly and says: 'What has the world
gained by the spreading of light? Were not the
earlier ages better than the present?' This is a spirit
of darkness, but not a spirit of the Lord, who is light
and truth. Unwise teachers, false prophets, would
declare their intolerant spirit and their darkness to be
light and testify in the name of religion against all
whose belief differs from their own; they would preach
religion and forget its first precept: 'What thou dislikest, do not unto others; love every man as thyself.'
What do these babbling hypocrites? They prune and
twist and turn the words of the Bible and the law, be
it the earlier or later law, be they the words of Moses
or of them who have drawn their knowledge from his
writings, till such meaning be accepted as they think
it good to apply to them. This is a spirit of night,
but not the spirit of the Lord. The word 'Nabi' is
used for the prophet, and really signifies Speaker,
Orator—but it is not the lips, the tongue, it is the act
that speaks; it speaks louder than the organs of speech.
And if God's spirit really rests on you, you will not
desire to be a mere orator, you will not merely declaim
of virtue in fine words and metaphors and you will not
bear your religion on your lips, without feeling it in

your hearts or showing it in yourselves. Speakers like
unto those should your actions be. Your whole life
should be one sound. * * What the inspired have spoken
will one day be fulfilled. One day, and though that
day should tarry, await it; that is the prophet's spirit.
Let us follow their example and never rest, till each
has fulfilled the command of his Father, to be a prophet
unto the Lord."*

The following are some extracts from Salomon's
sermon on "the spirit of the Mosaic religion," delivered
on Shabuoth, 1826. The feast of weeks asks of the
Israelite: "Does your religion, such as you
have it at the present day, offer all that is required to
make the life of man happy?" He answers with the
text; Deut. IV, 5-10: "For this is your wisdom and
understanding in the sight of the nations," as follows:
"The religion which I profess gives me all that is re-
quisite for a happy human life, as long as the welfare
of humanity is more than a dream, as long as human
virtue is more than a delusion. Israelites, if to be
happy is to be conscious of your greatness and dignity
as men, as the images of God, as immortal beings, then
your religion will suffice for you so long as human
reason will and can think. The very life-breath of our
religion is love and the image of the creator, which we
bear in ourselves, can never manifest itself more
worthily and more completely than in acts of love. For
it is only by love that we can become like him who
loveth all mankind. But you pause to reflect. Is it because perchance, another town, another country,
another continent lies between you and your fellow-
men? Ought a foreign city, or a strange land, or an
unknown region, then to be deemed a barrier between
hearts formed alike? Are not both they and you still
the creatures of God? Are you not still brethren? And
though one may dwell where the sun rises and another
where the sun sets, is not God the God of the whole

*Salomon: Twelve sermons translated by Anna Maria Gold-
smith, London, 1839, Charleston, S. C., 1841.

earth? Is not His name to be praised from the rising of the sun to the going down of the same? Love the stranger also as thou lovest thyself. Do you again hesitate? There lies between you, perhaps, something more than a continent—a different creed. But say, ye, who have feeling hearts, suppose, that of two, born of the same parents, the elder is tall enough to embrace their father while the younger can only clasp his knees, must not the older and stronger assist him who is yet too little and weak to climb to the parental bosom? Should difference in strength cause difference in fraternal love? My heart answers no, and so also speaks religion. This love will be meek and ready to assist enemies and offenders, tender and compassionate to the wretched and unfortunate, forbearing and indulgent to the weak and infirm, gentle and kind to those of lowly condition, who have the more need of love from their fellow-men, the more they appear to be without the love of their father in this, their earthly life. * * It is very possible to observe most punctually all the laws of Scripture, and yet to be as far removed from virtue as the east is from the west. * * The government commands you to do this and that, but what you may be thinking or feeling during your performance of the required action, or from what motives the deeds and actions may spring, is totally indifferent to it. It is not so with religion. The religion that is worthy of the name, demands something more than good deeds; it requires pure motives and holy feelings, for it is the aim of religion to purify our inward life. * * The Israelite is admonished to be holy, because God is holy (Levit. XIX, 2). You need but to peruse the laws that Moses delivered, to be convinced that they insist on the purest morality;* and hence this moral law of reason, will subsist to the latest age, however far mankind have advanced in science and civilization. Israelites! So long as virtue among men is something more than

*See especially Lev, Chapter 19.

a vain illusion, so long will your religion be capable of
ensuring to man a happy existence."

"It is the aim of the Mosaic religion to make of
us good and useful members of society. Men, however,
ignorant of the world and human life, act and speak as
though Israel still formed a separate and distinct state;
consequently they observe as parts of the universal
religion of Israel, institutions, which possessed value
in Palestine only, because there only they had spirit
and life. They require and inculcate the strict observance of these ceremonies, although by such observances
much of our own power to act usefully as citizens
must necessarily be destroyed. Besides this they envelop
the jewel of religion in so many folds, that numbers
of our brethren who cannot, or will not, penetrate the
covering, see not the jewel itself. Ignorance would,
perhaps, be pardonable; but there is—obstinacy.
Many, I grieve to say it, belong to the hypocrites, who
have more regard for their own wilfulness and
advantage than for our religious weal. They care not
whether some treasures may yet be saved from the
wreck, or all be lost in the bottomless abyss. Were
you real servants of God, true shepherds in Israel, like
those who have gone before you, your care would be
to save what is essential. You would be the first to
improve our Temples and the form of worship; you
would be the first to prepare for our youth books of
religion in which the husk should be distinguished
from the kernel. * * But, alas, you are like the woman
who feigned a mother's affection before the judgment
seat of Solomon, for ye say respecting the child that
was not destroyed in the night time, neither of us
shall have it. Yet you know what the real mother
did. She yielded the claim willingly to save from
destruction the child that had lain on her bosom.
(I Kings, III, 16-28). If religion really lies near
your hearts, teach it, and preach it in real purity
and simplicity, and divest it of all that can make us
ridiculous in the eyes of other nations. Divest it of all
excrescences and additions, so that it may again be

what it originally was; and all truly rational and wise
men may be forced to exclaim, in the words of our
text: 'Surely this great nation is a wise and understanding people.' "*

Such words, spoken in Europe sixty-four years
ago, are remarkable indeed.

The following extracts from his sermon on "The
Israelite's confession of faith," are timely. (Text,
Deut. VI, 4-9):

"But what should be the nature of this love of
God? The heathen thought they loved their divinities,
while they sacrificed to them their own children.
Many, even among those who acknowledge but one
God, have represented the destruction and annihila-
tion of self, as the proper proofs of love to Him. There
are many at the present day, who consider a disinclina-
tion to active life to be the same thing as devotion
towards God. Far be it from you, to entertain ideas
so erroneous."†

" 'Ye shall teach them diligently to your children.'
The word, in the original is used in reference to a
sharp-pointed arrow,‡ which pierces the heart easily,
but is very difficult to extract. Teaching and preaching are useless in themselves. Though you had
prophets like Isaiah for your preachers, men who
could speak with the tongues of angels, and though
each discourse were a master-piece, they could not
form you into perfect men. * * You must then impress
well on your children the truths of religion—at home.
For there the perversions of the world reach you not,
there you have no need to do homage to the absurdities
of the age, for fear of appearing in the eyes of men to
be 'behind the fashion,' or 'the improvements of the
times.' It is here that you can show your children

---

*Twelve sermons by Salomon, translated by Anna M. Goldsmith,
1839, pages 146, 148, 149, 150, 154, 155, 156, 161, 165, 166.

†Twelve sermons, page 181.

‡Deut. 32, 41 "veshinantom," Piel-form of "Shannan" Denom.
'shen" i. e. " tooth" or "sharp edge," "arrow" which pierces the
heart. See Ps. 64, 4, Isaiah 5, 28, Prov. 25, 18.

true examples of pious men and believing Israelites. And this is the pointed dart that enters the heart readily, but will not so readily be taken out."*

In the sermon: "Outward aids of religion," delivered in 1826, Salomon said among other good things the following, on the text, Deut. VI, 8-9:

"We are well aware that the same, or similar passages occur in the writings of the prophets, as also in the Psalms and Proverbs, which cannot be interpreted according to the letter, but are to be taken figuratively." (Ibid., page 192).† "In the holy Temple poetry, music and song were combined to elevate the moral feeling. Such physical aids do produce beneficial effects on the spirit. I need only remind you of the good that has been realized among us since the establishment of this, our house of God.   *   * The religion of the Israelites is great, is pure in its doctrines and truths; the ceremonies by which that religion is expressed must be in accordance with that greatness, that purity. That which is surperadded, and manifestly opposed to its spirit, that which offends the moral sense, shocks the feelings and disregards the laws of order and beauty, should not be accepted and practiced either in our domestic, or in our public worship. * * If reason is not exercised, then customs and ceremonies come to be considered as religion itself. Men then delight in vague feelings, and are satisfied if the heart is touched for a time, but not permanently improved. Many among the educated classes are disposed now to this mysticism, this visionary and dreamy state. (Pages 205-6).   *   * In Israel there are but too

---

*Twelve sermons, pages 185-189.

† Rabbi Samuel Ben Meir, (Rashbam) remarks to Exod. XIII, 9, which passage is also contained Deut. VI, 8-9, the following: According to the natural explanation the passage means to convey the idea, that the exodus from Egypt should be a memorial, a reminder as if it were written "upon thy hand," as we read in a similar passage, Salomon's Song, VII, 6: "Set me as a seal upon thy heart." The same, "between thine eyes," like jewelry, which a person wears as an ornament on the forehead." See also Ibn Ezra's note to Exod. 13.9, and to Deut. 6.8, and page 56 of my "Talmud" (1880, Berlin, Issleib).

many men and women, who are satisfied with this half-light and consider it piety. * * They adhere to empty, superstitious customs, to cabalistic mysteries and sayings and reject suitable and appropriate aids to virtue. Do you desire examples? I will give you some. The holy solemnization of the Sabbaths and Festivals, is to many among you, a matter of indifference; but you fear, ye observers of times, to commence a business, or to remove into a dwelling on certain days. Some of you consider prayer and devotion as objects of small import, but when you do pray, you fear to pray in any language except Hebrew, which you do not comprehend. You disobey the Mosaic ordinances for the Day of Atonement, without self-reproach, but you fear to be present at the service of the dead, (Haskardth Neshamoth) lest it should injure your parents, who are still living. Religious customs that would exalt the life, remain unobserved, but in cases of death, customs are observed which owe their existence to prejudices, which, probably, originally sprang from heathenism.* Why is this? Whence is this? Because imagination rules, and reason is become her handmaiden. Who can deny, that the outward distinction of festivals and fast-days may give a pious tendency and tone to the heart, and in this way lead it to religion. But if you do not also employ your reason, you might even thus find an excuse for dishonesty, when in fact it would be better even to make the day of the festival a day of work for honest maintenance, than thus to render religion a pretext for a recourse to fraud.† There ever were and are yet many

---

*Similar things are found even in this country It is appalling, how superstitious many so-called enlightened Jews are, whenever death enters their house.

†This reminds one of the passage in the Talmud "Make thy Sabbath a week day, but ask not for the assistance of men." In the same spirit Salomon said: "There is no law in the religion of the Jews to hinder you from devoting your powers to the state to which you belong, to the fatherland which protects you, at whatever hour or whatever day your services may be indispensably necessary." "Twelve sermons." (page 160). The principle

individuals in Israel, who imagine themselves to be
pious and better than the rest, because they observe a
vast number of ceremonies, whose whole meaning has
long since been forgotten; because they keep many
fast-days, utter many prayers, read much and often in
the sacred writings, as if the dead letter could open
heaven to them. And these things are held to be
religion, while religion itself is disregarded. Thence
the ridiculous blindness, with which so many look
down with contempt, on such as think differently
from themselves. Pride is concealed beneath their
tatters. The words in the Midrash are remarkable:
"Do not add to his words." (Proverbs). This means,
according to Rabbi Khijah: "Do not make the fence
around the garden a matter of greater import than the
garden itself, else it might fall in and destroy the
plants." Oh, deluded ones, they hope to be healed,
merely because they read the prescription of their
physician and frequently comprehend not the language
in which that prescription is written. No! To over-
value these means is just as sinful as to neglect their
use altogether."* Salomon was often compared with
Klaus Harms, and was also called the "Jewish
Draeseke," which was considered a great compliment
in those days.

It is impossible to enumerate here even the titles
of all the sermons of Salomon. Many of them appeared in pamphlet form, while the most select ones
were published in book form, as "Sammlungen,"
(selections of sermons). Thus appeared "Sermons in
the new Israelitish Temple at Hamburg, by Dr. G.
Salomon, first selection."†

---

is, however, not as new as it might seem. Mar Samuel taught more
than fifteen centuries ago "Dina Demalkhuta Dina": "The law of the
Government is law." See also Talmud Joma. 85: "The Sabbath
hath been delivered unto you, not you unto the Sabbath." (Cf "my:
"The Talmud," page 36.

*Twelve sermons, pages 205-269.

† Hamburg, 1820, Hoffman and Campe.

In 1821, followed a second and in 1825, a third "selection" of Salomon's sermons.

By special request of the ladies of his Congregation, Salomon published in 1825, a pamphlet: "The family life," in three sermons. Salomon relates in his "autobiography" that he was urged by his Congregation to publish weekly sermons delivered by him and by his colleague, Dr. Kley. Thus three volumes were published entitled:

"Collection of the newest sermons delivered in the Israelitish Temple at Hamburg, edited by Dr. Eduard Kley and G. Salomon.* The first volume contains fifteen sermons. The fifteenth sermon on the "Separation from those we love," based on Numbers, XXVII, 12-23, is beautiful in the extreme. In fact Salomon's greatest force as a preacher is manifested in sermons which appeal to the heart rather than to the mind, hence, in sermons dealing with sorrow and death.†

The second volume contains also fifteen, and the third volume thirteen sermons. In 1829 a new volume was added to these "collections," entitled "Festpredigter, fuer alle Feiertage des Herrn,"‡ which Salomon himself considers his best efforts. These sermons, twenty in number, are indeed models of simplicity and conciseness.§ Among the sermons published in pamphlet form, is one in memory of Israel Jacobsohn,‖ and another on, "Add nothing to it and take nothing away from it."●

Salomon's sermon "The desecration of God's name, in word and deed," delivered in 1846, created

---

*Hamburg 1826-27, Ahrons.

†Twelve sermons, translated by M. Goldsmith, p. 229.

‡Sermons for all the Holidays of the Lord, Hamburg, 1829, Nestler.

§This volume is dedicated to Dr. Leo Wolf, Philadelphia.

‖Sept. 13th, 1820, "The pious Israelite does not die.", Text Isaiah 51-3, "An Israelite in whom I glory."

●Aug. 29 l, 1839, text, Deut. 12.6. reprinted in Kaiserling's Bibl. Jued. Kanzelr, page 220.

quite a sensation, and was published at the request
of his Congregation. In this sermon he uttered
among other things the following words on
blasphemy: "If there are houses in Israel, in which
the youth is instructed in everything but religion, or
houses and schools in Israel, in which religion exists
in nothing but a mere mechanical work of memory, of
formulas and usages, a heartless occupation, oppressing
rather than reviving, then be sure, in such houses are
bred—from such houses come—blasphemers. How
then can we best conquer blasphemy?" To this he
answers: "Truth above all! Truth in particular in
the house of truth, before the God of truth! Do not
utter in your prayers wishes, for the fulfilment of
which you do not care; do not pray for things which
in reality you do not want, do not praise God for the
giving of laws and the promulgating of statutes, which
he never commanded.† 'No liar and no hypocrite
shall appear before God.' Thus scripture informs us.
And should there be found in your prayer-books
wishes, supplications and benedictions of that sort,
then do not rest until you have purified and purged
your devotional books."‡

Salomon was a pioneer in the sketching of Biblical
characters in a series of sermons from a Jewish point
of view. The first collection in this line was his
"Moses, the man of God," in twenty-one lectures at
Hamburg, 1835. Most of these discourses were de-
delivered in the year 1827

Two years later a second "collection" was published,
entitled:

---

†What sense is there in praising God by a special benediction,
because he had commanded us to wash our hands, to light the
Chanuceah candles, to read the Megilla, when we can find no
passage in the Thora where such orders were ever given? I could
add many more instances of this kind.

†See Kaiserling: Bibl. Jued, Kanzeledner, Berlin, 1870,
Springer, Vol. I, page 275, and my "Selbstkritik der Juden," second
edition, Leipzig, W. Friedrich, 1890, pages 8-9 and note.

†See Kaiserling Bibl. Jued. Kanzelredner, Geiger: Zeitschrift
fuer Juedische Theologie, where these lectures are reviewed by Dr.
B. Wechsler, (Vol. III, page 91-102).

"David, the man after the heart of God," in
twenty-six lectures.

The third collection of this kind made its appearance in 1840, and is entitled:

"Elijah, the enthusiastic prophet, the champion
of light and truth," in nineteen lectures.

In all these lectures Salomon often draws the
moral lessons from the historical material in an ingenious manner. Salomon edited, in company with
Rabbi Dr. I. Mayer in Stuttgart, the "Koeniglichen
Kirchenrath of Wurtemberg," another "Collection of
Sermons for the Holidays and Other Occasions."* A
certain M. Lowengard, writing under the nom de
plume of "Judah Leon," an orthodox student of
theology made himself "immortal" by a most ridiculous
criticism of these sermons from a so-called "philosophical" point of view.†

In April, 1847, Salomon was called to Strelitz, in
order to dedicate the Synagogue, where he delivered
two sermons; one on the text, Psalms LVIII, 2-5,
the other on Leviticus XIX, "Holy ye shall be." The
sermons were dedicated to the noble Grand Duke
George, who had received the Jewish preacher most
cordially.

Salomon deserves the undisputed credit of having
given to the Jewish sermon its specific Jewish
character by the good use he made of the Talmud,
Midrash and the later Rabbinical literature.

Another characteristic of Salomon's pulpit work
is his practical sense. He always deals with the vital
topics of every day life and with the burning questions
of the hour, which nowadays are painfully neglected,
evaded or ignored by the majority of the Jewish
preachers in Germany. They are, also, too smart, too
well versed in the arts of diplomacy, and afraid to take
a manly, bold stand on the questions of the day. There
was nothing of the least interest in the family, Con-

---

*Fest-und Casualpredigten, Stuttgart, 1813, Metzler.

†Judah Leon: Beitraege Zur Kritik der Reformbestrebungen
in der Synagoge, Stuttgart, 1841.

gregation or in public life, on which Salomon did not preach.   Hence his great influence inside and outside of his immediate field of activity.   Many charitable institutions, societies and liturgical reforms owe their origin to the pulpit of Salomon.   Many families were kept back from the baptismal font through his inspiring sermons; many Jews, who were indifferent to their religion, were won again for our cause by the impetus received from the Temple in Hamburg, because there they were taught that notwithstanding their lax practice of the Jewish ceremonies and forms they could still be good Jews.   There they heard for the first time, that right living and good conduct constitute the essence of our religion.   The words of the prophet seemed to have been fulfilled: "Behold, days will come, when I will send a famine, not a famine for bread, nor a thirst for water; but to hear the word of the Lord." (Amos VIII, 11.)

Therefore we most deeply deplore the fact that Prof. Graetz has hardly a good word to say for Salomon. While, for instance, men like Heine and Boerne, who have nothing to do with Judaism, inasmuch as they were apostates, occupy a space of forty pages, *hardly ten lines are devoted to Salomon, and these abound in ridicule, bitter sarcasm, scorn and detraction. While the professor concedes that Salomon was an "able preacher, well versed in Biblical and Jewish literature," (Ibid., page 417), he accuses him of having given to the Temple a perfectly Protestanical appearance and in consequence of his (Salomon's) self-complacency and want of modesty, a defiant character." In vain we look for the learned professor's proofs of these assertions.   Again: "With Salomon commenced the influence of the preachers in Germany; the pulpit took the place of the house of learning and from it not seldom the hollow-sounding word was heard, which concealed the thought or the want of thought.   The

*Graetz's Hist. of the Jews, Vol. XI, pages 368 to 408. Forty lines would have more than sufficed for them in a "History of the Jews".

peals of the organ produced shallow emotions and pushed into the background the earnestness and the wealth of thought of the original Jewish doctrine." (Ibidem). In this country and even in Germany the organ is a popular institution of almost every, even the conservative Synagogue. Further: "The eternal 'preaching' "—Graetz uses the sneering expression 'Gepredige," which is no German at all,—"became disgusting to deeper natures." "They did not prophesy a long existence to the Temple." As it is still flourishing, they were false prophets. "A would-be wag characterizes the little confidence the friends of the Temple had in its lasting success:" "The preachers in Hamburg are growing rich, and can, if things turn out badly, buy a Congregation. (Minjan i, e. worshippers)." Now, even if this, by no means good joke, had originated among the friends, and not, as was the case, among the enemies of the Temple, it would still be out of place in a "History of the Jews," which ought to deal in facts only. Yet, Graetz himself cannot help stating, that "now and then the Temple succeeded indeed, in bringing back to the fold some Jews, who were about to join the church." (Ibid., page 417). Is this fact in itself not sufficient to treat the Temple and its preachers less irreverently and more respectfully? It almost appears as if the learned professor had felt some regrets, some compunctions of conscience on account of the sneers and ridicule which he had heaped upon the Temple, its preachers and upholders on page 417 of his "History." For on page 418 of the same work we are unexpectedly treated to the following highly appreciative and complimentary passage concerning the Temple: "Nevertheless the merit of the Hamburg Temple is not to be underestimated. It has removed from the House of God with one stroke and without many scruples, the trash which had gathered around it during many centuries; it has swept away in youthful impetuosity the holy spider-web, which nobody had dared to touch, and it has awakened a sense for a regulated form of decorum, order, taste and simplicity during divine service." We now ask in the spirit of fairness, whether it would not have been in better taste, and, moreover, in the interest of historical justice, if Prof. Graetz had omitted the sneering passages quoted. On the occasion of the hundredth anniversary of the birthday of Moses Mendelssohn, September 10, 1829, which was celebrated in Berlin, Breslau, Hamburg, Dresden, Leipzig, Frankfurt, Dessau and other large cities of Germany, Salomon published a sermon, "Light and Blessing," and a book: "Monument of Remembrance of Moses Mendelssohn." (Hamburg, 1829). The first part is devoted to an interesting biography of the "Sage of Dessau," while the second part forms a selection of systematically arranged extracts from Mendelssohn's writings in eight chapters. The publication is dedicated to Joseph, the only one of Moses Mendelssohn's children, who remained faithful to the religion of their fathers, and to David Friedlaender, whom Salomon fittingly designates "the truest disciple of the immortal master." Joseph Mendelssohn highly complimented Salomon on his conception of his father's life. As a token of his appreciation he sent the author the autograph of Mendelssohn, containing a notice of the "Hamburg Correspondent," written in Mendelssohn's handwriting. That newspaper announces to the world that "in July, 1779, the Chief Rabbi of Altona had excommunicated all those Jews, who would read Mendelssohn's translation of the Pentateuch."*

Salomon was a religious poet. He belonged to the commission which was authorized in 1833 to publish a new hymn book for the Temple in Hamburg. Dr. M. Fraenkel and Dr. Wohlwill were members of the same committee. Up to this date the Temple had used the "Religious Hymns and Songs for Israelites," published in 1818 and 1821 by Dr. Kley. Among the

---

*His name was Raphael Kohn, born in 1722, died in 1803. He was the grandfather of Gabriel Riesser.

four hundred and seventeen hymns of the new hymn book, ninety-five were composed by Salomon.* The full title of the book is: "General Israelitish Song Book for Houses of Worship and Schools," Hamburg, 1833. This hymn book, while an excellent selection of religious songs, has one great disadvantage. The songs are, as a rule, too philosophical, deep and transcendental, a mistake which characterizes not a few Jewish hymn books. This fault of our Jewish devotional literature reminds one vividly of Zunz's witty remark: "Der Jude Singt Logik und Betet Metaphysik."† But in justice to Salomon it must be stated that the songs composed by him form, to a great extent, a praiseworthy exception in this respect, because they are, as a rule, plainer, simpler and appeal less to the mind than to the heart. In regard to hymns it might not be amiss to remark that the Jews could learn a great deal from the Christians, whose Congregational songs on account of their plain form and substance are often inspiring. Our Temple-music is, especially in the large Temples, highly artistic. We sometimes pay extravagantly high prices to our choirs, and yet a less expensive Temple-music and a few more inspiring Congregational songs would considerably diminish the chilliness so characteristic of our worship and might increase the attendance in our Synagogues. The audience would then become, instead of an inactive critic, an active participant in the service. How much less expensive would such an arrangement be for smaller Congregations!

The following hymn composed by Salomon may find a place here. It has seven stanzas in the original German. This translation is contained in the "hymns and anthems," adapted for Jewish worship, selected and arranged by Dr. Gustav Gottheil, Rabbi of Temple Emanuel, New York, (1887) on pages 98-99:

*Salomon's Autobiography, page 31.

†The Jew sings logic and prays metaphysics.

SOUL, WHY ART THOU TROUBLED SO?

———

"Soul, why art thou troubled so?
"Soul, why art thou so sore afraid?
"Feelst thou not the Father nigh,
"Him whose heart contains us all?
"Lives no God for thee on high?
"Loving, while His judgments fall?
          "Look above!
          "God is love!
"Soul, why art thou troubled so?
          "Heart and eye
          "Lift on high!
"Every tear that on earth flows,
"God, the world's great ruler, knows."

"Soul, why art thou troubled so?
"Why art thou so sore afraid?
"Art thou then of all forsaken,
"Standest thou on earth alone?
"All thou loved'st from thee taken,
"Nothing thou canst call thine own?
          "God is with thee,
          "Eternally.
"Soul, my soul, shake off thy dread!
          "Firmly trust
          "God the just!
"Never shall His word betray.
"Never shall His love decay."

"Soul, why art thou troubled so?
"Why art thou so sore afraid?
"From thy heart has fatal death
"Torn the loved ones thou wouldst save?
"Sawest thou them, with anguished breath
"Sink into the gloomy grave?
          "Death's last blow
          "Endeth woe.

GOTTHOLD SALOMON.

"Soul, have comfort in the Lord!
"Tears, take flight,
"For in light
"Walk the hosts that God adore,
"Blessed, blessed evermore."

Salomon proved himself also a religious poet in his "Parables."*

But his monumentum aere perennum is his "German Bible for the People and the Schools of Israel."† Salomon thus gave for the first time into the hands of the Jews a German translation of the whole Bible from a Jewish point of view.

It is a testimony to Salomon's intense perseverance and painstaking work. The translation, while ignoring in most cases the results of modern Biblical research, especially of philology, is based on the conception of the best Rabbinical commentaries and does full justice, both to the spirit of the Hebrew and German languages. Salomon's "Volks und Schulbibel" especially the Pentateuch, was criticised by M. Hess, of Trier and by Rabbi L. Schott, of Randegg.

In the answer to these critics and in his polemical writings, Salomon gives ample proof of his great controversial powers. Anton Theodor Hartman, professor of theology in Rostock, a prominent scholar in the field of oriental languages,‡ found in Salomon a foe worthy of his steel. In a pamphlet: "Eisenmenger and his Jewish Opponents," and in the fifth and sixth volumes of the "Archives of the Newest Legislature," in an essay: "Should a perfect Equality of Civil Rights be granted to all the Jews at present?" Hartman, an uncompromising enemy of Israel, threw suspicion on the oath of a Jew. Salomon replied in "Open Letters to Mr. Anton Theodor Hartman:"§

---

*Leipzig, 1819.
†Deutsche Volks-und Schulbibel, Altona 1817, Zweite Auflage 1838, Hammerich.
‡See his "Die Hebraeerin am Putztisch."
§Offene Briefe an Herrn A. Th. Hartman, Hamburg, 1835.

These five letters are remarkable for the thorough knowledge of Jewish literature he displayed, for the logic, and keenness of argumentation, for his shrewdness in discovering every weak point of his opponent, for the quick wit, irony and merciless sarcasm, with which Salomon unmasks the ignorance, littleness, miserable bigotry and animosity of the assailant of his co-religionists. To Th. Hartman's statement, based on the book of the orthodox Rabbi Loewenstein in Emden, that the Talmud is the code of laws for the Jews, Salomon plainly answered, "No!" "And if a hundred Rabbis," thus he continues, "should say so, what does it prove? Our Rabbis, even the oldest and most learned of them, are neither bishops nor popes." The conclusion of the fifth letter, where Salomon reminds the professor, or better the Christian world, of what the Jews cheerfully forget, provided the Christians forget some foolish expressions in old Jewish books, which not even the Jews—except a few scholars—understand, is a masterpiece of eloquence. He concludes thus: "Practice the love, of which in word and deed is preached so much in churches, and which is so often spoken of outside the church. * * Be thou a Christian, as I am a Jew, in this sense, and it will not be necessary to make our future salvation and present welfare dependent upon books, for the letter killeth the Christian and the Jew, but the spirit maketh them both alive."

These letters created at the time such a tremendous sensation that Hartman was compelled, by his students, to defend himself. They plainly told him that they would no longer attend his lectures in the University, if he should keep silent after having been publicly accused of ignorance. Hartman was thus put on the defensive, instead of the offensive. He then came out with a pamphlet: "Principles of Orthodox Judaism," to which Salomon replied in a "Second and Last Letter." He conclusively refuted Hartman's accusations concerning the national pride of the "chosen people," concerning their hatred of the adherents of other religions, recklessness in taking an oath, and cowardice. He showed by numerous quotations from the Biblical and later Jewish literature, that Jehovah is considered the father of the whole human family, irrespective of nationality or creed,* and that the kingdom of truth will slowly, gradually, but surely gain universal dominion in the whole world.

In those days Judaeophobia, Jew-baiting, or "Anti-semitism," as modern phraseology styles this idiosyncrasy, was nurtured, fostered and fanned by the German professors, who, sailing under the false colors of theological rationalism and political liberalism, made the Jews scapegoats and targets for their own narrow-mindedness. A Ruehs, Fries, Hartman and even a Bretschneider were not ashamed to attack Judaism with the rusted ammunition used by an Eisenmenger, Schudt, Wagenseil, and others. The school of the so-called "Jung-Hegelianer," with their merciless "criticism," commenced to attack Judaism and Jews under the guise of philosophy. The most prominent exponent of this clique was Bruno Bauer, who by his scathing and corrosive criticism of the "Evangelical History of the Synoptics" deprived Christianty of every historical basis, and regarded religion as the enemy of all development in the spirit of freedom. No wonder that he was expelled from the chair of the theological faculty for the expression of such views.

In 1842 he published in the "German Yearbooks of Science and Art," which was the official organ of the "Young-Hegelians," an essay on the "Judenfrage."† Bauer desired to prove, that Judaism and the modern government of nations are incompatible contrasts, hence, the emancipation of the Jews must be made dependent on their giving up their religion and nationality. It was the old sophistry in the garb of

---

*Leviticus XIX. 18, 19, 2., Exod. XXIII. 4-5, Proverbs XXV, 21-23, Sch.

†See Deutsche Jahrbuecher fuer Wissenschaft und Kunst, 1842, pages 274 and 282. It appeared in pamphlet-form in 1843. (Braunschweig.)

New-Hegelianism. It is the old story "les extremites se touchent." Here is an outspoken enemy of every religion, yet he would have the Jews give up their religion for—what? For the right to be possibly chosen to the office of a policeman or town-crier? Had Bauer taken the trouble to study the history of the Jews in middle ages, he would have known, that their religion was dearer to them than life itself.

Bauer's pamphlet elicited many telling replies from leading Jewish scholars, among others, a pamphlet from Gustav Philippson. * More thorough were the answers of Dr. Abrahm Geiger, Samuel Hirsch and the always ready champion, Gotthold Salomon. Geiger treated the relation of the Jews to the state in the different epochs from the historical-critical point of view and most cleverly refuted every one of Bauer's sophistic arguments.† Samuel Hirsch published a pamphlet: "Judaism, the Christian Government, and the Modern Criticism, Letters concerning the 'Judenfrage' of Bruno Bauer, Leipzig, 1843." Hirsch having been a Hegelian himself and endowed with a mind, eminently trained for philosophical argument, and having been well versed in the theological, historical and Rabbinical literatures, was especially fitted to demolish Bauer with his own weapons. This he most ably did, although his style of writing was a little too deep for the masses. This, however, was also the case with Bruno Bauer's style. Sentences containing from eight to twelve lines are by no means of rare occurrence in Bauer's pamphlet.

Salomon published a strong and popular pamphlet: "Bruno Bauer and his Superficial Criticism on the Jewish Question."‡ Common sense, knowledge of Jewish history and Rabbinical literature are the weapons which Salomon most cleverly used to destroy the unfounded hypotheses of Bauer. He shows the

*"Die Judenfrage, von Bruno Bauer," nacher beleuchtet. Dessau, 1843.
†Geiger's Wissenchaftliche Zeitschrift fuer Jueische Theologie, Vol. 5.
‡Hamburg, 1843, C. Rosenkranz.

inconsistency of Bauer, who, while denying Christianity, still clings to the hyper-orthodox notion that "Christianity is the fulfillment of Judaism." The prophecy which Salomon jokingly made, that he should not be surprised to see the iconoclast Bauer in the role of an editor of an orthodox Christian paper, became, indeed, later literally fulfilled. Bauer, the merciless demolisher of the Evangelical history of the "synoptics," joined hands with the pietists and feudalists as a contributor to the notorious "Kreutzzeitung.† He also published anti-Jewish articles in the conservative "State-Lexicon" of the inveterate Jew-hater Wagener, and advocated the theory of the "Christian Government." (Christlicher Staat). Still, Bruno Bauer and his ilk are forgotten and could not prevent the emancipation of the Jews.

A year later Salomon's polemic pen was again put to good use in the publication of a pseudonym pamphlet: "The Blue Book of Gottfried Sigismund," (Hamburg, 1844.) as a rejoinder to a most scurrilous publication: "The Black Book, by B. Carlo." The booklet is spicy, sprightly, witty and amusing in the extreme. It begins as follows:

"The greatest misfortune that the Jews have brought upon Germany in general and the good city of Hamburg in particular, consists in the large swarm of ignorant, good-for-nothing scribblers, whom the great question of Jewish emancipation has produced."

We come now to one of the most important periods in the history of the Jewish Reform-movement, namely, to the famous "prayer-book controversy," which, though originally a local affair of Hamburg Judaism, was destined to exercise the greatest influence upon the development of the Jewish worship. That Salomon did not remain inactive in this controversy will be seen.

In Chapter IV of this book, the reader will have noticed what a stir the first Hamburg prayer-book,

*This Berlin daily is the mouthpiece of the "Altconservative" or "Junkerpartei," the organ of Feudalism and Antisemitism.

"Order of Public Worship of the Whole Year," had
created.   Partly on account of the scarcity of this book,
but more especially in due consideration of the pressing
wants of a new, more advanced generation, the officers
of the Temple concluded to publish an amended prayer-
book.   The title of the new prayer-book was "Seder
Abodah," and it was introduced in 1841 in the Temple
of Hamburg and in its branch-synagogue in Leipzic,
where divine service was held during the annual fair,
(Messe.)

While the members of the Temple were in full
sympathy with the new prayer book, Bernays* of the
"German Israelitish Congregation," of Hamburg, came
out with three warnings, published in the three Synagogues of Hamburg, against the use of said prayer-book.
(October 16, 1841.) He literally interdicted it; declared
it "un-Jewish" and "sinful" to make use of it for the
sake of prayer, without, however, giving one valid
reason for this prohibition.   It deserves special mention that Rabbi Ettlinger, of Altona, did not sign this
document. +   Rabbi Bernays had proved his hostility
to the Temple on another occasion.   After the resignation of Dr. Kley as preacher of the Temple, in 1839,
and Dr. Frankfurter's election as his successor, the
administration of the Temple passed the resolution
to build a more spacious new Temple.   As the permission of the Senate of Hamburg was indispensable for
such a step, the Senate inquired about it of the officers
of Bernays' Congregation, who in turn asked for
Bernays' opinion on the question.   The "Chacham"
took the opportunity to prevent the grant of the desired
permission on the ground that the Temple-society was
sectarian.   He even went so far as to induce the Christian authorities to prohibit the use of the new prayer-
book, and thus to annihilate the Temple-society.
But he could not succeed in making the Senate a pliant

---

*In his attempt to imitate the Portuguese Jews he preferred the
pompous title of "Chacham" (sage).

+Later however, due to the pressure brought to bear on him, he
took sides with Bernays.

tool of his fanaticism. That these doings, especially
Bernays' "interdict," did not fail to create a painful
sensation, is a matter of course. Bernays' antecedents
were not at all in harmony with conduct so fanatical,
and so utterly unworthy of a man, trained in German
Universities and well versed in philosophical literature.
No wonder that people attributed his action to personal
spite against the Temple-society, which had drawn
away the best and most intelligent younger members
from Bernays' Congregation and had thereby increased
the membership of the Temple to the imposing number
of eight hundred! It cannot be denied that Bernays had
not justified the great hopes of the orthodox party and
that his inactivity and the peculiar style of his so-called
philosophical sermons had utterly failed to attract to
him the rising generation. More even than the "interdict" itself did its inconsiderate, insulting tone incense
the members of the Temple. Bernays charged the officers of the Temple with "frivolity and irreligiousness."* Even such calm, moderate and generally dis-
passionate men as Gabriel Riesser became indignant.
They saw in Bernays' step a flagrant violation of their
rights, "because the Chacham had no jurisdiction over
the Temple." The board of directors of the Temple
in a counter-declaration, (October 24,) charged Bernays
not only with "arrogance, impotent partiality, malicious ignoring of the contents of the prayer book," but
even with "ignorance in the theological-liturgical science." Bernays and his Congregation flooded the
Jewish Congregations of Europe with copies of the
interdict. This in turn compelled the Temple administration to call forth the opinions of modern Rabbis
and preachers on the subject. It shows the growth of
the Reform-movement, that, while twenty years pre-

---

*Bernays said in his "interdict" among other things, that the
"most arbitrary mutilation of our main prayers, intentional deviation from the Jewish mode of prayer and the most irresponsible
destruction of the spirit of prayer by abolishing and changing of
passages concerning our religious (?) future. "Redemption,"
"Messiah" "Resurrection," and a frivolous treatment of future hopes"
are manifested in the prayer-book.

viously, during the first "Hamburg prayer book controversy," only three foreign Rabbis had dared to come
forward publicly in favor of the prayer book,* no less
than thirteen, and the most famous Rabbis of Germany
at that, at this time boldly espoused the cause of
reform and progress. Aside from the two preachers of
the Temple, Salomon and Frankfurter, the following
Rabbis gave favorable opinions on the prayer book: J.
A. Friedlender, Holdheim, Levin Auerbach, Geiger,
Guttman, Kohn, Maier, Mannheimer, Philippsohn
and Stein. Zacharias Frankel, in full accord with his
"mediating" disposition and his customary indecision
gave an opinion which satisfied neither party. Geiger's and Holdheim's opinions are the most thorough
of all.

Salomon's opinion is contained in a small pamphlet
which thoroughly discusses the matter.†

The tone of this publication is earnest, and dignified. Salomon refuses the charges brought against the
authors of the prayer book, that in it they ignore the
three doctrines of Redemption, Messiah and Resurrection. He proves by numerous quotations from Biblical
and Rabbinical literature, that the prayer book is not
inconsistent with Mosaic-Rabbinical Judaism. In this
he proves too much, as it is not at all the province of
Reform-Judaism to be in every respect in harmony with
Mosaic-Rabbinical Judaism. The omission of the Mussaph
prayer which refers particularly to the ancient bloody sacrifices in the Temple of Jerusalem, of the prayer "Velamalshinim,"‡ (against the apostates) is, he continues, in
full harmony with the spirit of our age. He concludes
as follows:

*See chapter IV "Aron Chorin," page 76 of this book.
†Das neue Gebetbuch und seine Verketzerung, sine ira at cum
studio, (Hamburg, 1841.)
‡The following is a literal translation of the prayer: "O,
let the slanderers have no hope; all the evil-doers may be
annihilated speedily and all the tyrants may be quickly cut off,
humble thou them speedily in our days. Blessed art thou, oh God,
who destroyest enemies, and humblest tyrants." This is the
twelfth of the so-called eighteen benedictions, (Shemoneh
Essreh).

"Whether the author of the anathema thought more of his own cause than the cause and honor of God; whether he is 'not at home,' as many people claim, in the liturgical and theological literature, so necessary for a clear judgment in this matter, or whether he did not carefully read the work, so mercilessly condemned by him, we do not know. But we do know that since the existence of the Jews and Judaism no Jewish teacher has ever come out with a similar interdict. * * * We are convinced, however, that even this event will contribute ultimately to the promotion of enlightened religiousness in Israel."

Salomon devoted also a special sermon to the prayer book controversy, entitled: "It is dangerous to accuse a whole community of irreligiousness," delivered February 7, 1842. The text: "Abraham said, I thought there is no fear of God in this place," (Gen. XX, 8-11) is most appropriate for the occasion.

Dr. L. Auerbach, (Leipzig,) said: "The step of Bernays was not only hasty but also superfluous and useless; superfluous for his own orthodox Congregation; useless for the members of the Temple, who had been accustomed to a similar prayer book for twenty-three years in spite of the interdict of forty Rabbis." Auerbach protests most emphatically against Bernays' words, that "it had never entered the mind of a Jew to make use of this prayer book." This, if true, would exclude every member of the Hamburg and Leipzig Temple-people from the pale of Judaism! And yet, the most respected, most charitable and best educated men, (Gabriel Riesser and others,) were active members of the Temple! How much more tolerant were the Talmudists, who teach: "As long as a man does not worship idols, he has a right to be called a Jew. *

Such prayers only were eliminated as might tend to throw suspicion upon the patriotism of the Jews.

*See Maimonides on "Idolaters, II, 4, Talmud Megilla 13; my "The Talmud," pages 34-40, and my Prinzipien des Judenthum's chapter VII.

Similar passages are omitted in the Portuguese prayer book, which is considered strictly orthodox. For instance; the passage "And bring us back in peace from the four corners of the globe," or "Return, oh God, to Jerusalem, Thy City, in peace." Maimonides said: "Prayers can be recited in any language," and "The Mussaph prayer is not absolutely necessary."

The Messianic idea is well represented in the prayer book, hence Bernays' talk about "a frivolous treatment of the future of Judaism," amounts to nothing.

Joseph Friedleander, then eighty years old, comes to the conclusion that Bernays' utterances are not based on legal causes or liturgical reasons; and that the prayer book, which does justice to a purified and dignified service in accord with the demands of the age deserves to be recommended to every Jewish Congregation. He closes with the following beautiful sentiments: "I am the same for truth and justice from youth to old age."

Abraham Geiger gives the following opinion:* According to the Talmud the short prayer "Habinenu" is sufficient, so far as fulfilling the daily duty of prayer is concerned. Hence the omission of some prayers in the prayer book of the Temple does not justify Bernays' interdict, not even from the strictest Talmudical point of view. The omitted prayers were among those, that owe their origin to a later period. The ritual is different in German, Polish, Portuguese, Spanish, Provencal, Italian, Greek and other Congregations, and even in Fuerth, Frankfurt, Vienna, Metz, Bohemia, Bavaria, Wuertemburg and Russia, the mode of worship differs. Hence the discrimination as to what must be called a Jewish prayer book is arbitrary in the extreme. Aside from this there are no radical changes in the prayer book of the Temple, and even those pointed out in the :"interdict" concerning Redemption, Messiah, Resur-

*See Geiger: Der Hamburger Tempelstreit, eine Zeitfrage, Breslau; 1842, Leuckhardt, and Nachgel, Schriften I, pages 113-197.

rection,—which, however, have nowhere been designated as essential elements of the prayer—are very tame indeed. Hence the verdict is purely subjective and arbitrary, and the prohibition of the use of said prayer book is wholly unfounded and in glaring contrast with the laws of the Talmud concerning prayer.

In his pamphlet on the "Hamburger Templesteit," Geiger takes the Temple people to task for not going farther in the Synagogical reform than they did, and accuses them of inconsistency, half-heartedness and want of decision.

Dr. Samuel Holdheim, Land-Rabbi of the Grand-Duchy of Mecklenburg-Schwerin, has also published his opinion on the prayer book in pamphlet-form, entitled: "On the Prayer Book and its Use in the Temple," Hamburg, 1841. He proves that the custom of the Hamburg Templers, not to repeat the Shmoneh Essreh* twice, but to recite it with the reader, was advocated by Rabbi Gamaliel† and by Maimonides, who had introduced the same reform‡ in a Congregation where he resided.

In answer to an attack made upon him in the "Zeitung des Judenthums" Holdheim published an article § on the question of authority from which the following is an extract:

"I have, as Rabbi of my generation, the same right which the forty Rabbis had, who twenty-three years ago decided against the prayer book. The imposing number of forty proves nothing. Every one of them was only one. * * That these forty Rabbis voted against, and to-day only a few Rabbis vote for the prayer book is a problem easily solved. Although an impartial, liberal opinion is no longer considered heresy in our day, its advocacy has nevertheless for many a Rabbi unpleasant consequences, to defy which

---

*Eighteen Benedictions.
†Mishna Rosh hashana IV, 9.
‡Geiger: Wissenschafte Zeitschrift fuer Jued Theologie, Vol. II, pages 347-348.
§Zeitung des Judenthum's, 1842, No. 8, February 19th.

not everybody has the courage.   These forty Rabbis,
who in 1819 denounced the Hamburg prayer book,
reaped glory and honor, a kind of veneration from their
contemporaries, and as long as the advocates of Reform
make themselves unpopular by their course, the numer-
ical strength proves nothing for the truth and justice
of the cause in question."

Abraham Kohn, Rabbi of Hohenems, Tyrol, Austria, said:* "Judging from Bernays' interdict I expected,
indeed, that the prayer book—which I had not yet seen
at the time I read the interdiction—contained most
radical views on our religion.   But how surprised was
I when I saw the prayer book.   What a bold statement
it was that "the spirit of our prayer had been destroyed
there!"   I found indeed that the changes were intentional, but by no means "arbitrary."   On the contrary,
that they gave due consideration to the genuine and
pure spirit of Judaism as well as to the exigencies and
demands of our age.   Only such passages are eliminated and changed as are liable to foster intolerance, to
nourish conceit and false pride.   Furthermore, such
passages as are not compatible with refined taste, disturb order and decorum, and hinder devotion, are omitted.   Lastly, ideas, which the majority of our co-religionists do not believe and whose realization they do not
wish, are not contained in the new prayer book.   On
the other hand the prayer book strives to elevate the
sentiments of Judaism and humanity.   That the
lamentations on account of the loss of Palestine, Temple and sacrificial rites are partly omitted and partly
changed does not at all constitute a dogmatic question.
For it is known how little the prophets and psalmists
cared for the sacrificial worship.   The great Maimonides regards the ideas of Redemption and Messiah as
conveying the lesson that a time will come when the
knowledge of God will be universal and the kingdom of
righteousness and truth will be established on earth.†

*December 19th, 1841.
†Maimonides hilchot Teshuba, chapter IX and Melachim
chapter XII.

That our oppressed ancestors never forgot a prayer for Israel's restoration was due to their persecution and oppression by the surrounding nations. Where is then the *raison d' etre* for us to recite such prayers? Who expects or wishes in our days the re-establishment of a Jewish monarchy? The amelioration of the civil and social position of our co-religionists in Germany is nearer to the heart of the Jew in Germany than the restoration of the Davidian dynasty in Palestine. Aside from this it is an irrefutable fact that to a large majority of our co-religionists the belief in a Messiah means the hope, that all men, irrespective of creed, will recognize in Jehovah the Common Father of all mankind. The Talmud informs us that Jeremiah and Daniel changed a formula of prayer instituted by Moses, because they did not consider it right to utter before God, who is the embodiment of truth, convictions which they did not hold, because they did not want to lie before Him (*Joma 69 b.*) I deem it therefore my duty to recommend the prayer book to every Israelite and to express my heartfelt thanks to the Temple-society for its highly meritorious endeavor to give more life and truth to our liturgy. May it triumph over sanctimoniousness and indifferentism. While we regret that in many places nothing is done, to heal old wounds, it is still more deplorable, that even there, where a change for the better has already gained firm ground and borne noble fruit, a fight is made against it at the expense of truth and peace. But let us not fear their impotent efforts, for God is with us, the God of light and truth."

Dr. Isaac Noah Manheimer, of Vienna, passed the following judgment on the prayer book:(Vienna December 23, 1841).

1. "According to Rabbinical principles it is permitted to recite all the prayers—except the priestly blessing—in the German or in any other generally intelligible language."

2. "The abolition of the Pijutim and Selichoth is an indispensable condition of the complete restoration of our Divine service to its pristine dignity."

3. "Vehu Rachum"* (a long prayer for Mondays and Thursdays,) all *Jehi razon*; † the alphabetical register of sins committed during the year, "*Al chait*"‡ which plays so important a part in the prayers for the Day of Atonement, may be unscrupulously abbreviated or even entirely abolished."

4. "The only prayers for which the Rabbis of the Talmud claimed authority, integrity and validity are the Shema,§ with the prayers preceding and succeeding it; and the Tefilla."‖

5. "The only important change in the Hamburg prayer-book, which has, however, already taken place in the edition of 1819, is in the so-called Mussaph (additional) prayer for Sabbath-and Holidays. There the supplication for the 'restoration of the sacrificial service' is changed into "Hear our prayers, in the place of sacrifices."¶ Manheimer candidly confesses that a restoration of the sacrificial service and particularly of the bloody sacrifices does not belong to our Messianic hopes and expectations. He cites the prophets and Maimonides, who designated the sacrificial service as belonging to a childish stage of the people of Israel."**

He therefore considers Bernays' interdict as unjustifiable. The fact, that Bernays deems it necessary

---

*This prayer is composed of Biblical passages. Jarchi, Abudiraham and Midrash Shocher Tob to Psalms 22, speak of this prayer. Translated literally it means: "And He, i. e., God, is merciful."

†Prayer beginning "May it be Thy will, Oh God."

‡Literally "For the sake of the sin." This prayer was already known to R. Amraem and originated in the time of the Gaonim. The Portuguese have not so many "Alchait" as the Germans. Maimoinides knows only of one. R. Jeehuda Barzelloni (1130 p, C.,) was opposed to this prayer. (Zunz: Ritus, page 13). Many Rabbinical authorities object to the public recital of a detailed confession of sins, justly remarking, that it belongs to private devotion. The form of the "Al Chait" proves its late date.

§"Hear, oh Israel, the Eternal our God, the Eternal is one." It is our Credo. Talm. Berachot 13.

‖"Thefilla" literally "prayer," is used for the eighteen benedictions on week days and seven benedictions on Sabbath-and Holidays.

¶Manheimer is not quite correct. The old form is also retained in small print.

**Moreh Nebuchin (Guide of the perplexed), Vol. III.

to modify and to weaken the interdict of the Hamburg
Rabbinate in 1819, shows that he is not so sure of the
justice of his cause. But had he simply warned his
own followers, without attacking and throwing suspicion upon the honor and reputation of the Temple-
Society, which, in the twenty-two years of its existence
had shown itself worthy of Judaism, his course might
have been excused to a certain extent. But now it is
the duty of all those, who entertain the least hope for
the restoration of our religion and of a revival of the
spirit of our people, to raise their voice most emphatically against the narrow-mindedness, one-sidedness,
usurpation of authority and arrogance manifested in
his interdict by Bernays, who, being himself a child of
the new age, ought to have been the last person to be
guilty of such actions. The more indifferent the Rabbis
of Bernays' stamp have shown themselves in the
cause of improving our worship, and the more they
have looked on, while thousands upon thousands in
Israel have thus been estranged from the House of
God, the less right have they to give themselves the
appearance of heroes and champions of our faith in the
face of those, who, in order to stem the tidal waves of
apostasy and of threatened dissolution, were the first to
set bounds to the religious anarchy and lawlessness in
things divine. Manheimer, who was married in 1824
by a preacher of the Hamburg Temple according to
the ritual of the Temple, and who for two years, 1823-
25, had officiated as preacher in the Temple, says that
he is indebted to it for the richest everlasting impressions. There he received his inspirations for his
successful labors in one of the most influential Congregations of Germany. He says that he will never forget the sad impressions which the abstruse lectures of
Bernays and the utter deterioration and decay of the
service in the Synagogue, under the spiritual guidance
of Bernays, have made upon him, impressions which
have not left his mind to this day.

If the question of authority is to be considered of
greater import than argument and scientific result,

then he may safely place his authority based on the
confidence which he enjoys in the Congregations of the
Austrian monarchy, in matters pertaining to the Jewish rite of worship, in opposition to that of Mr.
Bernays.

Dr. Frankfurter, in a pamphlet: "Standstill and
Progress," with special reference to the Hamburg
prayer-book controversy, (1841) said: "The prayer-book
controversy is the old struggle between progress and
standstill. There was a time, when religious observances were a matter of inheritance from father to son.
Nobody thought of questioning their meaning and
significance; they were practiced, but they were dead
all the same.

"But with the awakening of a better spirit of the
age the Jews who took an active part in this awakening naturally had the pardonable ambition to rouse the
religious life from its stagnation. Hence parties were
formed, the one representing standstill, stagnation and
indolence, the other advocating progress, development,
change. The former opposed every deviation from
beaten paths. To them Mendelssohn was an infidel,
because he had translated parts of the Bible into pure
German instead of making use of the Jargon. They
cursed Wessely, because he had put himself on record
in favor of a better education of the Jews. The Talmud
and its commentaries constituted their world. Belonging to the past, they had no eye for the present
and future. Hence every argument set forth in favor
of the new wants and considerations was ignored by
them. They have done nothing because they were
fully convinced that no action was necessary.

"The friends of progress tried to enter into this new
spirit of the times, sought and found more appropriate
and timely forms for a religious life. The movement
was a strong, irrepressible demand of the time.

"What are the opponents of progress doing in this
second phase of spreading Reform? They sigh, lament,
complain of the decline of religion, while the representatives of progress are up and doing, to bring back

to the fold those who went astray. As a reward they are styled 'heretics,' 'infidels,' and 'neologuists,' by those who idly look on the 'decline of Judaism.'"

Frankfurter says of the Hamburg Temple: "It never intended to oppose the Synagogue in its imperishable truth; on the contrary it aims to strengthen our faith.

"And now a closing word to the opponents of progress. With lamentations, sighs and excommunications you cannot change the current of the age.

"You utter the reproach, that among the men of progress everything is not as it ought to be. But have you the right to overlook the real improvements for the better accomplished by those men? Is your idleness excusable in times like ours, when the religious apathy, indifference and indolence of the masses, so far as Judaism is concerned, are the rule of the day? Is it right, that instead of opening the eyes of the masses you try to deprive them of the light they have and to lead them backwards? Our Synagogues decline; what are you doing to support them, and to fill worshippers with the love of God and of His doctrine? The herd is scattered; what are you doing to gather them?

"If you want to accuse the present you must not yourselves do a crying wrong against it; when you accuse others of tearing down you must be able to show what you yourselves have built up, established, repaired. Where then are your works, which ought to testify for you and against us? Where?"

The following is the opinion of Dr. Joseph Maier, Kirchenrath, of Wuertemberg, and Rabbi of Stuttgart, (December 16, 1841.)

Dr. Maier is very systematic in pointing out most accurately in nine paragraphs the difference between the Hamburg and the old orthodox prayer-book. He then goes on to give, in four additional paragraphs, the principles which apparently have guided the authors and compilers of the Hamburg prayer-book, as follows:

1. The restoration of the dignity and simplicity of the original Jewish worship, hence the abolition of

Pijutim, and the removal of abuses. He criticises, however, the Temple for its inconsistency in many things. Such as the Kiddush* retained in its prayer-book, although according to Schulchan Aruch† it is unnecessary. Nevertheless the prayer-book is a good attempt at a returning from the abuse to the good old usage.‡

2. Revival of the devotion, which, in consequence of the long duration of the service and of the unintelligibility of the prayers, had almost utterly disappeared from the Synagogue. Hence the abbreviation of the many prayers, and of the reading portions from the Pentateuch; the introduction of German prayers, hymns and responses, which stimulate the activity of the whole Congregation in the service.

3. Elimination of all prayers and utterances, expressing intolerance and hostility against the adherents of other religions.§

4. Elimination of passages expressive of the desire of a return to Palestine and the restoration of the Temple in Jerusalem with its sacrificial cult. Now, while it is much to be regretted that in this respect the prayer-book is very inconsistent ‖ it must be taken into consideration, that a radical separation of the national from the merely human elements in our prayer-book is rather premature.

---

*A prayer spoken on the eve of Sabbath- and Holidays over the wine. "Kiddush" literally means "sanctification" of the Sabbath- and Holidays. It does not belong to the Synagogue at all, only to the house. By mere chance it was introduced into the Synagogue, (Pessachim 101, b.) and the Gaon Hai, and even Karo, (Tur, I, 269), favored its abrogation from the house of worship. In Palestine it was never introduced in the Synagogue.

†Orach Chajim, chapter 269, 94.

‡"Vom Missbrauche zum guten alten Branch." Zunz was the first to make use of this phrase in his "Gottesdienstliche Vortraege."

§The prayers "Velamalshinim" "Av Harachmeim" and several passages in "Abinu Malkenu," belong to this class.

‖As one instance I mention, that while passages like "Rebuild, oh God, Thy Temple as it was formerly," "Bring us back to our country, Palestine," were changed in accord with the principle, prayers like "Yaale Vejavau," which express the same sentiment, remained unchanged.

As long as the Shema and the Tefilla are not eliminated from the prayer-book, the Reforms touch only the Minhag (usage), concerning which, in all times, Congregations differed one from another.

We possess not one prayer in its original form.* The three years cycle in the reading from the Thora is already mentioned in the Talmud,† and deserves recommendation, because the too long Perikopes‡ make the service a burden. For the same reason the abolition of the "Haphtara"§ is in order, as the beginning of the reading of the "Hapthara" was usually a signal for the people to run out of the Synagogue. Aside from this the Haphtara was introduced only very lately as a substitute, at a time when it was forbidden to the Jews to read the Thora, which prohibition has long since been revoked.

The Talmud (Berachot 13) permits the recitation of the Shema and Tefilla in the vernacular. In a time as critical as ours the words of Maimonides ought to be taken to heart: "The religious authorities of every age have the authority to set aside temporarily even ordinances of the Mosaic law, whenever the preservation of the whole religion demands it, just as the physician is in duty bound to amputate a diseased limb in order to save the rest of the body."

In connection with the prayer-book controversy, The following passage from a sermon of Dr. Baernhard Wechsler, Chief-Rabbi of the Duchy of Oldenburg, delivered on the occasion of his inauguration into office in 1842, deserves mention: "How can our pretentions and our hopes of a recognition of our religion as a religion of the spirit and truth, be fulfilled, when men who occupy the position of leaders of large Congrega-

---

*As proof of this statement, see Zunz: Gottesdienstl. Vortraege, page 369.

†Megilla 29 and Maimonides on "Prayer," XIII.

‡Perikope or "Sidrah" means the weekly portion which is read from the Pentateuch every Sabbath.

§"Haphtarah" from "patar," "dismiss," "make free," (Christian-Catholic Missal), means the reading of a chapter of the prophets after the reading of the Thorah.

tions, intend to enslave religious opinions and to control them by force?" It is needless to say that the provoking steps taken by the Hamburg Rabbis against the prayer-book are most particularly alluded to. *   *   "I do not deem it right to keep silent here in this matter. For it is not the question of admitting a single Reform, but of the freedom of the whole spiritual process within Judaism. When they again commence to disturb the conscience with the old rusted weapons of the 'Issur,' (prohibition) and of the excommunication—then it is the duty of every Rabbi to warn in his circle and to defend the right of free religious conviction."

In the meantime the senate, under date of January 12, 1845, had publicly made known its decision, that the much talked of proclamation of Bernays, against the prayer-book must be removed by the administration of the Congregation of Altona. The Chacham and his followers resisted as long as possible compliance with this ordinance, but on the 2nd day of February, the "Modaah" (proclamation) was removed. A few days later, however, they affixed the closing passage of the said proclamation as a new "Modaah" near the entrance of the Synagogue, which read thus:

WARNING.

It is forbidden to recite the obligatory prayers out of a book, which was published here last year under the title: "Prayers of the Israelites."

Hamburg, Erev Shabbath (eve of Sabbath,) 10th Shebat, 5602. | Isaac, son of Jacob Bernays, Chacham of the German Israelitish Congregation of Hamburg.

This prayer-book controversy had thus brought the Hamburg Temple into more than local prominence, had weakened the influence of orthodoxy, not only in Hamburg, but throughout all Europe, and has even compelled the Synagogue to do something in the way of making the divine worship more attractive to the young generation and the female sex.

A similar struggle took place at the same time in England. Some German Congregations of London had introduced the sermon in the Synagogue in 1838 and were about to inaugurate other reformatory measures, when members of the Portuguese Congregation had resolved to "purify the worship from all prayers and usages not based on the original revelation."[*] But they did not intend to do things by halves, and therefore they applied in 1840 to Germany for an able preacher and scholar who would lead their steps in the right direction and who would defend the Reforms to be introduced with weapons from the armory of Jewish theology. They were, however, disappointed, as no German Rabbi possessing those qualities was willing to go to England. They then selected a young talented Englishman, Rev. W. Marks, who, in company with the well-known scholar Heimann Hurwiz, elaborated a new prayer-book. It was resolved to build a new Synagogue. This was the signal for a great storm. Influenced, no doubt, by the example of Bernays and his followers, the Rabbi of the German Congregation of London, an ignorant man, and the Portuguese Rabbi, Raphael Meldola, published an interdict against the prayer-book and its defenders. (May 10, 1841). In this proclamation (Azharah) the "Form of Prayer used in the West London Synagogue of British Jews,"[†] is styled "a great evil," "which should not be brought into a Jewish home." To recite the prayers from this prayer-book was called, "a sin and an abomination." This document was signed by some other Rabbis hailing from Lissa, and Krotoschin. The Reforms were so insignificant indeed, that the prayer-book would be considered orthodox to-day. With the exception of a few

---

[*]Jost. Geschichte des Judenthum's and seiner Sekten III. page 375.

[†]Edited by D. W. Marks, printed by J. Wertheimer, 5601, A. M. It shows, how little reformed the prayer-book was when even the date of publication was "Anno Mundi."

abbreviations,* the old Portuguese prayer-book remained unchanged.   This interdict was sent broadcast to all British Congregations and accused the new Congregation of heresy and schism.   But no attention was paid to this act of fanaticism.   Liverpool and Manchester returned the document, while in Portsmouth it was solemnly delivered to the flames, although those Congregations belonged to the London Rabbinate-district.†

After the West London Synagogue with its prayer-book had become an established fact, the members of the new Congregation did not intend to withdraw from the Mother-Congregation. But the "London committee of British Jews," at the head of which stood Sir Moses Montefiore, refused to recognize the new Synagogue as a Synagogue, and to register the same (February 8, 1842).   The object of this intolerant and unjust action was to prevent the members of the Congregation from entering into wedlock—according to his interpretation of the English law on Jewish marriages— or to make their marriages illegal. To this Francis H. Goldsmith, one of the directors of the West-End Synagogue, answered politely but firmly, that Sir Moses Montefiore is mistaken when he thinks that Jewish marriages need his consent.   Notwithstanding the fact stated by Montefiore, that "our spiritual church authority" does not regard us as Jews, no court of law can be convinced that a Synagogue, which has in its ritual the hymn "Jigdal,"‡ has forfeited its claim to be a Jewish institution.   Mr. Montefiore could have well afforded to testify that the house of worship on Burton street is a Synagogue, although he does not consider our Judaism as genuine as his.   Were I the

---

*Ezeh Mekkoman, Pittum Haketoreth, Bammeh Madekin Lecho Dodi, Velamalshinim, Velo Nessatto. In the Mussaph-prayer a few benedictions in the Thefillath Sheba (seven benedictions) are condensed.

†"London Globe," 1842, February.

‡This hymn contains the thirteen creeds, of Maimonides, which were reduced to three: Belief in God, Revelation and Future Recompense, by Joseph Albo, (Ikkarim).

president of the committee of deputies of British Jews,
I would not in the least hesitate to attest that members
of a certain Synagogue are Jews, although their
Judaism is not identical with mine in all points. In
answer to this Montefiore re-affirmed his position once
taken in the matter.

To this Francis Goldsmith replied, that he still
misses the reasons for Montefiore's decision and hence
is logically compelled to surmise that he cannot give a
reason for it.* The only reason why the committee
deemed it worth while to ask for the certificate must be
sought in the fact that they intended to live in peace
and harmony wtih the entire Jewish community of
England. Knowing, as they did, that they were Jews,
it did not so much as enter their mind for a moment
that anybody who acts as president of the committee of
British Jews would dare to dispute such apparent facts.
Neither have the members of the new Synagogue asked
for your testimony because of difficulties which they
might encounter in the performance of their marriages,
and without such attest. For such difficulties do not
exist at all. We do not go with our grievances before
parliament or before the courts, in order to spare the
public the spectacle, how Jews fight against Jews in the
courts. Our committee is still more afraid to furnish
to the opponents of the Jewish emancipation the weapon
that a prominent individual among the Jews, who had
rendered on one occasion† to the Jews an important
service, should surpass the most fanatic of these opponents in intolerant zeal, by denying to those who differ
a trifle in their religious opinions from his views, the
benefits which the legislation had guaranteed to them,
I mean the liberty to have their marriages performed
and registered according to their wishes. Therefore
the committee will not further insist on their rights.
But it has authorized me to inform you, that it protests

---

*Since times immemorial orthodox jews when asked for
reasons of a ceremony, have given the answer: "Man darf nicht
fragen." (It is forbidden to ask questions).

†He alludes, no doubt, to the Damascus-affair.

against Montefiore's refusal as an illegal act, preserving
for itself the right, either to deny the legality of such
action, or to ask parliament to take away from Montefiore the authority which he had so greatly abused. *

Montefiore forwarded the whole correspondence to
the Chief-Rabbi Hirschel and to the Beth-din for action.
(February 7, 1842). On the same date the answer
was sent to Montefiore urgently requesting him not to
grant the certificate to David Wolf Marx as Secretary
of the West London Synagogue, because the Rabbi and
Beth-din "do not consider it a Synagogue." This was
signed by S. Hirschel, Chief-Rabbi, David Meldola,
A. Haliva, Israel Levy, Aaron Levy and H. L. Bar-
nett. This action of Montefiore was in opposition to
the accepted Jewish law, which most emphatically objects to the appointment of a man as judge in his own
cause. Montefiore could hardly doubt that the men
who stated in their interdict "that no power on earth
had a right to change one jot of the ritual and that the
members of the new Synagogue are no longer Jews,"
would endorse his opinions. On February 14, 1842,
the committee of British Jews passed a resolution ratifying Montefiore's action, although he had not asked
them before; as was his duty. In consequence of this
the West London Synagogue openly rejected the "validity of the oral law," and declared it a one-sided interpretation. This question naturally produced quite
a lively controversy.

The prayer-book of the West End Synagogue was
published in two volumes and with the exception of
the omission of the prayer "Velamalshinim," differs
but little from the old prayer-book.   *   *   *
The abolition of the second holiday and of the calling
people to the Sepher, and the introduction of the Portuguese pronunciation cannot well be numbered among
the "prayer-book reforms." And yet, though these
reforms were so insignificant, the fanaticism and the
intolerance employed against those who attended the

*Zeitung des Judenthum's, Vol. VII, pages 180-183.

new West End Synagogue was something fearful. Poor people who attended the new Synagogue were deprived of the benefits of charity, and the sister-in-law of Montefiore was refused burial in the Jewish cemetery because her child was circumcised in the West-End Synagogue. It was even hinted by the orthodox Jews that her death was a punishment of God because she had belonged to the new Synagogue.*

Let us, after this digression, return to Salomon. In his practical spirit he took the prayer-book controversy as a basis for a forcible circular letter addressed to the "Rabbis, preachers and teachers, in German Israel, concerning the revision of our prayer-book."†

On October 18th, 1843, the twenty-fifth anniversary of the dedication of the Temple and of Salomon's installation into office was celebrated. Dr. Frankfurter delivered on the evening of the 17th of October an oration which gave a history of the struggle and success of the Temple, paying a deserved and high tribute to the labors and talents of Dr. Kley, Dr. Salomon and to the directors of the Temple. The celebration was concluded by a cantata, consisting of fourteen numbers, lasting an hour and a half, no doubt the longest musical piece ever rendered in a Jewish service. Next day, the 18th, Salomon delivered the jubilee sermon, in which he touchingly reviewed his experiences in Hamburg. Coming home from the Temple he found the directors and a majority of the members of the Temple at his house, waiting to offer their hearty congratulations. The president of the congregation, Dr. Maimon Fraenkel, addressed him and presented him with resolutions signed by the directors and a delegation of one hundred and sixty members, and a costly and substantial token of their admiration in the shape of a solid silver piece, representing the interior of the Temple, pulpit and tabernacle. On the curtain the following words are written: "Dem Herrn Dr. Gotthold Salomon, zu seiner 25 jaehrigen Amtsfeier als Prediger am

*Zeitung des Judenthum's, April 30, 1842. No. 18, page 363.
†Zeitung das Judenth's, 1842, No. 14, 19, 22.

neuen Israelitischen Tempel zu Hamburg, am 18 October, 1843, von seinen Verehrern." (To Dr. Gotthold
Salomon on the occasion of his twenty-fifth anniversary
as preacher of the Israelitish Temple at Hamburg,
October 18, 1843, from his admirers.) On the pulpit
the words were written: "The Lord Eternal hath
given me a tongue for teaching, that I should know
how to strengthen the weary with the word." (Isaiah,
l. 4.) There were other artistic inscriptions on a silver pillow: Salomon's German Bible and the verse
Nehemiah vii, 8; the prayer and hymn book, with the
Hebrew inscription of Psalm xlii, 9; a vivid representation of 1 Kings, viii, 4-6, is given with the inscription: "And Salomon turned his face and blessed the
whole assembly of Israel."

Aside from this Salomon was made the recipient
of a beautiful album containing the most excellent
maxims in poetry and prose, written in various languages, by his friends and admirers all over the world,
each bearing their signature. The following are only
a few of the names represented in the album: Draeseke, then the most popular Christian preacher, (Bre-
men); Boeckel, Rupp, Jacoby, Ammon, Niemeyer,
Rosenkrantz, Minister Von Struve—all prominent theologians or philosophers. Of the Jews I mention:
Cremieux and Salvador, in France. At the banquet
in the evening, Dr. Gabriel Riesser made an eloquent
toast. The "Zeitung des Judenthum's," of October
18th, 1843, says among other things: "It is Salomon
who has elevated the German Israelitish homiletics
from the stage of infancy to the high dignity, the
praiseworthy development and energy which it possesses to-day. He freed the Jewish sermon from the
imitation of Christian preachers and was the first to
make it an original product, belonging to Judaism. * *
He was the first to conquer the respect of Christians for
the German-Israelitish pulpit oratory. From Odessa
to Philadelphia the German sermon is an integral part
of the Jewish worship. Where is the Jewish preacher
who has not learned from Salomon?"

On September 5, 1844, Salomon had the privilege to dedicate the new Temple which his Congregation had built. He preached on the highly appropriate text: "Greater Will be the Glory of the Second Temple than the First." (Haggai, II, 9).

He called it a "Beth Tefilla," (House of prayer), a "Beth-Hamidrash," (House of Learning), and a "Beth-Hamikdash," (House of Sanctification). He published also for this auspicious occasion, with notes and documents, which contain a veritable mine of historical facts, a short history of the new Israelitish Temple at Hamburg during the first twenty-five years of its existence, (Hamburg, 1844).

Salomon traveled a great deal. In 1822 he visited Copenhagen, where he gained the friendship of Manheimer, with whom he was intimate, until death parted them. He preached in Copenhagen on Friday evening, 1822,* in the house of Nathanson, and so aroused the people that on the next day he was offered the position of preacher in the main Synagogue. In 1828 he received a call as Rabbi and preacher of the then much larger Congregation of Copenhagen; but owing to the urgent entreaties of the Temple people he remained in Hamburg and recommended to Copenhagen Dr. A. Wolff, of Giessen.

In 1829 Salomon visited his parents, whose old age he sweetened by his filial love. He also visited Dessau, after an absence of eleven years. He was deeply disappointed at the decline of the Congregation after Wolff's death and gave vent to his feelings on the subject in a sermon before the Congregation.

In 1834 he went to the sea resort of Heligoland for his health—and in his joy over his perfect cure he published: "Memoirs of the sea-bath at Heligoland," (Hamburg, 1834). In 1837 he visited Switzerland and in 1844-46 the Rabbinical conventions of Braunschweig, Frankfurt and Breslau. He preached in

---

*If I am not mistaken this was the first time that a Jewish sermon was held on Friday evening.

Frankfurt in the school-building (called "Real-schule," also "Philanthropin.") In 1846 he preached several times in the Temple of the "Reform-Genos-senschaft," of Berlin. A fine reception was tendered him in Breslau. He said he had never found a Congregation whose members were better educated, more refined and whole-souled than that presided over by Geiger at Breslau. Culture has not deprived the Jews of Breslau of their heart and naturalness as is the case in Berlin.*

In 1851 he visited the Industrial Exposition in London. Among other places he attended there the West-London Synagogue and he speaks in the most glowing terms of its preachers, Marx and Loewy. There he preached in German on August 12, 1851. That sermon was published in an English translation entitled: "The Three Elements of Israel's Welfare," and dedicated to H. I. Montefiore, E. Moccata, and Jacob A. Henriquez.

In 1853 Salomon visited Dresden, Prague and Vienna. He was surprised at the progress made in the German Synagogue at Prague, where he heard a hymn as sung in his Temple. In Vienna he was cordially received by his friend Mannheimer and was invited to preach on September 17, 1853. He preached on the significance of the month of "Elul" and was honored by a flattering letter and present in the shape of a golden tabatiere from the Vienna Congregation. The letter is signed by Joseph Wertheimer, who has a name in Jewish history, Heinrich Sichrowsky, Joseph Bieder-man and Moritz Goldschmidt. The date of Salomon's sermon in the Vienna Temple was engraved on the tabatiere. He greatly enjoyed the company of Werthei-mer, Szanto,† and the historian Wolff.

The idea of Rabbinical conventions originated with Dr. Abraham Geiger, who was to my knowledge the first Rabbi in this century who convoked a confer-

---

*See Salomon's letter to Mrs. Dr. Beer, of Dresden.
†Szanto was the founder and editor of the Vienna "Neuzaeit," one of the best and most advanced Jewish weeklies of Europe.

ence of Rabbis at Wiesbaden, as far back as 1837, "Zur Erhaltung und Fortbilung des Judenthum's und zur Belebung des Religioesen Sinnes."* But in 1844 Dr. Ludwig Philippsohn took up the idea of Geiger, without, however, giving credit to him, and brought it prominently before the public is his "Zeit. des Judenth's," as something brand new. He did the same with Geiger's idea, on a Jewish theological faculty, advocated by him as far back as 1835 in his "Zeitserift fuer Juedische Theologie," while years later Philippsohn palmed it off as an entirely novel scheme of his own. I do not in the least intend to detract from Philippsohn's merits, but in the interest of historical truth I deem it necessary to do justice to my teacher, Geiger, because in the able biography of Gotthold Salomon, published by Dr. Phoebus Philippsohn —which has rendered me a great service in writing this book—the credit for the idea of "Rabbinervesammulungen," is given only to Ludwig Philippsohn. Philippsohn sent out an appeal to the Rabbis, urging them to hold during the summer of 1844 a convention in a centrally located city of Germany. The first encouragement came from Dr. Herxheimer, Land-Rabbi of Bernburg, Anhalt; Herzfeld, Land-Rabbi of Braunschweig; Geiger, Rabbi of Breslau; Holdheim, Land-Rabbi of Mecklenburg-Schwerin; Kahn, Chief-Rabbi of Trier, who promised to be present. The Congregation of Braunschweig, induced by its Rabbi and in full accord with the government, declared its willingness to receive hospitably the representative Rabbis of the nineteenth century, and thus the first Rabbinical convention was held in Braunschweig, from the 12th to the 19th of June, 1844. Besides the Rabbis already mentioned, the following were members of this first convention: Dr. Mayer, Stuttgart; Dr. Salomon, Hamburg; Goldman, District-Rabbi, Eschwege; Samuel Hirsh, Luxemburg, later Philadelphia; Schott, Randegg; Sobernheim, Bingen; Wechsler, Oldenburg; Jolowicz, Koen-

---

*"For the preservation and development of Judaism, and for the sake of the revival of the religious sentiment."

igsberg; Bodenheimer, Land-Rabbi, Hildesheim; Ben-
Israel, Coblentz; Samuel Adler, Alzey, late Rabbi of
Temple Emanuel, New York; A. Adler, Worms;
Hoffmann, Waldorf; Heidenheim, Sandershausen; Ed-
ler, Aachen.

These Rabbinical assemblies had the purpose to
strengthen and encourage morally the Jewish Reform-
movement. Salomon and his colleague, Frankfurter,
were among the very few members of the convention
who from the nature of their positions in a Congregation, every member of which was a Reformer, could
afford to be more independent and outspoken than the
rest of the Rabbis, who were compelled to be more or
less guarded in their votes and utterances on account of
the many conservative members of their Congregations.
Salomon belonged to the extreme wing of Reformers
in the convention.

Rabbi Goldman made an earnest plea in the convention for the retention of the Hebrew language in
prayer. In this plea he pointed, by way of argument, to
the devotion which reigns supreme in the Polish Synagogues, while in the Temples of Hamburg and Leipzig decorum only is to be found. Salomon replied to this
argument as follows: "There are, I do not deny, pious
people among those who regularly attend the Polish
Synagogue, but is their fear of God the result of the
disorder in the Synagogue, of the unbecoming behavior, lack of decorum, the screaming, the noise and
the dead Hebrew letters, which are recited there? I
further ask, are there no scoundrels, no rascals, among
those who attend only the old Synagogue?   *   *
Alas, I know many of those, who, after having welcomed the Sabbath in the manner described by Rabbi
Goldman with the greeting: 'Come in Peace,' mal-
treat their wives and children a few minutes later and
incite quarrel and discord; I know a good many who
literally recite their 'Tikkun Shabath'* in the Hebrew-
Chaldaic-Syrian language. * * and even the twenty-

---

*A collection of devotional songs for the Sabbath.

four Mishnas of the tract Shabbath and who nevertheless immediately after the first 'Jeziath hashaboth shta-
jim shenen arbah'—readers, who are Talmudists, will
appreciate the sarcasm—sell two yards for four yards,
i. e., neglect the Biblical command 'not to do wrong
by false measure,' (Lev. and Deut.) And Mr. Goldman
wishes to recommend to us that kind of worship.''

He then enumerated the beneficial effects of the
Hamburg Temple, which Goldman had assailed, and
declared that the female part of the Congregation is not
benefitted by a Hebrew worship, and that even the
boys of the present generation have not the time to en-
gage in the study of the Hebrew language, without
neglecting their other studies.*

In the same year Salomon published a polemical
pamphlet,† a defense of the Braunschweig convention
against its numerous enemies. He uttered a manly
protest against Philippsohn, who attempted to play the
Pope, and against that spirit of his, which is so well
expressed in this country by the phrase "rule or ruin
policy." It is a deplorable fact, that Philippsohn's
undisputable merits in the cause of Judaism were not
a little overshadowed by his excessive egotism, which,
based on the autocratic principle, " I and none besides
me," opposed every measure which did not originate
with him, or did not turn out just as he anticipated.
This opinion about Philippsohn was led by Abraham
Geiger, by Dr. Leopold Stein, of Frankfurt, and by a
great many other leading Rabbis of Germany. My personal intercourse with him in Bonn, during the three
years of my ministry there, from 1878 to 1881, had
convinced me that those opinions were not the result
of personal bias and prejudice.

Salomon closes his pamphlet with the hope that
in the future "the staff of command and despotism
would be taken out of Philippsohn's hand."

---

*Protokolle der ersten Rabbinerversammlung. Braunschweig.
1844, pages 56-57.
†Die Rabbinerversammlung und ihre Tendenz. Eine Beleuch-
tung fuer ihre Freunde und Feinde. Hamburg, 1845.

Salomon delivered also a sermon in the Temple of Braunschweig during the Rabbinical convention, the following extracts of which may find a place here:

"Experience teaches us that persons who have never permitted this or that food for religion's sake to pass their lips, have not been able to guard them from uttering wickedness, lies, slander, curses and false oaths; experience teaches that men who are able to afflict their bodies with fasting did not possess the strength to fast in accord with the conception of the prophet, that is to loosen the fetters which wickedness has forged for the poor and unfortunate; that is, to give bread to the hungry, a roof to the homeless and to take care of those who are of our flesh, who are human beings and fellow men. * * God is most perfect, free of human frailties. * A weak, imperfect God does not lay stress on a perfect and pure conduct. If God is acknowledged as holy, then he requires holiness of us. If God is holy, then he does not permit himself to be bribed. * * It is not so easy to satisfy a holy God. We cannot win such a God by means of beautiful words or glittering actions, we must sanctify and glorify Him through every feeling of our breast, through every thought in our soul, through every work in our life. * * This is our divine service. * * Such divine service is more difficult than the one which is limited to the House of God or to ceremonies, be they ever so imposing. Thousands of rams, myriads of rivers of oil, repeated devotions and daily fasts are a far easier sacrifice than the sacrifice of one bad passion, and of one destructive, favorite desire upon the altar of the purified heart. Not one, and not ten high priests can consecrate you through their merits; not one and not ten saints can sanctify you through their virtue. Only your own piety, your own character can open the heaven unto you and plead your cause before the throne of God."

Salomon was also present at the Rabbinical convention of Frankfort-on-the-Main, (July 15 to 28, 1845). This convention was made more outspoken in its reformatory tendency than the first. Salomon had belonged to the important commission on liturgy, whose report* engaged the attention of the greatest number of meetings. He took part in the discussion concerning the Hebrew language in the prayers and said among other things: "Not a single one of our religious works or codes of law makes it obligatory for us to pray in Hebrew. Holy Scripture does not command us to pray at all, it leaves this holy occupation to the heart. Mishna and Talmud say plainly enough: 'Shema and Tefilla may be recited in every language. Even the Shulchan Aruch † permits the public service in every language. 'The Book of the Pious,'‡ recommends the recital of the main prayers in the vernacular, which people understand, and says that it is far better not to pray at all than to pray in a language which people do not understand.

"Even the Cabbalists hold the same opinion,§ hence there is actually no religious obligation to pray in Hebrew."

Concerning the question of the "Messiah," he most emphatically declared, that we do not believe in a personal but a spiritual Messiah, and showed by quotations from the prophets and later Rabbis† that the belief in a Messiah has always been considered figurative, signifying the far remote age of universal truth, light, peace and brotherly love.

Salomon attended also the third Rabbinical convention at Breslau.● The subjects under discussion were the laws concerning Sabbath-and Holidays. Salomon said that the words, "God hath made man plain, but they seek so many artifices," (Koehlet 7-29),

---

*Salomon was the only one of the committee who made a report.

†Orach Chajim 1014: "Yakhol lehisspallel bekhol lashon."

‡Sefer Chassidim, pages 588 and 785.

§The author of the Shelah, which is an abbreviation of "Shnai Luchoth habrith" (two tablets of the covenant). The book forms an Encyclopædia of Jewish-religious knowledge, and encourages asceticism.

‖Sanhedrin, 96 a, Jebamoth, 62 a, Maimonides.

● It took place from July 13th to July 24th, 1846.

have never been better verified than in the Mosaic laws of the Sabbath.   Later Rabbis have added mountains to the plain words of Exodus XX, 8 ff.

Salomon had an interesting family of five children. One of them, Dr. M. G. Salomon, was a phycician in Hamburg.   Salomon was charitable in the extreme, not only to his own kin but to strangers.   In his sermons he always advocated the cause of charity and was instrumental in the establishment of many benevolent societies and institutions in Hamburg, which are still existing and in a flourishing condition.   Especially the class who were ashamed to beg had always a good friend in Salomon.

His correspondence was very extensive, especially with Dr. Mayer, of Stuttgart; Manheimer, of Vienna, and P. Beer, of Dresden. *

For a time he was quite an enthusiastic Mason, the fruit of which was his "Stimmen Aus den Osten." † But he could not help finding out that mere talk about humanity is not humanity in fact.   He saw with sorrow the exclusion of the Jews from Prussian lodges, and gradually kept away from his Masonic brethren. His "Decalogue of the Mason," in poetry, is quite interesting.   In the year of the Revolution, 1848, in Hamburg also a "constituting assembly" was formed on the basis of democracy, and Salomon was elected one of the representatives.   But politics was not his sphere.

In 1854 Salomon celebrated his seventieth birthday, surrounded by his children, grand-children and friends.   Congratulations poured in from all sides. Dr. Leopold Stein, Rabbi of Frankfort-on-the-Main, honored him with an excellent poem for the occasion, and appreciative of his merits.

The last collection of his sermons was entitled: "Sermons for all the Holidays of the Lord," (Hamburg, 1855).   It cannot be denied that the warmth

---

*See Neuzeit, Vienna, 1862, No. 61-52, 1863, No. 1-4, published by Dr. Wolff, where some letters of Salomon to Beer are published.
†"Voices from the East," a collection of Masonic discussions, Hamburg, 1845.

and enthusiasm which characterized his first sermons
are absent. These last sermons address themselves more to the mind than to the heart.

Already at that time a disease of the nerves made
itself noticeable to Salomon. His memory grew
weaker. On March 13, 1856, his beloved wife, his
companion for forty-seven years, died. It caused him
a great inward struggle to resign his post on
account of the rapid progress of his disease. April 16,
1857, he delivered his last sermon, on the subject:
"Universal Good Will and Love of Family,". He
selected his text from Isaiah XII, 3, "And ye shall
draw water with gladness out of the springs of salvation," and said among other things: "I part after having preached the word of God for nearly four decades.
* * From our Zion, from our Temple, light has
spread over Israel. * * On the evening of my life it
is granted to me to behold Israel occupying a worthier
and nobler position within and without. Man has
grown, and thou, beloved Congregation, hast also contributed towards this progress. Thou hast practiced
and furthered the work of genuine humanity and of
true Israelitish religiousness."

In beautiful words he took leave of the administration of the Temple, which has always been ready "to
realize the sublime idea of genuine religion, and to separate the noble metal from the dross and the essence
from the rigid form." With enthusiasm he encouraged and blessed his colleague and successor in office,
Dr. Frankfurter, and the whole Congregation.

After his resignation the administration of the
Temple sent him a long and highly complimentary
letter, dated April 12, 1857.*

Salomon lived until his seventy-ninth year, but,
alas, his mental faculties were gone. After a sickness
of twelve days he died, November 17, 1862. His successor, Dr. Jonas, delivered the funeral sermon at the

---

*This document was signed by Dr. H. Frankfurter, at the time
President of the Commission on "Cultus," by Dr. M. Wolfsohn, B.
A. Simon, M. Isler and Dr. Leopold Reiss.

cemetery and immediately after the burial a memorial
service was held in the Temple, where Dr. Frankfurter officiated.   His oration* was worthy of Salomon
and of his eulogist, full of deep sentiment and dignified
appreciation of the activity of his deceased colleague as
man and preacher.   German and Hebrew mourning
chorals concluded the impressive memorial service.   In
several Jewish Congregations of Germany and other
countries memorial sermons and eulogies were delivered from the pulpits on the Sabbath after his death.
The press of Hamburg † and of other cities, ‡ paid the
highest meed of praise to the memory of the famous
preacher.

With Salomon died one of the last "Biurists," i. e.
one of those who, following Mendelssohn's example,
have translated parts of scripture into pure German on
the basis of the Jewish tradition and older exegetists,
and have added to it a Hebrew commentary.   He was
also the first who furnished to the people a perfect
translation of the Bible into German, printed in German letters.   His powers of labor were immense, and
perhaps the cause of his later brain disease.

The following estimate is given of Salomon by a
man, who, as a critic, is recognized by every Jewish
scholar of this century, I mean by—Abraham Geiger.
In his "Zeitschrift fuer Wissenschaft und Leben," in a
necrology on "Salomon," he said: "Salomon was the
first and most eminent Jewish preacher.   Mighty and
pleasant words burst from his heart and found entrance
into the hearts of others.   He felt more than he could
scientifically construe, what treasures the knowledge of
Judaism of all ages contained, and he knew how to

*It was published by Nestler and Melle, Hamburg, 1862, under
the title: "Rede bei der von der Direction veranstalteten
Todtenfeier fuer den seligen Herrn Dr. Gotthold Salomon am 20
November, 1862, gesprochen von Dr. Frankfurter."
†Das Neue Hamburg, No. 104, "Hamburger Nachrichten,"
"Freischuetz," "Reform," from November 18th to 20th.
‡Nationalzeitung, Berlin, November 20th, 1855, Zeitung des
Judenthum's, 1862, December 9th, No. 50, Geiger's Z. F. W. U. L.,
1863, Vol. II, pages 128-129.

find and to make use of them. The Jewish sermon gained a perfect mastery through Salomon." * *
"The Jewish sermon," which was very unpopular among the Jews, when Salomon appeared on the scene, "has now become a power in the midst of the Jewish Congregation; It now takes the first rank among the means of religious edification. That it has become so is the merit of Salomon and his compeers." (Vol. ii. p. 128-29, Breslau, 1863, Schletter). I refer to the following publications, to the authors of which I am greatly indebted in my labor: Salomon, "Selbstbiographie," Leipzig, 1863; Phoebus Philippsohn, "Biographische Skizzen," 3 Heft, "Gotthold Salomon," Geiger's "Zeitschrift," F. W. U. L; "Gotthold Salomon and Gabriel Riesser," vol. ii. pp. 125-29; Kaiserling, "Bibliothek Jued. Kanzelredner," vol. 1, pp. 142-73; "Zeit-des Judenth's," 1842; "Unsere Zeit, Jahrbuch zum Conversations Lexicon," vol. vii, p. 396, Leipzig, Brockhaus; Jost, "Judenthum und seine Sekten," vol. iii. pp. 336, 365, 370; "Selbstkritik der Juden," pp. 3-10, Berlin, 1880, Carl Duncker, second edition, Leipzig, 1890, Wilhelm Friedrich.

CHAPTER VI.

ABRAHAM KOHN.

Abraham Kohn's biography deserves special mention from the fact that, like a true priest (Cohen), he died in the service of God, in the cause of Judaism, a sacrifice upon the altar of conviction and devotion to God and humanity. He suffered the tragic death of a martyr, inasmuch as he was poisoned by his fanatic enemies, because he was a—Reformer. Born in 1806 (27th of Sivan) at Zaluzan, a little town in Prachim county, Bohemia, of poor but highly respected parents he had already as a child the desire and ambition to become a Rabbi, and to lift up his co-religionists. In accord with the custom of those days he studied the Talmud with the assistance of a tutor. But soon he knew more than his teacher, and at the age of twelve the youth, endowed with great talents, indomitable ambition and desire to learn, left his home in order to continue his Rabbinical studies at the feet of great Rabbis and masters in Talmudic lore and Jewish literature. Secretly, however, he devoted time and attention also to so-called profane studies, so that for two years he seldom slept more than four hours nightly. In Pisek he went most successfully through the examinations of the gymnasium, after which he studied philosophy, at the University of Prague. Like many Jewish students before and after him, he had to live for a long time on dry bread. Our present students of theology, especially in this country, have no idea what the pioneers of Reform Judaism had to undergo, as students, in the hard struggle for existence; and as

Rabbis in the hotly contested battle for their principles. The strain on Kohn was at last of such a character that it threw him upon the sick-bed, where he was for a long time in danger of death from brain fever.

In 1830 he appeared for the first time in public as a preacher. The occasion was the dedication of the Synagogue in Pisek. The effect of his sermon, in which he depicted the beauty of peace and harmony in the most glowing colors, can be best imagined by the fact that it induced two of the first families of the place, who had been enemies for years, to become friends again. Those who know from experience how intense such hatred is, especially among Jews in small communities, will best appreciate this incident. In Prague he preached quite often, until in 1833 he accepted a call as Rabbi of Hohenems (Tirol).

Although his Congregation had only ninety members, he found a good field, because just at that time the question of Reform commenced to interest the better class of Jews in Germany and Austria. Abraham Geiger came out at this time with his Zeitschrift fuer Juedische Theologie (Magazine for Jewish Theology, Wiesbaden, 1835), which was devoted to an earnest, scientific discussion of Jewish customs and ceremonies. Kohn was a contributor to this magazine, and his essay on the "Mourning Customs of the Jews" is not without interest yet. In his articles in this magazine, as in the "Zeitung des Judenthums," "Synagoge," by Dr. L. Adler, "Annalen," by Jost; in Busch's "Kalender," and in the "Centralblatt," he urged the abolition of observances which had no basis in Bible and Talmud, and are therefore detrimental rather than beneficial to the true interests of Judaism. He himself was, however, most strict in the observance of the ceremonies. He organized charitable societies and a society for the furtherance of trade and handicraft among the Jews. He introduced choir and other reforms in the Synagogue of his Congregation, whose best members considered it an honor to sing in the choir. He was particularly active in the school, and took especial delight in the education of the young, the future banner-bearers of Israel. His relation to the Congregation was that of a father rather than of a salaried officer. His sermons were attended by Jews and Christians. In this patriarchal state he lived and worked, when misfortune knocked at his door in the shape of a call tendered to him in 1843 by the very large and influential Congregation of Lemberg, Galicia. Two large Congregations of Germany honored him with a call at the same time, but his ardent longing to bring progress, light and reform to a section so benighted as Galicia induced him to prefer Lemberg. He would not have left his Congregation had he not known that the way there was sufficiently paved by him for reform and progressive development in order to make smooth sailing for his successor, whoever he might be. He felt within himself the power, energy and strong will to labor in a large sphere. In July, 1843, he went to Lemberg and impressed all the friends of progress and reform so favorably that his entrance upon his position was agreed upon for the next spring, as he did not want to leave his Congregation before he had secured a worthy successor. He left Hohenems in April, 1844, and arrived in Lemberg May 4th. The regret at his departure from Hohenems was general and sincere.

His position in the capital of Galicia was quite different from that in Hohenems. Here he had, it is true, the better and more intelligent classes on his side, but alas, they were not in the majority. In Hohenems he was Rabbi, and as such entitled to speak freely on all religious questions, and to attack authoritatively all abuses and superstitious customs which had crept into Judaism. His position in Lemberg was only that of "preacher and teacher of religion," while the Rabbinate there was orthodox in the extreme. In addition to this the great masses could not understand and sufficiently appreciate his philosophical sermons, and were not yet ripe for a Reform-movement. They had to be prepared for it by schools. Supported by the well meaning administration of his Congregation, Kohn was enabled to open in the year 1845 an excellent normal school, with a staff of efficient teachers. He himself took charge of the religious instruction in the higher classes, and acted as superintendent of the school. The success of this institution was so phenomenal, especially from the fact that girls received instruction in religion and Hebrew, things unheard of before, that the school rooms could not accommodate the numerous new applicants, many of whom had to be turned away.

Kohn's other duties consisted in the immatriculation of every birth, marriage, death and divorce within the Jewish community; in the supervision of all benevolent institutions and in delivering sermons at least twice a month. Though it can be seen that he had much more work than in Hohenems, he sought every opportunity to increase the sphere of his usefulness by addressing the people on all proper occasions, dispelling erroneous views, abolishing abuses of long standing, and enlightening them on the most important subjects. He did missionary work in the highest and noblest sense which this term implies. Two dozen of such Kohns to-day in Russia and the Russian-Jewish quarters of New York, Philadelphia and other cities would make Russian Jewish Ghettoes in America a thing of the past. His words, coming as they did from the heart, could not fail to enter into the hearts of his hearers, and created an enthusiasm for him which can be better imagined than described.

Meanwhile a new Temple was finished in 1846, and there Kohn preached. It was the rendezvous of the progressive element, at whose expense it had been built. At that time Kohn was appointed District Rabbi, which was a position of far reaching influence. He strove with his utmost zeal toward the elevation of his Congregation. The many tokens of esteem and appreciation shown him by high officials, and the wonderful growth of the so-called Reform party are the best proofs of his increasing popularity. But all this did not satisfy his holy zeal to become the benefactor of his people. Unlike others who, after having once attained

the goal of their ambition, bask in the sunshine of their
glory and self-sufficiently rest upon their hard earned
laurels, he was, like Mordecai, an "Ish," a true man, and
hence a true Jehuda. Not satisfied with being "great
among the Jews and acceptable among the multitude
of his brethren" (Esther, X, 3), "he was a promotor
of good to his people" (Ibid). He was not like some of
our co-religionists who, as soon as they become prominent in a certain sphere, "see the resting place that is
good" (Gen. XLIX, 15), indulge in their ease and with
a certain indifference look down from their lofty
heights upon the struggles of the poor unfortunate
dwellers in the valley. Abraham Kohn followed the
example of Moses, who, "just at the time when he was
greatest in Egypt"—I translate "vajigdal" in this sense
—went out to see after the welfare of his brethren and
looked on their burdensome labors," (Exodus II, 11.)
Kohn was greatly grieved to see that the Jews of Galicia were subjected to the most shameful, humiliating
and oppressing taxes for no other reason than that they
were Jews. The most outrageous and disgraceful was
the tax on meat and the candles used for the Sabbath
lights. The worst feature of these taxes was the disgusting fact that they were the hardest on the poor
people, inasmuch as they doubled the market price and
made living so expensive for them that many of the
poor Jews in Galicia did not eat meat during the whole
year. Following was the tax: For a pound of meat,
1½ kreutzer; a pigeon, or chicken as large as a pigeon, 2½ kreutzer; a rooster, hen or duck, 7 kreutzer;
a goose, 17 kreutzer; a turkey, 27 kreutzer. The taxes on candles were: A tallow candle for the Sabbath,
5 kreutzer; a wax candle, 15 kreutzer; a Jahrzeit candle on the anniversary of a death, 3 to 6 kreutzer; a
Channkah candle, 1 to 2 kreutzer; a candle for the day
of Atonement, 12 kreutzer; a candle for a wedding, 2½
florins; so that as two candles were necessary, it meant
a tax of five florins. Each family had to use two candles on the Sabbath, or at least to pay taxes for them,
no matter whether they were used or not. Another

evil in connection with this tax was that those who were taxed the highest were eligible in the directory of the Congregation. In consequence of this the number of candles determined in the Congregations their presidents, and in further consequence those who made it a business to lease the taxes, managed to elect their creatures and pliant tools into the administration of the Congregations. Even strangers and visitors had to pay this tax. At the least suspicion of false statements concerning the candles used in the house, the lessees had a right to demand on oath of the renter, attired in the garments for Jom Kippur (Reinigungseid), in the Synagogue, in the presence of the District Rabbi and District Commissary. *

Alas, too true, Jews could be found who paid a high price to the government for the yearly lease of those contemptible taxes, and in order to make as much money as possible out of them, they were merciless in their collection. They employed a most despicable system of espionage; set paid spies into the kitchens of poor Jews, or into the dining-rooms on Friday evenings in order to find out the exact amount of meat or of candles used for the Sabbath, and stooped so low as to bribe the Christian servant girls of well-to-do Jews, in order to prevent their employers from so-called "cheating" the government. Now Kohn resolved to abolish this disgraceful, and, what was still worse, demoralizing tax, and he succeeded. How dearly he paid for it, future events will show.

In conjunction with the leaders of his Congregation and other influential Jewish communities of Galicia and Austria, he went to work for the accomplishment of this aim. Twice in the fall of 1847 and in the spring of 1848 a deputation composed of the most prominent Jews in Galicia, headed by Kohn, was delegated to Vienna, in order to effect the abolition of these taxes, which were a dark stain on the civiliza-

---

*Jost: Neuere Geschichte der Israeliten, Vol. III, page 338, note.

tion of Austria. The delegates had a difficult task, because, sad and deplorable as the fact may be, it is nevertheless true, that from a Jewish, and of course interested, side, every lever was set in motion, and no stone was left unturned in order to throw every imaginable stumbling-block in the way of the deputation. Yes, hear it readers, in amazement! Jews, nay, so-called strictly orthodox Jews, brought every influence to bear upon a government in order to induce it not to do justice to the Jews; not to set aside one of the most disgraceful and tyrannical laws which the meanest kind of Antisemitism and mediaeval fanaticism could desire against the hated Jews. It was not the first time in our history that the words of the prophet Isaiah, "Thy destroyers, oh, Israel, come from thy own midst," were verified. But after a year of incessant and effective work Kohn and his supporters were victorious. The taxes on kosher meat and Sabbath candles were abolished. I mentioned the dear "penalty" which Kohn had to pay for this victory in the cause of the Jews. The enemies of progress commenced to be afraid of his growing popularity and influence. They had forwarded a counter-petition to Vienna stating that the abolition of these taxes was not at all necessary. Having failed in their purpose to influence the government, they resolved to make Kohn's stay in Lemberg unpleasant and burdensome in the extreme. The history of the Jewish Reform-movement is full of proofs that the enemies of a progressive development in Judaism have a most remarkable talent for the art of embittering the lives of Reform Rabbis. They insulted Kohn personally, but as this proved of no avail they heaped upon him the meanest and most ridiculous charges before the courts. Among other things he had to answer to one of those peculiar "saints" why he carried on the Sabbath day his handkerchief in his pocket instead of binding it around his body as the orthodox Jews do. All sorts of false accusations were also manufactured against him, which amounted to nothing. Naturally the better and educated classes vied with each other to make him forget these chicaneries and adversities, and the more the opposition showed itself in its true colors the more it lost its followers, and dwindled down to a small, insignificant clique. It was utterly discomfited by the additional blow that it met with a contumelious rebuff from the courts on account of its foolish and malicious charges against Kohn. One of the persecutors was even arrested on account of malicious slander and inciting the populace against Kohn. No sooner had the latter heard of this fact than he, like a true "priest who loveth peace and promoteth it," employed every means at his disposal to free his enemy from prison, and he succeeded in doing so by his personal interference and entreaties. But this act, instead of pacifying the scoundrels, embittered them the more, and seeing that all their wicked designs and miserable machinations against the noble man had failed, they did not stop at *murder most foul and cowardly.*

This is, to my knowledge, the only instance in Jewish history where fanaticism and religious bigotry were carried to such an extreme, for the attempt of murder against Baruch Spinoza was, at least, not successful. Toward the end of the summer of 1840 Kohn was about to publish a weekly under the title of "Der Israelitische Volksfreund" (The Israelitish Friend of the People). On the 6th of September, while busily engaged in this work, a villainous scoundrel poisoned his dinner. The Sabbath previous he had preached on the commandment: "Thou Shalt Not Murder." While the members of his family recovered, he twenty-four hours later (September 7th), after painful sufferings, succumbed to the effect of the poison, and died in the bloom of vigorous manhood, full of resignation to the will of God, a martyr to the principles of Reform-Judaism, a sacrifice upon the altar of his unshakable conviction in the ultimate victory of truth and justice.

Eight years later a volume of his sermons on the "Ten Commandments," together with a short sketch

of his life written by his son, Jacob Kohn, to which I
am largely indebted for this biography, was published
in the first volume of the "Jeshurun," a magazine ably
edited by a pupil of Dr. Kohn, Dr. Joseph Kobak, formerly Rabbi of Bamberg, Bavaria. These sermons
were all delivered in Hohenems, with the exception of
the one mentioned above, on the sixth commandment
(September 2, 1848), which was delivered to his Lemberg Congregation. I deem it right and proper to
place before the readers of this book a few extracts from
this, in some respects remarkable, last sermon of
Kohn. I say remarkable, because he could hardly
have preached otherwise had he known that one of his
fanatic enemies would murder him four days after the
delivery of his sermon.

"To murder a creature like ourselves, to kill a
human being, to shed the blood of an innocent man,
must still be prohibited to the shame of humanity!
There are wild beasts which tear other creatures,
which drink the blood of animals, but only against
strange species are they so cruel. * * Man only,
who is so proud of his privileges, calling himself the
crown of creation, the master-work of God, rages
against his own genus. * * You feel horrified at
this picture, yet it is not overdrawn in the least. Even
according to Biblical literature the first quarrel was ad-
justed by the murder of a brother. * * Pity, reason,
conscience, ought to preserve human nature from the
most horrible crime of destruction of human life. But
no! The Lawgiver and Judge of the Universe must
exclaim: 'Thou shalt not murder.' In order to in-
stil each and every one with disgust of murder and
bloodshed. The Mosaic law inflicted punishment even
upon the unintentional murderer. He had to flee to a
City of Refuge. Nay, more. In a city where murder had been committed and the murderer could not be
discovered, the elders had to wash their hands and to
proclaim aloud: 'Our hands have not shed this blood,
and our eyes have not seen it. Grant pardon unto thy
people Israel, whom thou hast redeemed, and lay not,

oh, God, innocent blood in the midst of thy people
Israel.' Happy are we that we obey such law. It is on
account of this obedience that murder and bloodshed
are of such rare occurrence, are unheard of among us.
Yes, we can say it with pride, there is no nation, no
religious society, which entertains such high regard for
human life as does ours. Among us even the deadliest
foe is safe; his life is sacred to us. But fanaticism is
capable of doing anything. What is there which hatred, wickedness, malice, are not liable to do? * *
But is he only the murderer who suddenly ends the life of
a fellow-man with a deadly weapon? 'He who deprives
his fellow-man of the means of existence kills him,'
said Ben Sirach. Sorrow, grief, affliction, neglect,
mortification, disregard, wound no less than daggers
and arrows. For anger, vexation and griefs are slow,
lingering poisons which gnaw on the marrow of life;
poisons which they only can administer who are very
near to us. How often do children thus shorten the
lives of their parents! Israel has been guilty of a similar crime since times immemorial against her best
friends, against her faithful teachers and guides, whose
lives are shortened by the eternal struggle with meanness and wickedness. In this sense Jerusalem was indeed a 'city which murdered her prophets.' Who had
surpassed Moses in sacrificing love for his people? But
how did they reward him, how often did they rebel
against him, and were about to stone him? The same
fate befell the prophets of God, because they did not
talk sweetly, because they saw things in their true
light, called things by their right names; because they
did not mind the exclamation of those who 'said to the
seers: Ye shall not see; and to the prophets: Reveal
not unto us true things; speak unto us smooth things;
reveal deceits.' (Isaiah XXX, 10). The last of these
men of God, Jeremiah, could hardly escape death, as if
he had caused the destruction of the Jewish commonwealth. That it was not better in later times is proven
by the remarkable opinion of the Talmud concerning
the 'popularity' of theologians and preachers. 'If

you find' thus the Talmud puts it, 'a Rabbi who is liked well among all the people of his town, then do not imagine that he is worthier and better than others; but be sure that he is derelict in his duty to reprimand them whenever the occasion demands it.' "

Aside from this volume of sermons, Kohn published "Six Sermons, Delivered in Hohenems, Prague, 1834," on the following subjects: 1. The Divine Blessing; text, Deuteronomy, VII, 13-15. 2. Prayer; text, Psalm LXXXIV. 3. The Power of Faith; text, Sachar, IV, 4. 4. Meaning and Significance of the Sabbath; text, Isaiah, LVIII, 13-14. 5. Charity; text, Leviticus, XXV, 35-39. 6. Israel, a People Chosen by God; text, Exodus, XIX, 3-6." He further published a sermon on ' True Heroes,'"* and on "How Can We Purify Ourselves Before God."† His inaugural sermon delivered in Lemberg, 1845, was based on the text: Maleachi, II, 6.

In Geiger's Zeitschrift he contributed scholarly essays on the "Jewish Mourning Customs," on the "Necessity of Popular and Juvenile Jewish Literature;" on "Music on Holidays;"‡ on "The Removal of Leather Shoes on the Day of Atonement."§ He was also among the progressive Rabbis who gave favorable opinions on the question propounded by the Congregation of Breslau, which was presided over by Dr. Geiger, concerning the compatibility of Judaism with free research.‖

In a sermon on the Second Commandment Kohn said: "Another still more dangerous idolatry is the worship of luck. The heathen had a Goddess of Fortune,

*The sermon was delivered in 1837, on Chanukkah, and was published in Dr. L. Adler's "Synagoge," Vol. I, pages 193-207.

†It was delivered on 1838 on the eve of the Day of Atonement, and published in "Synagoge" Vol. II, pages 326-336.

‡See Geiger's "Zeitschrift fuer Jued. Theol., Vol. III, page 214, IV, pages 29, 76, 165.

‖See "Rabbinische Gutachten ueber die Vertraeglichkeit der freien Forschung mit dem Rabbineramte, Breslau, 1842, (September). It contains opinions of Kohn, Herxheimer, Friedlaender, Chorin, Einhorn, Hess, Guttman, Wassermann. Kohn's opinion on the Hamburg prayer-book, see page 138 of this book.

whom they called 'Fortuna,' and whom they represented standing on a wheel with her eyes blindfolded,
thus conveying the idea that fortune is blind and
fickle, offering its favors often to the unworthy, and
again overturning those whom it had raised. Temples
and altars were erected to this Goddess. It is no longer the fashion to erect temples and altars. But has
this Goddess not gained strong following in our days?
Is she not to many the highest power, in which alone
they believe? 'Oh, if I had only luck!' 'If luck
would follow me,' is their daily devotion. 'If luck is
lacking, all endeavor is in vain,' this is their wisdom
and their confession of faith.   *   *   A man has
risen by industry, perseverance, talent, cleverness and
mental strain. They do not ask, 'How is it that the
man was so successful,' because for them it is a firmly
established fact, 'that he owes it all to his—good
luck.'   *   *   They must reap the fruits of
their doings, are punished for their recklessness, their
carelessness, inability, dishonesty and extravagance.
Whatever they commence does not go forward, they lament and accuse not themselves, they know well
whence it all comes—fortune does not favor them, they
have ever been persecuted by ill luck, were the target
of its maliciousness. Instead of bettering their conduct
and changing their mode of living, they try to concili-
ate their luck by gambling in the lottery, sacrificing
their last kreutzer ($\frac{1}{2}$ a penny), to the hostile moloch
of play.   *   *   Are you Israelites? Do you
believe in the one living God?"* In a sermon on the
Third Commandment Kohn said: "The name of God is
uttered most particularly in prayer, and considering
this the third commandment is referred to not only by
myself but also by the teachers of the Talmud. Is it
not contemptible blasphemy to utter lies before the
Holy One, to deny His benefactions and to complain
about sufferings, which we do not feel? And let me
be candid, such blasphemies are freely uttered by Isra-

---

*Dr. Kobak's Jeschurun, Lemberg, 1856, Vol. I, pages 34-35.

elites who are numbered among the pious of the land.
For many of the antiquated prayers contain legends
which nobody to-day accepts as facts, complain about
sufferings and persecutions, which God has ended long
ago.   *   *   Well may we exclaim to those who,
without devotion, and in an irreverent position, recite
formulas of prayer—I cannot call it praying—well, I
say, may we exclaim: Why do you blaspheme God?
Why do you take His name in vain?   *   *   *
It is not the mass of words which constitutes prayer.
Let the words of our ancient sages suffice us, 'God
requires only the heart.'"*

In a sermon on the Fourth Commandment Kohn
made the following timely remarks: "I am inclined
to translate the passage: 'It is your duty to work six
days in the week.'‡ That laboriousness belongs to
piety and fear of God can be easily proven.   *   *
Where is the least resistance against corruption and
vice? In the heart of the idle person. Laziness is the
beginning of all vices. 'The Eternal, thy God, will
bless thee in all thy labors and in all the works of thy
hands,' (Deut. XV, 10). Shall he also bless idleness,
laziness and carelessness?   *   *   A lazy man
will envy his fellow man, and in his jealousy hate his
successful brother.   *   *   He will rob, steal,
and defraud, he will borrow and not repay, in short he
will live like a freebooter at the expense of other people, until the arm of justice overtakes him.   *   *
In the best case he will be dependent on charity and
alms.   *   *   Is this not a crying wrong against
the burdened dispensers of charity and against the
really helpless, old, feeble and frail people, who are
thus injured?   *   *   *

"I explain the passage of the Talmud: 'He who
would not teach his son a trade, teaches him robbery,'†
as follows: He commits robbery on human society by

---

*See Jeschurun, Lemberg, 1826, pages 91-93. .
†It is generally translated: "You can labor," i. e., if you are in-
clined to do so.
‡Kidduschin 29.

not training his son for a useful occupation. This concerns us Israelites most particularly. It is well known that we are reproached with the vice of shunning manual labor. Alas, a portion of our co-religionists cannot be acquitted of this accusation. This reproach is made use of in order to deprive us of our civil rights. It is, however, our duty to defeat this objection by our deeds, to encourage by material support a useful activity among our poorer classes. It is a fact that Israelites, who spend the week days in idleness on the street, give not only offence, but bring about in the true sense of the term chillul hashem (desecration of the name of God)."[*]

Such was Abraham Kohn, whom Dr. B. F. Mannheimer, justly calls "a martyr of our time."[†] And yet Prof. Graetz, who devoted no less than forty pages to the Jewish apostates and renegades, Heine and Boerne, has not a single page, not a single sentence, not a single line, not a single word to say about poor murdered Abraham Kohn. No itinerant "schnorr-Rabbi" is too insignificant for a place of honor in Graetz's "History," if he has published the least Hebrew pamphlet on the most foolish question. But a martyr like Kohn is ignored. Why? Echo answers, "Why?" Most likely for the same reasons that Friedlaender, Jacobssohn, Chorin, Salomon and others, are disparaged. Had Kohn been orthodox or conservative, and had the Reformers poisoned him, Graetz would most likely not have utterly ignored the historical fact. That the learned professor utterly ignores men like Geiger, Loew, Einhorn and Samuel Hirsch in his work might be excused on the plea that, like the authors of the "Encyclopedia Britannica," he hesitated to pass judgment upon persons who were yet living, although he made some slight exceptions from this praiseworthy rule. But Abraham Kohn had been dead

---

[*] Jeschurun, sermon of Kohn on the "Fourth Commandment," pages 105, 110, 111, 112, 113, 114, 115, 117.
[†] Biography of A. Kohn, (Stettin, 1859). I am sorry to say, that I was unable to obtain a copy of this publication.

twenty years at least before the last volume of Graetz's history was written.   Even partisan historians ought to do a little justice.* I consider it a great privilege to have been instrumental in bringing the name of the noble martyr, Rabbi Abraham Kohn, before the English reading public.

*See my: Graetz's Geschichtsbauerei, Berlin, 1881, Issleib, pages 79-83 ff.

CHAPTER VII.

SAMUEL HOLDHEIM.

Born in 1806, in Kempen, Posen; died as Rabbi of the Reform Congregation of Berlin, August 22, 1860.

Samuel Holdheim was one of the most remarkable characters in the history of Reform-Judaism. In his life we see the gradual evolution from the lowest type of Jewish orthodoxy, such as to-day can be found in Russia and Poland, to the extreme wing of Radical Reform. He verified the saying: "*Les extremes se touchent.*" But this development was not by a single bound, but the result of a hard, inner struggle within his heart during a period of twenty years. The best proof of his sincerity can be found in the fact that in every stage of his religious growth he warmly and most ably defended the opinions then held by him, as if the possibility of ever changing them were out of the question. This is a praiseworthy trait of character, which is not found among time-servers and hypocrites. Few of our young Rabbis, especially in this country, have an idea what a consuming strain such a mental struggle must be for the mind and heart of a conscientious Rabbi. It is greatly to be deplored, that Prof. Graetz so utterly ignores this phase of character in Holdheim's career. Had he not done so he would never have spoken of him as "a man without an ideal," as of a "Mephistophelian nature," who "personified the spirit of negation," who "considered the Rabbinical profession as a milking cow."[*] He would not

*Graetz: History of the Jews, Vol. XI. page 563.

have represented Holdheim as a hypocrite, because he
observed conscientiously the Jewish ceremonies during
his ministrations in Frankfort on the Oder, and because
in the first few years of his Rabbinical career he was
not yet a Reformer.   He would not have reproached
him with "want of earnest conviction," (p. 564).   He
would not have been guilty of such unhistorical, biased and unjustifiable passages as, for instance, the following: "Holdheim, who formerly had no idea that
the divine service should be dignified, found all of a
sudden the disorder which had distressed him very little in Frankfort inappropriate in the Synagogues of
Mecklenburg-Schwerin, and was bent upon removing
everything from the worship which was not in harmony with the spirit of the age." (Ibidem).   Now it
is, to say the least, a broad assertion that Holdheim
"had no idea," when Rabbi of Frankfort, "that the
divine service should be dignified."   Even a superficial perusal of the little volume of Holdheim's sermons,
published in Frankfort in 1839* will convince the
impartial reader that Holdheim had already at that
time pretty strong opinions on the subject of our worship.
But, granting he had no decided convictions in Frankfurt, does he deserve to be reproached for introducing
the Wurtemberg (Reformed) order of the Synagogue in
his district? (Ibid, P. 565) And suppose the orthodox
Congregations of his district did not like it, why
was this more of a "violence done to the conscience"
than the interdict of Bernays against the Hamburg prayer-book, against which Graetz had nothing to
say?   Had the Professor treated the character of Holdheim with less hostility, he would never have penned
the following lines: "Since Paulus of Tarsus, Judaism
never had such an enemy within its own fold, who had
shaken its whole structure to its very foundations."
(Ibidem).   Holdheim, who is compared by Graetz to

---

*See pages 10, 12, 13, especially the introduction to Hold-
heim's sermons, and the discourse on: "The Two Important Institutions of Salvation," pages 8-10.

the actual founder of Christianity,* has done more
through his reformatory activity in Berlin towards checking the tidal wave of apostasy than Graetz and all the orthodox Rabbis of Prussia combined. The truth is, the
latter, by their uncompromising attitude and stubbornness, have driven to the baptismal font not a few of the
young generation. On the other hand it is statistically
proven that since the establishment of the Radical-Re-
form Congregation in Berlin, with Holdheim at its
head, Jewish conversions to Christianity became few
and far between. Hence the comparison with Paulus
of Tarsus, is, to say the least, not well chosen.

In the light of such patent facts it sounds almost
like irony when Graetz assures his readers on page 566
of his "History," that in the time of the Maccabees,
Holdheim, like Menelaus, would have advised the
Jews to worship the Greek Zeus; that in the age of
Hadrian, like a second Acher, † he would have recommended to the Jews the worship of Jupiter Capi-
tolinus; and in the period of Philipp, of Spain, and
Emanuel, of Portugal, he would have considered it a
praiseworthy thing on the part of the Jews to worship
the cross. A real historian deals only in facts and relates what a person has done. It is beyond the province of a historian to attempt to say what anyone
would or might have done under certain circumstances.
"The hidden things belong only to God." Had Holdheim, indeed, been without character and principle, as
he is represented by Graetz, then like many of Graetz's
disciples and other time-servers and sycophants, he
would have cast his lot with the powerful majority,
where honors, influence, material advantages and

---

*Not Jesus, but Paulus was in reality the founder of Christianity.
See my "Principles of Judaism compared with those of Christianity,"
pages 118-136, on the subject: "Origin of Christianity," chapter IV,
and my essay on "Jesus of Nazareth," in the "Menorah," August,
1889.

†"Acher" is a sarcastic name for Elisha Ben Abujah, who, according to a Talmudical tradition, became a skeptic, pantheist or
atheist. Literally translated the Hebrew word "Acher" means
"another."

chances of promotion were beckoning. But what has
he done? He left an influential position for life as
Land-Rabbi of Mecklenburg-Schwerin, where he, as
an officer of the government, was independent of the
will and whims of his Congregations. In the hope of
becoming a power for good on his own merits, he accepted the call of a small Reform Congregation at Berlin, which was hardly organized, and was surrounded
by enemies from within and without.* He thus cut
loose from old associations and cherished bonds. He
was cursed, reviled, sneered and laughed at, he became
a butt and by-word among the majority of his co-religionists. Having been recognized, even by his most
bitter opponents, as the greatest Talmudical scholar of
his time, he most assuredly could have done better
from a material point of view by playing† the "conservative" Rabbi. But no, he preferred to travel the
rocky road. He went to Berlin, thus passing the Rubi-
con and burning, as it were, all bridges behind him.
For "Kol Banaihoo lau Jeshubun." Those Rabbis,
who in the forties had run the risk of affiliating with the
"Reform-Genossenschaft, of Berlin," which is the
most radical Jewish Congregation in the world, with,
perhaps, the exception of the Sinai Temple of Chicago
—could not return to a Rabbinical office in another
Congregation in case of failure in this field of labor.
And yet Holdheim went to Berlin in order to build up
a radical Reform Congregation; he went there on the
strength of what? Was he a young man of prepossessing appearance, of fine physique, endowed with great

*The Prussian Government has been, on general principles, op-
posed to the Jewish Reform-movement.

†Graetz' school i. e., the disciples of the "Breslau Rabbin-
erseminar" have reduced hypocrisy to a fine art. With very few
exceptions they are masters in the unenviable art of "playing" the
"conservatives," in public and being radicals to the core. Graetz,
himself covered himself with the "Talith" during divine service,
while by word and pen he mercilessly attacked the belief in the
divine origin of the Bible. And such a man dares to call Holdheim
a "hypocrite" and "enemy of Israel." Kol hapossel bemumau
possel." (Some people blame in others their own shortcomings,
Talmud).

oratorical powers, social attainments, pleasant delivery, personal magnetism and all those little artifices which generally make the successful preacher? Oh, no. Yet he went to Berlin, simply on the strength of his ardent enthusiasm for the cause of Reform-Judaism, of his unshakable trust in its ultimate triumph and victory, of his unbounded confidence in the power of his argument and in the force of what he considered truth. Now I ask every impartial man, no matter how little he sympathizes with Holdheim's convictions, whether such a man deserves to be ranked among vile traitors, who, like Menelaus, have bartered away their religion for gold and sold their birthright for a mess of pottage? But let us turn away from such historiography to real historical facts concerning the life and the works of the much abused and little appreciated Radical Reformer, "Samuel Holdheim."

Samuel Holdheim was born in Kempen, Duchy of Posen, in 1806, and was educated according to the rules of the strictest orthodoxy of Poland, which sufficiently accounts for the great struggles within his own breast, before he arrived at his advanced ideas on religion.

He was sent to the "Cheder" (Hebrew school), according to the usual custom, and stealthily, only, he dared to read a German book, to do which in those parts of the world was considered sinful. Even the study of Hebrew grammar was regarded as a waste of time. Thus Holdheim devoted almost all his time to the study of the Talmud, in its dialectic and pilpulistic method. How successful he was in the art of wending his way through the labyrinth of the Pipul* is proven by the fact, that when a little boy, to the utmost surprise of the learned Rabbi, and the recognized luminaries of the famous Congregation of Kempen, he solved

---

*"Pilpul" is that rabulistic and sophistic manner of argumentation, which permits the logic to go astray, and acuteness of mind to take a crooked route. (See my Talmud, Denver, 1884, page 13). Heine calls it a "Fechtschule" a "Gedankenjagd um Mucken zu fangen" (a hunt after thoughts, in order to catch midges).

a most complicated Talmudical problem. No wonder that he soon acquired great fame as a distinguished Bachur, and that he was called to different places in order to instruct boys in the Talmud. But the greater his fame as a Talmudist became, the more he found out how little he knew of other things outside of the Talmud, and how very limited was his knowledge in the field of so-called "profane" science and literature. Like all self-taught men he improved every opportunity to study, tried to read every book within his reach, until he came to the resolution that he must study systematically. To accomplish this purpose he directed his steps toward Prague, which was the seat not only of Talmudical scholarship but also of a University. With a zeal and energy, of which only a Bachur is capable, he studied day and night, so that, in a comparatively short time, he mastered the classics and became well versed in historical and philosophical literature. Although a man in years, in order to quench his thirst for a higher knowledge, he did not deem it below his dignity to sit on a bench of the study halls with young students.

After several failures in his efforts to get a position, he was in 1836 elected Rabbi of Frankfort-on-the-Oder. This position he held until 1840.

At that time the position of Rabbi in Prussia was owing to the fact that the Rabbis as a rule were opposed to all progress in the domain of Judaism, most difficult. The tendency towards checking and curtailing the privilege and influence of the Rabbis was then general among the administrations of Congregations in Germany. In 1823—the same year, the Jacobsohn Temple had to be closed by order of the Prussian government, a ministerial rescript had deprived the Rabbis of all influence upon the Jews."*
This measure was greeted with applause by the better

---

†This rescript was based on the verdict of Gumpertz, an elder of the Congregation of Berlin, who called the Rabbis "Kausherwaechter," (Guardians of kosher-meat), thus conveying the idea that they were good for nothing else.

class of Jews, because a check of Rabbinical authority was looked upon as a triumph of progress. No wonder, as a progressive Rabbi was unusual in those days. The care for the stomach, the performance of marriages, divorces, Chalizah and similar ceremonies were about the only functions of the Rabbi "and other servants of the Synagogue." They were strictly prohibited from "teaching religion and instructing the youth." Similar reasons have caused the Jewish Congregation of Frankfort-on-the-Main to check the influence of the Rabbi, especially in the religious school, to such an extent, that Dr. Leopold Stein resigned his position rather than endure such a humiliating state of affairs. The same rescript plainly says: "Jewish Rabbis are no teachers of the Jews and cannot be looked upon by the state as teachers of religion in the sense of Christian clergymen." Hence the inspection or supervision of a "religious school," which is nowadays one of the main duties of the Rabbi, was refused to the Rabbis by the government.

Holdheim did his best towards bringing about a change for the better in this respect; towards overthrowing the wrong principle that "the Jewish religion is only tolerated." In the preface to the "Sermons," (1839), he bitterly complained of the humiliation to which the Rabbis of Prussia were subjected by the government and demanded the relegation of "this sad legacy of a dying age," to the past. While the Jews of Prussia were emancipated in 1812, their religion is not at all recognized, but is, on the contrary, still resting under the bane of mediaeval disgrace. He concludes, however, that the Rabbis themselves have created the erroneous impression that they had no interest in worldly affairs, and were utterly indifferent to the efforts, victories and defeats of the new age. He admitted that they lived in the dead past only, have become mummies without life and warmth, and were representatives of stagnant ceremonies. And yet Graetz wants to make the public believe, that a man who writes in this strain as Rabbi of Frankfurt in

1839, had "no idea that the divine service should be dignified." Holdheim continues: "The modern Rabbi must protest against such shameful conceptions. His Congregation must bear witness in his behalf, that decisions on the ceremonial law and performance of marriages and divorces do not fill the whole sphere of his usefulness. His main task and duty is, and will be, to teach religion and morality, not only theoretically, but through his example and character. This is of greater importance to Judaism than the explanation of the ceremonial law and the rendering of ritual decisions."

Holdheim was opposed to the usual custom of separating the office of preacher and teacher from that of the Rabbi. He was one of the first Rabbis who combined the functions of both in his person. In Prussia he surely was the first Rabbi-preacher. He, like Geiger, saw a danger to Judaism in that dualism, according to which two men, representing opposite religious views, should manage the religious affairs of the same Congregation; the one being identified with orthodoxy, the other standing for the principle of progressive development.*

In the pulpit Holdheim became the compromising mediator between the old "Derasoth"† and rationalistic, moral discourses and philosophical addresses. While the latter were excellent and fraught with good results in their day, it cannot be denied that their shallow moralizing tone, coupled as it was, with superficiality, lack of substance and vitality, did no longer satisfy the demands of a critical age. Holdheim's first sermon was delivered in 1836 in his native city, Kempen.‡ In a sermon on "Religion, Legality and Peace," delivered in Frankfurt, March 4, 1837, Holdheim advocated the necessity of Rabbinical Conferences and urged the

---

*See Geiger: "Ansprache an meine Gemeinde," Breslau, 1842, and Geiger's Nachgelassene Schriften, Berlin, 1875, L. Gerschel, Vol. I, pages 52-112.

†From "Darash" "seek, search." Dialectic argumentations on the Halacha.

*It was published in Berlin, (1836). The text was taken from Genesis I, 26.

Rabbis to heal the breach between the past and present of Israel. The sermon was favorably criticized.*

The following sermon on "Prayer and Instruction combined are the essentials of the Jewish divine service," (Frankfurt, 1837) is of special interest to those who were informed in Graetz's "History" that Holdheim had no idea in Frankfurt that the divine service should be dignified." (Page 564) In answer to this charge, which, if true, might stamp Holdheim as a hypocrite and time-server, the following passages, which could be greatly augmented, are quoted: "What would Isaiah say should he happen to enter our Synagogue on Sabbath or New Moon; what would be the result of his impressions? A, by no means, small part of the Congregation he would not see at all, and in relation to them he would address his words contained in chapter 29, 11. But among those present he would meet with a spirit of disorder, of stubbornness, of confusion. He would see how the practice of the most sacred ceremonies during services is disturbed by conversations and discussions about the most profane things; how the old people set the most destructive example to the young; how during the recitation of the prayers by the cantor, noise and unbecoming behavior reign supreme. He would notice things which would not be tolerated in a public place of amusement. He would see, how the most sacred of our religious functions, the reading from the Thorah, is ignored, and treated with contempt, inasmuch as during this part of the service the majority of the Congregation leave the Synagogue, while others indulge in conversation and laughter."

Now, if such words, which, by the way, furnish a most excellent and true picture of the Synagogueworship in almost every orthodox Congregation of Europe, are not yet proof sufficient for Graetz, that Holdheim had, even in Frankfurt long before he went

*See: Literarisches and homiletisches Beiblatt zur Allg., Zeitung des Judenthum's, 1838, July 21st.

to Mecklenburg-Schwerin, an "idea that the Jewish worship ought to be dignified," perhaps the following passage will be convincing: "The Prophet Isaiah would see how the calling to the Thorah (Aufrufen), is offered at auction to the highest bidder and is regarded as a performance, which furnishes the opportunity of showing favors or spite. He would see that the public instruction from the holy place is, to many, a stumbling block; that they try to give public annoyance by all sorts of disturbances and that they fill with disgust the attentive and devoted audience."

However, not only in his own Congregation, but whenever a measure was advocated, which promised to benefit Judaism at large, Holdheim supported it with might and main. Thus, when Geiger's idea of establishing an institution for the training of Rabbis was taken up again, Holdheim agitated the measure most forcibly in his sermons. He tried to interest the many merchants, who happened to be in Frankfurt during the mass, in the subject.

His sermons, entitled, "Gottesdienstliche Vortraege,"* are symbolical in nature. Even at that time he was already opposed to a "blind veneration of tradition." Among other things he said that we should not subscribe to doctrines which expect us to abjure all reason, to believe without research and to accept without the least investigation everything as holy and divine which has been given out as such by human beings.

Such utterances show that Holdheim, even in those days, was by no means an orthodox Rabbi.

Holdheim was engaged at that time in a controversy with Dr. Freystadt, who attacked Moses Mendelssohn on account of his statement, that the Jews have no dogma. In an article: "Have the Jews Dogmas?"† Holdheim tries to prove, that Mendelssohn had simply stated that the divergences of opinion in

---

*Frankfurt, 1839.
†See Zeitung des Judenthum's, 1838, Nos. 4-9 and Salamith, Vol. VIII.

Judaism concern ceremonial laws only and not doctrines of religion.

Another interesting article by Holdheim appeared in Jost's "Israelit. Annalen,"* on the "Oath of the Israelites in Criminal Cases."

In the mean time the Geiger-Tiktin controversy in Breslau has set many a theological and other pen in motion. Among others a Dr. Lowositz had published a pamphlet: "The Election of Rabbis," (Breslau, 1840), strongly condemning every progressive development in the domain of religion and consequently taking part against Geiger's election as Rabbi in Breslau. In reply to this pamphlet Holdheim published his brochure: "The Religious Progress within German Judaism."† He held the opinion that religious instruction ought to pave the way for Reform. "The way and method of teaching religion has always been subject in Judaism to the exigencies of the age, but the word of God was the same in every epoch of our history. Moses taught otherwise than the prophets, they otherwise than the men of the Synagoga Magna, they otherwise than the teachers of the Mishna, they otherwise than the sages of the 'Gmarah,' they otherwise than the Gaonim, and they otherwise than the later theologians and great men in Israel."

Dr. Lowositz in his reply‡ to Holdheim spoke of him in terms of great appreciation and the highest esteem. In the meantime the title "Doctor of Philosophy" was bestowed upon him by the University of Leipzig. He was soon recognized as an authority by both parties; by the conservatives on account of his immense Talmudical scholarship, by the progressive Jewish element on account of his modern education and apparent friendliness to their ideas. Jost pointed to Holdheim as to an important authority whenever a defense of Reforms and innovations from

---

*1839, No. 30-32.
†Der Religioese Fortschritt im Deutschen Judentum. (Leipzig, 1840).
‡Orient. 1840, No. 29-40.

the basis of Talmudical and Rabbinical literature was
necessary.* The Congregation of Posen asked for
his decision on the question, whether the son is entitled
to inherit the office of Rabbi made vacant by his
father's death. The "Orient" discussed his sermons
in seven successive numbers.†

In a "Memorial Sermon on the King Friedrich
Wilhelm III," June 23, 1840, Holdheim laid special
stress on the fact that the Jews of Prussia demand not
only equal rights but equal duties.

In his farewell address, August 15, 1840, he urged
his Congregation to elect as his successor a man who
was in full sympathy with the requirements of the age.

There are those who reproach Holdheim for his
rigorous decisions on religious questions. He answered
as a rule such queries strictly in accord with the Shulchan Aruch.‡ Those who censured him were wrong.
A judge or lawyer, who is asked to decide a question
in accordance with the law of a certain state, will give
his decision according to the law of that state and not
according to his private opinion on the subject, which
might be entirely different.

So, even so, a Rabbi is in duty bound to decide a ritual
question in accord with the Shulchan Aruch when
asked what the code teaches on that question. If,
however, he is asked for his individual opinion, he is
then at liberty to decide according to his own judgment.

---

*Jost: Annalen, 1840, No. 36, 1841, No. 51.

†See Literaturblatt des Orient, 1840, Nos. 35, 36, 37, 39, 47, 49, 50. J. A. Fraenkel, critic.

‡"Shulchan Aruch" means a "A table set." The work is divided
into four parts; (1). Orach Chajim (The Path of Life), which contains ordinances concerning the daily religious life of the Jew,
comprising 697 chapters. (2). Joreh Deah (The Teacher of
Knowledge), treats mainly on the dietary laws and contains 403
chapters. (3). Eben haezer (The Stone of Help) treats particularly
on conjugal life, marriage and divorce, in 178 chapters. (4). Choshen
Mishpat ("Breast Shield of Justice") in 427 chapters, treats on civil
and criminal law, comprising the entire field of jurisprudence.
(See more on this subject in my article the "Shulchan Aruch"
"Jewish Reformer," 1886, Nos. 12, 13, 14, 15).

The "Hezogthum," Mecklenburg-Schwerin, had granted to the Jews in 1839, a constitution, which was favorable to a progressive development of their religion. The "Statutes for the Religious Interests of the Israelitish Subjects" ordered the election of a "Land-Rabbi,"* who would receive two hundred thalers as an appropriation from the government, provided he should prove to be a man of modern culture. Negotiations with Holdheim led to good results, and on September 19, 1840, he was solemnly introduced into his new office as Land-Rabbi.

This position was more difficult and complicated than the one in Frankfurt, and the field of activity was larger: For Holdheim took charge of a combination of several Congregations, which vastly differed in their religious ideas. The "Israelitish Oberath," consisting of two officials of the government and five members elected by the Congregations, was a great support to him, but still there were opposing forces to pacify, and selfishness and apathy to combat.

The organization of schools, and especially the introduction of religious instruction for the young, were his first care, in Schwerin as it was in Frankfurt. This was no easy task, as the education of the young had so far been managed by ignorant "Shochtim" (slaughterers of animals), and "Chazanim" (readers of the prayers). The opening of the Jewish Congregational School in Schwerin, January 10, 1841, was, therefore, an important event in the history of Jewish culture in Mecklenburg. Holdheim called an able pedagogue and theologian as superintendent of the school, and the success of the institution was assured after the first splendid examination of the pupils. The example of Schwerin induced other Congregations to do likewise, and after a comparatively short time the Congregations of Wahren, Guestrow and Buetzow could boast of good schools, which they maintained at great sacrifices. As a matter of course the teachers of

---

*Land-Rabbi means the Rabbi of a whole state or province.

those schools did their best to improve and dignify the
worship in the Synagogue, which had been most sadly neglected. A report of Dr. L. Marcus, one year
after Holdheim's arrival in Schwerin, bears testimony
of the good work done by the Land-Rabbi.* Two
years later Holdheim introduced a "Synagogenor-
dung," (Order of the Synagogue), after the pattern
of the one introduced in Wuertemburg, which caused
some opposition, especially in the country Congregations. Holdheim visited, at that time, Hamburg.
While he admired the Temple and its service,† he
could not help noticing some inconsistencies in the
Hamburg Reforms. For instance, the abolition of the
daily worship, of the "Haphtarah" on the one hand
and the retention of the "Second Holiday" on the
other. He felt what Geiger so ably demonstrated, that
the prayer-book of the Temple was not based on scientific principles.‡ He also expected of the Temple
that it would eventually transfer the reforms from the
worship to practical life.§

Holdheim' "opinion" on the prayer-book is spoken
of on page 137 of this book. In consequence of an
anonymous article ‖ and a pamphlet,● Holdheim
felt called upon to write again on the Hamburg
prayer-book.** He also published a pamphlet:
"Accusation of Heresy and Liberty of Conscience, a
Second Vote on the Hamburg Temple Controversy."††
In a thorough, sarcastic manner he shows the utter
ignorance, arrogance and boundless fanaticism of the

*Jost's Annalen, 1891, page 359.
†Jost's Annalen, 1841, Nos. 45-46. "The new Israelitish Temple
at Hamburg."
‡Geiger: Der Hamburger Tempelstreit, Breslau, 1842. See also
Nachgelassene Schriften, 1875, Vol. I. pages 113-197.
§Wissenschaftliche Zeitschrift fuer Juedische Theologie, Vol.
III. page 151.
‖Zeitung des Judenthum's, 1842, No. 4.
● Jude und Nichtjude, eine Erwiderung auf die Schriften der
Triple-Allianz der Herren Doctoren Holdheim, Salomon and
Frankfurter, Amsterdam, 1842.
**Zeitung des Judenth's, 1842, No.8.
††"Verketzerung und Gewissensfreiheit ein zweites Gutachten
ueber den Hamburger Tempelsbreif, 1843.

pamphleteer, and takes occasion to protest against the inconsistent, vascillating and wavering attitude of Zacharias Frankel. In his polemics Holdheim made use of a shrewd strategem, to accept seemingly an argument of his opponent in order to conquer him with his own weapons, and then to demolish him entirely by proving the falsity of the argument. This he had learned from the Talmud. At that stage of his development he was of Mendelssohn's opinion concerning the ceremonial laws, especially so far as the Biblical precepts were concerned. Herein we see the main difference between Holdheim and Geiger, for whom, both as a scholar and a man, Holdheim had always held the highest admiration and reverence. *

For the sake of a just appreciation of both these great men, who take the front rank in the history of the Jewish Reform movement, I quote Geiger's words on Holdheim: "In our relation of love and high esteem during a quarter of a century, we most readily agreed on the justification of our divergent opinions, conceding to each other honesty of purpose both spiritually and morally, yet we knew always very well how to find the line where our views differed. Holdheim was of a dogmatic, dialectic nature; mine was, and is, decidedly and preponderatingly historical. Holdheim gained gradually an understanding of the progressive, spiritual life.† My labors in this direction have found in him, not only a zealous, but a penetrating, and, I dare say, sympathetic reader. Nevertheless he was not fully capable of entering into this way of thinking on subjects connected with historical religion.

*See Holdheim's estimate of Geiger in his: "History of the Origin and Development of the Jewish Reform-Congregation in Berlin." (Berlin, 1857: Julius Springer, pages 68-69). Geiger's influence on Holdheim's religious development was very great, and was gratefully acknowledged and appreciated by the latter. See Holdheim's "Gutachen" in "Rabbin. Gutachten Ueber die Vertraeglienkeit der freien Forschung mit dem Rabbineramte," Breslau, 1842; Ritter: "Samuel Holdheim," page 79 ff.

†Geiger' Wissensch. Zeitschrift, Vol. III, pages 216-17. See also Geiger's letter to Zunz, Nachgel Shriften, Vol V. page 182, and my Graetz' Geschichtsbauerei, page 82.

Therefore he was often compelled to change his views. Guided by his clear judgment, he always very readily yielded to progressive ideas, and indefatigably strove after the attainment of a new theological basis. Hence we cannot be surprised that on page 76 of his pamphlet "Verketzerung' und Gewissensfreiheit," Holdheim decidedly advocates the belief in the divine inspiration of the Bible.*

The great conflict in the "Geiger-Tiktin" controversy at Breslau exerted a powerful influence on Holdheim's religious development. More about this struggle in Breslau, which is the most important in the history of Jewish Reform, will be found in this book in the chapter on "Abraham Geiger."

Before reviewing Holdheim's important work: "The Autonomy of the Rabbis," we deem it proper to mention that it was Zunz's "Gottesdienstliche Vortraege" which has influenced Holdheim in the direction of Reform, a fact which Holdheim candidly and plainly confesses.†

Holdheim's literary labors were, as a rule, the outcome of some outside occurrence, and the work under consideration forms no exception to this rule.

In Mecklenburg-Schwerin the old practice of having all cases concerning marriage, divorce and inheritance, decided in accordance with Talmudical law was still prevailing among the Jews. To this Holdheim, on account of unavoidable difficulties arising from it, justly objected. Aside from this Geiger, Wechsler, M. Guttman, Karo, I. A. Fraenkel, had just then discussed the questions of "Chalizah"‡ (Lev. XV, 8; Num. XII, 14; Deut. XXV, 5-10), marriage and divorce. Added to this, new reactionary

---

*On page 65 of this pamphlet Holdheim seems to agree with Mendelssohn's opinions on the ceremonial law. (See chapter I, page 18 of this book).

†See Holdheim: History of the origin and development of the Jewish Reform-Congregation in Berlin, 1857, page 77, note.

‡See Lev. 15, 8, No. 12-14, Deut. 25, 5-10. See also: Geiger's Zeitschrift III, 1-13, Ansprache a. m. G. p., 26; Zeitschrift IV, Z. D. J., 1, 87, 90, 93; Literaturblatt, Orient I, 20-22.

laws against the Jews were about to be promulgated by the Prussian Government. All these causes combined induced Holdheim to publish his "Autonomy of the Rabbis and the Principle of the Jewish Marriage." (Schwerin and Berlin, 1843).

In the preface to this work Holdheim declared that the best proof that the Jews have no separate nationality is the fact that they do not want it. They feel insulted whenever their enemies accuse them of "national isolation." Just as the Jewish right of "excommunication" had been set aside by the Government at Mendelssohn's instigation,* because it had lost its vitality, so had the entire Jewish jurisprudence been abrogated. This was the basis of the political emancipation of the Jews, inasmuch as, instead of Palestinians and Orientals, they have become German and Europeans. He demanded from the Rabbis a "consistent separation of the religious precepts of the Pentateuch from the political and civil laws of Moses." The principle of Mar Samuel† in Nehardea, which was endorsed by the President of the School, Mar Ukbah, "The law of the Government is under all circumstances valid," must govern us. Hence in questions of marriage and inheritance the civil and not the Rabbinical law ought to be decisive. Even the ancient Rabbis, Holdheim goes on to say, made a distinction between obedience to the Mosaic law within and outside of Palestine, inasmuch as they allowed those observances which were especially applicable in that land, to fall into disuse after the exile. But they ought to have said whatever Jewish rite or law concerns Palestine is inoperative in other countries. Our duty to-day is to effect a consistent separation between matters of religion and civil or political affairs.

The three leading principles of Holdheim's "Autonomy of the Rabbis," are the following:

*Jerusalem II, 120-121.
†"Dina demalchutha dina."

1.   "The Antonomy of the Rabbis must cease. Religion, and religion only, is their domain. They have no title to be judges and lawgivers, or to usurp the rights of the state.

2.   "Separation of the religious precepts from the political and civil laws. In Palestine, where the Jews were a political body, religion and state were one. Hence Palestinian laws have no justification in the midst of the modern state.

3.   "Marriage is a civil act according to the doctrine of Judaism. Hence the law of the state attends to its civil and legal side. Religion, however, has the mission to be only the guardian of the home, and of the ideal side of marriage. Hence the forms ought to be of a more dignified and less business-like character."

This book created a stir in Jewish circles of Germany. Among the progressive element it was greeted with great applause. To many the idea that Judaism does not in the least collide with the demands of the modern state appeared almost a revelation, although the prophet Jeremiah had already expressed the same views long before Samuel of Nehardea, and Samuel Holdheim. Jeremiah exclaimed: "And seek ye the welfare of the city whither I have banished you; for in its welfare ye fare well." (Chap. XXIX, 7). Still the mere fact that a Rabbi had come out so plainly and boldly was a matter of pleasant surprise to the friends of religious Reform.

Yet they objected to several propositions and deductions of Holdheim. The idea that marriage is a purchase and barter was distasteful to all those who looked upon marriage as upon something more solemn and sublime. They disliked also the idea of the state meddling too much with the religious affairs of the Jews. They knew only too well how prone a government is to abuse power, and how very difficult it is to wrest from its grasp what it has once taken. Thus A. Bernstein, a publicist of prominence, who wrote under the pseudonym Rebenstein, criticises the "Autonomy."* While fully recognizing Holdheim's scholarship, ingenuity and acute penetration, he regrets that he cannot find a better remedy for the reform of the Jewish laws on marriage than the expedients offered by Talmudism on the one hand and by the intervention of the state on the other. All that was necessary towards bringing about a better state of affairs, would be, that the modern Rabbis should show the same courage in coping with difficult questions, which was manifested by the Rabbis of old. Have they not abolished old, even Biblical laws, and have they not instituted innovations whenever circumstances and the exigencies of the age rendered them imperative? The state, which is Christian, will never be a friend of Jewish Reform, hence we do not want its assistance,† because a solution of such problems is possible only on the basis of a full emancipation of the Jews, which the state is, as yet, unwilling to grant.

Bernstein claims that it is about time to confess openly what is meant by "revelation," "authenticity of the Pentateuch," so that our children may be spared the same conflict and inner struggle through which we have gone. Christianity cannot do without the belief in a supernatural origin of the Pentateuch, and in miracles. Judaism is better off in this respect. The Pentateuch is, not a revelation, but a testimony that our forefathers were imbued with the consciousness of God. The Pentateuch came into existence after the return of Israel from the Babylonian exile through the school of Ezra, and we, ourselves, after an exile of almost two thousand years, are living witnesses of a living consciousness of the sublime relationship that links us to God. Herein we find the true criterion for the measure of Reform. Those ceremonies and symbols which tend to strengthen this consciousness of God, deserve to be preserved, while all

---

*See Freund's Zeitschrift: Zur Judenfrage, 1844, Vol. II, pages 7, 25, 65-108.
†"Timeo Danaos et dona ferentes "I fear the Greeks, especially when they offer presents."

those which fail to promote the life of Judaism should
be removed and those which have been impaired should
be changed or reformed.

Bernstein's criticism of Holdheim created a great
stir.   Holdheim replied in Freund's Monthly,* in
which he, while dogmatically adhering to the old views,
plainly and boldly took leave of all those ideas which
he could no longer harmonize with the whole tendency of the age.   He comes to the conclusion that the
Rabbis of the Talmud, whenever yielding to the pressing demands of an age, have done so from necessity
and not because they were animated by "a true reformatory spirit."   They believed that the Bible in its integrity had been given for all time to come, and that
even those laws which are now out of practice would be
reinstated in due time.   According to Geiger's theory
the divine law has become a product of the creating
spirit of man and tradition has been placed above "the
Word of God."   Here we see that Holdheim could not
fully enter into the spirit of historical criticism.   He
was in danger of becoming a Karaite.   He wanted to
"save the supernatural conception of Mosaism and
Prophetism."   For he could not understand how it was
possible to "declare the Bible as a work revealing the
consciousness of God in man" and yet "speak of revelation."   He emphatically believed in a positive revelation.   And yet Holdheim was more reviled by
orthodoxy than any other Rabbi of this century.   It
has been pointed out at the beginning of this chapter,
how Graetz speaks of him, the same Graetz, who, so
far as the Bible is concerned, holds views so radical
that, compared to them, Holdheim's opinions were conservative in the extreme.†

As to marrriage Holdheim said, in his reply to
Bernstein, that only so far as the right of property can
be called holy, marriage is considered sacred in Judaism.

*See his article, Unsere Gegenwart, (Our Present), 1844, pages
149-171, 231-258, 313-340.
†See my: Graetz's Geschichtsbauerei, Berlin, 1881, Issleib,
pages 88-108 and 79-83 ff.

In his definition of Reform he still clings to Mendelssohn's view on the ceremonial laws, with this modification only, that whenever laws have lost their meaning on account of the exigencies of the age, then God himself, who has changed the times, has, as it were, caused the change or abolition of those laws. This is very ingenious, but a little too far fetched. Holdheim thinks that the institution of marriage would lose nothing of its dignity by being placed under the supervision of the state.

Dr. M. Hess, a warm friend of Holdheim, also objected to his "Autonomy" on the ground that it was not radical enough.* Rabbi Hess claimed that, as long as Holdheim believed in supernatural revelation and the literal inspiration of the Bible, he had no right to separate the religious precepts from the political laws of Moses. The idea of revelation must be regarded more philosophically.

Samson Raphael Hirsch, the champion of uncompromising orthodoxy, attacked Holdheim strongly.† Holdheim replied in a dignified manner.‡ He informs Hirsch that it is necessary to concede the purity of motives, even in an opponent, and that he was too profuse with his unjust suspicions. According to Hirsch's arguments it would be a religious duty of the Jew to obey the behests of the state, even if the state should prohibit him from keeping the Sabbath and Holidays; from circumcising his sons and from honoring his parents. Holdheim gradually abandoned the great Rabbinical mistake of the equal validity of all the Mosaic enactments and laws.

Zacharias Frankel was another opponent. In the Geiger-Tiktin conflict, when the question came up as to whether the persons who rudely disturbed Geiger's

*See Hess's Israelit des 19. Jahrhunderts, 1845, No. 19.
†See Hirsch: Zweite Mittheilungen aus einem Briefwechsel ueber die neueste Juedische Literatur, 1842.
‡Holdheim: Literaturblatt zum Orient, 1844, No. 28, 29, 30, Zweite Mittheilungen, beleuchet von Holdheim, Schwerin, 1844; Das Ceremonialgesetz im Messiasreich by Holdheim, Berlin, 1845, pages 125-132.

ministrations at the cemetery were to be punished,
both Frankel and Holdheim decided in the affirmative,
as a cemetery is a sacred place according to the Jewish
law. (1842). But now he attacked in a most scurrilous manner not only Holdheim's "Autonomy," but
its author. His strictures are full of personalities and
resemble those of Graetz in his impartial "History."
And yet the bitterest invectives against Holdheim had
to be omitted, because the censor did not permit the
article to pass in its original composition.* Frankel
accuses Holdheim of being, like Bruno Bauer, a Jew
hater, a juggler, a traitor to our religion, who would
sell Judaism for a mess of pottage, i. e., for the advantage of the emancipation of the Jews, and, to cap the
climax, he calls him a liar and a denunciator. If
calling names could demolish a literary and religious
antagonist, then Frankel would most assuredly have
triumphed over his adversary. Holdheim replied in a
pamphlet entitled "The Religious and Political in
Judaism." (Schwerin and Berlin, 1845).† Holdheim's answer, though quite severe, was more dignified
than Frankel's. He begins his reply with the assertion that Frankel reproaches him with having committed two crimes, one of which is the opposite of the
other. Holdheim is accused of having sacrificed the
ideal advantages of Judaism to the material welfare of
the Jews, and in the same breath his utterances are
called "denunciations," which tend to injure the material interests of the emancipation of the Jews. The
fact, however, is, that he deems it necessary to give up
false religious conceptions in the interest of religion itself, even though material advantages may be connected with these innocent views, which is just the opposite of Frankel's insinuations. He shows that Frankel
had committed the mistake of S. R. Hirsch with regard
to Jewish jurisdiction. His onslaught on the authority

---

*See Frankel's Zeitschrift fuer the religioesen, Interessen des
Judenthums, 1844, Heft. V-VIII, and Hess's Isr., des 19. Jahrh's 1845,
page 56.
†The title of the pamphlet is rather lengthy.

of the Talmud and the Rabbis makes him as little an enemy of Judaism, like Eisenmenger, as have Luther's attacks on Popery made Luther an enemy of Christianity. The preservation and progressive development of Judaism is possible then only, when our religion is purified from false conceptions, which are bound to hurl it sooner or later into the open abyss.*

A correspondent from Prussia gives a very favorable review of this pamphlet.† He praises Holdheim's indefatigable efforts to develop, to grow and to rise to a higher religions standard. The want of decision and outspokenness which is one of the characteristic features of Frankel is laid bare in all its nakedness with a dignity which favorably distinguishes the enthusiastic friend of truth from the hero of mediocrity.

Raphael Kirchheim, of Frankfurt, took the same stand as Frankel in his criticism of Holdheim's "Autonomy,"‡ to which Holdheim replied. The controversy created such a sensation and set so many pens in motion, that the editor of the "Orient," Dr. Julius Fuerst, had to refuse place to many contributors on the subject. Able articles were written by Dr. I. Gebhardt, Rabbi in Wreschen, later in Bromberg, (Posen), Dr. Wessely, a lawyer in Prague; Leopold Zunz, Adolph Jellinek, then at Leipzig; Leopold Loew, to whom Holdheim replied in an article entitled "The Ceremonial Law and the Kingdom of the Messiah," Orient, pp. 150-52. A Hebrew pamphlet: "Answer to the Evil-doers, Holdheim and his Friends, in thirteen Letters," Frankfurt, A. D. 1844, by a certain S. M. Heilpern, of Poland, contains 72 pages, and is full of very ingenious ironical onslaughts. The writer conceals, to a certain extent, his own views, but prefers Bernstein's outspoken, rationalistic denial of revelation

---

*Holdheim: Das Religioese and Politische im Judenthum, p. 88.
†Israelit des 19. Jahrh's, 1845, March.
‡Orient, Literaturblatt, pages 321 ff 405 ff, and Isr.des 19. Jahrh's 1845, No. 29. See also Orient Ltbl., 1844, No. 2, and pages 444, 749, 1845, page 25 ff.

to Holdheim's belief in revelation, accompanied by his destructible and sarcastic criticism of the tradition, with his belief in the revelation.

Thus we are justified, in considering the "Autonomy of the Rabbis," the most prominent Jewish literary event of the year 1843.

In the Jewish community of Frankfort-on-the-Main a Reform-movement took place at that time which could not fail to create a great sensation. Frankfort was distinguished among the Congregations of Israel, not only by its wealth, but more so by the high degree of intelligence and culture of its Jewish citizens. This was due, to a great extent, to the "Philanthropin"* and its scholarly, progressive and enlightened teachers, who, through the instrumentality of the "Andachtssaal" have exerted a most powerful influence in the direction of Reform. Of renowned Jews of Frankfort I mention: Abraham Geiger, J. Johlson, M. Jost, Michael Creizenach, Jacob Auerbach, Raphael Kircheim, Jacob Weil, E. Carmoly, Siegmund Stern, Leopold Stein and M. Stern, who have become part and parcel of Frankfort Judaism. Since 1815 the "Andachtssaal" has become the rendezvous every Sabbath of all those Jews who constituted the educated classes. Hence the tidal wave of apostasy which had swept over Judaism in North Germany did not strike Frankfort to any great extent. Neither could religious indifference play such great havoc there as in other Jewish communities, because congregational life there was always active. Those things combined may, in some measure, account for the fact that the most radical Reform movement in modern Judaism had taken its start in Frankfort. History proves that wherever indifference reigns supreme, interest for Reform-Judaism is seldom found. Quite natural. We try to improve, to repair only those institutions in which we are interested. Those who care nothing for

---

*"Philanthropin" is the name of the Frankfurt Jewish "Real-Schule," which is presided over at present by Dr. Baerwald.

Judaism, the atheists, the agnostics and materialists
will always oppose Reform; in many cases they plead
the cause of orthodoxy, because orthodoxy gives them
a good excuse for keeping aloof from Judaism which
they do not consider worth while reforming.   Reform
would make it obligatory for them to labor in its cause,
and to offer sacrifices in its behalf—sacrifices of time
and money.   This accounts for the apparently surprising alliance we often meet with in history between
orthodoxy, atheism and materialism.   Talmudists will
recognize the phrase "Jireoo ad shejisstaavoo," which
was employed by the enemies of everything Jewish.
This phrase, the translation of which would necessitate
a detailed explanation of a complicated old sacrificial
law, conveys figuratively the idea, that, as Judaism
has no future, the sooner it goes to ruin the better.
Hence it would be foolish to try to galvanize and to
revive the corpse by attempt at Reform.   It is a well
known fact, that the Ethical Culture Movement, inaugurated by Prof. Felix Adler, with whom I sat at the
feet of Abraham Geiger in Berlin (1871-73) takes this
view of Judaism.   Hence it is easy to understand why
the learned Professor, in his arraignment of the Pitts-
burg Platform, 1886, sided with Orthodoxy against Reform.   History repeats itself.   This also accounts for
the fact that the Reform-movement is not more powerful than it is in Europe, although the majority of
modern Jews do not better observe the ceremonial laws
in Europe than in America.   It is simply more convenient to be let alone, or to pay dues to a Congregation, and to be done with the demands of Judaism by
attending the Synagogue once or twice a year.   Expressions such as "Why should I bother with Reform
of the worship, I attend service only on Rosh-
Hashana and Jom Kippur, any service will suit me
for two days," are the answers one receives in the
large cities of Europe from the majority of Jews, whenever one broaches the subject of Reform.

   After this digression I will state that in the
Frankfort of those days—I am sorry to say that things

have changed there also, considerably for the worse since that time—indifference to the cause of Judaism was almost unknown. There were three parties: the moderate reformers, the radical reformers and the strictly orthodox. The radicals formed, in the fall of 1842, the Frankfort "Society of the Friends of Reform." (Verein der Reformfreunde), and came out with the following declaration of principles :—

1.   We recognize, in the Mosaic religion, the possibility of an unlimited development.

2.   The collection of controversies, treaties and precepts, usually called "Talmud," has no authority whatever for us, neither dogmatically nor practically.

3.   We neither expect nor desire the advent of a Messiah, who would bring back the Israelites to Palestine; we recognize no father-land except the one to which we belong by birth or civil relation.

In the programme accompanying these resolutions the framers of the same say that the past attempts at Reform have proven too insignificant. They agree that their principles are only theoretical and negative. They emphatically protest against the insinuation that they had been actuated by a desire to gain civil privileges over those who still cling to the old orthodox notions.* They want to preserve the Mosaic faith against stagnation and decay. They do not intend to establish a new sect, or even to disrupt the Jewish community. Their platform simply gives expression to the views which are shared already by a great mass of Israelites and publicly protests against many things which the world had been accustomed to regard as belonging to the religious confession of the Jews. They do not mean to destroy, but to save the kernel and essence of Judaism, even at the expense of priestly-theocratic ceremonial laws.

These declarations were sent broadcast to the Israelites of Germany and other countries, but the

---

*Already in the time of David Friedleander accusations of this character were hurled by the orthodoxy against the advocates of Reform (See page 25-26 of this book.)

orthodox party did not take notice of them until a member of the Frankfort Reform-Society omitted the circumcision of his son on the strength of those declarations. Then the "Reform-Society" was looked upon by its opponents as an "Anti-Circumcision-Society."

Now a fearful hue and cry was raised by the old and new orthodoxy. Salomon Abraham Trier implored the aid of the Frankfort senate in order to enforce the circumcision of Jewish children and quoted the Choshen Mishpat, (Chapter XXXIV, 24), according to which a father who neglects the circumcision of his son is unfit to be a witness in a court of justice. But the senate refused to decide this purely religious question. Trier, following the example of the Hamburg orthodox Rabbi, in 1819, sent circular letters to Rabbis, requesting them to give their opinion on the subject of the "New Sect" and as to what should be done with a "man, who from wicked motives, does not permit his son to be circumcised." Forty-one Rabbis gave their opinion in favor of circumcision, but differed greatly as to the measures to be applied against recusants, some regarding them as atheists, others as Jews. It was surprising to many that Isaac Noah Manheimer, in Vienna, who had taken the part of Reform in the "Hamburg prayer-book controversy," had sided with the most fanatic orthodoxy on this question. He went further than Michael Sachs and Zacharias Frankel, although they expressed themselves quite forcibly on the subject. Manheimer called the neglect of circumcision on the part of a Jew "treachery," "breaking the covenant," and threatened the recusants with expulsion, refusal of Jewish burial and loss of salvation hereafter. S. D. Luzzatto, of Padua, condemned the "Reform-Society," although he concedes that the aim of Judaism is the establishment of a universal religion, and morality for the whole race.* S. L. Rappoport, F. Gruenebaum, S.

---

*Literaturblatt Orient 1843, No. 51.

R. Hirsch, M. Adler, A. A. Wolf, and even outspoken Reform-Rabbis like Samuel Hirsch, Einhorn, M. Guttman, and Leopold Stein were dissatisfied with the Reform-Society. Einhorn* complained that the Society was a disturbing element in the development of Judaism which, just then, was about to enter on a successful career. In a time when unity and harmony among the friends of Reform was so very necessary, the Frankfort Society was disrupting the forces with its anarchistic "Confession of Unbelief" (Unglaubensbekenntniss). Twenty-eight of the Rabbinical "decisions" on the question of circumcision were published in manuscript. (1844). Geiger, whose "Zeitschrift" was the indirect cause of the declaration of principles, and of the formation of the Reform-Society, could not agree with its methods. The only Rabbi who lent his aid and the columns of his paper to the uncompromising support of the Frankfort "Reform-Society" was Mendel Hess, the Land-Rabbi of Weimar and editor of the "Israelit. d. 19, Jahrh's." He too concedes that the platform does not appreciate the "sanctity of history," and decidedly underrates the "living development in the Rabbis of former ages," but in substance he agrees with the Society. "It is high time," he said, "to speak out our minds. The opponents claim that the 'declaration' does not say enough, but something is better than nothing, and it was a good beginning anyhow. The foundation has been laid." As to the reproach that the platform is merely negative he ingeniously answers that all those who "do not believe" that our religion is rooted in the spirit and ethical kernel of the Mosaic teachings are "negative." He sees, in the lack of definitive assertions and positive formulas of the declarations, a re-

*Einhorn was opposed to the course of the "Reform-Verein" mainly because he considered inopportune. In his decision on "circumcision" in the case of a father, who in 1847 at Teterow, in the Duchy of Mecklenburg-Schwerin omitted on principle, the circumcision of his son, he took the part of the father. He did the same in a similar case at Horic, Bohemia. See Einhorn "Sinai." (Vol. II 699-763, III, 796-955).

deeming feature rather than a cause of reproach.
The platform does not "disturb the peace." This is
always done by fanaticism. The plank on the Messiah
casts no suspicion on orthodoxy, which is by no means
indifferent to the interest of the fatherland. Gabriel
Riesser, Creizenach, Goldschmidt, and M. A. Stern
were strong supporters and enthusiastic members of
the Society. Riesser advocated the idea that no
father should be compelled to have his son circumcised. A neglect on his part in this respect should
not be accompanied by evil consequences, so far as
political or civil advantages are concerned. Freedom
of conscience, Riesser claimed, must be respected
under all circumstances. Leopold Zunz, in a pamphlet on the "circumcision,"* (1844) warns also
against church discipline and so-called penalties for
heresy. He recognizes as an Israelite him who has
not been circumcised and would not debar him from
the use of the Synagogue. But he regards the
circumcision, not as a ceremony but, as an "institution" which belongs to the essence of Judaism. It is
with regard to this decision of Zunz, that Geiger
wrote his famous letter to him in which he called the
circumcision "an act of barbarism."†

Under such circumstances, at a time when public
sentiment was so strong against the "Reform-Society
of Frankfort," it required great courage to come out
publicly in its favor. But Holdheim was the man to
do it.

He published a pamphlet: "On the Circumcision
in its Religious-Domestic Relations."‡ He formulates
the three following questions:

1. Is the circumcision of such great importance
for Judaism that a child, born of Jewish parents, but

---

*His characteristic words are: "A Jew who is uncircumcised is
an uncircumcised Jew." (Zunz Gesammelte Schriften 1875) Frankfurt, 1844.

†Geiger, Nachgel Schriften, Vol. V. page 181-182; also page 202-
203.

‡Schwerin and Berlin, 1844.

not circumcised, cannot be considered as belonging to Judaism?

 . 2. Is the father, who neglects the circumcision of his son, or he, who, though not circumcised when a child, neglects the performance of this act in later years, to be considered an Israelite?

3. What have the Jewish religious authorities to do in such cases of neglect of circumcision; can they directly or indirectly interfere in the matter; have they the right—where they have the power—to enforce the circumcision or to cause the authorities of the state to enforce it?

He ingeniously proves, from Genesis XVII, 14, that all those Rabbis, who see in this passage that circumcision holds the same position for the Jew as baptism does for the Christian, were grossly mistaken. "For," argues he, "if circumcision is the condition of allegiance to Judaism, how can he, who, born of Jewish parents, neglects the same, be threatened with the penalty of extermination for this transgression, when the whole ceremony concerns Jews only? How can such a one be called "destroyer of the covenant," when he did not yet belong to the covenant at all until he had been circumcised? This demonstrates beyond any doubt just the contrary of what Frankel, Manheimer and all the opponents of the Frankfort Society claimed; namely, that it is not the circumcision but the fact of being of Jewish parentage which makes the Jew, as far as law is concerned. "It is strange," he continues, "that Moses speaks once only of the Abrahamitic circumcision, not even mentioning it in the Ten Commandments; fixing no civil penalty for its neglect in the penal code; while the Sabbath is mentioned dozens of times as a "sign of the covenant." But even the Talmud† considers the circumcised Jew still a Jew. Hence circumcision is a ceremony only like many others. He arraigns Manheimer, who, though at one time an enthusiastic admirer of David

---

†Chulin 1. Abodah Sara 27, A.

Friedlaender, and Israel Jacobsohn, has gone over to the camp of the fanatic obscurants. The fact that circumcision may be performed on the Sabbath is no proof of its higher significance because the sacerdotal and sacrificial rites were also performed on the Sabbath, rites, the restoration of which Manheimer had excluded from the Messianic hopes.* The argument that during the Syrian persecutions the Jews became martyrs for the circumcision, proves no greater importance for this ceremony, as they had also become martyrs for the dietary and other laws. The antiquity of the ceremony proves nothing as it was practiced among other Oriental nations long before it was instituted in Israel, and demanded of them a greater sacrifice. It was and is still performed, not on children eight days old, but on adults. According to strict Rabbinical consistency Manheimer and his friends could also be excluded from the pale of Judaism on the plea of heresy. The fact, however, is that only the idolater who denies the belief in one God, is excluded from the fold by the Talmud.† He answers Manheimer most forcibly and gives him a lesson in religious tolerance. Manheimer, to the surprise of many, who would never have deemed him capable of penning such lines, said, in his "opinion" on the Frankfort Society, that if a Jew should intentionally neglect the circumcision of his son he would decline to register this boy in the books of matriculation; that he would not admit him to the confirmation and not permit him to be called to the Thorah; that he would refuse to perform the marriage-ceremony at his wedding and that he would not permit his body to be buried in a Jewish cemetery.

Holdheim sarcastically asks the Vienna preacher whether he thinks that things were now the same as in the middle ages, whether he has forgotten that a

---

*See page 139 of this book, Chapter V. "Gotthold Salomon" and Rabbinnische Gutachten ueber das Hamburger Gebetbuch," 1842, page 97.

†Chulin 5 a, Megilla 13 a, Maimonides on Idolatry II 4.

Jewish "religious authority, vested with worldly power, was, thank God, a thing of the past." The Schulchan Aruch, "a code, which has today archælogical and antiquarian interest only can no longer be made an object of practical jurisdiction. Do not condemn, do not accuse people of heresy, do not use force, if you do not want to be laughed at in your impotency as ignorant mountebanks. How can you dare to play the part of judges in the Judaism of to-day which recognizes only teachers? * * And why is it just the question of circumcision which has so resistlessly animated you with hierarchical and inquisitorial desires, that you seem to have lost all calm reflection? Do you not know that Rabbinical jurisdiction in former times was empowered to enforce not only the circumcision but the practice of every other Jewish ceremony?"

Holdheim recommends to Manheimer, Rappoport and their associates, the reading of the Boraitha Kethubot, 85, where it is ordered that he, who would neglect the observance of Succah and Lulab, should be punished with thirty-nine lashes for the first offence and be whipped to death for a continuation of the same.* According to "Sefer Hamizvoth" the same penalty ought to be applied to transgressors of every other observance. Holdheim then goes on to say, that such intolerance and attempted force in matters of conscience means a step backwards far behind Moses Mendelssohn, who has proven beyond the shadow of a doubt, that the Mosaic penal code had nothing to do with the Mosaic religion; that force is out of the question in matters of religious conviction. It is one thing to attack theoretically the "Frankfurter" and another thing to put into practice an opinion entertained against them, and to refuse them the privilege of registration and confirmation. The mere fact that a person desires to be confirmed in the Jewish religion is in itself proof sufficient that he wants to be a Jew in his own

---

*According to this very few Jews in America would escape whipping, not even the members and some of the Rabbis of "orthodox" Congregations.

way.* As to marriage it is a well-known fact that a Rabbi is superfluous in this matter from the Jewish point of view. Refusal of marriage and burial smacks entirely too much of Catholicism. The Rabbis of the Talmud, who even permitted non-Jews to be buried in a Jewish cemetery "for the sake of peace" were far more in accord with the spirit of our humanitarian age than the half-Reformers: Mannheimer, Sachs, Frankel and their associates. The resume of Holdheim's writings on this subject is that it is not the circumcision but the birth, which constitutes a necessary element of allegiance to Judaism; that hence the father and the son who have neglected this ceremony have not ceased to be Jews, and that the only mission of the Jewish teachers of religion is to—teach. There was, to my knowledge, only one other Rabbi who expressed himself even stronger than Holdheim on the subject of circumcision and that Rabbi was Dr. Abraham Geiger. It has become the fashion to consider Holdheim more of a radical Reformer than Geiger. Even Dr. Kohler,† in his lecture on "Geiger, Holdheim and Einhorn, the three pioneers of Reform-Judaism"‡ holds this view, but Geiger's ideas on Biblical criticism and circumcision show that he was, de facto, the most radical Reform-Rabbi of his time. In a letter to Zunz, written almost half a century ago Geiger designated the circumcision as "a barbarous, bloody act which causes anxiety to the father and a sickening feeling to the mother." He holds "that the rough idea of sacrifice, once connected with this rite had vanished in our days when the ceremony is based on custom and fear only, and for these we are not willing to build temples."§

---

*He who rejects the belief in idols deserves the name Jew (Megilla, 13 a; Chulin 5 a; Maim., Idolatry II 4).

†Dr. Kaufman Kohler, the worthy successor of his father-in-law Dr. Einhorn, is one of the most prominent leaders of Reform-Judaism in America. He is one of the very few American Rabbis, who are recognized as scholars by scientists in Europe.

‡Zeitgeist, 1880, page 173 and 190, ff

§Geiger: Nachgel. Schriften V. page 181-182.

In 1849 Geiger proposed, in a letter to a friend,
(Wecusler) to bless the mother in the presence of the
child, which ceremony might, in time, supplant circumcision—it will be dropped by and by—just as the
introduction of confirmation has done away with the
"foolery" of the Barmizvah.* Holdheim, however,
ranges the circumcision among the ceremonies which
are not of a "political-national," but of a religious nature and which, therefore, will always possess validity.†

The following most remarkable question, which
according to the Midhash, a heathen philosopher had
laid before Rabbi Hosaia, deserves a place in connection
with this subject. " If circumcision is of such great
importance, why then was it not enjoined on the first
man?" (Midrash Rabba, Genesis, chapter 10).

But Holdheim did not agree with the platform of
the " Frankfurt Reform-Society" in all points.‡ In
1845 Holdheim published the "Ceremonial Law in
the Kingdom of Messiah." The Talmud, he argues,
claims for the Mosaic law validity for all time to come,
the laws connected with Jerusalem, Temple service,
sacerdotal and sacrificial rites are simply suspended.
The consistent logical application of this system is the
basis of a thorough reform. He strongly criticises the
Rabbinical view of the validity of the ceremonial law
for all time to come and claims that it is inconsistent.
For, if it be true, that all heathens will become mono-
theists in the Messianic age, what then is the use of a
ceremonial law which separates Israel from the rest of
the nations? He also criticises Dr. Herzfeld, who, in
his sermons on the Messiah, claimed that the Talmud
itself advocated the abolition of the ceremonial law in

*Ibidem V, 205-203: "Bar-Mizvah" is celebrated by calling a 13-
years-old lad to the Thorah, in order to recite, parrot-like, two Hebrew benedictions, which he seldom understands.

†Holdheim: On the circumcision and Ritter: Samuel Holdheim,
page 159; note.

‡See Holdheim: Reden Ueber dd. Mosaische Religion fuer denk
hude Israeliten, Schwerein, 1844, where the Reform-Verein is criticised.

the time of the Messiah, which Holdheim denies. It is a weakness of modern Rabbis to shield their advocacy of liberal views on religion by quoting certain passages of Rabbis in the Talmud, which, in most cases, do not express the ideas which they are said to convey. It is much better to advocate liberal views, even in spite of the Talmud. God has abolished all laws connected with Palestine and the Temple in Jerusalem, by the fact that he has taken away the land from our ancestors and has permitted Jerusalem and the Temple to be destroyed.

Herzfeld in an open letter to Holdheim* replied that passages in the Talmud, such as "all ceremonies will lose their validity in the Messianic age;"† or "all holidays will cease at that time," cannot be gainsaid. It is no less true that a great many laws, observances, statutes and precepts have been revised, amended and even abolished by the Talmudists.‡ The sentiment of this century is also entitled to be called a revelation. Holdheim rejoined again,§ saying, that it is a delusion to make the people think that their religious sentiment and that of the Talmud, which is diametrically opposed to that of the prophets, were identical. We must not judge the Talmud by a few phrases of the Haggada, which had very little practical significance, but by the whole system and combination of the Halacha‖ and its practical conclusions. The Talmud has developed the political-na-

*Israelit des 19 ten jahrunderts No. 25 and 33.

†Nidsh. 61. "Mizvot betailot leathid lavau."

‡See Numbers 18,27 compared with Chulin 131, Lev. 26, 13 compared with Maaser Sheni 5, 15; Exod. 12, 2 compared with Shalsheleth-Hakkabalah 14; Exodus 21, 24 compared with Baba Kamma.

§Israelit des 19 Jahrhunderts, 1845, No. 45-50.

‖"Halacha" literally "way, rule," means a discussion and legal commentary on the "Law." It was gathered by Rabbi Jehuda Hanassi, about 200 B. C. Although Moses emphatically interdicted any addition the 613 laws of the Pentateuch, (Deut. IV, 2-5), they have been augmented to the number of 13,602. The final decisions, which the Rabbis and students had to commit to memory on account of their practical bearing, were called "Halacha." See my "The Talmud," (Denver, 1884), pages 17-18.

tional side of Judaism, the basis of our reform must be universal monotheism and the sacred laws of ethics. Holdheim doubtless meant what is called nowadays "ethical monotheism."

One of the ablest and most penetrating criticisms on Holdheim's "Ceremonial Law and Kingdom of the Messiah" was written by Dr. David Einhorn, Rabbi of Hopstaedten, near Birkenfeld.* He demonstrates philosophically and theologically by means of telling arguments and quotations that the Talmudists were not so inconsistent as Holdheim represented them to be. Dr. Bernhard Wechsler† calls attention to the fact that we owe a certain gratitude to the Talmudists for the reforms inaugurated by them, no matter what the motives might have been. Holdheim replied in No. 12-13 of the Israelit.

Holdheim was a very prominent figure in the " Rabbiner-Versammlungen," (Conventions of Rabbis) at Braunschweig, 1844, Frankfort-on-the-Main, 1845 and Breslau, 1846.

We have seen that the first public demonstration of Reform-Judaism was made by the " Frankfort Reform-Society." It was composed of highly intelligent and well educated Israelites whose aims were worthy, but whose undertaking failed, because it was not backed by Jewish theological scholarship, and hence laid itself open to justifiable criticism.

A far greater influence was exerted by the " Rabbinical Conventions," because the slow but sure path of science and research was their guide.

These conventions were of very great significance for the beneficial development and healthy growth of Reform Judaism. Graetz's ridiculing remark,‡ on the first Rabbinical convention is in full accord with his

---

*Literaturblatt Israelit d. 19, Jahrh. 1846, No. 37. 38. 40.
†Israelit d. 19. Jhrh's 1846, No. 3. "Reformen im Judenthum."
‡"At that time the fashion of conventions and meetings came in vogue. The establishment of railroads had facilitated travel to larger cities. Thus the call for a Rabbinical convention received attention." Graetz' "History of the jews," XI. page 560. An excellent histriography. The railroads did it all.

customary unjust conception of Reform-Judaism, but will hardly influence thoughtful men. While it was naturally not quite possible for these conventions to solve all religious problems, they have done much to popularize the Jewish Reform-movement, to stir up the wavering and indifferent Jews, and to guide progressive Congregations in doubtful questions of religion. They represented the Jewish scholarship and were attended by the pillars of progressive Rabbinism. That the meetings were public is a fact worthy of notice. Every member of the convention was bound to introduce practically the results of the convention in his respective Congregation. The debates were remarkable for the very advanced ideas held by some Rabbis, who gained courage in the company of so many enthusiastic colleagues and felt inspired by the electrifying power of the free word spoken in public. It was not yet time to formulate a "declaration of principles,"* and attention was given to the practical questions of the day. Thus the Mecklenburg "Synagogue-Ritual," composed by Holdheim, was sanctioned by the convention. The resolutions of the Paris Sanhedrin of 1807, concerning marriage and divorce were adopted and especially in the question of mixed marriages, a more advanced position was assumed. The Sanhedrin declared: "Marriages between Israelites and Christians are binding and valid from a civil point of view" and deemed it necessary to add "that although such marriages cannot be invested with the religious forms, they shall not entail any disciplinary punishment,† (Anathema). This clause was simply a clever evasion of the main issue, as Napoleon's question was entirely different from the one they answered. The Braunschweig conference

---

*See Geiger's: Sendschreiben zur Rabbinerversammlung in Braunschweig, 1844. Nachgelassene. Schriften I, page 197.

†"Bien qu'ils ne soient pas susceptibles d'etre revetus des formes religieuses, ils n'entraineront aucun anatheme." (A. E. Halphern: Recueil des Lois, Paris 1851, page 25). Geiger: Nachgel. Schriften 11, page 239. Dr. Mielziner: the Jewish Law of Marriage and Divorce. Cincinnati 1884, page 47-48). As the Cherem had at that time not the least authority in France, this declaration was nothing but a blind and was made for effect.

manfully and decisively declared as follows: "The intermarriage of Jews and Christians, and in general the
intermarriage of Jews with adherents of any of the
monotheistic religions, is not forbidden,* provided that
the parents are permitted by the law of the state to
bring up the offspring of such marriage in the Jewish
faith.† The motion of Holdheim to appoint a committee for devising timely Reforms of the Jewish law on
marriage, which was an amendment of a similar motion of Jolowicz, was carried, and Herzfeld, Geiger,
Maier, of Stuttgart, president of the Conference, Holdheim and Bodenheimer were chosen members of this
committee.   Bodenheimer's motion that the Conference protest against the oath More Judaico,‡ which cast
suspicion on the trustworthiness of a Jew, was also carried.   The beneficial result of this protest was practically shown in the fact that soon after the conference
the oath More Judaico was abolished in the Duchy of
Braunschweig.   Holdheim's resolution to abolish the
prayer "Ko Nidre," on account of the many false conclusions drawn from it concerning the sacredness of the
Jewish oath, was also carried.   Committees were also
appointed on Maier's resolution to consider and report
the needed reform of the prayer-book and liturgy, and
on Dr. Samuel Hirsch's motion concerning the "revision or abolition of numerous dietary and Sabbath
laws."

Next to Geiger, Holdheim was the most striking
figure in the conference.   An eye-witness praises in

---

*It is of interest to know that it was Philippsohn who moved this
resolution. Philippsohn porposed also the introduction of solemn
Sunday-services for the benefit of those who work on the Sabbath-
day. (See "Kley Noch ein Wort zur Israelitischen Reform frage"
Hamburg, 1845. page 26, note.)

†Protokolle der Rabbinerversammlang in Braunschweig 1844,
page 23.

‡Literally in accord with Jewish law. A Jew was not permitted to take an oath except in the Synagogue in presence of the
Rabbi, who had to admonish him regarding the sacredness of the
oath. In some places the scrolls of the law were taken from the ark,
during the solemn admonition, and the one who took the oath had
to be clad in the garments worn on the Day of Atonement.

particular his modesty and kindness, independence and earnestness. He never stubbornly insisted on his opinions, but modified them and stood corrected whenever the occasion demanded. Hess, Samuel and A. Adler, Herzfeld and others surprised the public by the boldness of their advanced views on prayer, ceremonies, dogma and Talmud. The Conference declared unreservedly, that the "right of living, progressive development is deeply rooted in the Synagogue." Holdheim justly remarks that this Conference has paved the way and given directions for all similar assemblies. *

A protest from seventy-seven orthodox and conservative Rabbis—their number was later swelled to 116—against the resolutions of the Braunschewig Conference had only the effect of calling greater attention among the large number of educated Jews to the Conference and its aims. The Conference was even honored with an old-fashioned Cherem.†

A foe worthy of the steel of such champions as Geiger and Holdheim arose in the Rabbinical Conferences in the person of Zacharias Frankel. He, like a shrewd general, gathered around himself all the reactionary and conservative elements of Judaism, who, while opposed to Reform-Judaism, were ashamed to sail under the flag of uncompromising orthodoxy as represented by Samson Raphael Hirsch and others. He opened wide the door for a by no means small class of people, who, vacillating and afraid of every decisive step, are always on the fence. I mean the so-called "Halben" (half-hearted men).

It cannot be denied that not a few of those called in the Talmud "Zabuim,"‡ (literally "colored" but de facto hypocrites), have found a convenient shelter in

---

*Israelit d. 19. Jhrh. Literaturblatt, 1846, No. 20, review of Herzfeld's resolutions on the Reform of the Jewish laws of marriage.

†An excommunication was hurled against the Braunschweiger Rabbinerversammlung by the Rabbi Schreiber of Krakau, Galicia.

‡It means, "sail under different colors." A passage in the Talmud reads as follows: "Fear not the Pharisees, nor the Sadducees; we know them, but fear the 'colored' ones who act like Simri and demand reward like Pinehas."

the party led by Frankel, a party which to-day is powerful in Germany and is the cause of the decline of Judaism there. Starting from the basis of the "Volksbewusstsein," (sentiment of the people), claiming that, whatever is still living in the consciousness and sentiment of the people, must not be given up, Frankel, without offering proofs, jumped to the false conclusion that the people are conservative. He said that as soon as the people reject the Hebrew prayer, they must be given another language of prayer, even though the Hebrew prayer were recommended by the earliest teachers of the Mishna. He failed, however, to prove his bigoted assertion that the people are in favor of the old traditional customs. Judging from the fact that within the last five decades the Jews, not only in America, but even in Europe, have discarded most of the ceremonial laws, every unbiased observer must come to the conclusion that the sentiment of the masses, the "Volksbewusstsein," is rather opposed to the conservation of every old usage. Frankel, as a man of science, wielded a greater influence than the uncompromising and fanatic representatives of orthodoxy in Frankfort, Berlin or Vienna. But Frankel was half-hearted in whatever he advocated, whether it was a progressive or retrogressive measure. Therefore Geiger, Holdheim, Hess and their associates who wanted essence and not semblance, firm principle and not transient sentiment, mercilessly attacked his propositions, which they designated as lacking in firmness, manliness, consistency and character, and in which they saw attempts at introducing a hierarchy into Judaism.

Frankel attempted to usurp the role of the public lawgiver, censor and infallible Pope. He acted as if no one who differed from him could be influenced by pure motives. He blamed the Conference, which he himself had not attended, for having held their meetings in public, which criticism was in full accord with his lack of manliness and his hierarchal notions. Holdheim published a strong rejoinder under the title: "The first Rabbinical Conference and Dr. Frankel."

True to his method in controversy, he attacks Frankel
with his own weapons. He shows Frankel's inconsistencies in the most glaring light. Frankel claims
on the one hand, that the "sentiment of the people" is
the sole criterion for the justification of reforms, yet he
accuses the Reform-Rabbis of Jesuitical laxity, as soon
as they yield to the "sentiment of the people" and
abolish a ceremony which has lost its hold on this very
sentiment.* Holdheim condemns, in strong terms,
Frankel's dictatorial attempt to call a halt to those
who go further than he, and to fasten upon them impure motives. What right, he asks, has Frankel to
abolish the "Second Holiday," the "Meziza"† after
the circumcision, to modify mourning customs, to permit the eating of legumes on Passover if the "sentiment of the people" has to be considered? If Frankel
considers the sentiment of the ignorant, the reformers
have a right to consider that of the intelligent and educated people whose sentiments run in another channel.‡

On March 8, 1845, an appeal to the "Second Rabbinical Conference" to convene July 15th at Frankfort-
on-the-Main, was sent out by a committee, at the head
of which was Dr. Leopold Stein. In the meantime
Holdheim published his propositions concerning a Reform of the Jewish laws on marriage, and his studies
on the character of the Rabbinical oath. The liturgical and ritual question took up almost the whole
time of the second Conference. The attendance was
larger than it was at Braunschweig, and several Congregations sent to the Conference letters of congratula-

*See Frankel: Ueber Die projektirte Rabbinerversammlung in
the "Monatsschrift fuer diereligioesen Interessen des Judenths."
(Juni, 1844), "Die Rabbinerversammlung in Braunschweig, November, 1844; "Die Symptome der Zeit., (January, 1845).

†"Mezizah" is called that disgusting performance after the circumcision, when the Mohel sucks the blood, by which contagious
diseases are often imparted to the poor, suffering child

‡See on this subject: "The First Rabbinical Conference and its
Foes," by Dr. Mayer, President of the Conference; Frankel: Letter
to Dr. Mayer, Stuttgart and Salomon "The Rabbinical Conference
and Its Tendency," Hamburg, 1845.

tion, expressing hearty sympathy with its objects and ideas. The Reform-Society of Frankfort, and of a similar organization, just then started in Breslau, expected of the Conference more than it could reasonably do; inasmuch as it was the main purpose of the Conference to influence the whole community of Israel in the direction of Reform, and inasmuch as it had to contend not only with the opposition of the ultra-orthodoxy, but also with that of Frankel and his followers. The Frankfort-Society published a "third circular letter," (Drittes Rundschreiben). The "Breslau-Society" sent an address accompanied by 168 signatures, in which they asked of the Conference the abbreviation of the prayers, introduction of the vernacular and revision of the Sabbath laws. The Berlin Reform-Society was represented by three delegates, Dr. S. Stern, A. Bernstein (Rebenstein) and Simion. No less than twenty-two letters were addressed to the Conference. As can be seen from all this, the Convention at Frankfort had to contend with greater difficulties than that held at Braunschweig. The Conference lasted from July 15th to July 28th and had eighteen meetings, six of which were devoted to the question of the ritual, especially the language of prayer. The report of Dr. Maier on the liturgy was in the main accepted, German prayers and hymns, the use of the organ during divine service were not only permitted, but strongly recommended. A heated discussion took place on the question of the use of the Hebrew language in the service, which caused the withdrawal of Frankel from the Conference. He claimed that the retention of the Hebrew in the ritual is not only opportune and advisable, but necessary, legal and religious. The majority however, among whom were Geiger, Einhorn, the two Adlers, Holdheim, Salomon, Auerbach, Kahn and Maier, declared that the Hebrew language as the language of prayer, is neither legally nor absolutely necessary. These Rabbis added, however, that inasmuch as Congregations were not yet ripe for a total abolition of the Hebrew in the worship, it is opportune as an accommodation of the Congregation to retain for the present certain parts of the Hebrew service, but that it should be best to introduce a strict German Ritual as soon as the Congregations are ripe for it. Holdheim stated that the Hebrew language, far from being now a national bond of the Jews, is at present rather an impediment and check to the development of our religious life. Were Frankel right, then the Jewish law would not have permitted us to pray in any language but the Hebrew. Adler warned the people not to be guided in such important questions by sentiment but by truth. Talk about the holiness of the Hebrew language! What makes a language holy? Surely not the form, but its essence. A hypocrite and liar who prays in Hebrew desecrates this language, and he who expresses the purest and noblest sentiments in a German prayer sanctifies that language by its spiritual character. The fear that our Biblical literature would vanish from our midst, as soon as Hebrew ceases to be the language of prayer, is idle. The works of Homer and Hesiod are not forgotten, although people do no longer pray in Greek. It is not the language which immortalizes a work of genius, but vice versa.* As to the argument that the unity of Israel would be imperilled by the abolition of the Hebrew Ritual, he must answer that it is not the common language, but the common religion, the common confession of faith which truly unites the Israelites all over the globe. But there are weighty reasons for the introduction of the vernacular tongue in the divine service. It would do away with that lip-service which Isaiah so strongly condemned. It would stimulate the reading and studying of the Bible in the vernacular, while at the present time the people neglect the study of the Scripture in Hebrew as well as in German.

---

*He could also have added that the Bible is being studied more zealously among the Christians, though they do not pray in Hebrew, than among the Jews, who do pray in Hebrew. Two magazines are published by American Christians for the purpose of fostering the study of Hebrew.

Frankel withdrew from the Conference as soon as he saw himself defeated by the majority, and convoked a Conference of his own, which failed, however, to materialize. The Frankfort Conference recommended also the elimination from the prayer-book of every allusion to a political Messiah and to the sacrificial cult. Some minor matters on the abolition of Mikvah* and other laws concerning women, reports on the Sabbath question, on a home prayer-book, were partly discussed, partly consigned to committees for the next Conference.

The Third Rabbinical Conference was held in Breslau, July 13 to July 24, 1846. Holdheim at that time Rabbi of the Berlin Reform Congregation took a most radical stand on the Sabbath-question and declared in favor of its transfer to Sunday, wherever it has outlived the sphere of its usefulness and has succumbed in the struggle against the demands of life. He advocated this theory on the principle that the preservation of the Jewish religion is of far greater import than the claim of a certain day. In an "Open Letter" on the Third Rabbinical Conference,† he goes so far as to reproach the Conference, because it had not recommended a transfer of the Sabbath wherever such a radical change was identical with a restoration of a dignified and impressive celebration of divine service.

Quite a number of Holdheim's publications were the immediate result of the Rabbinical Conference. "The Oath in the Old Rabbinism"‡ was published by him in consequence of the abolition of the "Kol-Nidre-Prayer"§ by the Conference in Braunschweig. He stated, in this article, that the Rabbinical conception cannot be fully acquitted of the reproach that by its permission to annul a vow or an oath it encourages, to

---

*"Mikvah" is Hebrew, and means a ritual bath.
†Israelit d. 19, Jahrh's 1846, No. 46-48.
‡Isr. d. 19 Jahrh, 1844, No. 35 and No. 41.
§Israelit 1844, No. 47: Kircheim's reply to Dr. Holdheim; Israelit 1845 No. 2, Holdheim's answer to Einhorn; Orient 1845, No. 41, Holdheim against Kircheim.

some extent, a certain unconscious laxity with regard
to an oath. He reproached Frankel with having
rather concealed than uncovered the whole truth on
the subject of his book, "The Oath of the Jews."
This created a very animated controversy between
Holdheim, Einhorn, Kirchheim, Frankel and Rappoport. Frankel and Rappoport called him the worst
names and represented him as a bitter enemy of the
Jews, as a malicious slanderer and spiteful defamer of
Israel.

Rappoport even insinuated that all Holdheim
aimed at was the abolition of the Kol-Nidre-Prayer in
his Congregation in Schwerin, while it was *de facto*
abolished long before the publication of Holdheim's
articles on the oath of the Jews. Holdheim justly remarks that an attack on the Talmud must not
necessarily be prompted by hatred against Judaism,
but that an impartial, unbiased criticism of the Talmud can, in no way, affect the morality of the Jews.

Holdheim's "Propositions for a Timely Reform of
the Jewish Laws on Marriage," (Schwerin, 1845), were
laid before the "Second Rabbinical Conference." They
contain ideas similar to those expressed in his
"Autonomy." He claims that marriage and divorce
are simply civil acts from the Jewish point of view and
therefore badly in need of a reformation. He pleads
for the abolition of Chalizah, which has no meaning
for our times. He discussed the same important subject on the occasion of the Third Rabbinical Conference
with regard to Herzfeld's propositions.* He criticises
Herzfeld's proposition that the Kohanim (priests)
should no longer be prohibited from marrying a
divorced woman, but that they should be bound to
marry women of good moral reputation.† Every
privilege of a special priesthood ought to cease. Marriages forbidden to the priests should be forbidden to
all Israel or not at all.

*Israelit d. 19 Jahrhunderts, 1846, No. 20-21.
†Protokolle der Zweiten Rabbinerversammlung, page 334-348.
See Talmud Sabbath, 35, Maimonides Hichoth Talmud Thorah, I, 31

With regard to S. Adler's Hebrew essay on the
position of woman in Judaism, Holdheim published
"The Religious Position of Woman in Talmudical
Judaism," (Schwerin, 1846). He cannot agree with
Adler, that the Talmud prohibits woman on account
of her lack of earnestness from taking part in religious
worship. Women were placed in the same category
with slaves, deaf-mutes and little children.* They
were even excluded from reading the Shmah on Sabbath-and Holidays. Adler is right in declaring that
women are entitled to complete a quorum† for the
divine service, but it is vain endeavor to try to find
this artificially in the Talmud. Not even Adler's
great Talmudical scholarship could succeed in proving
this, simply because it is impossible to find our modern
religious sentiments and consciousness in the Talmud.

Another important publication is Holdheim's:
"The Principles of a Ritual, in Harmony with the
Present Religious Consciousness.‡ In May of the same
year he was asked by the Congregation of Toeplitz,
Bohemia, concerning his views on the abolition of the
Second Holiday. It is needless to say that he declared
in favor of the Reform.

In the meantime the Reform-Movement entered a
quarter from which it had been forcibly banished two
decades before by the order of the government, I mean
Berlin, where Mendelssohn, Friedleander, Jacobsohn
and Zunz had labored. Since the enforced closing of
the Jacobsohn Temple in 1823 by authority of King
Frederic William III, Jewish orthodoxy in Berlin has
had full sway, because it was justly regarded by the
Christian "pietistic" party as the best ally in its prose-
lytizing schemes. Even to-day, in this free country the

*See my article: "The Schulchan-Aruch and Rabbinical Law on
the Position of Women," Jewish Reformer, 1886, New York, No. 15,
reprinted in the "Jewish Spectator."

†Ten men constitute a quorum in a Synagogue (Minjan), but
even 10,000 ladies according to Schulchah-Aruch cannot form a
quorum.

‡Israelit d. 19. Jhrh's 1846, No. 8-13, 24-31.

missionary-fiends, mainly recruiting themselves from
Russian-Polish Jews, and the conversionists do all their
business in the Russian-Polish Jewish Ghettos of New
York, Philadelphia, Baltimore, Chicago and other large
cities. There existed in Berlin, so far as Judaism was
concerned, only uncompromising orthodoxy and indifference. With the ascendency to the throne of Frederic
William IV, a more liberal spirit made its entrance
into Berlin. This fact was proven by the victory of
Geiger in Breslau against Tiktin and other enemies of
progress, who tried their utmost to influence the government against the Frankfort Reformer. Naturally
the progressive element in Berlin considered the moment opportune for action. Even the administration
of the Berlin Congregation made the attempt to secure
for the Rabbinate a man of modern education in the
person of Dr. Zacharias Frankel, Chief-Rabbi of
Dresden. But Frankel did not accept the call, because he wanted to be Chief-Rabbi with full power to
act in all things pertaining to the spiritual affairs of the
Congregation. Thus Dr. Michael Sachs, of Glogau,
preacher in Prague, was called to Berlin, not as Rabbi
but as "Rabbinate-Assessor." He could drown the audience in a vast sea of flowery phrases, never ending periods, and romantic, mystic effusions. His Talmudic-
al-Rabbinical knowledge was, however, limited.
Sachs proved a fanatic of the worst type against Jewish
Reform and Reformers, so much so that his too marked
zeal was looked upon by many Reformers as artificial
and not quite sincere. His was a romantic nature; his
eye was dimmed by the mist of mystic illusions and therefore blind to the requirements of the new age. He could
have done great things in Berlin had he lived less in
the past and more in the practical present.* The fact
is, that the election of M. Sachs by the Berlin Congregation did not prove a fortunate acquisition, for the
conflict within the Congregation, instead of decreasing,
extended in intensity. The progressive element,

---

*See my Graetz's Geschichtsbaueri; Berlin, 1881, page 84-88.

which was utterly ignored in the whole affair, protested to no avail against the hasty election.* Of what benefit was the sermon to them if it was used as a weapon against progress and Reform? The same orthodoxy which triumphantly had pointed to the cabinet-ordinance of 1823 prohibiting the Jewish sermon in pure German, found all of a sudden in Sachs their mouthpiece. The German sermon which so long had been condemned as a Reform, was taken in the service of orthodoxy against Reform and Reformers. All gushes of verbosity, all the tinsel of glittering platitudes, all outbursts of sentimentality, all the ballast of Rabbinical quotations could not conceal the fact that the prayers were recited without feeling, thought and sentiment, and that the pulpit did not even attempt to become a power for good in the cause of progress and enlightenment.

The worship in the Synagogue, the system of education of the young, so far as Judaism was concerned, was worse in the large Jewish community of Berlin than in the smallest provincial town of Bavaria, Wuertemberg, Hessen or Baden.

In consequence of this sad state of affairs several influential heads of families in Berlin resolved to form a society of their own and to devise ways and means towards the realization of their hopes of perpetuating Judaism in its essential purity among their children. Dr. Siegmund Stern delivered a course of lectures,† which electrified the large audiences and filled them with new enthusiasm for Judaism and its glorious future. These lectures created a profound sensation, not because of their originality of ideas,—for the ideas were not new,—much less because of the deep scholar-

---

*The election of preacher took place in accord with an old regulation of 1750 and was contested. No less than two hundred of the most prominent and influential members of the Congregation have signed a document, which energetically pointed out the consequences of this step.

†See two volumes of these lectures on: "The Religion of Judaism" and "The Task of Judaism" (Die Mission des Judenthums," and "Die Aufgabe des Judenthum's," Berlin, 1845-46.

ship contained therein, but on account of the popular
attractive style, the wonderful delivery with which
Stern presented to the people the ideas, sentiments,
thoughts and feelings which so fully and fittingly expressed their own convictions. The success of those
lectures is mainly due to the time of their delivery, and
to their appeal to that which moved and filled the
heart of the audience. "Worte, die vom Herzen
kommen, gehen zum Herzen." They have reawakened
the pride of the Jews in their glorious past and
future and filled them with new enthusiasm for the
sublime mission of Judaism. Religion and life, said
Stern, are not, cannot and must not be in conflict, and
a religion not in harmony with the demands of life is
not religion, but pietism. This conflict is only apparent, not real. Judaism does not reject the justifiable and urgent claims of the progressive age, but ap-
preciates and recognizes them. Reform is aggressive
against those only who try to conceal the existing conflict between the present and past religious conception
of Judaism. We have to come out openly and boldly
before our co-religionists with our sentiments, feelings,
opinions, wants and urgent demands. Aside from these
lectures, Stern published essays: "Judaism as an
Element of the State-Organism," and, "The Present
Movement in Judaism, its Justification and its Significance."*

Stern's lectures were concluded on February 15th,
1845, and in the beginning of March meetings were
held for the purpose of forming a "Religious Association" on the basis outlined by Stern. A committee of
three was appointed to formulate an "Appeal to our
German co-religionists," in which the tendencies of
the new association should be clearly defined. Stern
and Holdheim give Bernstein due credit for having
greatly contributed towards making the "appeal"
largely instrumental in bringing about the wonderful
success attending the same. The appeal was published

---

*See Freund's Monatsschrift: Berlin 1845.

April 2, 1845, and avoided the fatal mistake of the "Frankfort Program" by laying the main stress on positive conviction, religious fervor and enthusiasm. The appeal was signed by thirty prominent Israelites of Berlin. No less than twelve of them were Doctors of medicine or of philosophy, a title which in Germany is indeed a proof of superior knowledge and higher education.

The appeal gives a graphic description of the existing conflict between inner religion and the outward form of its representation. It says: The consequences of this deplorable state are: Skepticism, indifference, pain and fear lest the rising generation should throw away both the shell and the kernel, the husk and the fruit. It is now high time for action. Before it is too late, steps must be taken to save the essential and important parts of Judaism at the expense of its dead, antiquated and superfluous forms and ceremonies. We yearn for a larger faith, we yearn for Judaism, we yearn for positive religion. We cling firmly to the spirit of the sacred Scripture. We cling firmly to the conviction, that Judaism will become the future religion of mankind. But we want to destroy the citadel of the dead letter, we do not want to pray for an earthly Messianic Kingdom, we do not care to observe forms which belong to the dead past. Imbued with the sacred essence of our religion we cannot maintain it in its inherited form, much less bequeath it to our posterity. And thus placed between the graves of our fathers and the cradles of our children, we cannot be deaf to the voice of the age calling upon us, the last ones of a great heritage, to be the first ones who shall lay the foundation for a new structure for us and for our generations yet to come. We advocate no secession, no breaking away, from the Jewish Community at large, no schism, no split, but unity is our motto. We call upon all those who think as we do to unite with us in truthfulness, in perseverance in our struggle, and in fidelity to ourselves."

This appeal could not fail to create a great sensation in modern Israel, not only in Berlin, but wherever the Berlin papers were read. Six months after its appearance no less than fifty-one Jewish organizations of Germany had given their joyful consent to the declarations, and many Rabbis and Jewish scholars had expressed their appreciation of and full sympathy with the movement. The manifesto fell like a bombshell into the camp of the romantic-orthodox school, which was suddenly made to realize that it did not control the field in the capital of Prussia. The fact that the movement for a thorough Reform originated within the Jewish Congregation of Berlin, and was backed by the best representatives of Jewish culure, naturally caused great consternation among the open and secret enemies of Reform. For the first time substantial proof was offered, that the ideas of progressive Rabbinism* were shared by the intelligent and cultured members of Jewish Congregations in Germany. The manifesto and its effect was a blow to Frankel and his consorts, who sneeringly exclaimed that the "religious consciousness of the people" (Volksbewustsein) was decidedly against Reform.

Quite a number of Congregations and individuals had joined the Berlin movement, and even Conferences of deputies preparatory to a Synod were held. The new Congregation increased rapidly, so that in a short time it numbered in Berlin alone two thousand souls. The second day of April, 1845, saw the foundation of the "Reformgenossenschaft." June 4, 1845, it was resolved to compile a temporary prayer-book for the approaching Holidays, and in a short time Stern, Bernstein, Simion and Lesser accomplished this work with great credit to themselves. The effect of the first service was so overwhelming, that it was resolved to have instead of a temporary a regular divine service, which resolution was carried into effect April 2, 1846.

---

*Geiger, Holdheim, Einhorn, Samuel Hirsch, Samuel and A. Adler, Hess, Wechsler and others.

Dr. Stern's impressive recitation of the prayers, the
music under the direction of Professor Julius Stern,
the excellent organ, the inspiring sermons of visiting
Rabbis tended to create enthusiasm for Judaism, not
only among the members of the new Congregation,
but among the visitors, many of whom attended the
services only from curiosity. The service was in the
main in German. Very few Hebrew sentences* were
in use. In sentiment, thought and feeling the worship was thoroughly Jewish, though not Palestinian.
The uncovering of the head during prayer created
more opposition at the beginning than all the other
Reforms. The Reader recited the prayers in an
oratorical form without any melody, the choir, composed of men and women, executed the singing part.
Geiger, Samuel Hirsch,† Gotthold Salomon and Frankfurter took active part in the arrangement of the new
prayer-book. All prayers expressing the hope of a return to Jerusalem, the restoration of the sacrificial
rites, and the transfer of the merits of the ancestors to
posterity were omitted. The spirit of sacrifice, which
is so strong in modern Israel, and the priesthood of all
Israelites found emphasis in the prayer-book. Israel's
mission among the nations was forcibly expressed, as
was the idea of the Messiah in its historical significance
in accord with the prophetical conception of the
Messianic age. Instead of lamenting the fall of Jerusalem a Thanksgiving-prayer was substituted expressive
of the sublime mission with which Israel was entrusted.
During the Holidays Dr. Philippsohn,‡ of Magdeburg,
delivered the sermons, six in number. The effect of
the solemn service silenced all opposition and hostility.
The future of the Congregation was safe and the

---

*Shmah, Kadosh and a few more.

†In a conversation held with him December, 1888, in Chicago, he
informed me, that the resolution passed by the Reform Genossenschaft to worship with uncovered head is due to his work. I refer
to my articles in the "Jewish Reformer," 1886, on this subject.

‡Philippsohn was in those days more radical than in later years.
He was in 1846 in favor of Sunday-services.

Minister of Prussia Eichhorn felt so friendly inclined towards it that no danger threatened from that side.

On the 2nd of April, 1846, a permanent service was instituted in a hall with a seating capacity of more than one thousand persons, and solemnly dedicated by Holdheim, whose sermon was published. (Berlin, 1846, Behr). Holdheim dwelt on the passage of the first appeal: "We yearn for a larger faith, we yearn for Judaism, we yearn for progressive religion."

The Reform Congregation tried hard to induce Geiger to accept the position of Rabbi. But he answered that he would not be the Rabbi of a part of the Jewish community. In accord with a resolution of September 10, 1846, Holdheim was called as Rabbi of the Berlin Reform-Congregation, and he accepted. Thus Holdheim left a position in a state where Judaism enjoyed the same official privileges as did Christianity. He gave up a position of "Land-Rabbi" which was paramount to that of a Bishop in the Church, and which was duly recognized by the government. When we bear in mind that in exchange he accepted a position in a society which had not even the privileges of an average Jewish Congregation, which was merely tolerated, and was looked upon with suspicion and distrust from all sides, we cannot help admiring his courage, firm principles and great self-confidence.

At this juncture it is desirable to point out the most distinguishing characteristic of the Berlin Reform-Congregation, a characteristic which no doubt was the cause of so little imitation outside of Berlin. This is its position on the Sabbath question, in which Holdheim had no part. The question of Sunday services had been settled in that Congregation long before Holdheim took charge of the Congregation, and Holdheim did not like the idea of abolishing the Sabbath services. He expressed himself on this subject as follows: "Concerning the Sabbath service, the prophecy of Dr. Bressler, that it would not be able to maintain itself and that the Sunday would be its heir, has also been fulfilled."* In the Third Rabbinical Conference in Breslau (1846), Holdheim had favored the idea of a transfer of the Sabbath, where it is necessary for the sake of saving our religion from certain destruction.† His speech at the Conference on the Sabbath question created a great sensation. He said: "The main idea of the Mosaic Sabbath is the word 'shavath,' i. e. rest. * * * The public sacrifice on the Sabbath was double as large as that of every day. Beyond this the law knows of no other way of celebrating the Sabbath. But rest is strongly urged, and to labor on this day is most severely prohibited.‡ Even apparently necessary and insignificant labors like the gathering of mannah, and the making of fire were forbidden."

He then shows that the Mosaic law does not enjoin the celebration of the Sabbath by divine service. It was only in the later course of historical development, in the prophetical, and more so in the Talmudical period, that aside from the negative side of the Sabbath by rest, a positive, active celebration, consisting of the reading of the Scripture and of divine worship, was introduced. Hence from the Mosaic point of view rest on the Sabbath was indeed a confession of Judaism, and the desecration of the Sabbath by labor was paramount to denial by act of the fundamental doctrines of the Jewish faith.§ Now our modern age, he continues,

---

*Holdheim: "History of the Jewish Reform-Congregation of Berlin," (Berlin, 1857, page 180).

†Protokolle der Rabbinerversammlung in Breslau 1846,page 159-73; See also Holdheim's "Predigten Ueber die Juedische Religion," Berlin, 1853, Vol. I, page 277.

‡Exodus XXXI, 14-15; Numbers XV, 32-36.

§Exod. XX, 8-11; Gen. XI, 2-3. Exod. XXXI, 12-17; Levit. XIV, 3-4; Ezech.XX, 16-20; XXIII 36-39. Three reasons: 1, God as Creator of the world: 2, God's Covenant with Israel: 3, Redemption from slavery of Egypt, are given for The Sabbath observance. According to this the Jews of America have given up long ago the Sabbath. And the so-called "Conservatives" are no better in this respect than the Reformers. These are and remain stubborn facts. See Dr.Samuel Hirsch's telling answer to the U. A. H. C., to the question as to what could be done towards arousing interest in American Judaism. (Report of U. A. H. C., 1886, page 1026).

does not share this view. The Israelite of our day who works on the Sabbath, does by no means deny the truth of his religion. Were this the case, then the great majority of the Jews in large cities would be heretics. The celebration of the Sabbath by mere rest from labor, as Mosaism will have it, does not convey to us the true idea of the Sabbath. For mere idle rest on the Sabbath cannot lift us up religiously or morally. Rest per se is for us only the means and condition for a celebration of the Sabbath by a spiritual elevation. Now as to the question what kind of labor is to be prohibited on the Sabbath, the answer is at hand. While from the Biblical point of view every labor disturbing the Sabbath-rest is prohibited, we from our point of view ought to prohibit every work which disturbs the Sabbath celebration. The Rabbinical Conference of Frankfort has given up the sacrificial worship, by eliminating every allusion to sacrifice from the prayer-book. In doing this the Conference has placed the higher conception of prayer above the outward symbols of bloody sacrifices. Has the Conference thus placed itself in opposition to the Bible? No. It simply maintains the view of a historical development. I also am not afraid to come before you with the expression of the last consequences of my opinion, although I shall not put it in the shape of a motion. I know full well that the large majority of the Jews will repudiate my words with indignation. But truth and conviction have a right to be heard in our convention. All our endeavors toward the restoration of a worthy celebration of the Sabbath are, alas, in vain, and there exists no thorough remedy, to harmonize the conflict between the celebration of the Sabbath and the demands of civil life, except the transfer of the Sabbath to a civil day. I protest against any concession to Christianity which might be inferred from this. I have only in view the possibility of a dignified celebration of the Sabbath. The wounds from which the religious life suffers, cut deep into the heart of each of us, and we will stand in need of good council

234 REFORMED JUDAISM.

and advice until the time shall have arrived which will
pronounce the only possible remedy."

Characteristic is Holdheim's argumentation on
this question from the basis of the Talmud. According to the Rabbis of old, the Sabbath laws have to
yield wherever and whenever a human life is in danger. Now, argues he, inasmuch as the Sabbath
is defeated in the great struggle against modern life,
the duty of self-preservation imperatively demands its
transfer to another day, in order to save it from
certain death. He claims that only they who observe
the Sabbath are justified in their protest against the
transfer of the Sabbath, because for them religion is not
imperilled, inasmuch as the Sabbath comes out a victor in its battle with life. Those not celebrating the
Sabbath are wrong in their opposition to a transfer,
because for them religion is in danger. They de facto
abolished the Sabbath, they do negatively, what the
friends of the transfer are doing, namely: They do not
observe the historical Sabbath. But they have to do
some positive act, provided they do not want to be utterly estranged from our religion. He proves from examples of Jewish history that such transfers had
been made without the least harm to religion, as in the
case of the Passah-sacrifice in the interest of those who
were unclean or in a far country. The Sabbathical
year and the year of Jubilee, which were based on the
Sabbath idea, have not been celebrated in the last two
thousand years. Yet this has done no harm to Judaism. While in this address he still maintains that
"the Sabbath has a determining influence on the preservation of religion," he goes a step further in his
sermons published in 1852 and 1853, in which he treats
the Sabbath as a "ceremony and institution" like other
ceremonies and institutions, which are subject to
change as soon as they do not fulfill their task and mission. "Judaism is not embodied in the Sabbath. The
Sabbath is a ceremony, an institution, one of the many
ways leading to the aim of sanctity, but it is neither
the only way nor the aim itself. *   *   *   The

embodiment of Judaism is solely and merely its ethical law. The precept: Holy ye shall be, for holy am I the Eternal, your God. * * We see in the Sabbath a day for our self-sanctification, but by no means the symbol and sign of our covenant with God. * * The celebration of the seventh day historically handed down to us is in conflict with all the relations of our civil life. Were Judaism embodied in the Sabbath, then we would have to sacrifice our life for that day. But this is not the case according to our conviction. * * The Sabbath is not the body of Judaism, without which it can not live. It is one of the many institutions which have undergone a change in the course of time. * *

Temple, sacrificial and sacerdotal service stood at one time higher than the Sabbath, and wherever they clashed with each other the Sabbath had to yield.* The temple evolved into the house of worship, the sacrifice into the prayer, the priest into the teacher. * * And so the Sabbath-celebration of the seventh day is transferred to another day of the week. * *

Shall Judaism, which has already experienced such manifold changes of form without injury to its life, die on account of this single change of a day? No. We think nobler, better of the divine power of Judaism. * * We are the historical Reformers, we repair the rents and cracks in the House of God.+ In a sermon on the Sabbath he says: "The seventh day, the historical Sabbath is de facto not being celebrated, and the question is not whether we should celebrate it or not, but whether, inasmuch as the seventh day is not observed at all, we should sanctify it on another day or not at all. * * In the Synagogue the celebration of the Sabbath is made use of for the purpose of decrying us as destroyers of Judaism, because we celebrate the weekly service on Sunday instead of Saturday, while the largest portion of the members of

---

*Abodah doche Shabbath.
+Holdheim: Predigten, 1853. "Die Risse and Spalten im Gotteshause. Vol. II, page 274-277.

the Synagogue can only boast of the fact that they attend divine worship neither on Saturday nor on Sunday. The words, 'In every place, where I shall permit my name to be mentioned, I shall come unto Thee, and bless Thee,' (Exodus, XX, 21), apply also to this very day. And while this day might not have the same power as the old Sabbath for the present generation, it will have it for your children and your children's children.*

*Holdheim: Predigten, 1852, Vol. I, pages 212-217; Dr. Samuel Hirsch in his reply to a circular letter addressed to the Rabbis by the U. A. H. C., May 1, 1885, (XII Annual Report of the U. A. H. C., page 1626), said among other things of the Sabbath question: "What is the Sabbath idea? Certainly no one thinks of transferring Saturday to Sunday. That would be as sensible as if you would transfer Monday to Wednesday. Further, nobody thinks of interfering with those who observe Saturday as Sabbath." "When or where Jews were persecuted, it was easy for them to celebrate Saturday as Sabbath. Every occupation was denied them, except such as were so much despised that a Christian would not undertake them. Therefore the Jews had a monopoly in their occupations, and people needing what could only be found among the Jews, had to choose a Jewish working day. "But how is it today? Thank God, every honorable calling is open to us, but we have a monopoly of none. In most cases—this cannot be denied—not working on Saturday would be the ruin of the whole business. In no case would and could the Jews fulfill their whole duty—that great duty to work six days for the good of humanity. Judaism proclaims two first and fundamental principles: First, man is on earth to work. Working constitutes his nobleness—distinguishing him from all other earthly creatures, who find their food prepared. (Moses I, 28): You shall conquer the earth. You shall overcome by your working the resistance put against you." "These Sunday services were not proclaimed a Sabbath service. No Sabbath prayer, no "Be Pleased O God With Our Rest" was prayed. These Sunday services must have been decried as an imitation, as a concession to Christianity. Friday evening lectures was the watchword, and it was declared, "Let people work seven days; God has to be satisfied with fifty out of a hundred." In a similar strain Abraham Geiger, although an opponent of a transfer of the Sabbath to Sunday, said some forty years ago: "We have a week day which is especially adapted for divine service, namely, the Sunday. Let us make use of it, if not every week, so from time to time. * * Let us not go too far through fear of concession to another creed. * * You make the Sabbath a day of work, the Sunday a day of recreation. Religion, however, should yield entirely on the Sabbath to the urgent demands of the present and on the Sunday to a stubborn clinging to the past? This is self-deception, through which the religious life is being wholly extinguished." (Geiger's "Nachgel - Schriften," Vol. 1, page 226). In a

On April 10, 1849, the "Religions-School," of the Reform - Congregation, which had been temporarily conducted by Bernstein, was definitely established and dedicated by Holdheim, who had come for this special purpose from Schwerin. He took as his text the appropriate passage: "We shall advance with our young and with our old, with our sons and with our daughters." (Exod. X, 9). He urged that it was high time to include the girls in the religious instruction, that this was a duty too long neglected in Israel. On August 28, 1847, Holdheim delivered his farewell address in Schwerin and as a token of the appreciation of him, a tablet of bronze was hung in the Temple bearing the inscription: "Dr. Samuel Holdheim, Land-Rabbi, 1840-47, has erected an imperishable monument for himself by his endeavors in the cause of religion, worship and school."

The promise of the grand-duke, that the cause of religious progress should be supported, and the conviction that his able successor, Dr. David Einhorn, would follow in his wake, made his departure less regretful to him. Einhorn entered upon his position on September 4, and Holdheim delivered his inaugura-

pamphlet of Julius Rosenthal: "Extract from Proceedings of Chicago Sinai Congregation, March 26 and April 9, 1885." Dr. Emil Hirsch said the following: "The Sabbath is a human want. Regardless of historical associations, it is planted in human necessity. Men need the periodical rest it brings. And as the day of rest it is the best opportunity to impart instruction on the higher problems of our nature—instruction which requires a teacher trained to impart it—the services on that day again correspond to a human want. The old Jewish Sabbath is dead. To successfully revive it, seclusion on the part of the Jews from the outer world in a new Ghetto would be the price. We cannot afford to pay that price. And therefore, to satisfy a purely natural craving, we utilize the day of rest—commonly observed— for the purpose indicated. Our Sunday services are not a transferred Sabbath, but a new creation. Einhorn had the following to say on the vexed question: "This we can, should and must do in order to arrest the evil, viz: Introduce a monthly Sunday service of a non-Sabbatarian character. Such a measure cannot, justly, be attacked from any point of view and will at the same time bring great blessing." Einhorn: Sermon delivered Shabuoth 1871, in the Temple Adath Jeshurun. (pages 312, 313, New York, Steiger).

tion sermon in Berlin on September 5. Both sermons were published, Einhorn's at Schwerin (Kuerschner), Holdheim's at Berlin. (B. Behr).

It was no small thing for Holdheim to give up a position as Land-Rabbi of Mecklenburg-Schwerin for one in an organization which was composed of so many intellectual and influential leaders, that it was a difficult task to be their leader. Aside from this the Berlin Jewish Congregation (Juedische Gemeinde) was in possession of wealth, power, of all charitable and educational institutions, basked in the sunshine of the Prussian government, and had in addition an eloquent preacher in the person of Sachs, who was most strongly opposed to Reform in general and to the new Congregation in particular. Aside from this the leaders and originators of the new Congregation, who had almost finished the whole work before Holdheim's arrival in Berlin, were jealous of their prestige, and by no means so ready for changes and modifications.

Holdheim published "The Religious Principles of Reformed Judaism, Recommended for the Examination and Acceptance of the Reform-Societies."* Concerning the Sabbath he expresses in this publication the views, that the "Reform Genossenschaft" in transferring the Sabbath-celebration from Saturday to Sunday has not departed from Judaism. He declares, that the "Genossenschaft" celebrates the same holidays at the same time as do the other Congregations. It is, however, strange that the most radical Jewish Reform-Congregation celebrates two days of Rosh Hashna to this very day, and that Holdheim could not influence it to do away with the second day of new year. Tranferring the Sabbath to Sunday and observing the second day of Rosh Hashaha i. e., the second first day of the year, is an anomaly indeed.

Holdheim was not only progressive, but extremely aggressive. Like the true Reformer he was not satisfied to rest on his laurels, but he made strong and

*Berlin, 1847 in seven chapters.

successful propaganda for Reform-Judaism. He was not only preacher, but Rabbi, and endowed with the same fervor and enthusiasm for his views as the most orthodox Rabbi is for his opinions. Thus he created great opposition to Reform on the one hand, but saved it from the bane of "indifferentism."

In 1849 the board of trustees on motion of Simion passed a resolution to send a memorial to the Prussian government pertaining to the oath More Judaico. Holdheim was commissioned to compose this document. He fulfilled this task by his publication, "Memorial of the Society for Reform," January 15, 1850, in which he asked for the abolition of the Jewish oath and proposed the formula: "I swear by God," with the closing sentence: "So help me God."[*]

Sachs, who before Holdheim's arrival in Berlin had been in favor of a Reform of the worship, became after Holdheim's election as Rabbi of the Reform-Congregation a fanatic opponent of Reform, and introduced into Berlin Judaism a sort of "Jewish Pietism," cant and sanctimoniousness, which, aided by bombastic eloquence and flowery, mystic phraseology, did not fail to exert great influence upon sentimental women.[+] Holdheim's only weapons were the honest word of truth, of sound logic and genuine Jewish theological scholarship. No wonder he had to deal with great difficulties, yet sincere and conscientious opponents gradually commenced to respect and even to appreciate him, though they could not agree with his ideas.

A decisive victory was won by Holdheim over Sachs and others on the inter-marriage question. The

[*]That he was successful in bringing about the abolition of the Jewish oath in Mecklenburg has been mentioned.
[+]See: Israelit. des. 19 t. Jahrhunderts, 1844. No. 3, Correspondence from Berlin In his "opinion" addressed to the administration of the Congregation (1846), Sachs considered the "lively and urgent demand of a Reform of the divine service" not only justifiable, but saw in it the welcome testimony of re-awakened interest for what had been overlooked before. In the second report he recommended the introduction of German songs in the service. See Einhorn's Sinai, (Nor, and "Schibboleth," a word to the Jewish Congregation of Berlin," (Berlin, 1865, Spaeth).

state attorney of Koenigsberg, Prussia, prosecuted Dr. Ferdinand Falkson, a prominent Jewish physician, who had married a Christian lady, on account of the decisions on the question rendered by the consistory of Koenigsberg and the Rabbinate of Berlin. Holdheim in his: "Mixed Marriages Between Jews and Christians," (Berlin, 1850), strongly criticised the decision of the Berlin Rabbis. His manhood is aroused against the "sentimental romantics of the Jewish orthodoxy," "denen eine schoen klingende Phrase, ein poetischen Blumenkranz, mit dem man die Leichen des Juedischer Mittelalters verziert, lieber ist, als gesunde Nahrung und lebenskraeftige Befriedigung fuer Geist und Herz." (Who prefer a well-sounding phrase, a poetical wreath of flowers, with which they adorn the corpses of the Jewish middle ages, to wholesome food, and to a vital, vigorous satisfaction for mind and heart).

In all his writings and in the Rabbinical Conference at Braunschweig Holdheim laid stress on the important fact, that the Talmudical-Biblical prohibition of mixed marriages has only in view foreign nations, but not the followers of another creed. He treats the subject as a question of liberty of conscience. In this spirit he wrote also against Dr. Schwab's "decision," concerning the "Reform-Genossenschaft of Pesth," which was presided over by Einhorn. It may be mentioned on this occasion that Holdheim was one of the few German Rabbis,* who officiated at mixed

---

*Das Gutachan des Herrn L. Schwab Rabbiner's zu Pesth ueber die Reformgnossenschaft daselbst, Berlin, 1848, page 17; See also my Open Letter to Prof. Maass, in Breslau, Koenigsberg, 1877, Prange. See also Holdheim's Autonomie der Rabbinen (1843), "Ueber das Religioese u. Politische (1845), Documente Ueber Gemischte Ehen," edited by Dr. Falksohn (Hamburg, 1847). The following Rabbis in this country officiated at marriages between Jews and Christians: Dr. Samuel Hirsch, his son Emil Hirsch, Sonneschein. Isaac Moses, and if I am not mistaken, Dr. Schlesinger, of Albany. Dr. Berkowitz' case in Kansas City cannot be called a "mixed marriage," as the groom embraced Judaism. The case created attention because Berkowitz received Mr. Gelat into the fold of Judaism without the rite of circumcision

marriages. In the fourth volume of his "Sermons" edited by Dr. Immanuel Ritter, the twenty-second and last address is entitled: "Sermon at a Mixed Marriage," on the text "Whither thou goest I will go." (Ruth I, 16-17). *

In 1854 Holdheim published anonymously a very instructive and interesting school book: "Religious and Ethical Teachings of the Mishna for the Use of Jewish Religious Schools." This text-book contains practical hints for every teacher of the Jewish religion. In 1857 followed the catechism entitled: "Haamuna Vehadaa," (Faith and Knowledge), which is not free from the shortcomings of so many similar text-books, namely, that it is written for philosophers and not for children. In the "Programmes" of the religious school of the Jewish Reform-Congregation Holdheim published in 1853 and 1860 two essays on Jewish religious instruction. His: "Prayers and Hymns for the New Year and Day of Atonement," (Berlin, 1859), are also too philosophical to become popular. Aside from this religious poetry was not his forte.

Not only within the limits of his Congregation, but in all important questions affecting Judaism. Holdheim exerted a great influence. He strongly opposed the idea of a Christian government, which, was advocated by the baptised Jew Stahl in his publication: "Christian Tolerance." Stahl maintained that Christianity had entered the stage of history as the religion of intolerance, and must necessarily be agressive towards all other religions. The government may be tolerant towards individuals but never towards religious communities. Being sure of its divine truth, how could it be tolerant towards the error which deprives God of His honor and robs man of his salvation? Holdheim, in his pamphlet: "Stahl's Christian Tolerance," Berlin, 1856, repudiated such an argument. He shows the great mistake of Stahl, who, looks upon justice, humanity and freedom of conscience

*Holdheim: Predigten neber die Juedische Religion, Berlin 1869, Julius Benziaan vierter Band, page 207-210.

as the result of atheistic philosophy. The Jewish government of Palestine had to be exclusive at the start, when it declared ethical monotheism as the religion of the nation. It had to be first strengthened and fortified in Israel in order to spread later as the religion of mankind and as a blessing for future generations. But during eighteen centuries Judaism has preached liberty of conscience, and "long before Jesus Hillel taught: 'What is hateful unto thee, thou shalt not do unto others,' this is the essence of our religion. The Roman Catholic Church had entered into the inheritance of the old exclusive Jewish theocracy, and now the Jewish apostate Stahl desires to introduce it into Protestantism."

In this book: "Moses Mendelssohn and the Freedom of Thought and Belief in Judaism, Berlin, 1859." Holdheim shows conclusively that Mendelssohn's statement that Judaism has no dogmas, simply means, that our religion protests against blind belief, encourages faith based on reason, a rational creed, the pillars of which are knowledge and conviction.

Holdheim's "History of the Jewish Reform-Congregation in Berlin"* gives an excellent insight into the origin of this organization. It is by no means an easy task to write such a book without bias and prepossession, especially when the author is an actor in the drama. But under the circumstances the author has done ample justice to his subject. One of the most important passages in this book is on pages 251-54, where he enumerates the results of the Reform-movement in Germany in general and of the Berlin Reform-Congregation in particular. He first points out the moral power of the very existence of the Berlin Reform-Congregation in those days. It checked in the first place that shameful and disgraceful apostasy, which was for a long time all the rage in the so-called high toned Jewish society circles of the Prussian capital, when parents were not ashamed to sacrifice their inno-

*Berlin, 1857, Julius Springer, 254 pages.

cent children to the Moloch of political advancement,
greed, social position and convenience. Thus the
Reform-Congregation became de facto the savior of
Judaism in the Berlin of that epoch. While it was in
Berlin a matter of daily occurrence that Jews sold their
birthright for a mess of pottage at the baptismal font,
it is a notable fact that among the members of the Berlin
Reform-Congregation, in twelve years only one case of
this kind had occurred. And why? Because the Congregation, composed of the best educated men and women
of Berlin Jewish society, had formed a strong public
opinion against renegades. People who cared little
what the orthodox and more or less Jewish masses
thought of such a step, were not at all indifferent to
the opinion of men and women who occupied great positions in the mercantile, scientific and artistic world of
Berlin, and who were members of the Reform-Congregation. Men and women who had the moral power to
withstand temptations were of course very severe in
their judgment against those who proved too weak
against the allurements of sin. Those who looked with
equanimity upon the verdict of the religious forum of
orthodoxy were mightily afraid of the verdict of the
moral forum of the Reformers. Thus the Berlin Reform-Congregation had exercised its beneficial influence in the direction just mentioned even upon the old
Berlin Congregation.

Another proof of the influence of the Reform-Congregation is that the directory of the old Berlin Congregation, owing to the great success of the religious
school of the Reformers, felt impelled to establish a
similar school. They had to do it, because the most
prominent members of the old Congregation had sent
their children to the school of the Reform-Congregation, where Bible, catechism and Jewish history were
taught.*

*I refer in this connection to an excellent article of Holdheim
in Einhorn's "Sinai," 1858, Vol. III, pages 901-929: "Der verbesserte
Religionsunterricht."

Another important work of Holdheim was published after his death, on the subject of marriage and divorce, and similar topics, written in Hebrew, and entitled: "Maamar Haisuth," Berlin, 1861. Its concluding portions were corrected by Dr. Geiger after Holdheim's demise. The idea of Sadducees and Pharisees, resurrection and kindred subjects are ingenious. The work owed its impetus to Geiger's "Urschrift und Uebersetzungen der Bibel," Breslau, 1857, but in the question concerning Sadducees and Pharisees, reaches a different conclusion from Geiger. The book created a stir in Jewish literary circles.

I call attention to a review of the valuable work by Dr. Herzfeld, in the Zeitung der Judenthum's (May, 1861). Holdheim himself regarded this work as the result of his most diligent studies, and sacrificed his health by his efforts to see its publication. He did not live to see it. A friend of Holdheim—I think I am not mistaken in saying Samuel Adler of New York—wrote to Einhorn concerning this book, as follows: "Holdheim is great and marvelous just on the subject of historical criticism, as is seen in the appendix to the book, which is of the greatest value to me. His theory on resurrection, which is for him the key to the understanding of the history of the Sadducees and Pharisees, is a veritable inspiration. And how he masters the Hebrew language! I am anxious to see whether the vacillating conservative school, which carries water on both shoulders, will have the courage to ignore this treasure." To this Einhorn remarks: "They will have this courage. They showed still greater courage by insulting Holdheim in his grave." (Einhorn's "Sinai," Philadelphia, September, 1861, vol. VI, page 266.)

Occasionally Holdheim was, like all great men, very sarcastic and unsparing, especially when hypocrisy had to be unmasked. Selig, later, Paulus Cassel, by the way, one of Dr. Sachs' most confidential friends and satellites, a few years before his "conversion to Christianity" had published an "Open letter" to the

Congregation of his native town, Giogau, in which he denounced in the strongest terms the appeal of the Berlin "Reform-Genossenschaft." He claimed that their desire to imitate Christianity and their ignorance of Judaism were the only motives of the Reformers. Instead of all criticism, Holdheim simply quotes Cassel's own words in this publication, which read thus: "Our religion did never care to keep those who forsake it; she dismissed the traitors either with regret or with contempt." (Holdheim Gesch. d. Jued. Reformgem, pp. 70-71, note; and Zeit. d. Judenth's, 1845, No. 26). Dr. David Cassel said in the pamphlet: ''Woher? Wohin?'' (Whence? whither? 1845), that the hatred of Talmudical Judaism is mostly found among those, who, in their early youth had devoted their time exclusively to the study of the Talmud, by which remark no other than Holdheim of Mecklenburg was meant, who, at that time, had nothing to do with the Berlin Reformers and their "appeal." Holdheim pays his respects to the zealous critic of the "Reformgenossenschaft" in his "Geschichte, d. Jued. Reformgem," and says among other things: "Mr. D. Cassel had published his 'Woher? Wohin?' in 1845. One year before that time he requested the author to give him a Rabbinical diploma (Hattarath Horaah), and expressed in his letters his great joy on account of the reformatory work, 'The Autonomy of the Rabbis,' which proclaimed so clearly the principles and sentiments which he (D. Cassel) had always darkly felt in the recesses of his heart. Out of this dark feeling of radical Reform has broken forth the light of new orthodoxy." (Ibid. p. 71, note 1). See also Dr. Beer's scathing criticism of Dr. Cassel's pamphlet.*

We have seen in Holdheim, as it were, a giant wrestling with the demons of prejudice and superstition, and conquering them. The development from the Jeshiba-Bachur to one of the most radical Re-

*Frankels "Zeitschrift fuer die religioesen Interessen des Judenthums," Breslau 1845.

form-Rabbis of his age was a remarkable evolution indeed, the outcome of great inner struggles and fierce battles within his own heart, and with enemies from without. Holdheim was always learning, and looked upon Geiger and Zunz as upon his teachers.* He well knew how to discriminate, even in heated discussions between principle and person, although he himself was treated most outrageously by his opponents, who often enough were his personal enemies.† Knowing that his motives were always pure, he could hardly comprehend, judging as he did others by himself, how men could suspect him of impure motives, and was naturally deeply mortified at the attacks so often made upon him by orthodox and half orthodox enemies.

Geiger said in the preface to a sermon of Holdheim published after his death: "Rarely was a man so suspected or attacked, reviled and treated with artificial contempt as Holdheim, but it was as if he had not noticed it; as if all the noise outside had passed over him without any trace. * * With all earnestness he defended his position; he never reviled his opponents, and never in his writings or sermons was he bitter."

In his later years he concentrated his main activity upon his sermons. They were systematic, logical, clear, concise, void of empty phraseology and verbosity, and Jewish to the core. He thus assisted his audience greatly in making easy the comprehension of his sermons, which were replete with philosophical and sublime ideas. He was accustomed to read his sermons, but in Berlin he memorized them. His voice was weak and his delivery not pleasant. But so far as substance is concerned, his sermons are among the best of the German-Jewish pulpit. They are published in four volumes. The first volume (Berlin, 1852), is dedicated

*See his "Geschichte der Juedishen Reformgemeinde," Berlin, 1857, pp. 11 and 70.
†It is, alas, still a dark stain on the escutcheon of Judaism, that especially Jewish theologians have not yet learned to separate in their controversies persons from principles.

to Dr. David Einhorn, the Rabbi of the Reform Congregations of Pesth, Baltimore, Philadelphia and New York; the second volume (Berlin, 1853), dedicated to the directory of the Jewish Reform-Congregation at Berlin, contains twenty-eight sermons; the third volume (Berlin, 1855), dedicated to Dr. Gotthold Salomon at Hamburg, contains thirty-one sermons. After Holdheim's death appeared eleven sermons prefaced by Dr. Geiger, and in 1869 Dr. Immanuel Ritter, his biographer, published a volume of twenty-two sermons of Holdheim.*

Holdheim's sermons are doubtless the clearest, best and most outspoken expositions of Reform-Judaism. An intelligent man unacquainted with the principles and doctrines of Reform-Judaism will find in these sermons a veritable mine of solid instruction and convincing argument. These sermons must be read, re-read and studied, in order to be fully appreciated. Holdheim's ideas of the Jewish Holidays will never lose their interest. His last sermon, which he was to preach on Rosh-Hashana, 1860, could not be delivered by him, as he died August 22d. His text was from Genesis, XXII, 14: "God Will See." The sermon was published with a preface by Geiger. In this sermon can easily be noticed his presentiment of death, and his consciousness of sinking vitality. But with the true calmness and resignation of a hero he speaks of the perishability of human life, of our perpetual work of grave-digging, in which we cover the impressions of yesterday with the solemn events of to-day. But "God seeth." He opens the graves, and the endeavor to make of to-day the grave of yesterday is vain, because the "Day of Memorial" lifts the cover from the coffin, in which the past life was hidden from us. This day opens before us our actions, tears the veil, which selfishness has woven around our eye, and calls

*Berlin, 1869, Julius Benzian. Eighteen of these sermons treat on the Jewish Holidays, one on Stern's departure, one is a Thanksgiving-sermon after a cholera-epidemic, one a marriage-sermon, and one a sermon at a mixed marriage.

to us, , 'God seeth." But also many a good angel ascends out of the graves of the past and joyfully greets
us. Let us keep him firmly, in order that he may ac-
company us into the new year, and let us not cease to
strive further after the good and noble, and if we feel
ourselves misjudged by men, who blacken what is pure
and darken what is glittering, let us always say to ourselves, "God seeth."

This sermon is also published in Einhorn's
"Sinai," Vol. VI, pages 302-310. The following are
the closing words of Geiger's preface, which
lose much of their force in an English translation.
Hence they may find here their place also in the
original: "Ueber den Graebern der Vergangenheit und
der Gegenwart wird die Zukunft immer mehr zur
reinen Erkenntniss erzogen werden. Was durch die
mit uns und nach uns Lebenden als Wahrheit hervorge-
arbeitet werden wird, das jetzt bestimmen zu wollen,
waere vermessen, ein solches Abschliessen waere der
ganzen Richtung des Verklaerten am Meisten wider-
strebend. Wer aber unter den vor und mit uns
Lebenden redlich, uneigennuetzig, geisteskraeftig und
mit wahrhafter, nicht kraenkelnder Gemuethstiefe
nach Wahrheit geforscht, das koennen wir heute schon
aussprechen und die unbefangene Zukunft wird es
immer mehr bekraeftigen. Und unter ihnen nimmt
eine gewichtige Stelle ein: Samuel Holdheim."*

Alas, Holdheim did not live to see the hour, in
which this sermon was to be delivered. On the 22nd
of August, he departed this life. It was on this occasion, that the intolerance of the so-called new-ortho-

---

Following is a translation: "Over the graves of the past and
the present the future will be more and more educated towards
a pure recognition. It would be presumptuous to determine now
what will be worked out as truth by those who live with and after
us. This would be mostly incompatible with the principles of the
deceased. Still, even to-day, we are permitted to point out those
who, living before and with us, have honestly and unselfishly
searched after truth. And the unbiased future will more and more
confirm this. And among these men Samuel Holdheim occupies an
important place."

doxy and the tolerance of the old school manifested themselves.

Following article of the "Zeitung des Judenthum's from Berlin on the subject, may find a place here: "A nervous disease of long standing and the excessive mental strains caused by the labors of the departed Holdheim on his Hebrew book ("Marriage and Divorce") brought about a weakness, and consequent death. In his delirium his spirit was continually at work searching and investigating. In his dreams he saw himself in the pulpit and at his desk, and when he awoke he regretted to be unable to write the newly discovered truths. On the evening of August the 22nd the directors of the Reform-Congregation met, in order to consult about the funeral. It was suggested, that the Congregation of Berlin should be requested to permit Holdheim to be buried in the row appointed for Rabbis. Dr. Waldeck conferred with Mr. M. who was of the opinion, that according to section 14 of the constitution of the "Burial-Society," Dr. Holdheim is entitled to a place in the row appointed for the Rabbis. He added, however, that it is appropriate to ask for the opinion of the hoary Rabbinats - Assessor, Oettinger. Mr. M., accompanied by Dr. W., went to Oettinger, informed him of Holdheim's death and of the desire of the Reform-Congregation. The venerable sage, over eighty years old, arose and slowly in short intervals spoke as follows:

"Holdheim is dead? — *Boruch dajjou emmes* (praised be the judge of truth). He was a great Lamden (Talmudical scholar). I have no objection to his interment in the row designated for Rabbis." On the evening of August the 23rd a letter of the directors was addressed to the "Burial-Association" requesting them to make the necessary arrangements for Rabbi Holdheim's interment in the row designated for the Rabbis of Berlin. Dr. Geiger, of Breslau, was invited to deliver the funeral oration at the grave and the sermon at the memorial service on Sunday, August

26th, in the Temple. This service was attended by a large number of orthodox Jews. While at the grave Geiger dwelt on Holdheim's personal qualities, his oration at the Temple was an exposition of the principles of Reform-Judaism, for which his deceased friend so enthusiastically labored more than a quarter of a century. The sermon created a deep impression.

"It must be remarked, that Dr. Sachs was at the springs, while all this happened. After his return to Berlin he took occasion in his first sermon to arraign forcibly the Berlin Congregation for having permitted Holdheim to be buried in the row of the Rabbis, and sent in his resignation to the directors of the Congregation. The directors answered Sachs in a dignified manner and left it with him to give them within three weeks a definitive declaration concerning his resignation. I, however, and with me thousands hope and trust, that the time will never come in Israel, when the Congregation will give up its autonomy and the Rabbi will be more than a venerated, experienced adviser." So far the "Zeitung d. Judenth's.

The Berlin correspondent of a New York paper had the following to say on the subject: "In mentioning Christian bigotry, I cannot omit for the sake of justice, to speak of the same quality manifested by a Jew. Dr. Michael Sachs, preacher of the Jewish Congregation, sent in his resignation because the Rabbi of the Reform-Congregation, Dr. Holdheim, had found his last resting place in the row of honor at the cemetery of the Jewish Congregation, which fact is looked upon as sacrilege by Dr. Sachs. * * He was doubtless convinced that his Congregation would rather exhume the body and rudely violate the honor due to the dead, than to do without his services. As soon, however, as Sachs noticed that he was mistaken in this supposition, he repented of the step. The New York correspondent of Einhorn's "Sinai" continues as follows: "Well may we ask with surprise how a man can permit himself to be carried away by the demon of arrogance to such an extent, especially in the metrop-

olis of intelligence, and in a state where the Jews had
to wage such hot struggles against Christian fanaticism?
We ask surprisingly, how Dr. Sachs, who once remarked from his pulpit that the "Pijutim were food (Futter)
for the people, and who in spite of his show* of orthodoxy, before the tribunal of genuine orthodoxy is considered no less of a heretic than Holdheim, could commit such a nonsensical act, by which he attacked in a
most comical manner the orthodoxy of the eighty
years old Rabbi Oettinger, with whose consent the
Berlin Directory acted?   *   *   This is one more
proof that the representatives of radical Reform are less
hated by the genuine than by the half hearted orthodoxy, because those who are outspoken in their convictions honor themselves by showing respect to their
opponents.   They, however, who have no firm convictions, attempt to replace the lack of self-esteem by a
false halo, by a hierarchical noise and bluster.   A Berlin jester made the following remark on this subject:
He hoped that the heretic Holdheim may be saved
from the bitter lot of giving to Sachs after a hundred
years, lessons in the Talmud.†

In this article Einhorn speaks of Holdheim as of a
"star of first magnitude," and informs us that an intimate friendship of fifteen years duration existed between him and the departed friend.   The first volume
of Holdheim's Berlin sermons (1852) is dedicated to
Einhorn.   As proof of Holdheim's character, Einhorn

---

*Dr. M. Pinner in two pamphlets proves, that Sachs was first a Re-
former then orthodox, then again a Reformer.   He says: "Sachs became, all of a sudden, veritably fanatic in his orthodoxy.   So he prohibited the most insignificant change in the worship of a temporary
Synagogue and denounced the Reformers in the most insolent manner from his pulpit, thus fanning the flames of partisan strife.   But
as soon as a new regime obtained power and the Reformers captured
all the offices in the Congregation, Sachs not only advocated Reforms in the worship, but arraigned from his pulpit the opponents of
the Reforms just as mercilessly as he used under the old regime to
assail the Reformers.   But this is not surprising, as Dr. Sachs was
originally a Reformer, and his agreement with the orthodox directory was merely artificial and necessary for the attainment of certain purposes."   Graetz extols Sachs, of course!

†It is a well-known fact, that the Talmud and Rabbinical lore
were not Sachs' forte.

relates the following: In spite of a bitter controversy
which was carried on among them in 1845 concerning
the oath, in which Einhorn had made use of many a
harsh word against Holdheim, the latter approached
him at the Conference of Frankfurt-on-the-Main, saying: "We both are struggling in the cause of Judaism."
—Nothing was further from him, than to force upon
others his opinion. He combined the keenest criticism
with kindness and leniency. He preferred the crudest
orthodoxy to the negations of a philosophical panthe-
ism, because, as he wittingly expressed himself, pov-
erty is preferable to a burden of debt. Holdheim manifested the greatest interest in the Jewish Reform-
movement on American soil, as is seen by his many
contributions to "Sinai." The main purpose of his
" *Maamar Haishuth*" was to carry the Reform-movement into quarters where German is not read. "And to
such a "*Gadol Bejissrael*" (great man of Israel) Sachs
denies a place of honor in the Jewish cemetery, the romantic Sachs, whose only merit consists in putting together nice phrases. Holdheim gained not only a
place in the "house of peace" ("Friedhof"), but a
place of honor in the battlefield of the modern history
of Judaism, where his name will radiate long after the
winds will have carried away the flowers of Sachs' so-
called poetry. Sachs, the haughty fanatic in kid
gloves, who has acquired some gold-dust from the
gold mines of Judaism, has only brought upon
himself the curse of contempt and ridicule by his intention to insult the mortal remains of the great dead, who
like his name-sake the prophet Samuel, standing at the
frontier of two worlds in Israel had buried with one
hand the corpse of Judaism, and had dug with the
other the richest treasures from the deepest recesses of
his mountains. In the detestable action of Sachs is
shown even his fear of the dead lion. He heard Balaam's cry of anguish.*

*"Oi mi jichjah mishmuel." See Geiger's ingenious explanation
in his "Urschrift," page 367. Einhorn alludes to the fact that Holdheim's name was also Samuel.

"The Berlin Congregation and the eighty year old Rabbi Oettinger honored only themselves by honoring the mantle which had fallen from Eliah, who had ascended to heaven." (Sinai, 1861, vol. VI). Yet Graetz raises to the sky the fanatic Sachs (History XI, p. 571-578), and slings mud at noble Holdheim, which proves beyond a shadow of a doubt that Graetz was no historian in the true sense of the word. Holdheim was buried among the Rabbis of Berlin, much to the discomfiture of a clique composed partly of romantic cranks and ignoramuses in Rabbinical lore, partly of hypocrites, who were not worthy to be mentioned in the same breath with Holdheim. The orthodox and conservative Jewish press gloated over the demise of this great champion of Reform-Judaism, and cowardly insulted the dead lion. But the better Jewish newspapers eulogized Holdheim as he deserved. Einhorn in his "Sinai" spoke of him as follows:

"Samuel Holdheim is dead. The great master in Israel, the high priest of Jewish theological science, the lion in the battle for light and truth no longer walks the earth among the living." In the number of November* Einhorn gave an interesting sketch of Holdheim's life and labors.

Geiger was called from Breslau to deliver the funeral oration at the grave and in the Temple. Dr. Immanuel Ritter, for nine years a colleague of Holdheim, and A. Bernstein spoke on the life of their great friend and master before the members of the Reform-Congregation. In a letter to Wechsler dated Breslau, September 6, 1860, Geiger speaks of his sincere friendship for Holdheim, although he did not approve of his unhistorical methods.   •

In spite of persecution, slander, hatred, malice and fanaticism, which even at this late date do not tire in belittling Holdheim's merits, the impartial historian cannot help placing him in the front rank of the pioneers of Reform-Judaism. His character was pure and

_____

*"Sinai," 1860, Vol. V, page 288-298.

unsullied, and his most implacable enemies — and they are numerous — have to concede this fact.

In the preparation of this chapter I am largely indebted to Dr. Ritter's "Samuel Holdheim." But a careful study of Holdheim's writings, of the Reform literature of those days, especially of Geiger's works, of the Jewish papers of this period, of the reports of the Rabbinical Conferences in the forties, and of the pamphlets on the origin of the Berlin Reform-Congregation, have taught me to be more just and less biased in my historical judgment, than were Graetz and Ritter. The former was prejudiced against, the latter too much prepossessed in favor of Holdheim.

CHAPTER VIII.

LEOPOLD LOEW.

TRANSLATED FROM THE HUNGARIAN OF DR. IM-
MANUEL LOEW, BY DR. WILLIAM N. LOEW,
ATTORNEY AT LAW, NEW YORK.

The biographical dates here given are authentic.
They are taken from Rabbi Loew's diary, from family
letters and memoranda in his own handwriting, all of
which are in the possession of the author of these
lines.

Leopold Loew was born in Czernahora, a little village in Moravia, one of the Provinces of Austria, on
May 22, 1811. He was the first born son of a poor, plain
couple, the only Jewish family in the village. From
his father's side he was a descendent of the famous
Rabbi Loew Ben Bezallel, of Prague, the hero of the
well known Gomel folk-lore or fable of olden times.
(1660). From his mother's side he was descended from
Mendel Krochmal, Chief Rabbi of Moravia.

He received a better education than usually fell to
the lot of Jewish boys in those days in Moravia. A
private tutor engaged for him and his younger broth-
ers, taught him. The Roman Catholic priest of the
village, who had taken a liking to the bright, wide
awake boy, taught him the national language and
music.

Loew showed a great inclination toward music and
had much natural ability in mastering it. Music and

song he always regarded as great educational aids, and
in his earliest Synagogual Reform programme, published in 1839, he dwells on their importance in the Synagogue and the school.

At the age of thirteen, he left his father's house to
enter the "Yeshivah." (High school for Rabbinical
lore).

The institution of the "Yeshivah" is fast dying
out.   Theological seminaries are rising in their place,
but the Yeshivah of olden days was the fountain at
which gigantic minds and heroes of deep thought and
learning like Loew, acquired that immense and profound knowledge of Talmudic lore for which they were
known.   He frequented three of these Yeshivahs;
Rabbi Joachim Deutschmann's at Trebitsch, later at
Kollin; Rabbi Moses Perls' at Kismarton; and Rabbi
Baruch Fraenkel's at Leipnik. In the year 1835 he was
made the recipient of his first "Hattarah," (certificate
of authorization to act as Rabbi), from Rabbi
Deutschmann, who described him as "the most intelligent scholar he ever had." His other hattarahs Loew
received later on from Chief Rabbis S. L. Rappaport of
Prague, Loew Schwab of Buda-Pesth and Aaron
Chorin of Arad.

In addition to his Talmudical studies he devoted
earnest and close attention to Hebrew grammatical
learning, so that he was able to write Hebrew with
classic beauty and power. He wrote Jewish poetry
with easy grace, and many of the classic poems of
Schiller were rendered by him into the language of the
divine psalmist.

In 1830 he left the Yeshivah and went to Bosko-
vitz to relatives, where he remained only a few weeks.
In September of that year he removed to Prossnitz, becoming the scholar of Loew Schwab, then the
Rabbi there, who, later on, became his life-long
friend and father-in-law. Here did he begin his studies of foreign languages such as French, Italian and
the ancient classics of Rome and Athens.

In all of these he acquired more than superficial proficiency, and a complete bibliography of his works must name articles of literary and scientific merit written in Hebrew, German, Hungarian, French and Latin.

In Prossnitz he received the appointment as Hebrew teacher. One of his pupils, Louis Schnabel,* of New York, at one time Superintendent of the Hebrew Orphan Asylum of that city, published in the "Deborah" a series of interesting reminiscences of those days, paying a tribute of grateful love to the memory of his beloved teacher. Mr. Schnabel cannot find words sufficiently eulogistic of Loew's great success as a teacher, leader, guide, and as a man of amiability and geniality. Instead of the stereotyped, long trodden way of teaching "Lainen"* and "Rashi," he taught the Bible pure and simple, in a manner which enables the student to understand and to appreciate it grammatically, aesthetically and archaeologically.

In 1835 he emigrated to Hungary. The year before that he decided upon this step, because the "Landes Rabbiner"—i. e., Chief-Rabbi of Moravia, had refused him a Hatarah on the ground that he, Loew, should never become a Rabbi with his, the Chief-Rabbi's aid, deciding that a man like Loew, who can read and write German and other languages, is not fit to become a Rabbi.

Loew went to Budapest, Hungary, and here he formed the acquaintance of Loew Schwab, the Chief-Rabbi of the large Congregation. He acted as private tutor in several Jewish families and in addition he pursued his studies.

In a table of hours showing his division of time it is made to appear, that his first lessons began at three

---

*Louis Schnabel, a Moravian, is the author of several interesting Ghetto-stories, which were published in the "Jewish Messenger" of New York. Sch.

†"Lainen" is a corrupt German expression for reading from the Sefer Thora (scrolls of the law). It designates also the attempts of young students of the Talmud, to "read" or find out the meaning of a Talmudic passage. Sch.

o'clock in the morning. For five years he worked very hard. Every branch of human knowledge was included in his curriculum. He studied mathematics and geometry, dogmatics, theology and philosophy, exegesis and hermeneutics, logic and psychology, ethics and metaphysics, the classics and the interpretations of the Scriptures, history and languages, natural history and natural philosophy, oriental languages and archaeology. None of these were taken up haphazard, but methodically and systematically.

One-sided philological, historical, philosophical studies then commanded and even now command almost the exclusive attention of Hebrew scholars. Loew was a close student. Dogmatics, ethics, catechetics and homiletics were fields on which he culled with observing eye, adapting their systems to his own studies.

In 1837 he graduated from the Lutheran Lyceum of Pressburg, and in 1840 he passed his examination as "Hauptschullehrer," at Vienna.

In the year 1840 he accepted a call as Rabbi of the Jewish Congregation of Nagy Kanizsa in Hungary and began his useful career of Rabbi, teacher and preacher.

One year previous he had begun his literary career with the publication of a Rabbinical-Reform programme, which caused men like Holdheim, Manheimer and Schwab to regard the young author with high appreciation. This programme was a preface to the great Aron Chorin's "Jeled Sekunim." It bears the name: "Die Reform des Rabbinischen Ritus auf Rabbinischem Standpunkte."* Thirty years later as the biographer of Aron Chorin and in a critical study—published under the pseudonym: "Dr. Weil,"—Loew erected a suitable and worthy memorial to his great friend and forerunner.

*See page 89, of this book, also Loew's Nachgelassene Schriften, Vol. II, edited by his learned son and successor in office, Dr. Immanuel Loew, (Szegedin, 1890). Sch.

In Nagy-Kanisza he began to carry out his Reform-programme. Synagogue and school, the two fields of his labor, soon showed the results of his beneficial efforts. Instead of the jargon sanctioned by custom, grammar and a correct language were introduced. The language of the country was taught, trade schools and girls' schools were opened.

In the year 1844 he began to preach in the Magyar tongue and to write articles in that language. He published them in the famous "Resti Hirlap," the foremost Magyar newspaper, edited by the Historian Szalay and later on by the world-famed Louis Kossuth. One of his articles was an answer to the latter, then only a lukewarm advocate of the rights of the Jews, for which lukewarmness and especially for some derogatory remarks Loew held Kossuth responsible. His Hungarian literary work of those days was almost exclusively devoted to awaken in the Magyar Jew a patriotic spirit and to educate and ripen his people for that position, which to attain, was the highest ambition of his life: the emancipation of the Jews in Hungary. His next efforts were directed to awaken a spirit of love and appreciation in the hearts of the Hungarian people and nation towards the Jews in Hungary. During these years he also began his agitation for a correct translation of the Hebrew Bible into the Magyar, a work finished about thirty years afterwards under the auspices of the "Hungarian Jewish Society."

Another aim of his life, set then, and ever afterwards most faithfully kept before his view, was to be an ever watchful guardian of his people and his religion against the attacks of the enemies of Jews and Judaism.

In the month of August, 1846, he moved to Papa, a city in the County of Veszprin, Hungary, having accepted a call from the large and important Jewish Congregation of that city. But the Jews of Papa, intimately connected with the Jews of Pressburg, could never forgive Loew for his audacity in spending almost two years in Pressburg, and instead of attending R. Moshe

Szofer's Jeshiba,* studying at the Lutheran Lyceum.
Here began Loew's religious martyrdom.

It is impossible to draw a correct picture of the
fight, which his call to Papa caused to break out. To
understand it fully, one must know the condition of
civilization of the Magyar Jews and Magyar Christians
of those days; one must have a clear insight into the
political organization of the Hungarian Comitatus-
System of that time. The protest against his election:
—the numerous charges against him, based principally
on the ground that he was a Reformer, caused a stir in
the town- and county meetings, went to the "Statthalterei" in Ofen, were referred to "Obergespans"
and Vice-Gespans to the "Lord of the Manor"
and ended finally with the election of Loew being confirmed and the numerous charges against him all being
dismissed. Some of his calumniators were even sent
to prison.

Loew's days in Papa were full of sorrow, full of
bitterness, but he felt no discouragement. He worked
indefatigably. He began his labors by consecrating
the new Synagogue and followed it up by organizing a
new school of four classes. He published the "Ben
Chananja," a monthly dedicated to the interests of Jews
and Judaism in Hungary, which publication he renewed
several years afterwards and continued for a decade,
making the "Ben Chananja" one of the foremost re-
ceptacles of Jewish thought in Europe. His "sermons"
were delivered in German, and occasionally in
Hungarian. While at Papa he became also Professor
of Hebrew at the Protestant Collegium of that city.
This was one of the causes that brought about such a
fierce opposition against him. His Congregation consisted also of people in whose eyes the very fact, that a
Rabbi should teach men who were to become "Gallochs"
(priests), or that a Rabbi should be seen in modern

---

*See about Moshe Szofer, page 77, of this book; also Loew: "Der
Jued. Congress" and, "Die Lebensalter."

dress* side by side with a Catholic or Protestant minister was considered a sacrilege. In the opinion of those fanatics, a Rabbi must shun society.

The Hungarian revolution caused the political martyrdom of Leopold Loew.

Loew became a chaplain of the national guard and went into the field of battle. His revolutionary sermons were by order of the government distributed among the army. Even to-day they are considered masterpieces of Magyar pulpit-oratory, and in handbooks of Hungarian eloquence, in Hungarian literary histories, they are referred to and cited as some of the best works of their kind within the range of Hungarian literature.

At the close of the war, Loew and his father-in-law, Schwab, the Chief-Rabbi of Pesth, were arrested by the Austrian military authorities and were sent to prison. Loew spent several weeks there. One by one his fellow prisoners were taken out and—shot or hung. The two Rabbis, however, were finally saved. The efforts of their faithful wives (mother and daughter) proved successful, and they were set free "for want of proof." But Loew was placed under a kind of police-supervision and was ever surrounded by "Spitzeils." (spies). In addition to the fact related below, showing how severely Loew was being watched by the police of Austria, the following anecdote is of interest: When Loew was pardoned he was ordered to include into the regular prayer for the emperor and the imperial family, a prayer for Haynau, the military commander of Hungary. Loew promised that he would do so. Years afterwards one morning, Loew, taking the newspapers into his hands, finds a telegraphic dispatch stating that Haynau had died. On the Saturday following Loew left out the prayer for Haynau. Within an hour after the close of the service of that day he was taken

*Loew always wore the picturesque dress on the Magyar: Top boots, an "Attila" reaching below his knees, a "Kossuth" hat with a tassel dangling over the rim of the hat.

before the military authorities and charged with having broken faith by having neglected to deliver the usual prayer for Hungary's military commander, who had saved his life. Loew tried to justify his act by showing, that Haynau being dead and buried, it would be a stupid thing to pray for him the same prayer as when he was alive and in office. The military authorities were "generous" enough not to punish Loew, but only to "reprimand" him, and ordered him to continue his prayers for Haynau until he (Loew) would be "officially" notified that he need not do so any longer.

The Jews of Hungary, however, their two foremost men being saved, were ordered to pay one million Gulden as a fine for their participation in the national cause! When Francis Joseph I had become king of Hungary, de jure, (1867), Loew became the spokesman of a committee which appeared before the king and requested him to remit the then still unpaid portions of this fine. The fine was remitted, and set aside as the National Jewish school-fund, out of which among other institutions of learning the Rabbinical Seminary in Buda-Pesth is supported.

Loew's participation in the Magyar revolution, his pamphlets and public letters, his inspiring sermons, that had been published and distributed broadcast throughout the land, were greatly instrumental in causing the independent revolutionary government to promulgate a law emancipating the Jews of Hungary. It was in 1849, when Minister Bartholomew Szmere read from the balcony of the Szegedin City Hall, then the seat of the government, the order: "The Jews of this land are recognized as citizens of this land."

A few days later the disastrous revolutionary war came to an end.

Loew returned to Papa, but remained there a short time only. Within a few hours after his almost miraculous release from imprisonment, his enemies began to embitter his life and to take steps to supply the "proofs" against him that were wanting before. He received a call to Szegedin, the great Magyar city of the Magyar lowlands, and accepted it. In the days following the Hungarian revolution it was for him not a matter of course to receive such a call, as it was not a matter of course for the Congregation to issue it. Both parties had to petition the government until finally the necessary consent was obtained. In December, 1850, he assumed the Rabbinate of Szegedin and filled it for a quarter of a century.

His salutatory, a sermon of great force, was published under the title "Die heiligen Lehrer der Vorzeit," and is a bold and manly Reform-programme of an enlightened mind and a truly religious soul. Two editions thereof went through the press.

In Szegedin Loew enjoyed the peace he had not known for years and his educational, literary and theological labors showed the beneficial influence of his happy surroundings. His foremost works were written there, and the longer he remained there, the more closely connected he became with his Congregation, which loved him, and with his city which honored and respected him as one of its most prominent citizens. While in Szegedin he received several calls from other Congregations. Yet, his answer was invariably, that he could not leave his Congregation and his city. Among these calls were those extended to him by the Jews of Lemberg, Galicia, the Congregation of Bruenn in Maehren, the Congregation of Bucharest, Roumania.

In 1871 he was called to Berlin to the "Hochschule fuer die Wissenschaft des Judenthums," just then opened, and in 1873 he was offered the Directory of the Rabbinical Seminary of Buda-Pesth.

The "Mafteach, an Introduction into the Holy Writ," was his first greater work published in Szegedin. It is a very comprehensive work of Jewish exegises.

In 1858 Loew began the publication of his "Ben Chananja," at first as a monthly, later on as a weekly journal, dedicated to Jewish theology. For ten years this magazine, published in a corner of Hungary, was one of the best exponents of Jewish thought and Jewish science.

In 1863 he was cited before the military tribunal, as Hungary was then under military rule. The government had issued an order relating to the consent necessary to be obtained from the political authorities before Jewish weddings were allowed to be celebrated, and ordered also a revenue tax to be paid in the form of stamps on and for the "Kethuba" (contract).

Loew criticised this movement of the government in unmeasured terms, and though his criticism caused a repeal of the order to tax the " Kethuba," he was sentenced to two weeks imprisonment, which imprisonment, however, the military commander of Szegedin suspended. "The orders of the government," he was told by the military auditor, "are not issued for the purpose of being criticised by you." "And yet," Loew replied, "the Minister of Finance repeals the rescript in consequence of this very criticism of mine."

Similarly did he fare when in 1863 he protested against the orders of the government appointing special Jewish overseers of schools, to be paid by the Jewish Congregations. In his protest he used the following language: "The Jews of Hungary do not beg, they ask not for charity in their religious or in their educational matters. They demand only what is their due." The government again felt itself constrained to retrace its steps. In spite of the fact that he was considered a "suspect," and that to every sermon of his, even at the graveyard, the military authorities sent a "controller," Loew was still a "persona grata." The purity of his character and his great learning were held in high esteem by " the powers that were," and on numerous occasions the government, which watched his very words, referred to him important questions relating to Jewish law, Jewish ritual, cult, customs, arising in Congregations, or before courts of law.

His written opinions upon these subjects, which fill a mighty volume, are perfect gems of deep thought and profound learning.

In consequence of these requests of the government, he edited a number of school books for elementary schools and wrote a Biblical history which his son, Dr. Tobias Loew,* rendered into Hungarian, and of which five editions went through the press. In response to similar requests, Loew published his famous study on the "Jewish Oath," being an exhaustive critical essay on the history of the oath of the Jews. Count Coloman Tissa read this essay at a meeting of the Royal Academy of Sciences of Hungary, and the "Jewish Times," (Editor, Moritz Ellinger, New York, 1872), published an English translation thereof in its columns. Another of his more important opinions furnished to the government was "The Jewish Cult," an historical and critical essay, which appeared also in English translation in the columns of the "Jewish Messenger." (Rev. Dr. Isaacs, editor, New York).

To name here all his works in this field would extend the boundaries of this biography beyond the allotted space. The "Augsburger-Allgemeine Zeitung" compares Loew's activity upon this field to that of the Gaons of old.

The "Ben Chananja" championed not only the cause of reformed, purified Judaism, but also the rights of the Hungarian Jew. When in August, 1862, Trefort, later Minister of Cult and Education in Hungary, in an academic lecture made a remark derogatory to the Hungarian Jews and to Jews generally, Loew addressed him in an open letter, which created a stir all over Europe. The great daily papers reprinted it and from the most distant parts of the civilized world came letters of thanks for his splendid defense.

In 1867 the Hungarian parliament emancipated the Magyar Jew. "Ben Chananja" had achieved one of the great objects for which it had been founded.

Its literary and scientific merits were recognized by the great Abraham Geiger, in his "Juedische Zeit-

*He held the office of Deputy Attorney-General of Hungary and died June 6th, 1880.

schrift fuer Wissenschaft und Leben," in the following
language:

"But 'Ben Chananja' confines itself by no means to
the important occurrences of the day; it enters earnest-
ly into deeper scientific questions and has furnished
many a noteworthy contribution to religious and to historic learning.

"The opinions of the editor upon manifold questions which not only touch matters of daily life, but
also important rites of religion, bear witness to his deep
insight into Jewish life and his profound learning on
historical and theological subjects. Such contributions
are of enduring value. 'Ben Chananja,' in almost every
one of its numbers, proves that in spite of all rigidity,
the later teachers, and not only the philosophically
educated ones, never sacrificed their own independent
convictions. This serves to enlighten history and to
strengthen the appreciation of the fact, that in Judaism
the free decision according to one's own convictions
never subjugated itself to the dead letter of the Talmud."

When in 1868 "Ben Chananja" ceased to exist it had
secured as co-laborers and contributors some of the very
foremost representatives of Jewish learning in all Europe, even the United States of America giving their
share (Dr. M. Milziener and the late Dr. Huebsch), to
the brilliant list. It ceased to exist, because, Loew
said, the Jews in Hungary being emancipated, it is not
fair that a newspaper devoted to their interests should
be published in the German language.

He devoted his time to his historical studies.*
Some of his articles relating to the history of the Jews
in Hungary are published as early as 1841 in Bush's
"Jahrbuch fuer Israeliten" (Isidor Busch of St. Louis,
Mo.) and in other periodicals and weeklies. "Die Jue-
dischen Wirren in Ungarn;" "Der Judische Con-

---

* He was a member of several Hungarian Historical Societies and
one of the judges designated to read the prize-histories of the City
of Szegedin.

gress;" "Juedische Dogmen;" "Das neueste Stadium der Ung. Jued. Organisationfrage," the ten volumes of his Ben Chananja, are rich repositories of his historical and critical studies in this field.

In 1870-71 he published his first volume of his "Beitraege zur Juedischen Alterthums-kunde," being two volumes of "Graphische Requisiten u. Erzugnisse bei den Juden," which were followed soon after by another volume "Die Lebensalter."

These two works crown his efforts in the field of Jewish archaeology, a subject upon which he was authority. In the "Literarisches Centralblatt," his "Lebensalter" was reviewed by the great critic Franz Delitzsch, who said: The author, among the Rabbis of Hungary the most prominent and also one of the most influential members of the Synod, proves in the work before us, not only his magnificent intimacy with the whole range of Jewish literature into its very narrowed corners, but also a rare knowledge of history which reminds one of D'Israeli's curiosities of literature; he is a surprisingly well read mind, who has a saying of Claus Harms as well as a passage of Heinrich Heine at his command; he masters his subject, which in its form, as built by him, is an architectural beauty, and in its style is an artistic gem, which teaches pleasantly and changes even abstrusities into playthings of charming causeries."

In April, 1889, the "American Hebrew," in an article on "Children in Jewish Literature," by S. Schechter, cites "Die Lebensalter" of Loew as authority upon the subject and says of Loew: "Dr. Loew was not very familiar to English Jews, but he was among the few Rabbis of the modern school who, besides their secular attainments, possessed a sound knowledge of the Talmud both in its Haggadic and its Halachic literature."

His third work upon the subject of Jewish archaeology, which was to appear under the title "Der Synagogen-Ritus," he did not complete. Part of it appeared after his death in "Frankel's Monatschrift."

A collection of his Magyar sermons published under the title "Beszedek" (speeches), received a full and very laudatory review in the "Jewish Times." The late Dr. Anthony Hofer—an attache of the New York Herald—was requested by the editor to review it.

Closely connected with Loew's Rabbinical life was the national life of his country. A collection of his published sermons, would show the political history of Hungary during the years of his Rabbinical career. I point to his addresses: "The Dawn of the Revolution," (1840-48); "The Heroic Struggle," (1848-49); "Vae Victis" (1850-63); "The Dawn of Constitutional Freedom," (1863-1867); "Constitutional Liberty and Jewish Emancipation in Hungary," (1868-1875).

He loved to celebrate national-political events in his Temple. His commemoration sermons, delivered on the deaths of Gabriel Klauzal, Baron Joseph Etvoes, and Szechenyi, three famous Magyar statesmen, were greatly admired.

Other occasions, as the opening of the first Hungarian Parliament, the coronation of the King, a wedding of one of his children, the dedication of a new Synagogue, (he dedicated fourteen Synagogues in Hungary), furnished themes for eloquent sermons, which were published and widely read.

His position in Szegedin was one of comparative ease and comfort, yet of constant struggle and care.

A three-fold martyr: Political, religious and literary, he was ever engaged in fight, now against ignorance, now against arrogance, now against the blind zeal of Chassidim, now against the impetuousness of the so-called Parnassim.

The Jewish Congress of or in Hungary knew him not among its delegates. This Jewish Congress was a pet scheme of the then minister of cult and education, Baron Joseph Eotvoes, a truly warm friend of the Magyar Jew. To bring about a concentration of the Jew and the Jewish Congregations of Hungary under the paternal care of the government was his plan, and the Jewish Congress was to discuss and prepare for it.

A very interesting condition of affairs arose in Hungary. Loew, the very foremost of Reformers, and the most orthodox Chassidim, were for once of the same opinion, to-wit: Both were opponents of the Jewish Congress. The motives of their objections were, however, different. Loew's opposition to the centralization of Jewish Congregations was based, among other reasons, on the fact, that, "the historic conditions under which a Jewish Congress in Hungary could and should organize the Jewish Church in Hungary, are not yet understood, and that the matter is in the hands of dilettants, who, however kindly disposed, forget, that the divine command 'in the sweat of thy brow shalt thou eat bread' applies here also and was not meant to refer to the bread we actually eat."

Loew was a member of the Jewish Synods held at Leipzig and at Augsburg. The New York World's correspondent said of him, in a pen picture, that his patriarchal appearance made him worthy the brush of a Rembrandt, while his learning and eloquence, his kindness and geniality, made him a beloved member of that noteworthy gathering. His reports to the Synod, as for instance his opinion upon the subject of riding on Sabbath- and Holidays, are full of profound learning and show a most scrutinizing examination of the subjects of which they treat.

Loew's social status in Hungary cannot very well be described by me. Jew and Christian loved, honored and esteemed him, and vied with each other to show and to prove it on every possible occasion. Generals of the army, ministers of the state, dignitaries of the church called on him to pay their respects to him. When Szegedin wanted the Roman Catholic Bishop Horvath to represent it in parliament, the city appointed a committee to urge the prelate to accept. As leader and speaker of this committee they named the Rabbi. On numberless occasions, at county meetings, political festivals, banquets of public bodies, it was always Loew who was invited and honored to be the spokesman. It was in Czegled, where he had dedicated the Temple, that the city and county authorities, headed by the Catholic and Protestant clergy, honored him with a torchlight procession. This very city of Czegled, ten years later, was the scene of a most disgraceful anti-Semetic riot.

Old peasants and peasant women, school-boys and school-girls would gather around him and happy was he or she who could get hold of his hand to press it with a reverential kiss upon it. He knew everybody and everybody knew him. With the clergy of the other denominations of his city he stood on terms of intimate friendship. The "probst" of Szegedin, hoary Anthony Kremminger, was happy, when, on an important occasion,—the installation of the Vicegespan* of the county,—he had a chance to toast his friend, the Rabbi, calling him by names of endearment and reverential respect.

Loew's Reform-programme was based on the teachings of what he called "the historical school." Beneath a picture of his, he wrote the following sentence: "Patience! the future of Judaism belongs to that school which can best understand the past."

No changes and innovations were even attempted by him, without educating his people to the high standard of intelligence and learning necessary to understand and to appreciate them and to know the why and wherefore thereof. On the 13th of October, 1875, he died.

Whenever a Hungarian Jew steps up to the ballot-box to exercise his constitutional right to vote; whenever he sees a co-religionist occupying a responsible position of honor and trust in public life; whenever he takes an oath without being compelled to humiliate himself; whenever Jews all over the world see Jewish learning appreciated, Jewish schools blooming, Jewish manhood and Jewish womanhood honored, they will

---

*An office similar but more influential than that of County-Judge in this country.

think of Leopold Loew, who did so much toward bringing about these happy results.

They will think of him, who was the greatest Hungarian Jewish patriot, the deepest Hungarian Jewish thinker, one of the most indefatigable and most successful workers for truth, light and justice. His memory will be blessed.

CHAPTER IX.

ABRAHAM GEIGER.

While comparatively little has been published on
the lives of the majority of the leaders of Reform Judaism, especially in the English language, Abraham Geiger forms an exception to the rule. Already in 1842 a
short biography of Geiger was published in the Silesian
lexicon of authors (Nowack's "Schlesisches Schriftstel-
ter-Lexicon," Breslau, 1842). The Brockhaus "Conversations-Lexicon" of 1846 and 1876 and Meyer's
"Lexicon" third edition, (Leipzig, 1876), contain interesting articles* on Geiger, as does also the Encyclopædia Britannica. Berthold Auerbach published a
most excellent article on Geiger in the "Gegenwart,"
(Berlin, 1874, Vol. II, pp. 291-93), Professor I. Deren-
bourg, of Paris, in the last number of Geiger's "Juedische Zeitschrift fuer Wissenschaft und Leben" (Breslau,
1875, Vol. XI, pp. 299-308), and Karl Emil Franzos
in the "Neue Freie Presse," (Wien, January 12, 1879),
reprinted in the "Israelitisches Germeinde-und Famili-
enblatt," (Nos. 12, 13 and 14, 1879), which I had published while Rabbi in Bonn. The "Jewish Times" (New
York) of 1874 and 1875 contains quite a number of
memorial sermons delivered in this country in honor of
Geiger. Dr. Einhorn's most excellent sermon is published in the collection of Einhorn's sermons edited by
Dr. K. Kohler (New York, 1879-80, Steiger). Dr. N.

*The articles of 1876 in both Encyclopedias were amended and
augmented by Geiger's learned son, Prof. Ludwig Geiger.

Bruell, late Rabbi of Frankfort-on-the-Main, published
also his sermon on "Geiger," delivered during a memorial service. Prof. Ludwig Geiger published "Abraham Geiger's Life in Letters"(Vol. V of " Posthumous
Works," Berlin, 1875, Gerschel; also a special edition,
Breslau, 1885, W. Jacobsohn & Co.) I published in
1879 "Abraham Geiger as a Reformer of Judaism."
In the English language a short sketch of Geiger's life
can be found in Henry S. Morais's "Eminent Israelites of the Nineteenth Century" (Philadelphia, 1880),
from page 92 to page 96. I am very much pleased to
see that this conservative author thus commences his
sketch: "Great among the greatest for originality of
thought and masterly ability in treating a variety of
subjects is Abraham Geiger. An imperishable evidence
of the depth of his understanding and versatility of his
powers he has left in his works upon which scholars
will long ponder, not only for the broad knowledge
they disclose of Hebrew literature, but also for the insight into Semitic languages that the author affords
the student. No better characterization of Geiger can
be given than the words which Dr. Herzfeld, of Braunschweig, once said to me: "Geiger was the teacher of
the teachers." Dr. Nehemias Bruell said of him :
"Later generations will look upon him as upon one of
the greatest teachers of Judaism, as the father of a new,
purified conception; as a man who, though at the beginning single-handed, whom a few only followed,
against whom many fought, yet, undaunted and sure
of victory, had advanced in the path of truth, and has
become a guide to all who strive higher, and a blessing
to all Israel. * * Side by side with the names of
Hillel, R. Jochanan b. Saccai, Saadia b. Joseph, Mose
ben Maimon, Asaria de Rossi, Moses Mendelssohn, will
radiate forth in all its brilliancy to the remotest times
the name of Abraham Geiger."

No less an authority than Dr. David Einhorn called
Geiger "the most prominent teacher of Judaism in our
generation" ("Sermons," page 91). As it is not easy
to do full justice in an English translation to the fol-

lowing classical passage of Einhorn's sermon on "Geiger," I also quote it in the original German: "Und an der Spitze der Maenner solchen glorreichen Strebens und Gotteskampfes stand Abraham Geiger; er, der mit dem Schwerte seines reichen Wissens wie kein Anderer es verstand, Wege durch Felsen zu brechen und die eisernen Riegel vor der Pforte unserer Schatzkammen zu sprengen; er, der mit dem Zauberstabe des Genius, in unserem innersten Heiligthum. in der ,Bibel, neue Welten der Wahrheit erschloss, und mit tiefblickenden Seherauge in die verborgensten und entlegensten Theile unserer Geschichte eindrang, um das Judenthum zu verherrlichen und den Nachweis zu liefern, dass, und in welcher Weise aus den Splittrn des juedischen Geistes der Reichthum der Religionen aller gebildeten Voelker geflossen." ("And at the head of the men of such a glorious ideal and struggle in the cause of God stood Abraham Geiger; he who understood better than any other how to break paths through and to burst open the iron bars before the gate of our treasurehouses; he who disclosed with the magic wand of genius new worlds in our innermost sanctuary in the Bible, and who with eyes of a penetrating seer entered into the most hidden and remotest parts of our history, in order to glorify Judaism and to offer the proof that and how the wealth of the religions of all intelligent nations had come from the splinters of the Jewish spirit." But the mere fact that Einhorn in speaking of Geiger had taken as his text, "And there was light—that means Abraham Geiger,"* proves more than anything else what a high opinion this great Reform-Rabbi of America must have entertained of the hero of this chapter, whose disciple the writer of this book had the privilege of being from 1871 to 1874 in Berlin.

A most remarkable pamphlet, "Modern Judaism, its Emancipation and Reform as brought about by the Merits of Lessing, Moses Mendelssohn and Abraham Geiger," by the Danish Professor Frederic Nielson,

---

*He alludes to the name "Abraham" and to Isa. LI, 2.

translated from the Danish into German by E. Schuh-
macher (Arensburg, 1880), while written in an orthodox
Christian spirit, does full justice to Geiger, and is important for the keen appreciation it manifests for modern Judaism.

Abraham Geiger was born in Frankfort-on-the-
Main, May 24, 1810. His father, Rabbi Michael Lazarus Geiger, was a scholar and highly respected in his
Congregation. Every Sabbath he delivered a "Drasha"
(lecture), which he usually read before young Abraham
on Thursdays. Geiger's mother, "Roeschen" (nee
Wallau), while not agreeing with the religious opinions of her son felt very proud of him and greatly
rejoiced in his fame. His brother Salomon was his
teacher, and is always spoken of by Geiger in terms of
deep reverence. The great talents of the boy manifested themselves very early. At the age of two years
he was already well known among the Jews of Frankfort for his wonderful brightness, and when three years
old, he could do what the majority of American-Jewish
boys cannot accomplish—namely, read Hebrew and
German. At the age of six years he studied the Bible,
the Mishna and the Talmud. When nine years old he
created a sensation in the city of Mayence,
and was honored by excellent testimonials from
the Rabbis of that city. Of plays, he knew nothing,
a fact which he deeply regretted in later years. From
his sixth to his eighth year he attended a school, the
teachers of which were ignorant and the pupils naughty
in the extreme. They hated and envied him on account
of his "pride"—he took no part in their mean tricks—
and prominent faculties. Hence he left that school
where he could profit nothing and only lose his good
manners. Mathematics and the Talmud were now his
favorite studies. His father and brother Heyman were his
teachers. The Talmud engulfed his whole attention
to such an extent that he would not even read a book
written in German. Touchingly he writes in his diary
concerning this time: "Woe, woe! How have you fled,
the years of my childhood! Neither were lessons of

morals inculcated into me, nor was my body strengthened by means of physical exercises, nor was my soul
ennobled by instruction and education. Woe! they
are gone! Come back, that I may make use of you!"
Geiger was strictly orthodox up to his tenth year. But
already in his eleventh year doubts began to awaken
in his breast. He was prohibited from reading the
history of the Jews. He obeyed this instruction, but
he read Becker's "Handbook of History," and the
reading of Greek and Roman history caused him to
pause and think. So, for instance, his orthodox
conscience was troubled by the question whether it
might not be possible that, just as well as Minos had
ascribed his doctrines to Jupiter, Lycurgus his to Apollo,
Numa Pompilius his to Emperia, so might Moses have
ascribed his to Jehovah. But, in accord with Talmudical dialectics, he answered these questions satisfactorily
to himself claiming that those heathen legislators in
ascribing their laws to their Gods had imitated Moses,
who was inspired by God. At the age of twelve he was
"loved by fools, respected by ignoramuses, honored by
the orthodox," but "pitied by the educated classes of
Jews," as he graphically puts it. The Rothschilds paid
for his instruction in Latin and Greek. At his "Bar
mitzvah" he delivered a "Drasha" (essay on a Halachic
subject) which was full of Talmudical subtleties, and
a German sermon, during the delivery of which some
pious men had covered their faces with their hands.
After his father's death in 1823 he became utterly disgusted with the Talmud, and his friends, Ludwig
Braunfels (his nephew), Max Loeb, S. Bruehl and
Ignatz Elissen confirmed him in his views. On the
other hand, his family wanted him to become a Rabbi,
without, however, being aware of the change which
had taken place in his views. Thus he was very
unfortunate indeed, as he was not fashioned for a
hypocrite, and yet had felt within himself the ambition
for theological activity. It must be said, however,
that his mother did notice the change which had taken
place within him.

April 28, 1829, Geiger arrived in Heidelberg, where he devoted himself in full earnest to the study of classical philology and Oriental languages, under the guidance of Professors Umbreit, Creuzer and Herrmann. Aside from this, he studied the Syrian language, without in the least neglecting his Talmudical studies, and continued his labors on the Mishna, which he had commenced July 21, 1827. At that time already he was aware of the fact that the spirit of the Mishna is different from that of the Gmara, inasmuch as it does greater justice to the rules of sound logic, and does not indulge so much in rabulistic sophistry and idle argumentation. He also studied anthropology under Daub, and history of literature and culture under Schlosser. Nevertheless, he was not satisfied with the opportunities for study offered to him at Heidelberg, and left, therefore, for Bonn, where the celebrated Orientalist Professor Freytag, filled the chair of Oriental philosophy. On his way to Bonn he stopped at Carlsruhe, where the Jews greatly displeased him. There he met Dr. Berthold Auerbach, who remained his lifelong friend. Geiger's original intention was to give up the study of theology in Bonn; but his short stay in Frankfort, where new interest was just then manifested in religious matters, induced him to devote his life to the enlightenment of the Jews. He did not want to go to the Wuerzburg Jeshiba, which he called in his diary the "well-known Jesuit institution;" so he wended his way to Bonn, where he arrived Oct. 28, 1829.

The causes of Geiger's wavering irresolution as to the continuance of his theological career were two:—In the first place the conditions of Judaism in Frankfort, where he found two extremes, the radical and hyper-orthodox Jews (Nachgelassene Schriften, Vol. I, pp. 298-299) were far from encouraging. Secondly, the few Jewish theological students, whose acquaintance he had made in Heidelberg, disgusted him entirely with the Rabbinical career. In a letter to Prof. Paulus, he speaks thus on the subject: "I found Jewish theologians in Heidelberg who walked in darkness, and the thought of the many obstacles which would be laid in my way by such theologians, and the battles I would be compelled to fight with them, embittered me against the study of theology, and Oriental languages engrossed my attention." (N. Schr. Vol. V, p. 47.) If he could have known of the struggles awaiting him in Breslau, he could not have written better and more to the point.

In Bonn life began to be more interesting to him. He mingled more with the people, although he shunned the well known societies of the students as they flourish in every German University, because he wanted to study and not merely to be called a "student." But he met there Jewish theologians, who brought back his taste for and reconciled him again to the Jewish theology. I mention as belonging to this circle, S. Scheyer, Samson Raphael Hirsch, his intimate friend, but later his most fierce and bitter opponent, Ullman, later Rabbi in Coblentz; Gruenebaum, still Rabbi in Landau (86 years old); Frensdorff, later Director of the "Seminary for Teachers" in Hannover, Rosenfeld, Hess and others. "Hirsch," Geiger said in his diary, "has been dragged into a peculiar mode of thinking, through Bernays in Hamburg, has accepted his excessive veneration of the Bible, and his after-philology, in the explanation of the same."

These students had formed a Society December 6, 1829, in Geiger's room, the object of which was to preach every Sabbath alternately, and to criticise rigidly these sermons. It was to my knowledge the first society of its kind in modern times. Geiger praised Hirsch's extraordinary eloquence, keen penetration and quick perception. Hirsch spoke well of Geiger's sermon (January 2, 1830), and for a year they read together cursorily the treatise on sacrifices in the Talmud (Sebachin). "Thus," the diary continues, "a mutual esteem and love has grown. I esteemed his excellent faculties, his rigid virtue, and loved his good heart; he respected my talents, loved my frankness and my youthful cheerfulness." I mention this on account of the fierce opposition which sprang up later among the two friends. Geiger mentions that he redeemed Ullman from his orthodoxy.

How zealously he had studied can be judged from the following curriculum. He studiously attended the lectures of Brandis, on logic, of Calcker on introduction into philosophy, of Freytag on the Arabic language and exegesis, of Welker on classical philology, of Niebuhr and Huellman on history, of Haase on anthropology, of Bobrik on philosophy. Aside from this he studied metaphysics, physics, rhetoric, psychology, read Herbart's writings with Scheyer, and in company with Frensdorff and Rosenfeld devoted a great deal of time to the study of the Talmud. And yet, he found time to give private lessons, partly gratuitously to his friends, partly for the sake of improving his financial condition; to read thoroughly the German classics, and to take interest in political questions which necessitated a more than superficial reading of the daily press. He was a great enthusiast for political liberty. Concerning the affairs of Judaism in those days, he complains of the atheism and immorality, of the lack of religious instruction and of the general ignorance of the young. He denounces the worship of the dead letter and the materialistic tendency which was en vogue among students of theology who considered the office of Rabbi as a milking cow. The following is an interesting characteristic of his friends in Bonn, of Samson Raphial Hirsch he says, that he indulges in philosophical speculations in the pulpit; of Ullman, that he is too sentimental; that Hess has no idea of what a sermon is, that Frensdorff preaches to scholarly, and that Rosenfeld is shallow, continuing: "We have no inspiring patterns, no masters whom we could follow. If only a Jewish Seminary should be erected at an University where exegesis, homiletics, Talmud and Jewish history should be taught in a true religious spirit, it would be the most fertile, and most instructive institution." This was written August 22nd, 1832, which proves beyond a shadow of a doubt, that Geiger was the very

first among all the Jewish theologians of the nineteenth
century, who advocated the important idea of founding a Jewish Theological Faculty or Seminary, for the
education of Rabbis. This is a significant historical
fact, because the versatile editor of the "Zeitung des
Judenthums," Dr. Ludwig Philippsohn, tried fifteen
years later to claim the origination of this idea for
himself. See also an article of Geiger on this subject
in his "Wissenschaftliche Zeitschrift fuer Juedische
Theologie" (1835), which was published later in
pamphlet-form. In the meantime he continued his
grammatical and lexicographical labors on the Mishna.
Lessing's theological writings, had an inspiring effect
on him, and his "Wolfenbuettel Fragments" awakened
in Geiger the thought of a similar work in the domain
of Jewish theology. Indeed he published in 1856 a
work, "Leon Da Modena," which reminds one forcibly of
Lessing's "Wolfenbuettel Fragments." Gabriel
Riesser's little pamphlet "On the Condition of the Professors of the Mosaic Faith in Germany," exercised a
great influence upon Geiger, and in a letter to S. R.
Hirsch, then Rabbi at Oldenburg, he expressed himself in the most sanguine manner as to the effect of
this book in creating a spirit of union and in eradicating the demoralizing usury among the Jews. It is
significant that Geiger deemed it necessary to add,
"Do not consider this matter too worldly and not becoming your position." (Nachgel. Schriften, VI, page
49). How times have changed! Geiger the student
an enthusiast for harmony and union among the
German Jews, while S. R. Hirsch devoted the labor of
his life to dismember and to tear asunder the Congregations of Israel, a work which his disciples and
followers still pursue. It speaks well for Geiger, that
already as a student he felt disgusted with Heinrich
Heine's sneering and jeering railleries, while Boerne's
earnest love of liberty was sympathetic to him.
(Nachgel. Schriften V, page 39). Yet the so-called
historian Graetz speaks enthusiastically of the
apostate Heine. Geiger was highly esteemed by the

celebrated Orientalist Prof. Freytag, on account of his proficiency in the Arabic and other Semitic languages. Mostly on Geiger's account the University of Bonn offered a prize for the best work on the question: "What has Mohammed taken from Judaism."* The prize was awarded to Geiger, August 3rd, 1842. This excellent book secured him also the diploma of Doctor philosophiae in 1835.

To his intimate friends belonged the Oppenheimer family in Bonn; Elias Grunebaum, then a student at Bonn, who was for the last fifty-six years District Rabbi of Landau,—Geiger speaks of him as a "philosophical head full of earnest will and warm zeal for theological studies;"—I. Dernbourg, of Mayence, now Professor of Hebreu Rabbinique on the Ecole des Hautes Etudes and membre de l'Institut in Paris, and Heinrich and Solomon Hertz, of Cologne. In spite of his lack of time Geiger started a "Society for the Furtherance of Culture among the Jews in Bonn." This society drew him into controversies with the fanatics of that old community.

Now the question arose with Geiger, how to find a suitable field for his activity. For a Reform-Rabbi of Geiger's calibre, sixty-one years ago in Germany, this was by no means an easy task. He applied for the position of Rabbi, then vacant at Hanau, and preached there June 16, 1832, but was not elected on account of his advanced views. He did not belong to the class of the "smart" Rabbis of to-day, who in their trial-sermons follow the maxim of that French philosopher who said that "the language is given for the purpose of hiding the thoughts." Still, in November of the same year (1832), he was elected Rabbi of Wiesbaden. He was at that time engaged to be married to Emilie

*The original question of the philosophical faculty was formulalated as follows: "Inquiratur, in fontes Alcorani seu leges Mohamedicae eos, qui ex Judaismo derivandi sunt." The Commentary of the English Orientalist Sale and a few extracts of Beidhavi's Commentary, made by Prof. Freytag during his stay in Paris, were all of the material of which Geiger could make use in his difficult work.

Oppenheim, of Bonn, a highly educated lady, on May
25, 1833. But he did not marry before July 1, 1840, as the
salary in Wiesbaden—four hundred Gulden (about one
hundred and thirty dollars), per annum—did not permit him the luxury of marriage.

Though the Congregation was small, it contained
quite a number of intelligent Jews, who were in favor
of progress and Reform. Geiger had to preach, to give
religious instruction to the older pupils, to supervise
the elementary instruction of the teachers, to perform
wedding-ceremonies in neighboring places, and to officiate at funerals. He preached every Sabbath, because,
as he expressed it in a letter to Gruenebaum, "he wanted the sermon to be regarded as a necessary part of the
divine service." (December 29, 1832). We must not
forget that a great many Jews considered the sermon simply in the light of an unnecessary addition to the service.
Geiger was a fiery, enthusiastic and forcible preacher,
for whom preaching was no labor, but a pleasure. He
was beloved by his Congregation, established in 1835
an "Israelitschen Maenner-Krankenverein," (Society for
the Purpose of attending to the Sick), published an
"Order of the Synagogue," which abolished abuses in
the worship, and fought against the obsolete form of
the Jewish oath. Through teaching the Confirmation-
class he gained great influence upon the young. He
had several Conferences with his Frankfort friends
Creizenach, J. S. Adler, Jacob Auerbach, Dernbourg,
F. Flehinger (Rabbi of Merchingen), Darmstadt and
others, in which important questions concerning the
welfare of Judaism were discussed. This was virtually
the first Rabbinical Conference of modern Judaism, and
surely the forerunner of all succeeding Conferences.
This fact is also of historical importance, as Dr. Ludwig Philippsohn claimed to be the instigator of the
modern Rabbinical Conventions in the interest of
Reform-Judaism.

But all this was not sufficient for Geiger's scope of
action. He studied most zealously the philosophical
and theological literature of the day, especially "The

Life of Jesus," by David Friedrich Strauss. He divined fully in his letter to Jacob Auerbach on this work, that this Strauss would revolutionize the Christian Church (January 9, 1837). Geiger intended to publish, in company with Frensdorff, Dernbourg and others, the works of the Jewish philosophers of the middle ages.

But the time was not yet ripe for a work mapped out on such a grand scale, although Geiger was ready to do his share of the work.

He was, however, more fortunate with his other venture, the publication of his "Wissenschaftliche Zeitschrift fuer Jeudische Theologie," (Scientific Journal for Jewish Theology), although he had very little encouragement. September, 1832, before he had occupied a position, he wrote to Frensdorff on the subject of this periodical. Starting from the valuelessness of "Sulamith," which had outlived its usefulness,* he claimed, that the time had come for a scientific treatment of Judaism, no matter what the results might be.

In spite of disappointment and discouragement the Zeitschrift was published, the first three volumes from 1835 to 1838. The first two numbers of the fourth volume were printed in Frankfort (Sauerland's Verlag) and the last two numbers in Stuttgart (Brodhag). Following is a partial list of the contributors to the Zeitschrift: Salomon, Kley, Rappoport, Mannheimer, Creizenach, Zunz, Abraham Kohn, Bloch, (Buchau), Herxheimer, and Joseph Aub (Rabbi of Bayreuth, Mainz, Berlin), Leopold Stein, Gruenebaum, Dernbourg and Jacob Auerbach. The fact that such a galaxy of the brilliant intellects of Israel contributed to the periodical is the best proof that it had really filled a long felt want. It advocated the progressive development of Judaism, and tried to prove historically the origin and growth of the Jewish ceremonial law. By this

---

*The tendency of the Salamith is thus characterized in his letter. "It says to the Christians: 'We Jewish children are no more as naughty as we have been. We behave better, we imitate you, and are, therefore, worthy of our rights.'"

critical method it was easily shown how a great many
of the ceremonies, customs and usages of the Jews and
their *raison d' etre* in certain circumstances, had outlived the sphere of their usefulness in our age and
amidst occidental surroundings. Reform is nothing
new, as changes have taken place in all ages and climes,
in accord with the demands and exigencies of the times.
On account of the dispersion of Israel among all nations, their religious institutions were by no means free
from non-Jewish influences. It was in particular
pointed out where Reform was needed. This system
is justly designated as historical-critical, based as it is
on scientific research and investigation. Therefore
Geiger deserves to be styled the creator of a scientific
Jewish theology, which has placed the Jewish Reform-
movement on the firm basis of science. The little there
was of this movement before Geiger, was merely the
result of an aesthetic want in the service of the Synagogue. It simply touched the surface, but did not enter into the very spirit of Judaism. Thus practical
questions of Jewish life were treated in the Zeitschrift,
for instance the "Jewish Customs of Mourning," "Music on Sabbath and Holidays in the Synagogue," "Removal of the Shoes on the Day of Atonement and on
the Ninth of the Month of Ab, and during the Blessing
of the Priests," by A. Kohn; "The Holidays," by
Bloch; "The Chalizah," by Guttman; "The Position of
Women in the Synagogue," by Geiger, and others.
These things may appear insignificant to-day, but they
were momentous questions in those days, and the mere
fact that Rabbis often of small Congregations had the
courage to give freely their advanced opinions on these
subjects has done wonders toward establishing the
principle of a scientific Reform and toward creating a
warm interest in this movement, even in circles where
Reform was either utterly unknown or was not deemed
worth while thinking of. For, so long as the Reform-
movement was in the hands of a few preachers, school-
teachers and private men, the official Judaism, as represented by the Rabbis, took hardly any notice of it.

Geiger's agitation, however, emanating as it did, from a Rabbi, aided and abetted through his Zeitschrift by Rabbis, did not fail to call attention and to produce a certain consternation in the camp of orthodoxy. Just imagine for a moment that at a time when to be a Rabbi and to be strictly orthodox were identical terms, quite a number of young Rabbis, under the leadership of Geiger, dared to throw the gauntlet to the powerful and influential orthodoxy of Europe, and to advocate Reform in their official capacity as Rabbis, thus investing the despised and hated Reform-movement with Rabbinical authority. This was a very bold step indeed sixty years ago, because unheard of before in the checkered history of Judaism.

But the Zeitschrift, while in the main devoted to the internal affairs of Judaism, and to a scientific research into its history and literature, did not neglect to fight valiantly for the emancipation of the Jews. I only mention Geiger's forcible and classical refutation of A. H. Hartman's hostile assaults against the Jews. Geiger justly held the opinion that outward oppression is always the source of stagnation, stability and retrogression within.* A glance at the miserable state of affairs of Judaism in Germany to-day, where officially orthodoxy holds sway, while practically atheism and indifference are rampant, prove the truth of this view.

Geiger's prize-essay: "What has Mohammed Taken from Judaism?" was published in book form in 1834 in Bonn. The celebrated Orientalist, Sylvester de Sacy of Paris, and other eminent scholars spoke highly of it, and helped to establish Geiger's literary reputation. He published also interesting articles in the "Universal Kirchen Zeitung," of Darmstadt, and in other journals.

But his main object to bring the progressive Rabbis of Germany together in convention, was not lost sight of and he worked undaunted by obstacles, until

---

*See Zeitschrift, I., 552-567, 340-357; II., 78-92, 463-473, and my "Der Fortschreitende Rabbinismus." (Konigsberg, 1877), and page 130 of this book.

he succeeded. Thus, in August, 1837, the first Rabbinical Conference was held at Wiesbaden. It was attended by Drs. Geiger, Kohn, of Hohenems; Mayer, of Stuttgart; Bloch, of Buchau; Wasserman, of Muchringen; Wagner, of Mannheim; Herxheimer, of Bernburg, Aub, of Beyreuth, Stein, of Burgkunstadt; Guttman, of Redwitz; Loewy, of Fuerth and Wechsler; Friedlaender, of Brilon, then eighty years old, Gruenebaum, of Landau, Hess, of Eisenach, came too late; Selz, of Uehlefeld and Neubuerger sent excuses, but declared their sympathy. While we cannot chronicle great tangible results of this Conference, the mere fact that the most intelligent and cultured Rabbis of Germany had assembled to discuss subjects pertaining to a Reform of Judaism, was in itself a result of important consequences for the future. True, their orthodox opponents ridiculed it, saying, that nothing was done. The same thing was said by the orthodoxy after every similar assembly in the last fifty years. But it was, to say the least, a proof of courage, and self-denial, that those Rabbis were not afraid to attend such an assembly which was called together for the purpose of advancing the cause of progress and Reform among the Jews. Loewy, Guttman, Kohn, Bloch, Wechsler, Herxheimer and Aub are complimented by Geiger in his letter to Jacob Auerbach, (August 22, 1837), for their zeal and activity. It was resolved, that practical questions should be discussed in the Zeitschrift and that the Rabbis should give their opinions and final votes on them. Loewy, Mayer and Stein were appointed a committee to publish a home prayer-book in accord with the demands of the times. The report spread by the orthodoxy, that the members of the Conference were ordered by the government to disband proved of course untrue.

But it cannot be denied, that notwithstanding these results Geiger did not occupy the position to which he was entitled. Not only was his salary so poor, that he could not afford to marry his beloved Emilie Oppenheim, of Bonn, but neither his literary nor his Reform aspirations could find realization in the small Congregation of Wiesbaden. (See Geiger's Nachgel: Schriften, pages 77, 80, 81 and 101.)

No wonder that he applied for the position in Gothenburg (March 6, 1835). But owing to the denunciations of his orthodox "friends" he was not elected on account of his "heresy." It must be said that Geiger, in his application for the position, did not in the least attempt to conceal his ideas. In 1838 he gave up his position in Wiesbaden, to the great regret not only of the government, but also of the Congregation, which is proven by the letters addressed to Geiger by the two bodies.

But now the time seemed propitious to Geiger's orthodox enemies to vent their spite and to wreak their vengeance on him. In the Zeitung des Juden- thums of August 18, 1838,* he was slandered by an anonymous, who said that Geiger was compelled to resign his position in Wiesbaden on account of his "im- moral character." This coward went so far as to sus- pect him politically. Gabriel Riesser and the Board of Trustees of the Wiesbaden Congregation felt called upon to answer that contemptible correspondence in a manner highly flattering to Geiger. When the office of "Land-Rabbi" was created in Wiesbaden, the position was again offered to him. His relations to his Con- gregation was always most pleasant. When he cele- brated his twenty-fifth jubilee as Rabbi, (November 21, 1857), he was made the recipient of an elegant present and of a complimentary letter from his former Congre- gation in Wiesbaden, and when the new Temple was finished, Geiger was called to Wiesbaden in order to dedicate it August 24, 1869. His sermon on that oc- casion, "Israel's Spiritual Life," was printed and repub- lished in his "Nachgel. Schriften, Vol. I, pp. 434-444."

---

*It was in bad taste on the part of Philippsohn, the editor of the paper, to publish an anonymous slanderous correspondence against Geiger, the successful candidate in Breslau. The very fact, that Philippsohn was also a candidate for the Breslau position, ought to have prevented him from publishing the libel.

Shortly before his departure for Wiesbaden he published in his Zeitschrift an article "The Author and the Rabbi," (Vol. I, pp. 492-504), which may be considered as the programme of his coming struggles. The drift of this article is, that the author has the whole community of Israel as his audience. Therefore he has not only the right, but the duty to consider the disagreements and divergencies of the entire community of Israel. He has the privilege to express his opinions, no matter how much they may differ from those generally accepted, and time must show whether his arguments are convincing. He is bound to call forth opposition, but this will only help the cause he represents. Absolute truth and the eventual dominion of the idea must be his ideal. But the same author will have to employ a different method in his quality as Rabbi of a single Congregation. Then and there he must accommodate himself to the desires of the members, and in view of his success in practical work, he will be satisfied with what he can accomplish. He will make use of existing circumstances to the best of his ability. A man of peace, he will labor in the field which is not at all touched by partisan strife. While as author he may oppose certain customs and usages, he will make good use of them for the same purpose in his quality as a Rabbi. In short, while the aim and object of the Jewish author and Rabbi are identical, the means to be employed are naturally different. As long as both labor in the cause of the ultimate realization of the Jewish religious idea, they fulfill their mission. It is, therefore, not hypocrisy or inconsistency, if a man, who as author advocates progressive measures of Reform, is conservative in his Congregation.

This view was sustained by the most prominent Rabbis of Europe during Geiger's troubles in Breslau.

GEIGER IN BRESLAU.

Notwithstanding the fact that Breslau could boast of a comparatively large number of cultured Jews, orthodoxy in its strictest form had still full control there

in the beginning of the fourth decade of this century.
Rabbi S. A. Tiktin held full sway in the Jewish Congregation of Breslau. As an instance of the tyrannical
way in which Tiktin availed himself of his power, I
call attention to the following fact. A Jewish printer
by the name of Sulzbach, was about to print M.
Brueck's reformatory publication on the "Rabbinical
Ceremonies," but S. A. Tiktin, like a censor of the inquisition, prohibited Sulzbach from doing so. This
was possible in Breslau in the year 1836. The book
was published, anyhow, by the bookseller Schultz at
the instigation of the lexicographer, Dr. W. Freund,
and did not fail to create a great sensation on account
of its bold criticism of the Rabbinical additions to the
the laws of Moses. Geiger published a thorough and
favorable review of this book in his "Zeitschrift," * which
fact was the cause of numberless annoyances and evil
consequences for the young Rabbi.

When the desire to introduce German sermons,
and a reformed service in the Synagogue of Breslau
could no longer be suppressed, the general attention
was directed upon Geiger. He declined, however, to
accept the position of a mere preacher; he wanted to
be Rabbi. I have tried to explain in the chapter on
Holdheim, that it was not a question of vanity, but of
principle, why Holdheim as well as Geiger, insisted on
the title of "Rabbi." In the meantime the "Rabbinats-assessor" Falk of Breslau died (1838) and the
vacant position was advertised. The advertisement
called for "theologians endowed with Biblical, Talmudical and scientific scholarship," who were "capable
of delivering instructive and edifying sermons on each
Sabbath." Of twelve applicants for the position, four
were found worthy of special consideration, namely:

Drs. Ludwig Philippsohn, Samuel Holdheim,
Solomon Herxheimer, and Abraham Geiger. At the
instigation of the committee, the latter was invited to
stop in Breslau on his trip through Germany and to

*See pages 63-65 of this book.

deliver several sermons in the Synagogue. Geiger
replied that it is not his custom to deliver
trial sermons, but that he would be willing to
preach once. He arrived in Breslau July 17th, and
was invited to preach July 21. Rabbi Tiktin received
also an invitation to be present on the occasion of
Geiger's sermon. But Tiktin's party lost no time in
trying to prevent the sermon. They called the attention of the Chief of Police Heincke to the fact that the
king had prohibited the delivery of German sermons in
a Jewish house of worship.* He referred them to the
government, went to hear Geiger's sermon, and coming home from the Synagogue, found the answer from
Berlin, that Geiger should not preach. Geiger's sermon was electrifying, and produced the greatest enthusiasm, although very many of his audience had become utterly indifferent to religion. He preached on
the text "Generation goeth and generation cometh, but
the earth stands forever" (Kohelet I, 4), and pointed
out that in the midst of eternal change the spirit only
is immutable. Israel is always the same, so far as the
basis of its spiritual existence is concerned, although
the manifestation of this fundamental thought has
been different at different times. Israel, in the times
of the prophets, was another than the Israel in the
dispersion, and the Israel of to-day is again another, so
far as customs, usages and observances are concerned.
Therefore the outward form must not be idolized, because it is changeable. The prophets say: "It has
been said unto thee, oh man, what is good, and what
thy God expects of thee, nothing but 'to do justice,
love kindness, and to walk humbly before they God.'"
(Micah VI, 9). Now, suppose you would answer: I
have practiced numerous ceremonies, but I was not
always just, then you have neglected the eternal for
the sake of the perishable. Straw, stubble, chaff and
wheat disputed once, each of them exclaiming: 'For
my sake was the field sown.' The wheat, however,

*This was done after the Jacobsohn Temple in Berlin had been

said: 'Wait until the owner of the field arrives.' As soon as he came, he threw away the straw, burnt the stubble, and let the chaff fly away. But he most carefully gathered the wheat. Now it is not necessary to throw away the chaff before the wheat is ripe. Thus it is with the forms and ceremonies, the bearers of the spirit. As soon as the spirit has departed from them, they are like straw, stubble and chaff, useless in the cause of piety. Institutions change with the times. When you gather water in a reservoir and shut it up carefully, you will find after weeks the same drops. But is it the same water? Why no! It is a stagnant pool. The taste is gone. So it is with the lifeless form, which cannot be preserved, after its spirit has departed. Only the husk changes, not the kernel and essence."[*] In consequence of this sermon Geiger was elected as second Rabbi and "Rabbinitsassessor" of the Breslau Jewish Congregation, July 25th, 1838.

Now one might think that the election excitement being over, things in Breslau went on quietly and smoothly. But this was not at all the case. On the contrary, the machinations of the enemies of progress in general and of Geiger in particular, were just now commencing in full earnest, and on a most extensive scale. Before Geiger's election his opponents found fault with him on account of most ridiculous trifles. Thus they objected to the gown he wore in the pulpit, because it was made of velvet and not of silk, which was the fashion among the Polish Rabbis. They found fault with him because he folded his hands and directed his eyes heavenward while praying, and because he said "Abraham" instead of "Avrohom," "Isaac" instead of "Jizchak," "Moses" instead of "Maushe," and so forth.

After his election, however, these comparatively harmless tactics were changed, and a fierce, bitter, yea,

[*]This sermon was published in pamphlet form (Breslau 1838, Friedlaender) and is reprinted in Geiger's Posthumous works; Vol. I, pages 355-360.

desperate fight was made against him, in which means most foul were employed to serve the end, all of course "*ad majorem dei gloriam.*"

All efforts were made to prevent the sanction of Geiger's election by the government.   In Prussia, the government has the power to veto the election of any clergyman.   In Geiger's case such a nullification of his election was the more plausible, as he was considered a foreigner in Prussia—he was a Frankforter—and was in need of naturalization papers.   Four individuals had so far forgotten every sense of decency and shame, as to make themselves guilty of political denunciation, which is called "Messirah" and is considered in the Talmud one of the worst crimes, equal to murder, incest and idolatry (Talm. Jerusch. Peah 1, 13).   Now these four champions of the Talmud importuned the Prussian government not to naturalize Geiger, because he was not only an innovator, but a dangerous demagogue, who aimed at the destruction not only of the church but of the state.   These "Watchmen of Zion" added the sin of bearing false witness against their fellowman to the crime of denunciation.   But not satisfied with this dirty piece of work, Rabbi Tiktin and his henchmen hired a baptized Jew, Franz Karl Joel Jacoby, to write a promemoria against Geiger.   The Prussian ministry demanded of Geiger an explanation of the charges of heresy brought forward against him.   Geiger answered thoroughly, and proved to the satisfaction of the government the ignorance and maliciousness of his accusers.   The following passage of Geiger's excellent reply may find a place here: "What, however, demonstrates, beyond a doubt, the malicious intentions and the evil designs of the traducers, is the manner of their attempt to bring into disrepute in the eyes of the government, all those who happen to be opposed to their private opinions.   Not capable of doing battle with the spirit, they would like to make use of the sword of the laws, by stamping every view differing from theirs, as the result of revolutionary ideas.   It is revolting in the extreme, that people should arrogantly impute to men whom they owe their better civil condition in the state, a 'passion for innovations' and 'malevolence;' that people in their malicious cowardice and mean deceitfulness dare to say of men who always defend them against hostile attacks, that they cause themselves to be used as tools for a revolutionary movement.

Geiger went in the meantime to Bielefeld and Frankfort, where he came in contact with the Prussian ambassador, whose opinion was required as to Geiger's political record. He answered that nothing of any damaging character could be found in the records at Mayence, and that having read the "Zeitschrift" he could not help being astonished at the ability and vast scholarship of Geiger as manifested therein.

In order to be nearer Breslau, Geiger went to Berlin, where he remained from September, 1838, to December, 1839. He conferred with the ministers Altenstein and Rochow, and with Alexander von Humboldt, whose powerful influence greatly benefitted his case, and who remained his life-long friend. Among other acquaintances of note, which Geiger had formed in Berlin were: Bettina v. Arnim, Max Ring, who wrote an excellent poem on Geiger, while presenting him in Breslau with a costly cup in the name of the Congregation; H. D. Oppenheimer, Ludwig Bamberger, and Leopold Zunz, in whose house he was always a welcome guest. The leading men of the Berlin Jewish Congregation had done absolutely nothing, although they were requested by the Congregation of Breslau to interest themselves in behalf of Geiger and his just cause, which was also their cause. This fact is in keeping with the character of the Berlin Jews, who deemed themselves very crafty in doing—nothing.

The following extracts of Geiger's letters during his stay in Berlin will always remain interesting reading. In a letter to Jacob Auerbach he says among other things: "Neither the government nor the Jews will weaken me in my firmness. The former would like to get rid of me in roundabout ways. But this will not do, they have to say clearly and definitely,

'We do not want you,' or they have to accept me.
I give a year of my life and even more. * * that
the Prussian government may speak out clearly and
decisively as to its measures toward Judaism without
subterfuges. * * They would like very much to
tire me out, so that I should throw away the pittance,
which would give them a chance to pose as the lovers
of justice; yes, I would go, would have gone long ago
if it had been only my own affair. As it is, I will
carry the matter through to the very last moment.
These gentlemen, as well as the faint hearted Jews, are
mistaken in me. My perseverance is a cause of embarrassment to their weakness and to their tricks, and
they confess already that they are embarrassed. * *
I am much too proud to attack Philippsohn as an opponent of mine. * * That I do not like the Jews
of Berlin you know by this time through Mr. M. It
is here where a person learns to know what indifferentism means.* They are here very strong in negative action only. * * They say that the cancer
must not be cut out, a little scraping is sufficient.
This may look nice for a time, but the cancer continues to eat. * * I know that I will accomplish
more in creating religious interest and in weakening
indifferentism than all these men who talk so positive-
ly. * * Please give my pamphlet on the 'Establishment of a Jewish Theological Faculty' no
further attention. Let it sleep as does the faculty.
The latter walks, thank God, in the realm of the
sainted souls, and has fled from his friend Philippsohn
and his consorts. Its enemies would not have done it
any harm."†

In a letter to M. A. Stern, dated August 2, 1839,
he says: "The embarrassment of the government
grows on account of my perseverance, aided by the
constancy of the Congregation in Breslau. The latter

---

*This remark is just exactly as true to-day as it was fifty-one
years ago.

†Letter to Jacob Auerbach, dated Berlin, June 13-21-t 1839 (Posthumous Works, Vol. V, pages 140-142).

acts indeed nobly. No trouble and no costs are avoided—you can well imagine that I do not live here at my own expense—in order to bring about a favorable result. Even if the decision of the government should turn out against me, the attention and sympathy which the matter has produced, cannot help bearing fruit. But should the result be favorable, great things have been accomplished, and I hope to do much in a Congregation of such importance as the one in Breslau.*

Of his relation to Zunz, Geiger says in another letter to Stern, dated November 14th-16th: "My personal intercourse with Zunz I would not give up for any price. I have indeed learned of Zunz very much, and to have won in him a friend, not only a literary associate, is saying a good deal, and is also of importance. * * While I always paid serious attention and love to the history of Judaism, I have made it more of a specialty, owing to the impulses of Zunz and my intercourse with him." From different reasons Geiger discontinued the publication of his "Zeitschrift" temporarily (1839). But he hoped that others would follow in his footsteps, but in vain. He writes to Stern in the same letter. * * "The main thing is that most of these Rabbis, and just the ones who occupy prominent positions, and who could exercise great influence upon others have learned too little. * * Philippsohn, for instance, possesses practical sense and versatility, but ability and the purity of character are lacking."

In a letter to Stern, dated December 6th, 1839, he informs Stern of his final success in the matter of naturalization, and continues: "I must confess I am proud of the fifteen months spent here and of their successes; many others would not have had the perseverance and the self denial necessary for such a protracted stay."

Geiger's enthusiasm for his chosen field was so great that no matter how things might have turned

---

*Geiger: Posthumous works, Vol. V, pages 142-145.

ont, he would have remained Rabbi. He expressed himself on the subject as follows: "Should I fail, owing to the slow course and to the stupidity of the people, I will know how to get through the world, but I shall remain Rabbi, even without an office. I know so well how I can be a useful member in the history of Judaism, that nothing can perplex me now."*

November 6th, Geiger was officially notified that his election in Breslau was sanctioned by the government. On December 24th he went to Breslau, and on January 2nd, 1840, he entered upon his position. He bound himself to preach almost every Sabbath, to supervise the educational institutions of the Congregation, and to care for the religious instruction of the young.

On January 4th he delivered his inaugural sermon. Not a few of his former opponents became his friends. He married July 1st, 1840, in Frankfort, where he was invited by the Congregat on to preach, and was presented with a diploma as Rabbi. His trip to Breslau via the cities along the Rhine, and by way of Berlin was a triumphal march. His reception in Breslau July 16th was a grand affair, giving testimony of the sincere affection which united Rabbi and Congregation, a bond which in consequence of mutual struggles in a sacred cause becomes always firmer.

Geiger's wife, Emilie, understood perfectly how to make her house the social center of the Congregation. For years the members of the Congregation, old and young, rich and poor, assembled on the first Wednesday evening of every winter month, and on Purim evenings, and these receptions or jours fixes were looked forward to with the greatest pleasure by the best element of Breslau Jewdom. Geiger's married life was blessed with two daughters and two sons, Dr. Berthold Geiger, Attorney at Law, in Frankfort-on-the-Main, son-in-law of Dr. Jacob Auerbach, and Doctor

*Geiger: Posthumous works, Vol. I, pages 7-25; see also Dr. Geiger's pamphlet: "Die Letzten Zwei Jahre" (Breslau 1840, Friedleander).

Ludwig Geiger, Professor of History at the University of Berlin. He is the author of numerous historical works, and editor of his father's posthumous writings. At present he is editor of a magazine in the interest of the history of the Jews, which periodical is subsidized by the "Deutsch-Israelitischen Gemeindebund," (The Confederation of German-Jewish Congregations). The fact that Ludwig Geiger and not the so-called historian Graetz was intrusted with this important task, shows the true importance which is entertained in Germany of Graetz's historiography.

But those who think that Geiger had smooth sailing in Breslau, after his victory over his unscrupulous and fanatical enemies, are very much mistaken. Inspired by S. A. Tiktin and his satellites, an anonymous pamphlet was issued, entitled: "The Election of Rabbi in Breslau." The author of this stupid publication was a certain Davidsohn, who was paid by the orthodox party of Breslau for his tirade against Geiger. In reviewing the libelous pasquinade, Geiger alludes to a Talmudic passage, and sarcastically translates it as follows: "David's son comes then only, when the intellect is gone and when the money has given out."[*]

Geiger refutes in the strongest possible terms the foolish fashion—and this may be a hint to the orthodoxy of our days—of introducing into Judaism terms which belong to Christianity exclusively. Judaism knows no "orthodoxy" or "heterodoxy," because the questions agitating the different parties within Judaism do not touch dogmas, but the ceremonies. Since time immemorial even those Rabbis who most strictly complied with the practice of every observance and usage, held the most radical views on inspiration, revelation, miracles, personality of God, resurrection, immortality of the soul, supernaturalism, and so forth.[†]

---

[*] This obscure passage speaks of the coming of the Messiah, who is called in Talmudical phraseology: "Son of David."

[†] It would lead me too far to give even a small number of passages proving this important assertion. They can be found on pages 127-128 of my "Principles of Judaism compared with those of Christianity" (Leipzig, Baumgaertner, 1877); and in my "The Talmud from

The writer of this pasquinade reproaches the Prussian Ministry in unmeasured terms for having sanctioned Geiger's election. He is convinced that if the just (?) complaints of the orthodox Jews had reached the throne of the king, and if the dissenting opinions of Geiger had been known to the highest authorities, it would have been needless for him to write on the subject. The fact of the matter is that the enemies of Geiger had left no stone unturned in order to oust him. At first they appealed to the government of the province of Upper Silesia, then to

the point of view of Modern Judaism" (Berlin, Issleib. 1880). But some instances may find a place here: "Who knows, who ascends the heaven, returns and tells us"(Talm. Makkoth, 23). "A time will come when all religious laws and ceremonies will lose their validity" (Niddah, 61). "God never came down from heaven to earth, Moses and Elijah never ascended the heaven" (Succah, 5). "Israel has no longer to expect a Messiah, for the prophecies concerning the Messiah were fulfilled through Hezekiah" (Sanh. 99). Many Christians and a great many orthodox Jews are of the opinion that the so-called Biblical criticism is the work of modern theologians, a product of the Nineteenth century. Nothing of the kind If they will please go back fifteen centuries, they surely will be nearer the cradle of this so-called "new science." In the middle of the third century Simon ben Lakish, the great Talmud teacher, decided that Job never existed but was a poetical creation, and furthermore, that the names of the angels were borrowed from a foreign people (Babylonians, Persians), by the Jews during the exile. By the way it may be mentioned, the highly-gifted Gaon Saadiah, who flourished in the ninth century, unequivocally placed reason above the Bible and the Talmud, and explained away many of the "miracles," for instance the speaking serpent in Paradise, Balaam's ass, the witch of Endor, and so forth. His contemporary, Chivi of Balk, explains the crossing of the Red Sea by the Israelites as "ebb and flood," the manna as a sort of resin emitted by the sweating of certain trees, the radiant face of Moses as caused by too much fasting, and he plainly denies supernatural revelation. Isaac ben Salomo, another contemporary, maintains that Gen. XXXVI. 31: "These are the Kings of Edom, who reigned before kings in Israel existed," had not been written by Moses, but at the time of King Josaphat. Moses Gikatilia brings prophecies of Isaiah in connection with the events of his own time. Samuel ben Chofni, Abulwalid (Jonah ben Ganach), ben Jasus (Jizchaki) belonged to the same critical school. Abraham Ibn Esra, born 1093, died 1167), is the first who boldly acknowledges the Babylonian origin of the so-called "Second Isaiah" (chapters 40-66), and hinted at difficult passages of the Pentateuch, thus attacking the authenticity of the same Spinoza explained these interesting passages. (See my lecture on "Spinoza," Chicago Inter-Ocean, December, 1883, and my "The Talmud," a series of lectures delivered ih Denver, pages 40-41. Denver, 1884).

the minister of the interior, then to the king, then they attempted to effect Geiger's removal from office.

He then accuses the representatives and members of the Breslau Congregation of frivolity, because they had elected Geiger, arraigns them that money leads the fashion with them, and contradicts himself in the following sentence, where he concedes that they possess a higher education and are imbued with a strong religious sentiment. Geiger was right in saying "Davidsohn came after he had lost his senses."

The author comes then to Geiger, and brings forth eight accusations against him, which would be entitled to a place in the "Curiosities of Literature." *

First Accusation: — Geiger has approved the abolition of the Fast of the Eve of Passover, for the benefit of a first-born son. Now, Maimonides and numerous Rabbis of the middle ages, disregarded this usage.

Second Accusation: Geiger does not observe the customs of mourning between Passover and the Feast of Weeks. The observance, not to shave one's beard in the "Sephira," i. e., the seven weeks between Pessach and Shabuoth, is of very late origin, and meaningless. †

Third Accusation:—Geiger disregards the custom of holding vigil on the night of the Feast of Weeks. This is a foolish cabalistic usage, which is not even mentioned in the latest codices.

Fourth Accusation:—Geiger called the observance of Tashlich‡ an invention of the people, which was not deemed worth while to be mentioned in the codex.

---

*There is no conservative Rabbi in America who is not guilty of the offenses of which Geiger is here accused.

†See Dr. Landsberger's "Heathenish origin of the custom not to marry between Passover and the Feast of Weeks. (Breslau, 1889, Schletter: also Geiger's Zeitschrift, Vol. VII).

‡Some of the hyper-orthodox Jews go in the afternoon of New Year (first day) to a river or dyke and throw pieces of bread or cake into the water, reciting the verses, Micah VII, 18-20. On account of the expression "cast all their sins into the depths of the sea," the ceremony is called "Tashlich."

Fifth Accusation:—Geiger should have said that the processions, with branches of palms and myrtle-branches on the Feast of Booths, were nothing but expressions of joy, as the whole festival is the "time of our joy." Geiger has proven this assertion.

Sixth Accusation:—Geiger should have said that the washing of the hands after leaving a house, where a corpse lies, is meaningless. Horrible s'n, this!

Seventh Accusation:—Geiger had said, that the prayer at sight of the moon should be shortened thus: "Praised be he who always reneweth the moon." The only wrong I can see in Geiger, is that he did not denounce such a prayer as idolatry and moon-worship.

Eighth Accusation:—Geiger had asserted, that the removal of the shoes is no act of reverence and respect among us, on the contrary, ill-mannered. Hence, is the custom that the Aaronites remove the shoes while blessing the people (Duchenen) objectionable. He also mentioned that the Biblical command that the priests should bless the people daily, was practically abolished and limited to three holidays only.

I have mentioned these "accusations" in order to show how ridiculous they were.

He finds also fault with Geiger's criticism of S. Raphael Hirsch's "Nineteen Letters,"* in which Geiger strongly arraigned the disgusting idolatry of the Jewish ceremonies, which is mentioned in these letters. Among other things, Geiger said; "It is very funny indeed to call a man an atheist because he writes two words or touches a candle on the Sabbath." The pamphleteer further accuses Geiger of "wicked superciliousness" and of "conceited rationalism," because he expressed doubts as to the Biblical origin of the custom to have "Mezuzoth"† on the door, and of

---

*These letters appeared, 1836, under the pseudonym "Ben Usiel," second edition, 1889, Frankfurt.

†Doorpost. (Deut. XI, 20.) On a piece of parchment are written the passages, Deut. VI, 4-9; XI, 13-21 (inclusive), and on the back the word "Shaddai" (Almighty). According to Isaiah LVII, 8, its origin seems to be heathenish.

laying "Tefillin"* (phylacteries) on the head and hand.
A less ignorant writer would have known that already
Rabbi Samuel Ben Meier,† the grandson of Rashi‡, not
only expressed such doubts eight hundred years before
Geiger, but went further than Geiger by declaring
plainly and unmistakably, that the passages, Exodus
XIII, 9, Deut. VI and XI, must not be taken literally
but figuratively, just like Canticles XIII, 6, "Engrave
them like a seal on thy heart." The Samaritans do
not lay "Tefillin" and have no "Mesusoth."§

In conclusion, Geiger censures most severely all
those who talk for pay about things of which they
know nothing. His biting sarcasm against the "Beer-
heteb‖ scholarship" of the modern orthodoxy, which,
utterly devoid of the knowledge of the origin and
history of religious customs, is always at hand with the
hue and cry: "It is a Mizveh; it is written," must be
read in order to be appreciated. He calls this sort of
learning a "curse to Judaism."●

The struggle in Breslau became more intense and
made the suspension of Tiktin necessary (1842). But
this was rather the signal to a renewed fight, in which

---

*Tefilin, "Tefilla" (prayer). There are two kinds, "Tefillin shel
Gad" (of the hand) and "Tefillin shel Rosh" (of the head). On pieces
of parchment are written the following passages: Exod. XIII, 1-11;
Exod. XIII, 11-17; Deut. VI, 4-10; Deut. XI, 13-22.

†He is known as "Rashbam," and complemented the Talmudical
labors of his grandfather, Rashi. He was one of the "Tossafists"
(Baale Tossafot) and a clear sighted commentator of the Bible,
which is best proven by his rationalistic explanation of Mesusa and
Tefillin

‡His name was Salomon ben Isaac [1040-1105], a disciple of Jacob b. Jakar in Worms, and Isaac b. juda in Mainz. He commen-
tated the entire Bible and Talmud, and it has always been a matter
of surprise how one man could accomplish such a gigantic work
and tremendous task all by himself. Zunz was the first to do him
justice.

§Because they take the passages in a figurative sense, like Prov.
III, 3; VI, 22; VIII, 3; Isaiah XLIX, 16. See Geiger, Zeitschrift der
Deutsch Morgenl. Gesellsch., Vol. XX, page 570.

‖Literally, "well explained." The book is a compendium containing the numberless Jewish customs and observances.

●See Geiger, "The last Two Years; Letters to a Befriended
Rabbi."

fair means and foul were used to harass Geiger. Tiktin's followers were especially embittered on account of
the ovations offered to Geiger by his Congregation.
Here is the translation of an address presented to Geiger and signed by every member of the Breslau Congregation: "Of our own accord we approach you from
the midst of your Congregation, which highly reveres
you, and which feels happy on account of your pious,
God-fearing activity, in order to express to you plainly
and candidly, our deep veneration and love in a time
when, alas, you have to fight hard struggles against
the unholy weapons of those who accuse you of heresy,
and against the poisoned arrows of slander and cal-
umny. We also give vent to our deep indignation on
account of the unworthy attacks with which blind passions overwhelm you. The pure and holy fire of enthusiasm for the genuine Judaism, which inflamed you
to show, with scientific keenness and clearness, the
eternally true kernel of our own faith, will encourage you
to continue your Rabbinical activity, which you have
begun so gloriously and carried on so happily in the
interest of strengthening the religious spirit in our
Congregation and in the community of Israel at large.
You will accomplish your noble work in spite of the
hostilities with which earthly interests and passions
obstruct your way. You may be sure of the thanks
and the veneration of all noble men and of the
blessing of God, who is a God of life and light, and
who will grant all-powerful protection to your work.
So mote it be. Signed, The Members of the Israelitish Congregation of the City."

No wonder that such an address, signed by every
member of the large Congregation, did not fail to fill
the hearts of Geiger's enemies with fierce wrath and
violent anger. Did not this address unmistakably
convince them, that all their tricks and machinations
had produced the contrary effect? Instead of depriv-
ing him of the respect and confidence of the people,
these intrigues had made him most popular, and his
name a household word in Breslau. We can easily

understand that such a feeling must have been galling
to the small but active band of fanatics and hypocrites
who constituted themselves as the saviors of Breslau
Judaism in those days. Their impotent rage knew no
limits. They became desperate, lost their heads,
committed one foolishness after another, and simply
made themselves ridiculous. For, was it not foolishness—yea, madness on their part, even to dream of the
possibility that the Prussian government would remove
Geiger from his position as Rabbi of so prominent a
Congregation, which had just as one man publicly demonstrated that they loved and worshipped him?
Was it not ridiculous to imagine for a moment that
the government which two years before, at a time when
Geiger was comparatively a stranger in Breslau, had
sanctioned his election, would now undo its actions in
order to please a few fanatics who had an axe to grind?
And yet Tiktin and his party petitioned the Prussian
ministry to remove Geiger, after a most successful
activity, from his office, in the face of the fact that he
had done more for the Congregation and for the cause
of Judaism in two years, than Tiktin and all Silesian
and Polish Rabbis had accomplished during their life-
time. If ever it proved true that "Quem Deus vult
perdere eum dementat,"* it proved so in this case. In
order to succeed, eight Rabbis of Posen and Upper Silesia—Eger,† Israel and David Deutsch, J. Caro and
others,—were induced to declare that Geiger was not
only unworthy to occupy a position of Rabbi, but even
to be admitted as a witness in a court of justice.

---

*Whom God wishes to destroy, him he makes mad.

†His father, Rabbi Akiba Eger, born in Eisenstadt, November,
1751, was Rabbi in Maerkisch-Friedland, and Posen. He could have
wielded a powerful influence for good but he used his influence in order to prevent the regulation of the school system among the Jews
of the province of Posen. He thought he had done a great thing in
freeing the Jews from military service, not knowing that he had in
this way hurt the cause of the Jews in Prussia, by giving rise to the
belief in the accusation that the Jews were cowards and unwilling to
shed their blood for their country. While he was considered a saint
by the ignorant masses, he was not able to make Posen a prominent
seat of Jewish learning. His scholarship was limited, his "opinions"

These eight pygmies acted as if Judaism had a tribunal of inquisition, and as if they had constituted this tribunal. In two pamphlets: "Darstellung des Sachverhaeltnisses in seiner hiesigen Rabbinats-Angelegegenheit," by S. A. Tiktin;[*] and "Entgegnung auf den Bericht des Obervorstehercollegium's der hiesigen Israeliten-Gemeinde ueber die Rabbinats-Angelegenheit an die Mitglieder,"[†] by the same author, Geiger is most mercilessly attacked as a man who systematically works to destroy the pillars of Judaism in a manner never done before, and who, in spite of all this, "does not blush and is not ashamed to officiate as Rabbi." (p. 16). More than this, Geiger is branded by these eight zealots as an infidel, who must be despised, shunned and separated from the community of Israel, and whose word as a witness before a court of justice is unworthy of belief. (p. 26).

To such an outrageous insult Geiger had to answer, and answer he did in a manner worthy of a Geiger. He delivered an address before his Congregation, which he published under the title, "Ansprache en meine Gemeinde."[‡]

One of the great complaints of Geiger's enemies has been that he was not satisfied with the position of a "preacher" or "lecturer," but that he insisted upon the title "Rabbi." Geiger was right in his action, as was Holdheim in a similar case in Berlin. Had the Reformers given up their titles as "Rabbis," the Reform-movement would have gained no stronghold in

----

on religious subjects did not betray a man of brains. He was one of those Rabbis who strongly condemned the Hamburg temple service. (See Geiger, Posthumoes Works," Vol. II, page 259). His son simply inherited from him the position of Rabbi in Posen, although he was a — nonentity. See page 190 of this book, Chap VIII. Holdheim. Akiba Eger died Oct. 12, 1837.

[*]Presentation of the affairs pertaining to his Rabbinical office. Breslau, 1842.

[†]Reply to the report of the Board of Directors of this Congregation, in matters of the Rabbinical office. Addressed to the members. Breslau, June 19, 1842.

[‡]Address to my Congregation, (Breslau, 1842), also published in Geiger's Posthumous Works, Vol. I, pages 52-112. (Berlin, 1875, Louis Gerschel, London, Asher & Co.)

the Congregations. Geiger, when coming to Breslau,
acted like a gentleman toward Tiktin, while the latter
behaved like an ill-mannered, uneducated "Rebbele."
Geiger called on Tiktin in company with Robert
Dyhrenfurth, president of the Congregation. Tiktin
requested Geiger to call on him again next day, but
alone. Geiger complied with this request, but was
told that Tiktin was not at home. Geiger left his
card there, and before leaving Breslau, he took leave
of Tiktin. As soon as Geiger had entered upon his
duties in Breslau, he asked of Tiktin, through Scheyer
Eliason, when his visit would be most welcome.
Tiktin's rude answer was that he did not desire
Geiger's visit. Who then disturbed the peace of the
Congregation, Geiger or Tiktin?* When Geiger was
requested to deliver a sermon at a wedding, at which
Tiktin was to officiate. Tiktin staid away. Although
Geiger never failed to attend Tiktin's addresses, which
were full of insulting allusions to Geiger and the
officers of the Congregation, Tiktin always absented
himself when Geiger preached, although his sermons
were utterly free from personal polemic. Even on
holidays he did not attend the Synagogue, notwithstanding the fact that the directors of the Congregation proposed to him to preach on the first day, provided he would come to the Synagogue on the second
day, when Geiger preached. Nevertheless did Geiger
not tire in trying to bring about a more harmonious
feeling. At a banquet where both Rabbis were
toasted, Geiger answered the toast, saying among
other things, that while he and Tiktin may differ in
their religious views, both of them are laboring in the
interest of the preservation of our religion. After the
speech he approached Tiktin. But all this was of no
avail with that haughty and conceited Rabbi, whose

---

*It is, however, a mistake to imagine for a moment, that Tik-
tin's ungentlemanly conduct towards Geiger was influenced by the
difference of religious opinions. No, it was simply meanness and
jealousy. For Tiktin had treated his colleague Falk, fifteen years
before, in the same way. Falk, however, was orthodox,

scholarship was by no means great. Whenever Rabbinical functions like Chalizah and Get (ritual divorce) made the presence of both Rabbis necessary, Tiktin intentionally slighted Geiger, in order to show him that he did not recognize him as a Rabbi. These insults occurred so frequently that at last the board of directors of the Congregation was compelled to inform Tiktin, that a continuation of these gross insults to his colleague, would be followed by Tiktin's suspension from his office. And, as Tiktin stubbornly refused to carry out these directions, he was suspended (1842).

It was a principle with Geiger and with all other Reform-Rabbis to oppose strongly the division of the functions of the Rabbi and of the preacher. Wherever such divisions existed, the Rabbi was regarded as the representative of stability and stagnation, and the preacher as the representative of progress, development and Reform. This state of affairs was bound to create and to keep alive two opposing parties in the Congregation; the party of stabilism, represented by the Rabbi; the party of progress, led by the preacher. Thus discord and dissension were perpetuated and nurtured. How right Geiger was, is best proven by the fact that nowadays such a division of the Rabbinical office is almost unknown.

Geiger was peaceably inclined. He even sacrificed his Zeitschrift "for the sake of peace," but having found out too late, that his peace-offerings were not appreciated by his bitter enemies, he commenced its publication again.

The following is another proof of the "piety" of Tiktin and his henchmen. On April 3, 1842, the funeral of Heyman Oppenheim, a prominent member of the Congregation, took place. Geiger was requested to deliver a funeral sermon. Whether Tiktin was also asked to do so, is not known. Still he spoke, but instead of delivering a funeral address, he cowardly abused his privilege in order to vent his spite against Geiger and his friends, whom he insulted in the most outrageous manner. He incited the mob to such

an extent, that, when Geiger was about to begin his
sermon, the tumult became so tremendous, and the
wild noise and excitement so fearful, that Geiger was
almost thrown into the grave. With his usual calmness and tact, he simply said: "I do not wish to disturb the rest of the dead; depart in peace." Who
then disturbed the peace? It was not until after this
scene, that Tiktin was suspended. Geiger preached a
sermon on the Sabbath following this outrage,
admonishing the hearers to preserve peace, and warning them against the "unholy fire" of fanaticism and
selfishness.

Sunday following this impressive sermon, three
so-called "messengers of peace" made their appearance
in Geiger's house. Naturally he thought that they
had been sent by Tiktin, in order to apologize in his
behalf for the affront offered to Geiger by Tiktin's
miserable behavior at the funeral. But how disappointed was Geiger when these messengers revealed
their mission. They—or better, Tiktin— had the af-
frontery to ask of Geiger that he should declare his
willingness to give up in future, his co-operation in
the functions of Chalizah and ritual divorces; in other
words, Geiger should resign his prerogatives, privileges,
rights and duties of Rabbi for the sake of pleasing an
ignorant fanatic and malicious enemy, who was his in-
ferior in every respect. One of the jesuitical mediators
proposed as a kind of a compromise, that if Geiger
would promise never to be present at such functions,
Tiktin—how gracious!—would grant him the right to
be present, would even condescend to eventually invite
him to attend, knowing, of course, beforehand, that
Geiger would not come. Geiger, an honest, straightforward man, who despised crookedness and trickery,
most indignantly declined such an arrogant pretension,
and emphatically declared that a peace based on hostile
sentiments cannot last. He said that Tiktin possessed
not the least authority to grant or refuse him Rabbinical rights and privileges after the directory of the
Congregation had decided the matter. At the same

time he was willing to forget Tiktin's insults and even to go to him, or to meet him on neutral ground, in order to offer him his plan of reconciliation. Again Tiktin declined. Geiger nevertheless proposed to him the plan, that they should alternately officiate in Rabbinical functions, which arrangement, however, need not interfere with the members of the Congregation, should they perfer Tiktin or Geiger for the performance of their function. Even this plan, which had formerly met with Tiktin's approval was now rejected by him.

Such systematic stubbornness on the part of Tiktin, forced the directory of the Congregation to enlighten the Congregation as to the true state of affairs. Thus appeared the "Report of the Obervorstehercollegium to the Members of the Congregation on the question of Rabbi," (Breslau, 1842, May 25),* in which Tiktin is, of course, blamed for his unjustifiable action. The fact was, that Tiktin wanted no rival and no competition. Geiger's so-called "heresy" served Tiktin simply as a cloak to conceal his selfishness. This is proven by the fact that he already raised the cry of "split in the Congregation" when for the first time the question of engaging a second Rabbi came up, who, "by his religious conduct, would be able to gain the approval of Tiktin."

We have mentioned how Geiger was excommunicated by eight Rabbis of Upper Silesia and Posen. Geiger sarcastically asked those Rabbis whether it is not both foolish and wicked to use in our enlightened age bulls of excommunication instead of instruction and conviction? "Are these Rabbis, Tiktin and consorts, so utterly blind as not to know that by using such means and weapons, their contemporaries will leave them more than ever before to their isolation? Do they still imagine that all they have to do, in order to make harmless the destructive criticism of their system, is to wrap themselves in their Polish gowns?

*Bericht des Obervorstehercollegium's an die Mitglieder der hiesigen Israelitengemeinde ueber die gegenwaertig vorliegede Rabbinats-Angelegenheit. Breslau, 1842.

Of what avail were the bulls of excommunication and the burning of the writings of Moses Mendelssohn and Hartwig Wessely ?

"They failed, although the Rabbis who in those days undertook the battle against progress and culture, were men who did not step directly from the dry goods shop and slaughter house into their Rabbinical chairs,* but had devoted a whole life-time to their studies." Such pygmies as Tiktin and his abettors were the last ones who could check the wheel of progress with their impotent hands, by mere noise and the cry of heresy. Those peculiar saints of Posen, Beuthen and Lublinitz accused Geiger of being a "Karaite" and a "Sadducee," which proved their recklessness and ignorance in judging men and things. For Geiger was all his life-time the strongest opponent of the "Sadducees" and "Karaites," just because "the Sadducees idolized the letter of the Bible," and the "Karaites" clung to the letter without paying the least regard to the spirit.† The other reproach that Geiger had attacked the "tradition" is another proof of the ignorance of his opponents regarding Jewish history, as the principle of "tradition" is simply the prin-

---

*Geiger alludes apparently to the despicable manner in which ignorant sons inherited in those degenerate days of orthodoxy, the Rabbinical positions of their fathers—Tiktin was one of this species—by means of nepotism, and even by the lavish use of money, in order to corrupt voters, just as it is done in political primary elections in this country. In Hungary, Poland and Russia, these methods are still en vogue in many Congregations. This deplorable system is well described in the following forcible language: "We do not find fault with the views of these men (Abraham Bing, Wuerzburg; Jacob Lissaer, Lissa; Akiba Eger, Moses Sopher, Pressburg), as they could not entertain others and were honest, but it is foolish to find in this, greatness and holiness. Consistency is easy when we do not see, or do not want to see the other side of the question. Pygmies only take their places, reduced storekeepers or the sons, according to the principle of heredity. Whenever a system has become rotten, but is not yet entirely subdued, these are its last supports. (Geiger: Lectures on Jewish history, from 1830 to the present day, meaning 1850, delivered in Breslau in the winter of 1849-50; Posthumous Works, Vol. II, page 259.

†See Geiger: "Wissenschaftliche Zeitschrift fur Juedische Theologie" Vol. I, page 36; Vol. II, page 114; "Judaism and its History," Vol. I, Lecture VII, (Breslau, 1864, Schletter) translated into Eng-

ciple of continuous progress and development, as opposed to the slavish worship of the letter of the Bible. We, who live within the Jewish Reform-movement and labor in its cause, are not only adherents of the tradition, but the rings in its long, endless chain. The eight "infallible" Rabbis claimed also that the contents of the Talmud are "eternally binding." No man who has the least conception of the science of Judaism would be guilty of such a ridiculous utterance, as the Talmud never was and never intended to be considered as a code of laws.* These "scholars" must have felt the weakness of their faulty argumentation, for at the end of their brochure they say that their system needs no defense against a Dr. Geiger, and can be as little shaken by him as can a rocky wall be shaken by a little boy (Darstellung, p. 29). History proves that the "rocky wall" has become very shaky indeed. On page 31, they threatened "measures which would be incalculable in their consequences." Very convincing arguments, indeed ! Justly, Geiger replied: " It is very convenient to envelope ignorance with the nimbus of holy inviolability, but such love of convenience must not be looked upon as conscientiousness and religious zeal."

Geiger was a worker; he preached more, instructed more, delivered more lectures than was his duty. What has Tiktin done in the seventeen years of his ministration in Breslau ? He quarreled with the Congregation because they wanted him to deliver twelve lectures during the year. He insisted that, in accord with his contract, six lectures—addresses on different occasions included—was all they had a right to expect. Such were the " saviors of Judaism" in those days.

---

lish by Dr. Maurice Mayer (New York, 1866, Thalmessinger & Cahn). The "Karaites" were the followers of Anan, son of David, of Babylonia. They worshipped the letter of the Bible to such an exaggerated extent, that they would freeze for twenty-four hours each Sabbath, and would sit in the dark Friday night, because it was not permitted to kindle fire on the Sabbath in Jewish dwellings.

*See my "Talmud." (Denver, 1884), pages 7-8.

The directory of the Breslau Congregation did not remain idle, but sent circular letters to the most prominent Rabbis of Germany and Austria, asking them for an expression of their views on the compatibility of Judaism with free research, and whether a man who holds a free, scientific, Jewish-theological conviction, and advocates the same in his Congregation, school and publications, is fit to officiate as Rabbi.

Seventeen Rabbis, all recognized as great scholars, answered in the affirmative.

These "opinions," which we consider among the most important contributions to the literature of "Responses" on Jewish subjects,* have been published by the Breslau Congregation in two parts. The first part† contains the "opinions" of Rabbis, Drs. Friedlaender, of Brilon; Chorin, of Arad; Holdheim, of Schwerin; Wechsler, of Oldenburg; Kohn, of Hohenems; Herxheimer, of Bernberg; Einhorn, of Birkenfeld; Hess, of Stadt-Lengsfeld; Guttman, of Radowitz; Wassermann, Muehringen, now "Oberkirchenrath" of Wuertemberg, Stuttgart. The second part (Breslau, March, 1843), contains the opinions of Drs. Levi, of Giessen; Aub, of Baireuth (later Mainz and Berlin); Cahn, of Trier; Maier, of Stuttgart; L. Adler, of Kissingen, later Cassel; Stein, of Burgkunstadt, later Frankfurt; Elias Gruenebaum, of Landau. Loewy (Fuerth), Schlesinger (Sulzbach), Gosen (Marburg), had also sent "opinions" and answers, but requested the Breslau Congregation not to publish them. Frankel (Dresden), Rappoport (Prag), had sent evasive or condemning replies. Ullman (Crefeld) declined to express himself, "in order not to give new fuel to the flame." Philippsohn was the only one who did not consider it worth while to even answer the request of the Breslau Con-

---

*The "opinions" on the Hamburg Temple prayer-book-controversy pale into insignificance when compared with this collection.

†Rabbinische Gutachten ueber die Verraeglichkeit der freien Forschung mit dem Rabbineramte. (Compatibility of Free Research with the Office of Rabbi.) Leopold Freund: Breslau, September, 1842.

gregation.   The fact is, that Philippsohn has proven,
during his long career, a secret enemy of Geiger, although he did not deem it good policy to come out
openly against him as long as Geiger was living.   But
hardly had he closed his eyes when he attacked the
dead lion, saying in his "Zeitung des Judenthums" that
Geiger was no theologian.   I have resented this cowardly insult, promptly and most forcibly, in my "Juedische Gemeinde-Zeitung" (Bonn, 1879), during my ministration in Bonn, where Philippsohn lived.   In his
review of my book, "Abraham Geiger as Reformer of
Judaism" (1879), Philippsohn made the above remark,
and this, too, in the face of the fact that authorities
like Prof. Dernbourg, Berthold Auerbach, David Einhorn and numerous other scholars had justly ranked
Geiger as the most prominent theologian of the nineteenth century.   Philippsohn could never forgive Geiger his mental supremacy and recognition by all the
leaders of thought.   Like all small men, he was vindictive and conceited in the extreme.   His maxim was:
"I and none besides me."   His motto was "rule or
ruin."   From the very moment when Geiger was
elected Rabbi in Breslau, for which position Philippsohn was a candidate, the latter proved hostile to the
former.   This animosity had increased with every new
success which Geiger attained, and it capped the climax in the statement that Geiger was no theologian.
The Talmudic passage: "Men blame in others the
faults which they themselves possess," applies well to
this case.   For in theological Jewish circles it is well
known, that while Philippsohn was a classical philolo-
gist, a most versatile journalist and quite eloquent as a
preacher, Jewish theology and Rabbinical lore were
not his forte.   Hence, he was surely the least competent man to criticise Geiger in such a sweeping way.

    Geiger occasionally expressed himself quite strong-
ly concerning Philippsohn's shallowness and lack of
principle and character; but he gave him credit for
what he had accomplished.   In his lectures on Jewish
history, delivered in Breslau in the winter of 1849-50,

Geiger, after having given an analysis of the scope of his Zeitschrift,* said among other things: "Thus several newspapers were established, the Universal-Kirchenzeitung of Hoennighaus (1837), and in the middle of May of the same year, the Allgemeine Zeitung des Judenthums, by Philippsohn, in Magdeberg. But it wanted to be a paper, more in order to satisfy than to stir up. Hence, it avoided decision and outspokenness in those points where it feared to lose a part of its readers. Aside from this, the personal notice of the editor was pushed forward too much, while the paper, with ill-concealed animosity, opposed notice of other persons of whom its editor was afraid, lest they might overshadow him. But the merits of versatility and industriousness cannot be taken away from the editor, who also took hold of other questions, delivered in 1848 lectures for workingmen, became secretary of the board of trade and published a commercial paper, by which, however, no Jewish Reformer is lost."†

The "Rabbinical opinions" on the question of the compatibility of free research with the office of Rabbi, are of the same importance for modern Judaism as were the "theological opinions" on Bruno Bauer's heresy for modern Protestantism.

Dr. Friedlaender (Brilon), then eighty-five years old, declared that neither the Mishna nor the Talmud contained divine revelations, and the laws found there are simply subjective views of individuals, without the least binding authority. The oldest Rabbis have introduced reforms and have even abolished laws of Moses. Hence is Geiger fully entitled to be a Rabbi, even though he attacked the Talmud. Chorin (Arad), seventy-seven years old, expressed himself even more forcibly. Truth, not ceremonialism, is the irrepressible demand of the age; hence, free research and untrammeled investigation are necessary. Reforms were introduced already in Biblical times. The circumcision

---

*We call attention to the fact, that Philippsohn's "Zeitung des Judenthums" was published two years later than the Zeitschrift.
†Geiger: "Posthumous Writings," Vol. II. page 271.

was set aside under Moses* and the Day of Atonement under King Solomon.† The prophet Elijah, although no priest, offered sacrifices on hills, which was an infraction upon the law of Moses. Hillel has abolished the year of release (Shmittah), an important Mosaic law. Rabbi Gershom ben Judah prohibited, in the eleventh century, in the Rabbinical Synod at Worms, the Levirate marriage.

One of the first and most thorough opinions was given by Holdheim. As Rabbi Eger, of Posen, was the representative of the most rabid opposition to Reform, Holdheim took his opinion as a starting point for his argument. Eger declared everyone who does not subscribe to the Talmudical interpretation of the Bible a heretic and unfit to be a witness, in fact an outcast from the community of Israel. In a masterly and irrefutable manner, by means of the Talmud, Holdheim proved the fallacy of Eger's views. He showed conclusively how Eger had confounded Talmud and tradition. He further demonstrated how Geiger, in his struggle against the Jew-hater, Prof. Hartman, at a time when his orthodox traducers had indulged in their *dolce far niente*, not even knowing of the dangerous assaults against Judaism, had already scientifically explained the difference between Talmud and Tradition. The principle of Tradition is not stagnation. It has not a tendency to make us slaves to the dead letter of the Bible, but rather disposes us to enter into its spirit and is in itself the result of a progressive development within Judaism. The Talmudists themselves never claimed infallibility for their views. Therefore they tried to find in the Bible a support (*Assmachta*) for their opinions. Now the same genius which moved them moves the Rabbis of our days. And if they could find support in the Bible for their innovations, the

---

*He doubtless means that the "generation of the wilderness" were not circumcised; and yet Moses made a covenant at the end of his life, with those uncircumcised Israelites. (Deut. XXIX, 8).

†He apparently alludes to 1 Kings, VIII, 2-6. The Talmud remarks that in that year the Day of Atonement was not celebrated.

Rabbis of our days will also, if necessary, find such support. Geiger, is, therefore, not a Karaite, who denies Tradition, but he heartily favors and scientifically advocates its growth and spiritual development. Holdheim arraigned the nine Rabbis from Upper-Silesia, who, in contradiction to their motto: "Love truth; love peace," instead of trying to refute and convince Geiger, insulted and denounced him. He censures those bigots who, in their contemptible spirit of hatred and revenge, were not ashamed to demand of the directory of the Breslau Congregation the removal from office of a man whose scientific writings they were too ignorant to understand and too stupid to appreciate. In answer to Tiktin's "Darstellung," (representation), in which he had accused the directors of the Congregation of having elected, as second Rabbi, a man who "denies the Traditional Judaism and whose vocation seems to be to eradicate and to destroy it forever," Holdheim gives a true estimate of Geiger. To Geiger, who had abandoned the method of narrow-minded casuistry, in order to promote a higher and more scientific study of the Talmud, belongs among the Rabbis of the new era the merit of being the first critical investigator.

He it was, who had recognized in Rabbinical Judaism a historical growth, and he, endowed with a thorough knowledge of the material and with critical acumen, had the ability to bring order and system into the chaotic mass of details, and to find out the moving spirit of every epoch. The directory of Breslau deserves, therefore, credit for having called such a man to take charge of the spiritual welfare of the Congregation, the more so, as Tiktin, like the rest of the orthodox Rabbis, had done nothing to revive and to lift up its declining religious spirit. A man like Geiger among the old and the young will awaken enthusiasm, and inspire ardent love for our time-honored heritage. A man of science, who, like Geiger, is imbued with religious earnestness and fervor, is the right man for the place in a large and intelligent Congregation. Geiger is just

the man, who "in a time when religious indifference
and materialism go hand in hand, combines in a rare
degree great power of mind with warmth of heart, profound scholarship with a popular style. Geiger is the
right man to fan the spark of religion to a burning
flame and to repair the damage which had been done in
consequence of long neglect and of an utter want of
every spiritual care."

Dr. Wechsler said that to deny to our age the
right of introducing reforms, is to drive away the intelligent Jews from Judaism. Theology is a science and
demands free research. Kohn (Hohenems) thinks that
the lamentations of orthodoxy about religious decline
are false and greatly exaggerated. The many new
Temples which are being erected yearly, and the great
interest which is generally taken in the introduction of
reforms and improvement in the service, give the lie to
these hollow pretenses. Indifferentism is the result of
rigid Rabbinism. The Talmud is not law, but merely
a source of theology. Herxheimer makes the distinction between Geiger, the author, who has the right of
applying full criticism on religious questions, and
Geiger, the Rabbi.* Einhorn (Birkenfeld, late Baltimore, Philadelphia and New York), said: "The Talmud is neither infallible, nor was it at any time accepted as Jewish law; hence, not even a practical disregard of a traditional ceremony by a Rabbi could
make him unfit for the office, as long as it is the outcome of his scientific research." Hess (Weimar) defended the most radical reform by the necessity of the
progressive development of tradition. Not only the
religious authorities, but even the masses have a voice
in the introduction of reforms. Stabilism decays in
consequence of its inconsistencies. Guttman (Redwitz,
Wuertemberg), finds the term "tradition" too far extended, inasmuch as the Talmud had increased the 613
laws of Moses to no less than 13,602. Geiger's activ-

*This is Geiger's own point of view. Zeitschrift, (Vol. I. pages
492-504; Posthumous Writings, Vol. II. page 207).

ity deserved the highest recognition, considering the
fact that his traducers, who style themselves "the pillars of Judaism," are a set of lazy drones. Wasserman
calls attention to the fact that from the point of view
of Rabbinism, nobody can be now-a-days an orthodox
Jew. In the olden times, liberal Rabbis have criticised
the most essential doctrines of Judaism, but no attempt
was made to read them out of the fold. Hirsch
Fassel* (Prossnitz, Maehren) proves from the point of
view of strict orthodoxy, that free research is not only
permitted, but is demanded by the Jewish theology.
Nobody has a right to expel a Jew from a Congregation. Levy (Giessen) considers free research and
timely innovations in the domain of Judaism necessary.
Aub looks upon the largest portion of the Talmud as
upon human work, which has never been made a law.
Cahn claims that though the office of Rabbi necessi-
tates the execution of prescribed forms, it is needless
for him to believe in the necessity of those observances.
Full of righteous indignation, he arraigns Tiktin and
consorts as follows: "You act as if you were the saviors of Judaism. Conscienciously and boldly we say:
You have done nothing for the preservation of our religion. Yes, you are the cause of the frivolous spirit
which here and there is found among the Jews in matters of religion. The following passage in Tiktin's
'Presentation' is without doubt true: 'But what
more could I do at the sight of the fatal destruction not
only of traditional but of Mosaic Judaism, in order to
check the raging torrent of religious and moral annihi-
lation—what else could I do than protest?' Does he
not condemn himself by his own words? Lo! such
dangers threatened Judaism, and he could do nothing,
and has done nothing, except protesting within the
four walls of his room! If it was indeed so bad as all
this, and he was really in earnest to check the "raging
torrent," why, then, does he trade and barter with the
directory of the Congregation about the number of ser-

*His "opinion," on account of some technicalities was not pub-
lished in the "Rabbinische Gutachten."

mons he is bound to preach during a year? Why does
he object to preaching twelve times during the year?
Suppose the by-laws of the Congregation call only for
six sermons during the year? Can six sermons during
the whole year suffice to check such evils as they exist
in Breslau, according to Tiktin's own statements? In
this case he ought to have delivered sermons continually, every Sabbath, every new moon, every fast- and
holiday, whenever an opportunity arose, in order to
admonish and encourage the people, regardless of circumstances, to preserve morality and religion. He
ought not to have rested, and the pulpit ought never
to have been vacant on those days. He ought not to
have been satisfied with "examining a few poor children in his room," but ought to have instructed the
young in the truths of our religion, in order to guard
it from the destructive spirit of the age. This he
ought to have done by all means, instead of laying the
hands in his lap, merely looking on, regretting, crying,
lamenting and protesting. Is he not ashamed before
his own followers to pose as the preserver and pro-
tector of our religion? What has Tiktin and consorts
done? Nothing! What for the elevation and morality of the Congregations? Nothing! What for the
schools? Nothing! What for the divine service?
Nothing! What for eradicating prejudice against the
adherents of other religions? Nothing, nothing at
all! These are no idle charges, but all Congregations,
officers and governments must agree with us in this.
We modern Rabbis do not claim, like Tiktin and his
consorts, to be the only saviors of Judaism. Far be
this from us! We are free from such conceit. But
we can claim, that we strive after the good, and that
we work with might and main, and do our best in
order to further and establish it on a firm basis. We
can truly say that we zealously labor in the cause of
education and divine worship; that we do not neglect
our duties; and that we do more than merely take our
salary. This, too, will be attested by all Congregations where modern Rabbis officiate, and by all officers

and governments. But they could accomplish much
more, and their activity would be a still greater blessing were it not for the deplorable fact that, alas, in
almost every Congregationt here can be found just such
men as Tiktin and consorts, who impede our every
step forward, disturb us in our good work, and when
we make the least attempt for a beneficial change,
they suspect us as infidels and belittle us in the eyes of
the masses. Acting on the maxim, ' To sit idly by and
do nothing is the best,' they pose as the saints of the
land, as the thirty-six pillars of the earth, with whose
demise the world will go to ruin.''

In order to justify himself for not delivering German instead of ''jargon'' sermons, Tiktin said on page
7, that ''such sermons are prohibited by the Prussian
government;'' and then he jesuitically adds: '' It is
not my business to investigate the fact that German
addresses are delivered in the Synagogue nevertheless,
in some Jewish Congregations of the Fatherland by
preachers who are expressly engaged for this purpose,
even where the Rabbi stands at the head of the cultus.'' To this Dr. Cahn pointedly remarks: '' Had
Tiktin excused his failure to deliver sermons in good
German, on the plea that he was not capable of doing
so, because he belonged to the old school of Polish
Rabbis, he would have been honest, even if he had
argued that in his opinion sermons delivered in the
'jargon' were more effective than classical German discourses; and nobody would have found fault with him.
But his attempt to represent all modern preachers,
Rabbis and theologians as criminals who break the laws
of the land on every Sabbath and holiday, or whenever
they deliver a German sermon,* is most cowardly,
fanatical, contemptible and worthy of a disciple of

---

*The prohibition of German sermons in the Synagogues in Prus-
sia after the forcible close of the Jacobsohn-Temple in Berlin, (1823),
was caused by the Jewish orthodoxy. The government cheerfully
complied with this request, in the hope of disgusting the educated
Jews with the Synagogue worship and of driving them into the fold
of Christianity. Alas, this hope has not proved to be an idle one.
See ''David Friedlaender,'' pages 33-36, this book.

Loyola. The purpose of this hypocritical remark was the wholesale suspension from their offices, by the government, of all modern Rabbis and preachers, a consummation which would have made again ignorant Polish Rabbis such as Tiktin, Eger and consorts, masters of the situation in Prussia."

It is interesting that Cahn speaks in his "opinion" of Chalizah and Get as of "meaningless, senseless and most burdensome precepts for our time."* He also mentions that the modern Rabbis are more scrupulous in the performance of ceremonies in strict keeping with the old laws, than are many orthodox Rabbis; although the moderns may hold advanced opinions on the validity of those ceremonies.† He calls attention to the humbug which is practiced, for a consideration, of course, with the so-called "Kosher-letters," for wine, etc., by a number of orthodox Rabbis. To-day, half a century after Dr. Cahn's publication, this swindle with "Kosher-letters" is carried on in our enlightened age, in the city of New York, by a so-called self-styled Chief Rabbi, who is recognized as such by not one intelligent Jew of America. Could Dr. Cahn have foreseen how the henchmen of this "Chief Rabbi"—lucus a non lucendo, a man who is utterly ignorant of any living language, and has, so far, not even given proof of his supposed scholarship in Hebrew and Talmud—like a horde of voracious wolves, pounce upon the poor dupes and innocent victims of superstition, in order to divide the spoils acquired by means of a shrewd design, the "plomb," he would have expressed himself still stronger on the subject than he has done.

*"Rabbinische Gutachten," Vol. II, page 27.

†In this connection I mention that while Rabbi in Bonn, a "Shochet" wanted the Kabbalah (permission to kill animals according to Jewish rites). As he was ignorant of Hilkhoth Shechitah, I refused to give him the permission. Surprised, he asked me for my reasons, as I was known to belong to the Reform-Rabbis, who do not consider Shechitah "min hatorah," which fact had, of course, nothing to do with the case. The strangest thing, however, was, that the orthodox Rabbi Auerbach gave him the Kabbalah for three chickens and a few thalers. This happened in 1879.

Dr. Maier, of Stuttgart, styles Tiktin's defense of the neglect of his official duties toward his Congregation, "unworthy," which cannot but fill with indignation even his friends and followers. "Was perchance, Moses hunting up cabinet orders and old rescripts of the government, prohibiting him from instructing his people when they came to him, mornings and evenings, in order to hear his teachings and decisions? Did he look for rusty statutes, on the strength of which he could get out of the fulfilment of the duties toward the people? Did he anxiously deduct the lessons and instructions which he had given to them? Tiktin is no pastor in accord with the word of God: for such a shepherd feeds his flock with knowledge and intelligence (Jerem. III, 15), and does not refuse the nourishment for which it craves." Maier ably refutes the argument of Tiktin and followers, with the good Jewish maxim that Judaism has never in its history punished opinions, ideas, views and doctrines, but actions, deeds, practices and performances. Not one of these fanatic Rabbis, even charges Geiger with an action which might be regarded incompatible with the position of Rabbi. All they claim is, that his principles are heterodox. While it must fill a man with pain to see that men utterly devoid of scientific culture, who do not even occupy a standing as Talmudical scholars, have the brazen impudence to give a verdict against purely scientific researches, to deprive the author, on the strength of their onesided judgment, not only of his honor but of his salvation; it is very pleasing indeed to know that one lives outside of the range of such zealots. If these people had the power, as they have the will, they would declare as dishonorable the best and most intelligent portion of Israel, and would deliver them to the funeral pile.

Mendelssohn has demonstrated* that Judaism grants to the scientific inquirer the widest scope, the

---

* "Jerusalem," pages 14 and 52.

fullest freedom of research. Josephus* informs us that the Sadducees, though differing widely in their religious views, from the Pharisees, were never deemed unfit to hold offices, as long as they performed their functions in accord with Pharisaic custom. On the eve of the Day of Atonement the high-priest had to take an oath that he would perform the ceremony of the Abodah in accord with Pharisaic, and not in accord with Sadducaic usage. (Mishna, Joma I, 4). How much less then could Geiger be removed from his office when his actions did not justify such fanatic measures? True, the people stoned once a priest on Succoth, because he poured out the water upon the earth, instead of pouring it upon the altar.† Had he poured it upon the altar, no harm would have befallen him, which shows that actions and not opinions were punished. Rabbi Joseph Colon,‡ the great fanatic, deposed Rabbi Moses Capsoli of Constantinople from his office, not on account of his disbelief in Talmudical principles, but on account of his illegal performances in matters pertaining to Jewish marriage laws.§ But this was done at a time when Rabbinical power and tyranny had reached its zenith. Hence, the removal of Geiger would be a matter unheard of in Jewish history. Aside from all this, Geiger is neither a Sadducee nor a Karaite, neither a Copher (atheist) nor an Apikores.‖ This is another reason why the accusations of Tiktin and consorts fall to the ground.

---

*Josephus, "Antiquities," Vol. III, page 12.—The Sadducees denied the belief in future reward and punishment. See on this important subject: Geiger: "Judaism and its History," translated into English by Maurice Mayer. Pages 158-170.

†Talmud Succah, page 46.

‡Joseph Colon (born in France) was Rabbi in Mantua, Italy, in the fifteenth century. He had a bitter controversy with Messer Leon (Judah ben Jechiel), a physician and philosopher in Mantua in 1840, who published a Bible-rhetoric (Nofeth Zufim). Both were expelled from Mantua by the Duke, on account of their quarrels. Colon published a commentary on the Pentateuch.

§See "Responses of Joseph Colon," No. 83, 84; and "Responses of Rabbi Salomon ben Adereth," No. 180.

‖Apikores, from the Greek, "Epicur," means in Rabbinical language, "skeptic."

Rabbi Eger, whose only merit it was to be the son of Akiba Eger, who inherited the Rabbinical chair of Posen, proved both his contemptible character and his ridiculous ignorance by applying the following passage of Maimonides to the case of Geiger: "He who does not believe in the oral tradition   *   *   belongs to the class of infidels and free thinkers (Apikorssim) whose life is in everybody's hand, *i. e.*, it is permitted to murder him.* Now this coward actually incited fanatics to kill Geiger.   Is it then any wonder that during the notorious funeral sermon of that other worthy, for whose person Eger entertained such affection ("birds of a feather flock together"), the mob was about to throw Geiger into the grave?   No, it was simply the natural consequence of Eger's second argument, which reads thus: "As soon as it is known that a man denies the tradition, it is permitted to throw him into the pit.   He who would kill such a man, fulfills a holy duty by putting offense out of the way."

But it would be an insult to the memory of the great philosopher Maimonides to imagine for a moment that he meant what men like Tiktin, Eger and others of this ilk inferred from his words.   This clique, which, thank God, has lost its influence upon the better class of Jews, would treat Maimonides not a whit better than they treated Geiger.   For the writer of the "Moreh Nebuchim"† was, for his time, to say the

---

*Maim., Hilchot Mamrim, Chap. III, Sec. 1-2.

†"Guide of the Perplexed," published 1191, deals with the perplexities of religious belief, tries to harmonize belief with reason. In this work, Maimonides opposes the tendency to materialize God and to localize his favors. He holds sacrifice to be a lower state of religious worship, and that the sacrificial system of the Jews had only the object in view, to wean a people living in the midst of idolatrous nations, from worse, and to lead them to better things. But in his opinion the value of sacrifice, like the value of prayer, lay in the fact that it was merely a means to an end, and not the end itself. Sacrifice, he held, was at one time designed to teach self-denial and practical repentance.   Prophecy he explained as a natural development of man's intellect, a kind of genius, or inspiration. He expressed similar rational views on the belief in angels and demons. Now, it was just such fanatics as Tiktin, Eger, Caro, Deutsch, who bitterly persecuted the philosopher Maimonides. Just as these Polish Rabbis called the aid of a Christian govern-

least, just as enlightened and liberal in his religious views as was Geiger for his time.

The alleged passage of Maimonides applies only to those men who deny the oral law, in order to indulge undisturbedly in their levity and the lust of their heart.* But Maimonides did not speak of men who devote their life-time to the study and research of the Thora, who practice its precepts, although their scientific conviction compels them to doubt the justification of certain ceremonies. Were Eger and the other Polish zealots right, then Maimonides would be the first to deserve all the penalties which these worthies wanted to inflict upon Geiger.

Blind belief has never been encouraged by Judaism. Even with regard to the doctrine concerning God, which is surely very important, we are commanded: Know, therefore, and reflect in thy heart, that the eternal is God (Deut. IV, 39). Mark well, " Know," not blind belief. The Hebrew language has not even a term for " belief." And we should blindly believe in the infallibility of human traditions ? " I, for my person," continues Maier, "consider the belief in the authority of a man just as much idolatry as any heathenish idolatry. For where is the difference, whether I bend my knee before a lifeless idol of wood or stone, or before the dead letter of a Rabbi Akiba, or Rabbi Tarfon ?" The most prominent teachers of Judaism

---

ment to remove Geiger from office, so the bigots in Maimonides' time denounced him to the Catholic Dominicans, who burned his writings. But Maimonides and Geiger are immortal, because "the works of the pious and righteous men bear fruits," while "the actions of the evil-doers bear no fruit. "The name of the wicked rots." Were it not for Maimonides, the names of his contemporaneous persecutors would have been forgotten long ago. Were it not for Geiger, not a human being would know to-day the existence of such obscure individuals like Tiktin, Eger and other nonentities. As to Maimonides and Geiger, every impartial and honest historian is bound to apply the Biblical passage: "And the wise shall shine like the brilliancy of the expanse of the sky, and they that bring many to righteousness shall be like the stars forever and ever."—Dan. XII, 3.

(See Sec. 3 of the chapter quoted by Eger. This "honest" "servant of the Lord" has no doubt "forgotten" to quote also the third section. See also Ikkarim, I, 2.

recognize the authority of reason in matters of religion.*

And does not the Talmud itself contain the strongest criticisms? If the Talmudists always ask: *"Mina lan,"* "Why is this," "whence follows its justification?" then we surely have the right to the same critical inquiry. There was never a time in Jewish history when the authority of the Talmud was officially recognized by the community of Israel. The same Maimonides† whom Geiger's enemies cite against Geiger, plainly says, that only the precepts of the Bible, and not those of the Talmud, can claim divine origin. In conclusion Maier said: "The best refutation of the slanders against Geiger was offered by the Breslau Congregation, which threw them into the waste basket. The efforts of the obscurants, from Upper Silesia and Posen, to prevent the religious and scientific regeneration of Judaism, can do no harm. When in the last century among the Jews an attempt was made to stop the only well-spring of science, it proved a dismal failure. And yet, the combined influence of the most prominent Rabbis of Germany and Poland, among whom were giants of Talmudical lore, was brought to bear in order to check the movement of the Mendelssohn school. How much less can pygmies of the Eger type expect to succeed in a similar undertaking at a time when science has become a powerful stream in Israel? It will carry them away and bury them in the depths of its floods."

Dr. L. Adler, Kissingen (he was thirty-five years Land-Rabbi of Hessen-Cassel), pleads for free research

---

*Bachja ibn Bakuda: Introduction into "Choboth halevovoth," Sadia Gaon in his "Emunoth Vedeoth" (Faith and Knowledge) Eliah Del Medigo in his "Bechinath Hadath" (Examination of the Jewish law), and others.

† Sefer Hamizvoth, second radix, with notes of Nachmanides and Hurwitz. See commentary page 7b. The same opinion is expressed even more forcibly by R. Jehuda Halevi, Kusari III; 39. The Talmud itself is the best proof against stagnation and stabilism. Hillel denied the belief in the coming of the Messiah. Fortunately for him Tiktin and Eger were not living then, else they would have insisted upon his removal from the Rabbinical office.

and proves that even the Talmudists had introduced reforms.

Dr. Leopold Stein strongly arraigns Tiktin for his attack on the German sermon and for his neglect to preach every Sabbath and holiday. He solemnly protests against Tiktin's attempt to represent the Reform Jews as a new "sect." Only dogmatic differences make the formation of "sects" necessary. There existed only one sect in Jewish history, namely, the "Karaites." Jews who do not observe many ceremonies, have not, on this account, ceased to be Jews, and are no separate "sect." The learned Rabbi, Dr. Geiger, far from denying the "tradition," has proven in his Zeitschrift, that we owe to the Talmudists, in opposition to the "Sadducees" and "Karaites" the principle of a progressive development of Judaism.* Only such people as practice sinful idolarty with every letter of the Talmud, can place the critic of the tradition in the same category with him, who denies it.† Stein says, that the time for merely protesting, as Tiktin and followers do, has gone by long ago. Since fifty years, when the old Rabbis protested against the reading of Mendelssohn's translation of the Pentateuch, protest is the only weapon of orthodox Rabbis, but this weapon has become rather rusty in our days. For time is mightier than their protests. A man once saw a carriage without a coachman, slowly passing by him, instead of taking the seat of the missing coachman and becoming master of the horses, he cried "halt! halt!" So often did he repeat this cry, that the horses began to be aware of their power and freedom, and in a wild dash they ran away with the carriage, caring little for the calls "halt! halt!" which that foolish man kept on repeating long after the horses were out of hearing of his voice. Even so have the old Rabbis acted in the last fifty years. It was in their hands to make themselves masters of the situation, by becoming leaders of

*Zeitschrift fur Juedische Theologie I, 36 ff.
†We consider the very expression "denial of the tradition" a proof of utter ignorance as to the meaning of "tradition."

the Reform-movement. With a little discretion and
tact they could have directed its course more successfully. But they have missed the excellent opportunity.
They did not move along with the tide, but remained
standing on the same spot calling "halt! halt!" to
the wheel of progress, protesting, lamenting and crying. They have made a most egregious mistake.
The horses left to themselves without a master ran
away. Now it is too late. Their cries "halt! halt!"
have no effect at all: are not even heard.

Under such deplorable circumstances the younger
generation of Rabbis, had to do something in order to
save the carriage from utter destruction. Seeing the
poison of apostasy and indifferentism spreading and
well nigh eating up the marrow of Judaism, beholding
the empty benches in the Synagogues, the neglected
schools, the flocks going astray without the care of
wise shepherds, they went to work, to repair the great
damage, to stem the dangerous tide of apostasy, and to
save what could be saved. And, thank God, their efforts are crowned with success. Thousands of our co-
religionists, who felt themselves strangers in the House
of God, find themselves again at home, wherever
beneficial Reforms in the worship have been introduced.
In all our Reforms we have the welfare and perserva-
tion of our religion at heart. We believe with Maimonides, that there are times when a member of the body
has to be sacrificed in order to save the whole body
from utter decay. The demand for Reform is so general
among the masses, that not even the unanimous *dictum*
of all the present Rabbis would be powerful enough to
check it. The attempt of Rabbi Eger and his associates
to exclude the Reformers from the pale of Judaism, is
therefore, to say the least, foolish, in the extreme.
Thank God, these men are powerless. Such men as
Dr. Geiger are of the greatest benefit to the cause of
Judaism, which is badly in need of just such men in
our days. The more burdensome we make Judaism
for the people, the less they will care for it.

Dr. Gruenebaum, Landau, proves that the very stupendous growth of the ceremonial laws from 613 in the Pentateuch to several thousands in the Talmud* is a most radical Reform. For is it not in contradiction to the words of the Pentateuch: Ye shall not add and ye shall not take away? (Deut. IV, 2).

By the citation of about a dozen instances† he conclusively proves that the Talmudists have abrogated, not only Rabbinnical, but Mosaic laws, consequently Tiktin and consorts, who claim that "no human authority is permitted to set aside or even to modify Talmudical precepts and prohibitions" are sadly mistaken indeed. Just the contrary from what they so apodictically assert is true. Far from doing a wrong it is the duty of Rabbis to follow the good example set by the great teachers of old and to introduce beneficial changes and Reforms in accord with the urgent demands of the times and the necessities of localities.

In a most thorough manner he demonstrates historically the utter ignorance of Tiktin and consorts as manifested by their unscientific statement that the Talmudical explanations of the Biblical laws are of divine origin." Freedom of research was valued so highly even after the establishment of the Sanhedrin in Jerusalem, that it was forbidden to write the interpretations of the law, in order to give a chance to other hermeneutics, in cases where the exigencies of the age rendered them imperative. It was only owing to outside oppression that the Mishna and later the two Talmuds were permitted to be collected and written. Fanaticism from without palsied every free activity and productive power of the Jews. "The misery and barbarism of the times, which made beggars even of the Greeks and Romans," said the scholar and genius Zunz, "exercised the same influence upon the Jews."‡

*See Maimonides Sefer Hamizvoth, rad. I on this subject.
†Mishna Berachoth, Chap. I, Maasser Sheni II, 2, Talm. Beza, fol 5. Tosafoth Jebamoth 86b, Sota 48a.
‡Der Zeiten Noth und Barbarei, die selbst Griechen und Roemer zu Bettlern machten, uebte auf die ungluecklichen Juden gleichen Einfluss.

This simple historical statement must take away from the Talmudical laws the nimbus of divine origin. But as the Rabbi of Posen belongs to the class of people who cannot comprehend the plainest historical argument, it is a good thing that the Talmudists themselves corroborate the truth of this argument. If then Tiktin and consorts condemn Geiger, they must also condemn Maimonides, Albo and a host of the greatest leaders of Jewish thought in all ages and climes. Hence Dr. Geiger is more in accord with the "tradition" than his traducers of Lissa, Posen and Lublinitz. They are guilty of the sins which, in a spirit of ignorance and arrogance they imputed to Geiger.

We have dwelt at some length on these "opinions" because they are of the greatest importance for a thorough understanding of the Jewish Reform-movement, and because it is the first time that the English reading public will have the opportunity of getting a clear insight into the struggles which the leaders of modern Rabbinism in Europe had to undergo. For Geiger stands for the principle of Reform-Rabbinism. He was the sun, the other Rabbis were satisfied to be considered the stars, and gladly received their light from him. In the conclusion of his opinion Dr. Aub appropriately used the following phrase:

"Rabbi Dr. Geiger, in whom we venerate the first representative of the scientific Theology of Judaism."†

As is often the case in history an event took place just at that critical time, which gave room for the general belief that peace would be established once more in the Breslau Congregation.

On March 20th, 1843, Tiktin died, and Geiger did honor to his memory in spite of all that had happened. The Prussian Ministers Eichhorn and Arnim re-

*Rabbin. Gutachten II, page 11, "Dr. Geiger in dem wir den ersten Repraesentanten der wissenschaftlichen Theologie des Judenthums verehren" The fact that Philippsohn, envious of Geiger's greatness, was not ashamed to write that "Geiger was no theologian," changes nothing in the matter.
†See Israelit of the 19th century, 1843, page 64.

jected the petition of his opponents and refused to remove Geiger from office.

But peace was not restored, owing to the agitation of the orthodox party. They wanted a second Rabbi. On Geiger's recommendation Dr. Fassel was invited, preached on trial and was elected (February 25th, 1845), but did not enter upon his position.

Now the opponents of Reform worked with might and main, to dismember the Congregation by inducing the members to refuse their payment of their dues.

As the radical element of the Congregation was also in favor of a split as the only means of a lasting peace, G. Tiktin, the son of S. Tiktin, was elected as Rabbi of the orthodox party.

Geiger's salary was materially increased in consequence of this arrangement. But the conservative element was so well represented in the administration of the Congregation, that it retarded the work of Reform. This fact became partly the cause of Geiger's acceptance of a call to Frankfurt, his native city. Geiger himself was also in favor of a split in the Congregation. He was convinced, that it had to come sooner or later in every large Jewish community. As early as 1842 he expressed these views in a letter to Jacob Auerbach, dated April 18th. "The healthy portion even if numerically small will develop in time in its solidity and harmony with the age, while the sickly and unsound portion will be swept away by the waves of the new era. In London the split is a fact, in Hamburg it cannot be kept back, and in Frankfurt it will come to pass in a short time."*

In 1843 Geiger received a call to Petersburg through Dr. Max Lilienthal of Riga, later of Cincinnati. But Geiger refused to leave Germany. In his letter to Lilienthal he said: I love Germany, although its institutions exclude me, the Jew. Does love ask for a reason? I feel myself interwoven with its science

*Geiger: Posthumous works Vol. V, page 161.

its spiritual earnestness, and who will cut in twain the nerve of his being?*

In 1849 Geiger was requested by his Congregation to publish outlines and a plan to a new " Prayerbook."† In accord with the principles contained in this pamphlet the famous prayer-book of Geiger appeared in 1854.‡

The spirit of progress, with due regard to the historical basis permeates this prayer-book. All prayers are eliminated, which do not express the true sentiment of the worshipers. The service is shortened considerably. The second edition of the prayer-book, which came out 1870 is more reformed than the first. It is used in Frankfurt, Bonn, where the author of this book had introduced it under great difficulties, and in a very few other German Congregations. Geiger's principles on the Jewish service are thoroughly expressed in his "Theses to the Synod at Leipzig," 1869. A few points, however, which are not contained in those theses, may find their place here. The exodus from Egypt can no longer occupy such an important place in our prayers, as it used to occupy. The same is the case with Amalek, Haman and the sufferings in middle ages. As the language of prayer, Geiger concedes, that the Hebrew is not our mother-tongue. The second holiday is not Biblical.

Of special interest to our readers will doubtless be Geiger's opinion on the vexed question of Sundayservice. I therefore copy in full an article, which I published five years ago on this important subject in the "Jewish Reformer,"§ January, 1886, and which

---

*Posthum. Works, V, page 165.

†They were published only for the Congregation. (Breslau, 1849, Leop. Freund, 36 pages). In 1861 they were reprinted under the title: "Necessity and Measure of a Reform of the Jewish Divine Service."

‡"Israelitish Prayer-book for the Public Worship of the Whole Year, Sabbath and Holidays Inclusive," with a new German adaptation (not translation). (Breslau, 1854, I. Hainauer 570 pages).

§Dr. Kohler, New York, and Hirsch, Chicago, were the editors of that excellent weekly.

was at the time extensively copied by the Jewish press
of this country:

ABRAHAM GEIGER ON SUNDAY-SERVICE.

Dr. Geiger said in his pamphlet "Nothwendigkeit
und Maass einer Reform des Juedischen Gottesdienstes,"
—"Necessity and Limitation of a Reform of the Jewish
Divine Worship," (Breslau, 1861):

"The holidays, when celebrated in a more dignified form, will surely attract a large part of the Congregation to the houses of worship, but I do not expect the
same from the Sabbath. It will always remain a comparatively small circle, which will attend the divine
service, even if it should be conducted so as to answer
all the demands."

These prophetical words, although spoken twenty-
six years ago in Germany, corroborating the saying
"the wise man is more than a prophet," cannot be
taken as a weapon against Reform. For Geiger explains this utterance as follows:

"Here in particular, we must exclaim in relation
to Reform the fatal words, 'Too late!' If in the
generation preceding ours the needs of the spirit and of
the heart had been considered, if the divine service had
not been made entirely indifferent, yea repelling to the
thinking, intelligent classes, the inclination of the heart
might perhaps have been powerful enough to draw
people to the house of worship on the Sabbaths in spite
of many obstacles. But now the stream of life has
overflowed its dams. Complaints or reproaches, will
not be strong enough, to lead it back again to its old
channel. The grown people attend to their business,
the children go to school,* and the House of God has
to rely upon a small, firm circle, of accidental visitors.
*   *   Now we ask ourselves: Shall we therefore bear ill-will against life? Shall the House of God
not offer its blessings, because they are not appreciated
as they ought to be at the time and hour when they

---

*In Germany the Jewish children attend school on Saturdays.

are offered? Shall the youth be punished by being deprived of all edification, because the parents send them
to school on this day? * * Should we not rather utilize
every opportunity offering itself to us, in order to win
back the masses to the House of God and to religious
life though it be at a time which so far has not yet
been used for this purpose? Our ancient teachers
thought so. For those, who could not attend service
on Saturday morning, they substituted a solemn
service on Saturday afternoon, Monday and Thursday
mornings. Let us follow their example. There is one
week-day, which is especially appropriate for divine
service, because the general business-pursuits are suspended on that day, namely *Sunday*. Let us make
use of it, if not regularly every week, but at least from
time to time. A solemn *Sunday-Service* (and be it only
once a month) will answer the purpose of giving to a
large part of the Congregation the opportunity of a
common devotion, without infringing upon the right
of the Sabbath. Do not go too far in your apprehen-
sion, that such a service might be construed as a concession to other denominations. I honor this shyness,
whenever urged in opposition to the shallow aping,
the begging before the doors of others. But, when you
once have given way to the general custom in all other
affairs of life, then do not boast of a steadfast perseverance and of insisting upon your peculiarity just in that
one point, which concerns neither your gain nor your
pleasure, but the religious food of so many. You
make the Sabbath a day of work, the Sunday a day of
recreation. Religion, however, must yield on the one
hand to the needs of life, and on the other to the
prejudice of the past. This is self-deception, through
which religious life is being stifled entirely."

Geiger is also opposed to the blessing of the people
by the so-called "Kohanim" (priests), to the "Sefirath
haomer,"* and considers earnest, solemn music a
good substitute for the blowing of the Shofar on New

*Numbering of 49 days between "Passover" and "The Feast of
Weeks."

Year's day. At any rate the Mishna deems three flourishes of the cornet (Tekia, Terua, Tekia), suffi- cient. The Lulab on the feast of Succoth can be dis- pensed with, as the feast is no longer an agricultural country-holiday, which was its original meaning.

Geiger's word made itself felt in every important Reform-movement.

We have dwelt at length in our biographies of "Chorin" and "Salomon," on the Hamburg-prayer- book-controversy in 1818 and in 1842. Geiger, when asked by the Temple people to give his "opinion" on the prayer-book, published a pamphlet: "The Hamburg Temple Controversy, a Question of the Hour."* He was, however, not satisfied with merely justify- ing the Hamburg ritual, but he criticised the Temple for doing things by halves. He said: "The Temple has missed the great opportunity to make itself the banner-bearer of scientific religious progress, in the domain of modern Judaism." Geiger emphatically ex- claimed. "Free from all retarding elements, respon- sible only to its enlightened members, they could have well afforded to handle questions which were delicate, yea, dangerous for others less fortunately situated. They could have exercised a great influence in the di- rection of scientific Reform in Judaism. Instead of this the literary activity of the Temple centered in the publication of the sermons of its preachers. While many of them are excellent contributions to our homi- letics, the principle of a scientific Reform in Judaism is not treated with that full consideration, to which it was entitled at the hands of the independent Hamburg preachers. Not only that the laborious work of build- ing up a Jewish theology on the basis of historical criticism received no support at the hands of the Tem- ple, but its representatives looked down upon this new movement as antiquated and superfluous, as if the di- vine service were the alpha and omega of all progress

---

*Der Hamburger **Tempelstreit, eine** Zeitfrage, (Breslau, 1842. Nachgel-Schriften. Vol. I, pages 113-197.)

in Judaism. The fact, however, is that the Hamburg Temple is already regarded as an "innocent institution," the worst thing which could befall it. The Temple, or at least its prominent leaders had so little understanding and appreciation of a scientific Jewish theology, that they openly advocated the long exploded idea, that a Rabbi has to practice every observance of the Shulchan Aruch, because he is Rabbi.* In its joy over its great victory in the matter of worship, the Hamburg Temple rested on its laurels, and intoxicated by success, became indolent and indifferent as to future greater possibilities of Reform-Judaism. The drift of Geiger's criticism is in brief this: The Temple owes its origin to its opposition to the Hamburg Synagogue. Having accomplished its object as an opposition-establishment, it has lost every interest in a progressive movement within the Synagogue on the basis of a scientific Jewish theology, which justly recognizes its representative in Abraham Geiger and his school.†

Geiger considers the second new prayer-book of the Temple entirely too conservative, and sees in it little progress in comparison with the prayer-book published twenty-three years before. In certain points it is even retrogressive, among other things the service instead of being shortened is lengthened. The hope of the re-establishment of a Jewish kingdom in Palestine finds expression in the prayer-book, the formula "May our eyes see it, when thou, O God, returnest to Zion" is retained. The passage "Oh, let shine forth a new light on Zion, that we may all speedily behold its light," which is wisely omitted in the prayer-book of 1819, is printed in small type and in parenthesis, but without the German translation in the prayer-book of 1843. How inconsistent! How timid! The same

*This is to this very day the only argument of our orthodoxy in Europe as well as in this country.

†This criticism is just. As proof I mention the fact that whenever a reformatory measure came to a discussion at the Rabbinical Conferences in the forties, the Hamburg preachers exclaimed: "Oh, this has been introduced or abolished in our Temple many years ago."

procedure is noticeable in the prayer, "and restore the service to the inner part of thy house, and the burnt-offerings of Israel and their prayers mayest thou accept in love and favor." Aut-aut. The purpose of such proceeding can only be to cast suspicion on those prayers without showing the proper courage of eliminating them, which is not worthy of an organization like the Hamburg Temple. While the Abodah* is omitted from the Jom Kippur service, which fact might be regarded as a protest against the animal sacrifice, this impression must leave us when we notice the retention of the main part of this historical recitation, in which bitter complaint is made that "now we have no high-priest, no sacrifice."

Another point of difference between the prayer-book of 1819 and the one of 1842 is that, while the former omitted the service for Minchah on Sabbath- and holidays, the latter retained it, which is retrogressive rather than progressive.

How a prayer-book of an organization which boasts of having fully emancipated itself from the yoke of Rabbinism, can contain the prayers: "Praised be thou, God, who hast commanded us to recite Hallel,"† or to "light the Channeca lights," or to "read the book of Esther,"* is utterly incomprehensible. For it is a well known fact that the Bible knows nothing of these commandments. The fact that these benedictions are printed in small type, in parenthesis, and without the German translation, makes the matter still worse, demonstrating that the authors were well aware of their glaring inconsistency.

But a very strong testimonium paupertatis for the Temple is contained in the following passage of the preface to the new prayer-book: "The Temple differs from other Israelitish Congregations in but a few

*Literally "Service" in the Temple of Jerusalem. This prayer describes in full the service of the High-Priest on the Day of Atonement.
†Prayers for New-Moon and Holidays.
‡It is recited on the festival of Purim.

forms of its ritual, not, however, in religious doctrines.
"What does the term 'other Israelitish Congregations'
mean in a time of struggle, transition and
changes like ours, which is not ripe for fixed religious
dogmas? But if it means, as it apparently does, that
the prayer-book is in principle at one with the traditional
and official mode of worship of the majority of Jewish
Congregations, then this declaration is simply not true.
For notwithstanding its glaring inconsistencies, the
views of the Temple on personal Messiah, sacrifice,
divine authority of the Rabbinical ceremonial laws, are
most decidedly at variance with the masses of so-called
conservative Congregations. *

But, if it were true that the only differences consists in "a few forms," then we might almost be justified in exclaiming: "Quel bruit pour une omelette."

The time has gone by, when the salvation of
Judaism is dependent upon mere outward embellishments of the service, which might, after all, prove to
be luxuriant death-chambers of our religion, if they
are out of all touch with the entire new religious conception and scientific spirit of modern Judaism. If the
Hamburg Temple intends to exercise a lasting influence
upon modern Judaism, it has to make itself the living
organ of the spiritual development of Judaism.

The experience of the last fifty years has proven,
that Geiger was right. To-day the Hamburg Temple
wields less influence in the Judaism of Germany than
it ever did. It still exists, vegetates, is for all we know
in a flourishing financial condition, as its members are
rich, but that is all. Its preachers are men of very
mediocre talent, unknown in literature, and cannot
bear comparison with men like Salomon, or Kley.

In the chapter on Holdheim we have dwelt
at length on the "Frankfurt Reformverein." †

*The new prayer-book and its opponents (Das neue Gebetbuch
and seine Verketzerung, Hamburg, 1841). See chapters on "Chorin"
and "Salomon" in this book; also Geiger: Posthumous Works, I,
pages 101-168.
†See pages 204 ff. of this book.

Geiger, while taking a warm interest in the movement as he did in everything pertaining to Reform-Judaism, did not favor the means employed by the Society, and was opposed to its revolutionary spirit. This Reform-movement had utterly ignored a historical development in Judaism. He characterizes it as follows:

"But also a revolution was not wanting. Those who had been separated long ago from the Jewish Congregations desired at last to give full and public expression to their views. But removed entirely from the historical ground this task became rather difficult. The "Reform-Society" of Frankfurt, and the "Friends of Reform" (in Breslau), were right in their struggle, but as soon as they intended to build up, they were not capable of constructing a new building out of mere negations, which offered nothing new.* The only new deed which emanated from the Society was the abrogation of the circumcision.† While Geiger, as we have seen before‡ was by no means opposed on principle to a schism within Judaism, he was not in favor of forcing a split. The Reform of the whole community of Israel was his bean-ideal, even though such a consummation was in the very nature of things

---

*The same holds good with regard to the "Ethical-Culture-Movement" in this country, which can claim not a single new idea not contained in the Jewish prophets. We challenge Prof. Felix Adler, to prove by one single instance, that his teachings are superior to those expressed by Micah VI, 8, and dozens of similar passages. It is far easier to pose as a founder of a new religion than to prove the necessity of a new religion. It has indeed been proven, that wherever Reform-Judaism has able and scholarly representatives—I point particularly to Chicago, where Hirsch holds the fort—ethical-culture is no success. It is the remarkable vigor of Reform-Judaism in America, which is a matter of great disappointment to our Ethical-Culturists. Hence their coquetry with our ultra-orthodoxy—les extremes so touchent—and their triumphant cry, that Judaism is dying out, although they know it best, that if it is dying, it is a mighty lively corpse indeed.

†Geiger's Posthumous Works; Vol. II, page 272.

‡See his letter to Jacob Auerbach, (page 331 of this book); also Posthumous Works Vol. V, page 191, and letter to Wechsler, Jan. 1st, 1849.

slow, up-hill work.* Another mistake of the "Reform-Verein" was, that it intentionally ignored the theologians, who in such a question as the abolition of circumcision were entitled to a hearing.† Geiger estranged many a friend from him on account of his opinion touching the Frankfort Reform-Society.

In Breslau a similar movement was attempted, where in a declaration signed by a number of prominent men the following demands were made:

(1) "Abolition of the belief in a personal Messiah; (2) of the dietary laws; (3) of the laws which cause the conflict of the Sabbath with the demand of every day life."‡ But only the Berlin "Reform-Genossenschaft" proved a success.

After Holdheim's death the Berlin Reform-Congregation was so anxious to induce Geiger to become

---

*It is for this very reason that he twice refused the position of Rabbi in the "Reform-Genossenschaft," of Berlin. Conscientious regard for the historical continuity of Judaism did not permit him to cut loose from the Jewish community at large. (Geiger's Zeitschrift, III, pages 216-218; also Posthumous Works, V, page 246, letter to Wechsler, and page 231 of this book.

†Geiger's letter to Stern, June 11, 1844; Posth. Works, V, page 174, Freund's "Zeitschrift zur Judenfrage in Deutschland." (Breslau, 1844, pages 109-116).

‡Breslauer Zeitung, April 4th, 1845. Later on they resolved to transfer the Sabbath to Sunday. Geiger published a pamphlet: "Nine Years Ago and To-day," (Breslau, 1846), in which he boldly advocated his views. He was then attacked in five "open letters," which followed one another in rapid succession, and were considered as Freund's work. In answer to this appeared: "Address of the Majority of the Breslau Isr. Congregation to Dr. W. Freund." (Breslau, 1846). See also: "True Report Concerning the Last Events in This Congregation," (Breslau, 1846), anonymously, but written by Geiger, and "Israelit d. 19. Jahrh.," 1846, No. 17 ff. In a letter to a friend March 8, 1861, he writes: "Within the Congregation I struggle, I conquer or succumb, and have the good consciousness that my struggle has stimulated powerful germs, which, after my strength is broken, will produce fertile developments. * * * I have declined such a position several times. I have refused the position as preacher in the Temple of Hamburg at a time when I had resigned my position in Wiesbaden, and when the chances for my naturalization in Prussia and of entering upon my position in Breslau were very doubtful indeed. I have twice declined the position in the Berlin Reform-Congregation, the first time under very difficult and precarious circumstances in this city." (Breslau).

Holdheim's successor, that they even offered to re-transfer the Sunday to Sabbath.

Geiger's motto was: "The Reform has to emanate from Rabbis and Congregations," but not from the Congregations alone. He advocated this opinion in a lecture entitled: "From Whom Shall Reforms Emanate?" delivered March 28, before the Breslau Reading-Society. Therefore was Geiger, heart and soul, in favor of the "Rabbinical Conferences," and was an enthusiastic member of the First Rabbinical Conference in Braunschweig. He expresses himself on this subject as follows:

"Revolution is not successful in religion, which demands not only tearing away of what is antiquated, but ennobling of what is existing, and of creating new things, when necessity demands it. This method was employed by the Rabbinical Conference, and it was the right way, notwithstanding the fact, that different stages of Reform were represented. These Conferences were checked in their development, long before they were given sufficient time to mature. Their motto was: 'Change, Reform, not Revolution.' They had to fight to the right, and to the left, but if they had had three years longer for their work, the fruits would have been seen ere now."*

The fruits at any rate are seen in the growth of Reform-Judaism, particularly in this country.

It was impossible for Geiger on account of official business to be present at the Braunschweig Convention at the beginning of the Conference.† But when he arrived June 18th, he was greeted with great enthusiasm by all present. "All surrounded"—thus a contemporary describes it—"the little man with the penetrating look and the long hair, as if he would have been a saint. All welcomed him most heartily, as if they wanted to say: You are our pioneer, you first opened unto us

---

*Posth. Works. II, pages 272-273.

†He had sent a highly enthusiastic letter to the Conference, which was published in pamphlet-form; also in Posth. Works. I, page 197-202. See also my Isr. Gemeinde-Zeitung, No. 28, Vol. IV. 1879.

the way of critical research, of progress in Rabbinism.
It is you, who first proclaimed the idea of a living development in Judaism." He had been elected even
before his arrival, a member of the committee for the
revision of marriage-laws. He took part in the eleventh,
last meeting, offered a resolution to create a fund, in
order to defray the expenses of Rabbis attending the
Conferences, and to have the Protocols of the Conference published in book form, the money to come
from subscriptions. He was elected to the committee
on S. Hirsch's resolution to abolish and revise a
number of dietary- and Sabbath-laws.

In the second Rabbinical Conference, Frankfurt,
1845,* he was present during the whole time. He
was Vice-President, and acted as President in the very
important eight meetings when the question on the
Messiah was discussed. The Conference voted him its
thanks for the very able manner in which he presided.
He strongly opposed Frankel, who declared that according to Jewish law, the Hebrew language had to be
used in prayer. He argued against mentioning the
sacrifices in prayer, and against a special celebration of
the Rosh Chodesh.† He offered resolutions aiming at
the establishment of Jewish theological faculties and at
the publication of good devotional books for the home
use. He was elected on the committee for both reso-
tions,

The third and most important, because most decisive and active Conference, was the one held in Breslau, to which Geiger had invited, aside from the members present at former Conferences, the Drs. Zunz,
Sachs and Leopold Loew.

I refer to a resume of the resolutions of the Breslau Conference, which I have published in the "Yearbook of the Central Conference of American Rabbis,"
as a member of the Committee on Publication, (Cincinnati, 1890, pp. 95-100).

---

*From July 15th to July 28th.
†The beginning of the month is usually celebrated by reciting
Hallel and Yaale vejavo.

Dr. L. Adler offered, in the name of the Conference, a vote of thanks to Geiger for the "just, kind and clever" manner in which he presided over the assembly in the midst of some very exciting debates, when the most burning questions and vital subjects were discussed. Through this Conference the Breslau Congregation became renowned throughout Germany as the banner-bearer of Reform-Judaism and scientific Jewish theology, and the bond which united the Congregation with its celebrated spiritual leader became stronger than ever before. Geiger's introductory and closing addresses of the Conference were masterpieces of oratory and scientific expositions of the aims and aspirations of progressive Rabbinism. In the introductory speech Geiger said among other things, that we do not meet here for the purpose of fettering the Congregations, of interfering with the religious freedom and autonomy of the people. Even if such authority should be given to us, we would not accept it, knowing as we do that true religious life can devolop there only, where the fullest freedom of conviction reigns supreme. We are here simply as representatives of the science of Judaism, who, assisted by our observations and experience in office, are able to recognize the wants of the Congregations, and to propose to them the necessary means of supplying the needs of our age. We are not here as clergymen in contradistinction to the so-called laymen. Such conceptions are utterly unknown in Judaism.

But we are here as men well versed in the history of Judaism, we are here to exchange our views as brethren in the Rabbinical office, and to offer the result of our discussions and council to our Congregations. We are here, not merely for the sake of abolishing, solving, setting aside and destroying. Our "task" is to strengthen our religion in the spirit of truth, and only where it is necessary we shall not be afraid to remove the crusts and shells. It is a destruction for the sake of building up.

After an excellent resume of the labors of the Conference, and the closing address of Geiger, the work of

the Conference was concluded, alas, not to be resumed
until after twenty-three years in Cassel (1868)* where
the preparations were arranged for the Synods in Leipzig (1869), and in Augsburg (1871).   Twenty years
have again passed, but the religious state of affairs in
German Judaism is so miserable, the hypocrisy, cowardice, and selfishness of the Rabbis† of the so-called
Reform-Congregations in Germany, so contemptible,
and the indifferentism, atheism and apostasy of the
masses so frightening, that there is hardly a hope for a
change for the better in the near future.   The Rabbis
—there are very few exceptions but exceptatio con-
firmat regulam—as a rule preach their weekly sermons,
do a little teaching of the young, and let well enough
alone.   The few scholars among them study in their
libraries and publish occasionally a book on some philological, archæological, philosophical, or at best exegetical subject, which has no bearing on the practical religious life of the present.   They are very cautious and
shrewd, these Rabbis.

To touch burning questions of the day might be
followed by unpleasant consequences, might compel a
man to show his true colors.   But it is just this, that
these "wise Rabbis" most carefully avoid.   Hence
German Rabbinism of this day offers, with very few
exceptions, the deplorable and anomalous sight, that a
Rabbi will pose as the most radical critic of the Bible,
and yet be afraid to express his true opinion on the
dietary laws or on some obsolete Jewish custom.
Much less will he dare to disregard publicly a Jewish

---

*The fourth Rabbinical Conference, which was to be held in
Muenchen, was not held, owing to the political fermentation of
those days.   After the Revolution in 1848 the reaction in Germany
was so powerful, that liberal religious movements could not hope to
be successful.   The Protocols of the Breslau Conference were edited
by the committee (Geiger and his friend Prof. M. A. Levy.) (Breslau, 1847, Leuckart, 517 pages).   Geiger published also a condensed
report concerning the work of the Third Conference of German
Rabbis.   (Breslau, 1846), and in reply to orthodox attacks he published a defense of the resolutions on the Sabbath-laws, entitled:
"The Third Conference of German Rabbis."   (Breslau, 1846.)

†The majority of them were graduates of the Breslau Seminary,
which has become a Jesuitical Institute under Frankel and Graetz.

custom which he considers antiquated. The old, bold, courageous Reform-Rabbis, of Germany, whose names are honorably mentioned in this book, are no longer among the living, and the present young generation of Rabbis are fanatic orthodox* or noncommittal.

But let us return to Geiger. The Reform-movement did not entirely occupy his labors. Aside from his literary work, he let no opportunity pass by, without utilizing it for the benefit and welfare of the Jews, for whose political emancipation he had always evinced the same interest as he had shown for their spiritual and intellectual elevation. As this book is in the main devoted to the Jewish Reform-movement, we cannot treat thoroughly this side of Geiger's labors. Suffice it to say, that he had several conferences with King Frederic William IV, (1841), with Minister Eichhorn, (1843), in behalf of the Jews. He published several pamphlets, among others: "Rabbinical Opinions on the Duty of the Jews to Serve as Soldiers," (Breslau, 1842), in which he justly considered the exemption of the Jews from the duty to defend their country, not in the light of a favor,† but as an insult. In the city of Breslau he also resented promptly in the press every attempt to wrong the Jews.‡ Politically he openly espoused in meetings the cause of liberalism.

It is needless to say, that he never neglected his literary labors. Aside from his "Zeitschrift"§ he published a: "Grammar and Reader to the Language

---

*The pupils of the orthodox Seminary, presided over by the hyper-orthodox Dr. Hildesheimer in Berlin. They bind the handkerchief around their body so that God might think it is a belt, carry no umbrella on the Sabbath, a. s. f.

†The orthodox Jews wanted such a "favor" because soldiers cannot keep the Sabbath and the dietary laws.

‡Breslau Zeitung, 1884, No. 28, when a hospital for the citizens of the "Christian denominations" was to be erected. His protest caused a change in the by-laws.

§The Zeitschrift, however, did not come out regularly, as it was too much of a strain for Geiger, who had to write almost every article. The fifth volume in four fascicles was published in 1843 and 1844, of the sixth volume in 1847 only three numbers were published. Fifteen years later it appeared again regularly.

of the Mishna,"* (II parts, Breslau, 1845). "The
Northern French School of Exegesis in the Twelfth
Century." "The Anthropomorphism in the Hag-
gaidah and the Rabbis of the Arabic school," on the
"Family Kimchi"† and Juda Halevi.‡ These labors, in
which Geiger shows also his remarkable talent as a
translator and poet are highly praised by Tal-
landier§ in the "Revue de deux Mondes." Another
exegetical work of great merit is his: "Parshandatha,
the Northern French School of Exegesis," (Leipzig,
1855). "Samples of a Jewish Defense Against Christian
Attacks in Middle Ages,‖" among which the pamphlet
on the Karaite: "Isaac Troki, the Apologist of Judaism
at the Close of the Sixteenth Century," was published
separately.¶ Among his multifarious monographs
deserves special mention, his: "Moses ben Maimon,"
with a Hebrew supplement under the title: "Iggereth ha-
Shemad leha-Rambam;"** "Joseph Salomo Del Medigo," his letter to Serach ben Nathan, translated and edited
with notes, German and Hebrew.†† Geiger's mono-

---

*The attempts of attacks against the book by Graetz were most
promptly resented by Geiger in several articles: "Samples of a Conservative Criticism" (Israelit of the nineteenth century, Nos. 5-6,
1845 and Nos. 5-10, 1845). The book found entrance into German
Universities.

†See introduction to Geiger's Hebrew writings.

‡Posthumous works, III, 34-97-176.

§1853, Avril 15th, p. 381.

‖Deutscher Volkskalender, 1851, 1856, 1859, Posthumous Works,
III, pp. 178-223.

¶ Breslau Jahrbuch 1853, in pamphlet form (Breslau, 1853), Kern,
44 pages, and Posthumous Works, III, pp. 178-223.

**"Studien," edited by M. Breslauer (Weigert & C. Breslau, 1850).

††Berlin, 1840 (W. Wilzig), 104 pages in German, 80 pages in Hebrew, see Melo. Chofnajim and Posthumous Works, III, pp. 1-34.
Jos. Sal. Delmedigo, born June 16, 1591, descendant of a family of
scholars, studied medicine in Padua, devoted himself zealously to
the study of science of mathematics, in which he greatly excelled,
and to the Kabbala. He was body-physician of the Prince Radzivill,
near Wilna, and traveled extensively. Geiger was the first to prove
Jos. Delmedigo's liberal religious views, by bringing to light his famous letter to Serach, which is full of biting sarcasms against the
benighted Rabbis of his day. His views on angels, prophecy, creation, Bible, Talmud, Kabbalah, were rationalistic. Graetz, true to
his unjust method to throw mud at all those who did not belong to
the orthodox Polish school of Rabbis, belittles the merits of Josef

graph on: "Leon do Modena"* is dedicated to the memory of Isaac Samuel Reggio. This book is most remarkable and deserves more than mere passing mention. Leo da Modena was a man, who under the cloak of defending the Talmud, most sarcastically criticised it, and with biting irony attacked the letter-worship and ceremonialism of his age. He was in this respect the forerunner of Gotthold Ephraim Lessing, who employed the same method in attacking the Bible and Christianity in his: "Wolfenbuettel fragments" which, though published under the name of another are his work. L. D. Modena had of course to be very cautious in his polemic, and therefore he published so-called refutations of "heretical views." But the "refutations" were so lame, childish and ridiculous, that they rather strengthened the cause of his "apparent opponent." In this way L. D. Modena attacks the custom of laying Tefillin, the second holiday, the dietary- and vigorous Sabbath-laws,

---

Delmedigo. Dr.David Cassel, in his "Guide for the Instruction in the Jewish History and Literature" (Leitfaden fuer den Unterricht in der Jued. Geschichte und Literatur, Berlin, 1875), mentions Delmedigo's letter thus: "Delmedigo's true ideas are now known through his letter to a Karaite, which was published recently" (p. 97). It would not have hurt Cassel in the least to give the credit for bringing this letter to light, where it was due, although Geiger was not a favorite with the former satellite of Michael Sachs. (See also Geiger's Post-humous Works, II, p. 195).

*"L.D.M., Rabbi of Venice, and his Losition to the Kabbalah, to the Talmud and to Christianity"(Breslau, 1856, J. M. Kern, 63 pages in German, 34 pages in Hebrew). L. D. M. was born 1571, in Ven-ice, died 1648 in Venice, where he filled the position of Rabbi. He was a most fertile author, published a "Hebrew-Italian Lexicon," a "Mnemotechnic," a "Warning against Gambling," which was trans-lated into the Latin and German, and anti-Kabbalistic and anti-Talmudic writings "Ari Nohem" (the roaring lion, and "Shaagath Arje" (the bellowing of the lion). See my Jued. Literar. Centralblatt No. 1 (Koenigsberg, 1876), on Leon da Modena. It is needless to say that Graetz attacks L. D. M. in an unworthy, or better, in a "Graetz"-worthy manner. He calls him the worst names, "hypo-crite," "blasphemer," "despiser of Judaism." (Graetz' History of the Jews, X, p. 139).

the endless prayers,* the Shechitah, even the fasting
on the Day of Atonement. For this only can be the
meaning of his remark, that everybody should fast in
accord with his physical and mental strength. He is
particularly bitter in his censure of the excrescences of
Rabbinical Judaism, which is a sin against the words
of Moses: "Ye shall not add to it," and advocates
the return to the plain, genuine, old, and pure Biblical
Judaism.

Geiger's philosophical labors include the following: The Ethical Basis of the Book on the "Duties of
the Heart,"† and "Jewish Poetry of the Spanish
School."‡ Besides numerous articles on Rabbinital literature contributed to Hebrew periodicals, § he
adorned the great "Journal of the German Oriental
Society"‖ with contributions which show his vast
erudition in the field of Syriac lexicography and Samaritan literature. No less an authority than Dr.
Adolph Neubauer, Professor of Oriental Languages in

---

*This is done in the following ingenuous argumentation. The
Talmud prescribes that he who goes on a dangerous journey, has fulfilled his duty by reciting a short prayer. To this L. D. M. adds, "We
Jews are always in danger." (See also Posthumous Works, Vol. II,
pp. 189-194).

† Breslau, 1853, June 3rd, an introduction to E. Baumgarten's
edition of Bachja Ibn Bakuda's "Chovoth halevovoth" Wien, 1853,
pp. 13-22.

‡ Leipzig, 1856, Isr. Volksbibliothek, III, and Posthumous Works
III, pp. 224-251. Highly interesting translations from the Hebrew
into German poetry are given by Geiger of the poets: Salomo Ga-
birol, Juda Halevi, Juda Charisi, Isaac ben Ruben, Moses Ibn Esra,
Abraham b. Meir Ibn Esra, Juda b. Isaac b. Shabthai, Meir b. Tod-
dros Halevi, Isaac Polkar, Sal. b. Ruben Bonafed.

§ Kherem Chemed, Ozar Nechmad, Hechalutz, by Schorr and
others.

‖ As it is out of question for us to dwell at some length on
these labors, we simply record the titles of the essays: "To the
Theology and Exegesis of the Samaritans," lecture delivered by Geiger before the Congress of Orientalists in Breslau, September 30th,
1857." "To the History of the Talmudical Lexicography, Vol. XII,
pp. 142-149, August, 1857;" "Why does the Book Sirach belong to
the Apokryphs?" Vol. XII, pp. 536-543, April 4th, 1858; "The Legal
Differences between Samaritans and Jews," Vol. XX, pp. 527-573,
Frankfurt, December 24th, 1865; "Jewish Terms in the Syrian Literature," Vol. XXI, pp. 487-492, Frankfurt, November 25th, 1866.

Oxford, England, ranks Geiger as "the highest living authority on Samaritan literature."*

But all this did not yet suffice for Geiger's enthusiasm for diffusing the science of Judaism. He therefore found time to give lectures to candidates of Jewish theology on history, literature, Chaldaic language, introduction into the Mishna, and other subjects. Dr. Landsberger (Darmstadt), Friedman (Manheim), Goldstein (Posen), Cohn (Schwerin, now Berlin), Schoengut, Mauksch and others were fortunate enough to hear these lectures.† Aside from this Geiger lectured regularly before the "Reading Society" on scientific subjects, which had nothing to do with Judaism.‡

But Geiger discontinued his lectures for the following reasons. We have often mentioned how enthusiastically Geiger always worked for the establishment of a Jewish theological faculty, for the realization of an idea which originated with him. Now, after long, weary waiting, the great dream of his youth seemed to approach its fulfillment. He found at last the right man in the person of Commercieurath Jonas Fraenkel, Breslau, who was ready, at Geiger's earnest solicitation to endow such an institution. But in this instance again the prophecy was verified. "Thou shalt see the promised land, but thou shalt not enter into it." By all sorts of intrigues, machinations, and tricks, Geiger who was destined by Fraenkel to become the leader of the new Institution, was passed over, and instead of him the conservative Zacharias Frankel was elected Director of the "Seminary." Unfortunately the founder of the Institution died, long before it was given over to its destination, and the executors of his will simply betrayed the sacred trust placed in them, by the establishment of a "Jesuiten-Anstalt,"* where hypoc-

---

*In order to do full justice to Geiger's literary labors, a special book of great dimensions would have to be written

†Some of them are published, Posthumous Works, II, pp. 1-32, 246-274.

‡Geiger: First and Second Report of the Jewish "Society for Teaching and Reading" (1843-1844).

*Hot-bed of Jesuitism. The methods of the Jesuitical Seminaries of the Catholic Church are employed there. The system of espion-

risy and cant are at a premium. This treacherous act has done incalculable harm to the cause of Judaism in Germany, and is the reason why Judaism in Germany of to-day, thirty-eight years after the establishment of this Institution, is in a worse plight than it was before the existence of the "Breslau Seminary." We say it —and we challenge anyone to disprove this important statement—that the Breslau Seminary has hurt most severely, not only Reform-Judaism, but Judaism in general, at least in Germany. Things there are so bad, that the number of Jewish apostates is daily increasing, while at the time when Reform-Judaism in Germany was at its zenith, a case of apostasy was a rare occurrence. "By the fruits the tree can be recognized." As the disciples of the "Breslau Seminary" occupy the prominent positions in Germany, they, the gardeners of the vineyards, must be made responsible for the deplorable fact that the garden is in a worse condition than before they took charge of it. An Institute, where the students are expected to come every morning with their Talith and Tefillin to the Synagogue of the "Seminary," where the one who screams louder than his fellow-student, while praying, has better prospects of getting a stipend than the other who may know more and study more and whose character is nobler; an Institute, where the system of espionage is encouraged, where a student who would write on Sabbath would be denounced to the director of the Seminary, and be punished by losing a stipend, such an Institute is bound to breed hypocrisy, Jesuitism, nepotism, flattery, intrigue, and all those qualities which do not make for righteousness.

------

age is en vogue. The students, who can best play the hypocrites, are preferred in the distribution of stipends and other benefits, and are sure to be recommended to the best paying positions, while those endowed with great talent, industry, perseverance and character have to take a back seat. But for this very reason the latter class are few and far between, and belong to the rarae aves in Breslau. As a rule they do not stay long there, the atmosphere does not suit them. More than half of Geiger's disciples in Berlin belonged to this class.

There is many a man in Germany who, although belonging to the best disciples of the Breslau "Seminary," and endowed with great oratorical powers, is condemned to eke out a miserable existence in some cross-road town, just because he could not give up his manhood and independence, just because he spurned the idea of acting the hypocrite. Men of such calibre are literally persecuted and hunted down there by the "powers that be." *Nomina sunt odiosa*, but we could give the names of at least three or four of Breslau "Seminarists," who have undergone and are still undergoing just such sad experiences.

The trouble with the "Seminary" is not so much that it represents conservative Judaism, but that it is colorless, and that the majority of its graduates are orthodox in orthodox Congregations, and Reformers in Reform-communities. Hence they represent no principle at all, and are consistent only in their inconsistency. Is it then any wonder, that the Congregations, presided over by such Rabbis, are getting more and more indifferent to Judaism. Was not Graetz, the power behind the throne in the 'Seminary,' himself a type of the whole system at work there? There was a Professor of Jewish history, who in the notorious eleventh volume of his "History" fanatically condemns sermons in the vernacular, music and choir in the Temple, and other innocent Reforms, slings mud at every advocate of Reform, and raises to the skies every Polish tramp, who has published the most worthless trash. Now people might think this Professor "conservative" and on the strength of this almost pardon his injustice. But in the first and second volume this very same Professor appears as "radical of the radicals," treats the Bible, the five books of Moses not excepted, as the *most faulty bungling work*, speaks of Joseph, Moses, miracles and revelation as legends. Now look at this picture and then look at that. One must of necessity be false.* If then the teacher sets such an

---

*See my Graetz' "Geschichtsbauerei" (Berlin, 1881, Issleib), especially pages 88 to 108.

example of principle and consistency, what can be expected of the pupil?

It can well be imagined, how disappointed Geiger must have felt not only on account of the personal injustice done him, but more so, because the establishment of a conservative Seminary, was justly looked upon as a blow aimed at the Reform so ably and enthusiastically advocated and represented by him. Since that time he has been no longer firmly opposed to the idea of leaving Breslau, although he had refused the position offered to him as Director of the Frankfurt Philanthropin.

Geiger's "Religious-School" started in 1843 was a great success and caused him much joy, as did the yearly confirmatin. Public spirited as he was he took great interest in almost every important Jewish organization of Breslau, charitable or educational. Poor students found in him a great friend. He assisted them directly and indirectly, He was often called upon to dedicate Synagogues.

In 1844 he lectured before the Congress of Orientalists in Dresden on the: "Value of the Study of the Mishna for the Hebrew and Syriac." In Muenchen and Wiesbaden, where he delivered sermons, he received great ovations and honors.

The year 1857 must be considered the most important in Geiger's eventful life. For in this year his life-work, his monumentum aere perennium was completed, his: "Urschrift und Uebersetzungen der Bibel in ihrer Abhaengigkeit von der inneren Entwickelung des Judenthum's."* In the same year he also celebrated the twenty-fifth anniversary of his Rabbinical career.

The "Urschrift" this chef d'oeuvre of Geiger is the fruit of twenty years' labor, and presents a critical investigation of the Bible. The work was considered epochal on account of its original and revolutionizing

---

*"Urschrift (means original manuscript), and Translations of the Bible in their Dependence upon the inner Development of Judaism" (Breslau, 1857, 500 pages).

theories on the Bible, on the development of Judaism
and its contact with Christianity. Geiger has proven
in this work, that the political and religious struggles
of the Jewish nation and the different political parties
had much to do with the text of the Bible. The
numerous conflicts and contradictions of the Bible are
explained by the fact, that they were intentional
partisan changes of the different political parties which
existed before the canon of the Bible was concluded. Two
of these parties are described in a new original manner,
entirely different from current ideas, and exploding
former notions. Even to this very day the Sadducees
are represented as Philhellenists, i. e., friends of Greek
customs, who had placed themselves beyond the pale
of Judaism, who had embraced new Grecian refine-
ment, who had become utterly denationalized as
Epicureans, Sensualists and worldlings, who neglected
all religious interests. The Pharisees, on the other
hand, have also assumed a false meaning. It was
particularly through the influence of Christianity, that
the Pharisees were, and among the masses are still, regarded as narrow-minded men, who strained at a gnat,
who would indulge in outward worship, without being
animated by true, inward piety, without capability for
more exalted, religious ideas. Some went even so far
as to place them in the same category with hypocrites,
bigots and fanatics. It was the merit of Geiger's
"Urschrift" to have thrown new light on these subjects. Geiger proves that the "Sadducees"* constituted the priestly nobility, vested with power, and

---

*Zadokites, from "Zadok," the high priest, a friend of the Da-
vidian dynasty, Joshua b. Jehozadak, the high priest, was
a leader of the exulants who returned from Babylonian captivity
(Haggai, Sacharia, III Ezech. XXXIV, 23-24; XXXVII, 24-25; II
Chron. XXVI, 16; I Chron. XXIV, 9-20; 12-28, 16-39, 27-16, 29-22,
5-31, 6-35; II, 24-26; Nehem. XII, 10-11; Esra VII, 1; Nehem. XI, 11;
I Chron. IX, 11; II Chron. XXXI, 10-13). They were also called
"Zaddikim" the righteous   *   *   *   because they were also
judges. The high priest was styled as "Malkhizedek" "the king of
justice." Thus "Zaddik" became a title for "prince," Psalm CXIII
118, CXXV, 2; Psalm CX; Isaiah XLIX, 24-25; LX, 21-22. See Geiger: Urschrift und Uebersetzungen der Bibel, pp. 20, 38, 57, 83, 293,
221, 101, 264, 215, 102, 202, 493.

placed above the masses, made their own personal interests paramount to all others. The "Pharisees," on the other side, constituted the very body of the people, were representatives of true democracy. Their exertions were directed toward the establishment of equal rights for all classes. Their struggle was one which is repeated in all times when great interests are at stake, a struggle against priestcraft and hierarchy, against the prerogatives and privileges of individual classes. It was also a battle on the side of the Pharisees for the great principle, that outward qualities do not exclusively constitute a claim to higher moral standing, but that the prize belongs to inward, religious conviction and moral worth. Thus the Pharisees were virtually the progressive party of the people, opposing the Sadducees, who formed the aristocracy, held all offices, basked in the favor of the court, were priests themselves, or connected with the priestly families, were in possession of power and influence which they strove to retain. The means which the Pharisees were compelled to employ, seem, at first sight, not to bear out Geiger's new views concerning them. But when examined more thoroughly in the light of those times and circumstances, they fully correspond with Geiger's theories. In order to oppose the priests successfully, it was of the utmost necessity at that time to claim priestly prerogatives and privileges for the masses of the people. They would not assign higher duties to others, lest they were obliged to ascribe to them also higher distinction. Hence the Pharisees said:

"We, the people, are as holy and occupy the same exalted position as you, the priestly and aristocratic party. Hence the Pharisees took upon themselves from political reasons all the numerous priestly laws of purity (dietary laws), and many others, which were formerly observed by the Sadducees only. True, they went too far in this, and were thus the cause of the multifarious, burdensome additions to the laws of Moses, of which the Mishna and Gmarah are full.

Geiger proves this by numerous instances. He further demonstrates, that two schools existed within the Pharisaism, the old and the new Halacha.*

The old Halacha is the norm of the Sadducees, while the numerous additions of laws, observances, customs and usages made by the Pharisees form the new Halachah. These differences can most clearly be noticed in the laws on purity, sacrifice, Temple-service and in the penal laws.† The decline of Sadduceeism is shown in the Samaritans,‡ and Karaites,§ their natural heirs in blind letter-worship. After the destruction of the Jewish commonwealth and the burning of the Temple in Jerusalem, the Jewish nationality was broken, and Sadduceeism was dead. For the occupation of the priests was gone, their ministrations in the Temple with the sacrifices were no longer wanted. Not a shadow of worldly power was left. No more contention for office and distinction, no more separation from and no more elevation above the masses. The Sadducees vanished from history. The Pharisees of the strict school of rigorous observance still existed, and were represented by the Shammaites, those men who thought to effect the sanctification of the people by rendering the yoke of the law heavier and heavier. After the destruction of the Temple their gloomy sentiment, continually looking backwards towards the ancient customs and institutions, strove to gain the ascendency, and advocated destructive asceticism. But the progressive school of the Hillelites, who paid

---

*Literally it means "walk," from the Hebrew word "halach," to go. Although Moses emphatically and energetically interdicted any addition to the six hundred and thirteen commandments of the Pentateuch ("Ye shall add nothing and take off nothing"), these precepts have been augmented in the Talmud to the imposing number of 13,602. The final decisions, which the Rabbis, judges, students and leaders were obliged to commit to memory on account of their practical importance, were called Halachah. See my: "The Talmud" (Denver, 1884), pp. 17-18.

†See Geiger: Urschrift, pp. 134-135, 151, 158, 173-176, 263, 270, 272, 351, marriage laws, 868 and 473.

‡Geiger, Urschrift, pp. 77, 80, 138, 139, 262, 372, 415, 468, 473.

§Urschrift, pp. 106, 119, 168, 168, 395, 420, 437, 467, 479.

higher respect to sentiment than to vigorous laws, who consulted the time and yielded to its pressing demands rather than to obsolete usages and antiquated customs, saved the spirit of Judaism from perishing and prepared it to enter successfully upon its marvelous pilgrimage through the world. Geiger then goes on to give a most minute description of the factors which were at work in shaping the text of the Bible, its translations and the later literary monuments of the Jews. With the instinctive intuition of the true genius he points out the numerous changes of the text, which were made by the opposing parties of Judaism at different periods of our history, in order to serve their partisan purposes, in order to make the text of the Bible what seemed to be most advantageous to their party-interests. The German term "tendenzioese Aenderungen" covers the ground better than any English word we know of. Following up this line of argument for an unbiased explanation of the Bible, Geiger shows the same method in a scientific appreciation of the Talmud. He sees in the Talmud, which is regarded by so many as the very embodiment of stagnation and ossification, a stupendous innovation upon the simplicity of the Bible-religion, and the grandest possible proof of the progressive development within Judaism.*

---

*Geiger expresses himself on the Talmud as follows: "In general, his (the Jew's) spirit was never bent down in him, however much depressed his outward carriage. While in dark ages bishops and knights were entirely devoted to ignorance, and the difficult art of reading and writing remained something foreign to them, this remnant of the dispersed Jews still preserved an aspiration to spiritual development, often but a one-sided one, which would not always keep pace with progress in life, but still it was a spiritual energy which forever saved their freshness. Canonization of ignorance has never been the rule in Israel. Science now and then took a crooked route, their acuteness sometimes went astray, their mind now and then adorned itself with worthless tinsel, but it was ever active. Gigantic works of darker and brighter times are before us, productions of thought and profound spiritual activity, and they awaken our reverence. I do not endorse every word of the Talmud, nor every idea of our teachers of the middle ages, but I would not lose a tittle thereof; they contain an acumen and power of thought which fill us with reverence for the spirit that animated our ancestors, a

We do not claim to have given to our readers even a faint synopsis of a work like Geiger's "Urschrift," which he himself had considered the work of his life. The ideas held forth were adversely commented on by scholars of the opposite school, and the author had to face a raging storm, on account of the radical views on the Bible, advanced for the first time in Jewish history by a Rabbi in office. Especially Frankel and his school were merciless in their strictures. The same school, Graetz in particular, have since then made Biblical-criticism a favorite occupation.

But Geiger had the satisfaction to find soon his work appreciated and recognized by scholars whose reputation was established in the world of letters. Dr. Neubauer said: "The chief merit of Geiger's researches in regard to this branch of study is his powerful analysis of obscure Talmudical passages." Professor Schenkel has in his world-renowned "Bibellexicon," (1872), virtually adopted Geiger's researches on "Pharisees." Schenkel is one of the most prominent Christian theologians of this century. The "Volkszeitung" of Berlin, said that the "Urschrift" offered for the next ten years entirely new material for important critical research. The "Kreuzzeitung," the organ of the Junkerpartei,"* attacked the work in strong terms, while a Professor of Catholic theology, Krueger in Braunsberg, made Geiger's results the basis of his book, "De secerdotum apud Judaeos nobilitate"† and acknowledged this fact in a letter of thanks to Geiger. The "Revue Germanique" contained a most excellent article on the "Urschrift," and Holdheim was full of enthusiasm about the work. The study of the book he said regenerated him scientifically, and inspired him to the publication of a work in Hebrew

fullness of sound sense, salutary maxims, a freshness of opinion often bursts upon us that, even to this day, exercises its vivifying and inspiring effect upon us." (pp. 284-85.) (Geiger, "Judaism and its History," pp. 284-85. My "Talmud," pp. 13-14).

*The party of the ultra-orthodox old Prussian nobility.
†On the priestly nobility of the Jews.

language.* The "Protestant Kirchenzeitung," the organ of scientific orthodoxy had in No. 44 an essay: " The Result of the Jewish Investigation on Pharisees and Sadducees," (Nov. 1st, 1862), in which Geiger's views are fully indorsed. Brockhaus's "Conversations-Lexicon" of 1864, contains an article on "Apokryphs," based on the results of the "Urschrift." Professor Dozy of the Leyden (Holland) University in a book: "The Israelites at Mekka" and another Dutch scholar A. Juynbell in his "Relation of the Kingdom of Juda to the Assyrian Power" in the years 741-711, have also based their researches† on Geiger's "Urschrift." A disciple of the great French savant Renan, Isaïe Levaillant asked Geiger's permission to translate the "Urschrift" into the French, saying, that Renan, whose secretary he was, promised to find a publisher for the work. "Renan," he said in his letter, "before leaving Asia, charged me to inform you what a sympathetic reader you have in him."‡ Of other renowned Christian German Professors, who have accepted Geiger's theories on the: "Sadducees and Pharisees" may be mentioned: Holtzmann in the second volume of the, "History of Israel" by Weber and Holtzman, Hanne in Hilgenfeld's periodical, Haussrath in Gelzer's Monthly, and Keim in his, "History of Jesus of Nazareth," in the first volume, (1867).

These instances, which could be augmented, go to show, that the "Urschrift" of Geiger is next to Zunz's "Gottesdienstliche Vortraege der Juden,"§ the most prominent Jewish publication of this century. How many of our American Rabbis know of the ex-

*Holdheim's "Maamar Haishuth" is meant. See p. 244 of this book.
†Both works were published in Holland in 1863. See Geiger's Zeitschrift, III, pp. 150-151.
‡"M. Renan, m'a chargé avant de partr de vous remercier de toutes les charmantes choses que vous lui avez envoyées et de vous dire quel lecteur sympathique vous avez en lui."
§Berlin, 1832. For scientific Jewish theology Geiger's Urschrift is even of far greater import than Zunz's "Gottesd. Vortr."

istence of this literary monument of modern Judaism? How many possess it, how many read and study it? Few, very few take sufficient interest in exegetical studies concerning the origin and development of our Biblical literature. And yet, without such studies the history of Judaism cannot be comprehended. If this book shall have the effect of inducing our young American Rabbis to devote a part of their time to the study of Geiger's "Urschrift," even at the risk of reading a few chapters less of Spencer, Huxley and others—the author will feel himself greatly rewarded. "Look up to Abraham (Geiger), the father of modern Jewish theology!" I remember, that at the celebration of Geiger's last birthday in Berlin, Dr. Emil G. Hirsch, then a student of the "Hochschule fuer die Wissenschaft des Judenthums," spoke of his intentions to translate the "Urschrift" into English. It would only be a debt of gratitude, if Geiger's disciples in this country and in England should undertake this praiseworthy task. True, it would be too difficult a work for one man. But four men like Emil Hirsch, Felix Adler, Samuel Sale, and the author of this book, all disciples of Geiger, could easily accomplish such a labor of love. The thanks of the scientific world of England and America would surely follow.

Next to the publication of the "Urschrift" the year 1857 was epochal in Geiger's life on account of the celebration of the twenty-fifth anniversary of his Rabbinical career. (Nov. 21st). This event became a great holiday for the Breslau Congregation and community. Congregations, (Wiesbaden, Posen and others), Magistrates, friends, and students vied with one another in making this day a feast. Presents and congratulations poured in from all sides. Among dedications to the Jubilee I mention in particular the one written by the celebrated poet, Berthold Auerbach, Geiger's life-long friend. It begins with the Hebrew quotation from Genesis, XXVII. 27: "See the smell of my son is as the smell of the field which God has blessed." He concludes thus: "In your work as a

scholar and in your religious activity is a breath of the
field, always fresh, invigorating as the air of nature.
May it continue to enliven you and everything emanating from you." Lazar Geiger, Dr. Honigman, Prof. M.
A. Stern, (Goettingen), Ferdinand Cohn, (Breslau) also
sent beautiful poems and dedications.   The celebration
lasted three days, Friday, Saturday and Sunday.   In a
letter to Jacob Auerbach, dated Dec. 3, 1857 Geiger
says: "I may speak of days of feast.   *   *   The
recognition, which I have received, is, to say the least,
a full recompensation for all my labor and painful
struggles.   The author, as a consistent representative
of a scientific system, has been celebrated by his followers, the undaunted progressive Rabbi has been
celebrated by the Congregations, more than he deserved.   But I appreciate even still higher, that it has
been demonstrated, that the man was not lost in the
author and Rabbi.   Men participated in the festivities,
who do not sympathize with my radical views, who
not seldom were my opponents."*

But, alas, for the inconstancy of human happiness! Geiger's beloved wife Emilie, to all appearances
enjoying good health on this day of gladness, had
already then suffered of a disease, to which she succumbed three years later, Dec. 6th, 1860.†

Geiger could never forget this hard bereavement,
and the name of his beloved wife was always mentioned
in the prayers after meals in his house.   During her
sickness in Berlin, Zunz and his wife proved themselves true friends.

The more Geiger threw himself into the vortex of
scientific labor on account of this sad loss. He resumed
again this "Zeitschrift fuer Wissenschaft und Leben,"
which was uninterruptedly published until Geiger's

---

*Posthumous Works, V. pp. 221-22.
†The following epitaph, written by Geiger, adorns her grave:
"Was du gewesen,-Wird nie verwesen,-Bleibst wie hinieden, Im
ewigen Frieden,-Vor Gottes Throne,-Des Mannes Krone der Kinder
Wonne-Des Hauses Sonne." ("What thou hast been will never die.
Thou remainest before God's throne in eternal peace. As thou hast
been here, the husband's crown, the children's joy, the home's sun.")

death. It was a quarterly Review and invited as contributors the "Biblical searchers of all denominations." Indeed Christian Professors like Noeldecke-Strassburg, world-renowned Orientalists, like Wright in London, Chwolson in Petersburg; Walz, New York; Fleischer, Leipzig; Delitzsch. Leipzig and other European authorities honored Geiger's Magazine with their contributions. Those of our readers, who are no strangers to the literature of Oriental philology are aware of the fact that the men just named belong to the recognized authorities of the Nineteenth century. Of Jewish scholars, who contributed to the "Zeitschrift" I mention Zunz, Prof. Dernbourg, Steinschneider, Prof. Luzatto, Wechsler, Prof. Goldzieher, Gruenebaum, Prof. Harkavy, Prof, M. A. Levy, Prof. M. A. Stern, Jacob Auerbach, Samuel Adler, N. and A. Bruell, K. Kohler, Landsberger, Kirchheim, Prof. Ludwig Geiger. Prof. Neubauer,* L. Baer, Schorr, Erlich, Wolff, Wiener, Kaiserling, Wolf, Vienna, Triber, Aub, Rothschild, Kohn, Prof. Schiller-Szinessy, Baerwald, Felsenthal, Tobias Cohn, D. Oppenheim, Lebrecht and others. Geiger's literary correspondence was very extensive. In the same year, (1860), he undertook a journey through Switzerland and a greater part of Germany, where he formed interesting acquaintances with Prof. Lazarus, Sprenger, Valentin, Buedinger-Weil, Hitzig, Benfey, Bertheau, Noeldecke, and renewed the friendship with Stern, Frensdorff and others.

In consequence of Dr. Leopold Stein's resignation the position in Frankfurt was offered to Geiger repeatedly, but he flatly declined out of consideration for Stein. He even urged Stein to make peace with the Frankfort Congregation, and to remain in office after a special committee had been sent to him from Frankfort entreating him to accept the call, Jan. 4th, 1863. But after a petition of members of the Frankfort Congregation to reinstate Stein was not acted upon, and

---

*Prof. Adolph Neubauer (Oxford), said that Geiger was doubtless the "highest living authority" on Samaritan literature.

the position would have been offered to another, Geiger did not feel it incumbent upon him to dismiss another deputation, headed by his friend Dr. Elissen, therefore he accepted the position in his native city, (February 7th, 1863).

It is needless to say, that enemies of Geiger, most particularly those who tried in season and out of season to embitter his life in Breslau, were the first to speak of Geiger's ingratitude towards the Breslau Congregation in leaving it, and of the "wrong" done to his friend, Dr. Stein, by going as Rabbi to Frankfort. Indeed a pasquinade full of the meanest slanders, aspersions and insinuations reflecting on Geiger's character was published in the same year in Breslau by an anonymous assailant, under the title: "Dr. Geiger and His Removal From Breslau to Frankfort."[*] This libelous pamphlet had only the effect to make Geiger, who still wavered,[†] owing to the entreaties of his Breslau friends, immovable in his resolutions, and with a heavy heart he saw no other way than to send in his resignation to the Breslau Congregation, (March 13), which was accepted April 13, to take effect August 1st.

There are those who claim that Geiger ought to have remained in Breslau. After the treachery of the executors of the Fraenkel-endowment in basely betraying the trust placed in them, cheating Geiger out of the office of director of the Breslau Seminary and making of it a hot-bed of Jesuitism and hypocrisy, it is rather surprising, that Geiger remained in Breslau so long, without being disgusted. Aside from this his wife had died and his isolation became more oppressive. Now Frankfurt was the place of his birth, where he had relatives and old friends. And, last but not least, he laid the flattering unction to his soul, that the

---

*Breslau 1863. There is reason to believe that Graetz and his clique were not ignorant of the personality of the nameless coward.

†He had even written to Frankfort, requesting the Congregation to release him from his promise to accept the position, but this request was not granted.

Rothschilds and the numerous other Frankfort Jewish millionaires would be easily influenced by him, as their Rabbi, to establish in Frankfort a Theological Institution for the education of consistent Reform-Rabbis, which would stand under his guidance and sole control. Later events will show that the Psalmist was right in saying: "Do not trust in the rich." In a letter to Stern,* Geiger said: "If I could only succeed in establishing in Frankfort a Rabbinical Seminary in accord with my ideas. And this is after all the most important motive of my removal." Geiger's departure from Breslau was equally honorable for the man who officiated there twenty-three years as for the Congregation. On July 4th, Geiger delivered his farewell-sermon before an audience which filled the Temple to its utmost capacity. On July 7th, a banquet was tendered to him, at which toasts, poems and costly presents of magistrates and friends gave proof of his great popularity. The ladies of the Congregation, his pupils, and the Societies over which he presided, overwhelmed him with presents, addresses and tokens of love and respect. In a letter to Stern of January 25th, 1863, Geiger writes: "The poor children shed tears on hearing that I intended to leave. Many Guelfish court-pastors would like to see such tears, but they are only shed because they remain in their places." On July 9th Geiger left Breslau, and after a sojourn of a few weeks in Colberg, a summer-resort, he arrived Aug. 9th in Frankfort. Of the numerous poems to Geiger the one entitled: "Abschieds-grurs" (Farewell Greeting), by Dr. S. Meyer, Breslau, July, 1863, is touching in the extreme. We excerpt the following lines:

"Wem drang's nicht einmal in die Seele tief, wenn ihn der Mutter traute Stimme rief? Dass er noch einmal in dem heil'gen Raum, Geniessen moeg, der Jugend gold'nen Traum; die Mutter hat sich nicht des

---

*June 17th, 1863. Posthumous Works, V. p. 263.

Kind's zu schaemen, und will den grossen Sohn, zurueck sich nehmen.''

GEIGER IN FRANKFORT.

Had Geiger been the man to seek a resting-place after long struggles and hot contests, he could not have found a better place than Frankfort, the town of his birth. But he felt disappointed, that the main object of his accepting the position, namely the establishment of a Theological Faculty, could not be realized, although he left no stone unturned to bring about such a consummation. True, his sermons, his religious instruction imparted to the young and his confirmation-classes were a source of joy to him and of general satisfaction to his Congregation. But he found nothing to fight for, and hence the enthusiastic combatants of the palmy days of Breslau were wanting, in short, Geiger was not in his element. His plan to form a: ''Society for Jewish Affairs,'' was not successful, although D. D. Adler, of Cassel; Landsberger, of Darmstadt; Goldschmidt, of Leipzig, Cahn, of Mainz, Aub, of Mainz, Rothschild, of Alzey, Goldman, of Birkenfeld, Suesskind, of Wiesbaden, Wittelshoefer. of Floss, Wertheim, of Berlin, Koenigswarter, of Paris, were present in Frankfort to hold a discussion. The absence of contention gave Geiger an opportunity to devote more time and attention to the science of Judaism. He was pleasantly surprised by visits of old and new friends such as M. A. Stern, Berthold Auerbach, Edward Lasker, Prof. Dozy, of Leyden, Prof. Staehelin, of Basel, Joseph Dernbourg, of Paris, M. A. Levy, of Breslau. Jacob Auerbach and Raphael Kirchheim belonged to his most intimate personal friends in Frankfort. In a letter to Wechsler Geiger writes: A man who has been accustomed for twenty-three years to be the center of the Congregation will meet in Frankfort with many centrifugal forces and also with men who wan t to be centers themselves. Frankfort * * cannot so easily be made

enthusiastic."* In saying this, Geiger does not mean
that he was less popular in Frankfort than in Breslau.
But no man can accomplish in eight weeks the work of
twenty-three years. Geiger continued in Frankfort
his lectures on "Judaism and Its History."† In a
letter to M. A. Levy he said, that Graetz has "no
historical intuition" and in a letter to Stern he calls
Graetz "a charlatan of the first water."‡ A strong
expression, but a man like Geiger knew what he was
saying. Whenever an eminent scholar died (Luzatto,
Frankfurter and others) he complained, that there are
no good men to take their places.

The following letter is practically important for our
own circumstances in this country just now, when we
are grappling with the question of the wholesale immigration of Russian Jews. Geiger's ideas on the Roumanian Jewish question are bold and in pleasant contrast with the sentimentalism which is so often paraded in our Jewish Press. In a letter to Saniel Markus,
of Bucharest,§ he is just as outspoken in this matter as
he is in everything else. He took great interest in the
Roumanian Jewish question, and interested the Berlin
Jewish Congregation and his own Congregation in the
matter of sending petitions to the King and to the
Chancellor. Indeed, the King of Prussia and the
Prince of Hohenzollern, father of the reigning prince
of Roumania, promised to do their best in the matter.‖

But at the same time Geiger did not shut his eyes
to the seat of the evil. In two articles entitled
"Spirit and Money," he forcibly raised his voice
against "political missionary activity." No nation
can be regenerated by another. "Civilization cannot be
imported, and can be acquired only by hard labor.
Who has ever assisted the Jews in Germany? Did they
ever ask the mediation of France, England or America?

---

*October 15th, 1863. Posthumous Works, V, p. 255.
†Breslau, Schletter, 1862-1865.
‡Posthumous Works, V, p. 257.
§Posthumous Works, V, p. 297-299. March 17th, 1868.
‖See Geiger's Zeitschrift, VI, pp. 81-86, 160, 289.

Much as we sympathize with you Jews in Roumania, it is not well if you always wait for outside assistance, and thus show how little confidence you have in yourselves. Go to work energetically, as we in Germany have done and are still doing. Continual complaints lose their force and degrade. * * Work and labor in your own cause. * * Be doubly watchful over yourselves, so that prejudice against you can find not even the semblance of a cause. * * But the worst possible thing is, when you never cease to beg for money. As soon as a house is on fire in Galicia, the whole west of Europe and America are expected to pay for the damage done. When a crop in Persia is bad, an appeal is made to all the Jews, and when a mob of Roumania ruins a few houses, then all Israel should establish insurance-societies. *

Geiger did not object to alms-giving as such, but to its abuses. "It only relieves temporarily," he continues, "without stopping the sources of the evil. These sources are: Ignorance, fanaticism, intolerance, hostility to culture and civilization. Just keep on throwing away thousands and thousands of thalers by sending them to Jerusalem. They encourage and nurture barbarism, laziness, fanatic fury and savagery.† Out of the midst of the land itself must emanate the powers and forces of civilization and regeneration. The imported article will never accomplish the work.‡

Geiger felt most painfully the isolation of the progressive Rabbis who were in favor of Reform. Again he instigated a movement tending to revive the Rabbinical Conferences of 1844 to 1846. The following is a synopsis of a most excellent article on the present situation: "The Resurrecting Rabbinical Conference."§ "I say to-day, what I said more than thirty years ago. The Jews as a whole have advanced, but Judaism does

---

*Geiger's Zeitschrift, X, pp. 161-165, 220.
†Even the hyper-orthodox Sir Moses Montefiore, was excommunicated by this gentry, because he dared to establish schools in Jerusalem.
‡Wissensch. Zeitschrift, X, p. 218.
§Zeitschrift, VI, pp. 161-171, July 10th, 1868.

not keep pace with the progress of the time.   *   *
The Congregations do not know what they want and
do not want what they know.   The intelligent Jews do
not wish to be disturbed from their rest, and are therefore ready to make the most disgusting concessions.*
*   *   There must be found some remedy, no matter
how many attempts are accompanied by failure.   *   *
Public discussions are growing to be a pressing necessity.
The new results of scientific research must no longer
remain buried in the library of the student, or in some
magazines read by specialists, but they must become
public property of the masses.   We entertain now rad-
ically different ideas on the Bible and the Talmud,
from those we entertained two decades ago.   This
knowledge must be imparted to the people.   *   *

"We must, by means of public discussion, try to
eradicate ignorance.   It is ignorance which induces
some to cling anxiously to the most obsolete forms.
Others again through ignorance, are led to believe,
because they do no longer practice effete customs and
antiquated ceremonies, that they cut loose entirely
from the fold of Judaism, and many a Rabbi is afraid
to abolish a custom which had lost its meaning in our
days, because he does not wish to act single-handed,
not knowing how his Congregation will look upon his
step.   Therefore discussions on such questions by the
Rabbis, and the presence of representatives of Congregations at such discussions would be considered as an
expression of the will of the Congregation.   There are
things where a change or total abolition are urgent demands of the time.   *   *   All this impelled me, in
company with others, to revive the Rabbinical Conferences.   Twenty years ago it was necessary to have
only Rabbis admitted as members of such assemblies.
But even then worthy scholars like Jost and Zunz were
invited to the Conferences.   In our day, however, we
need not hesitate to admit men who are well versed in
the Jewish literature, even if they are no Rabbis.

---

*This is a true picture of the state of Judaism in Europe in our
days.   Not so in America.

Dr. Philippsohn, acting on Geiger's suggestion, called a Conference to Cassel, which convened August 11th to 13th, 1868, and was attended by twenty-four Rabbis. The question of public worship occupied them almost exclusively. While they did not act on this question, they passed the resolution to hold in 1869 a Synod in Leipzig, which should be composed of Rabbis, Jewish scholars and representatives of Congregations. Geiger's influence can be seen in this resolution. He strongly opposed the idea of admitting to the Synod delegates only, who were elected by Congregations to the Synod. In an article: "The Conference in the Cassel"* he said: "The Conference did well to oppose the idea of electing delegates. Such a clause is useless, because even the decisions of delegates are not invested with legal power, and it is dangerous, because not the men of principle, but the men of mediocrity, would constitute the majority of the delegates. What? Just those sincere men, who are not satisfied to swim along with the current, but who, following the dictates of their conscience, are not afraid to do battle for their conviction, if needs be, should be kept away from the Synod? Should not the men of genuine firmness of character, who never flinch and never waver in their convictions, be entitled to take part in discussions, the very object of which is to strengthen principle and to vivify conviction?

"What is the use of all compromises, of all successes, if faint-heartedness is nurtured, and the living impulse of the spirit is killed?"

Thus the Synod at Leipzig was held.†

Geiger was not over-elated over the results of the Leipzig Synod, because over-cautiousness, timidity and want of courage characterized the assembly. He missed in it justly the spirit of the Rabbinical

---

*Zeitschrift. VI, 241-247. See also a very interesting article by Dr. Wechsler on the "Cassel Conference," Zeitschrift, VII, pp. 70-74.

†See my "Report on the First Synod of Leipzig, June 29th to July 4th, 1869, In the "Yearbook of the Central Conference of American Rabbis," pp. 100-111, (Cincinnati, 1891, Bloch Publishing Co.)

Conferences held in the forties. Comparing the Philadelphia Rabbinical Conference, which met November 3rd to 6th, 1869,* with the "Synod," Geiger candidly admits that the Leipzig Synod was not satisfactory,† that indecision was one of its great defects. He said that Philippsohn's bombastic resolution betrayed too ostentatiously a desire of creating a sensation and producing an effect outside of Judaism, but that it was inconsistent, devoid of force and principle, so far as the inner development of Judaism was concerned. It was even worse than valueless, inasmuch as it put upon the transactions the stamp of superficiality and shallowness. These declarations and the discussions on the divine worship showed a careful evasion of principles and burning questions. In short, the Synod was afraid to appear liberal, had the courage to recede a few steps, and was so bold as to appear conservative.

Of the Philadelphia Conference Geiger speaks very enthusiastically. "Here we meet with flesh of our flesh, spirit of our spirit. The men who controlled this Conference are Germans who crossed the ocean, who brought to America their knowledge and theological point of view, who still are intellectually nurtured from the sources of its spiritual life, but who in free America are enabled to a more consistent and more energetic activity. Here are names of sterling characters in their former homes in the fatherland, very dear, brave old friends. There is the worthy, considerate S. Adler, there is Einhorn, always aglow with youthful, noble zeal, who has already gone through his development in Schwerin and Pest, and feels now invigorated in the fresh air of America. There we find also the straightforward, candid Hirsch."‡

Just at that time Geiger was requested by the Frankfort Congregation, to publish a prayer-book.

---

*In a book on "Reform Judaism in America," we will have occasion to say more of this Conference.
†Zeitschrift, VIII, pp. 5-6 ff.
‡He was Rabbi in Philadelphia, at Knesseth Israel Congregation.

This work was done on the basis of the theses laid before the "Synod" and scientifically argued in an essay entitled: "Plan for a New Prayer-Book."* Dr. J. Auerbach and Raphael Kirchheim assisted Geiger in this work, which was however not finished in Frankfort, but in Berlin, where it was published in 1870 in two volumes under the title: "Israelitish Prayer-Book Second Edition, Berlin, L. Gerschel's Publishing-House."

But Geiger's literary activity in Frankfort was not exhausted with the question on worship. Aside from four sermons and "Congratulation to Zunz on the Occasion of his Seventieth Birthday," a very important historical document for the lives of both these great men,+ he contributed to Loew's "Ben Chananjah," to the "Zeitschrift der Deutsch - Morgenlaendischen Gesellschaft" on Syrian and Samaritan philology, and published his "Zeitschrift," where most of the articles emanated from his pen.

The lectures: "Judaism and its History," which were delivered by Geiger before selected audiences in the winter-months of 1863-64, and 64-65, are his most popular works. They were mercilessly attacked, particularly on account of his bold opinions on the "origin of Christianity," ideas which were never before expressed by a Jewish theologian. But even his opponents like Delitzsh‡ in Leipzig could not deny the originality and philosophical independence of his ideas, the stupendous scholarship stored up in these works and the brilliancy of his descriptions of the different epochs of Jewish history and literature. This work does not pretend to be a "History," but gives outlines of Jewish history and culture. The first volume contains "A Review of the New Labors on

*Zeitschrift: "Our service," VI, 1-21, which caused a highly interesting controversy between Geiger and Dr. Joel, his successor in Breslau." See Dr. Joel: " Zur Orienirung in der Cultusfrage," and Geiger: "Zu Schutz und Trutz," Zeitschrift, VII, pp. 1-59.
+ Posthumous Works, I, 296-308. Geiger calls Zunz his master and teacher. August, 1864.
‡ Jesus and Hillel, Leipzig, 1864.

the Life of Jesus," in which Renan's and D. F. Strauss's works on this subject are ably and strongly criticised. To the second volume is appended an "Open Letter to Prof. Dr. H. Holtzman."[*]

In 1867 Geiger published: "Salomon Gabirel and His Poems,"[+] which opened to the public the view into an entirely new realm of literature. We see here a great poet and gigantic mind wrestling with the unfathomable mysteries of life. Geiger's translations from the Hebrew into elegant German are masterpieces of poetical genius, and generally recognized as such.

In 1866 attempts were made by the friends of Reform in the Jewish Congregation of Berlin to induce Geiger to accept the position of Rabbi in that city. Berthold Auerbach's first letter to Geiger on this subject is dated February, 1866. But Geiger's enemies published a pamphlet, in which extracts from Geiger's "Urschrift" were put together without system and sense, in order to prove his heresy and unbelief. It took three years of incessant struggle and alert watchfulness on the side of the liberal and progressive party, before their purpose of electing Geiger as Rabbi of Berlin became realized (September, 1869). This result was not a little due to the labor of his friend, Dr. Aub, who in his "opinion" on the compatibility of free research with the office of Rabbi, given 1842, spoke of Geiger as "the first representative of the scientific theology of Judaism."[‡]

The only thing which induced Geiger to make a change from Frankfort to Berlin was the assurance given him that he would find in Berlin the long looked for opportunity to teach students of theology in the

---

[*] Breslau, 1865, Schletter's Verlag, 203 pages.

[+] Leipzig, Oscar Leiner, 148 pages.

[‡] See page 312 of this book, and Rabbin, Gutachten, II, p. 11 (Breslau, 1842). Dr. Aub was one of the teachers of the author of this book. My book: "The Self-criticism of the Jews" (Die Selbstkritik der Juden) Berlin, 1880, second edition, Leipzig, 1890, was dedicated to him.

"Hochschule fuer die Wissenschaft des Judenthums."* Without this firm promise he would not have accepted the position.

GEIGER IN BERLIN.

The general fear that Geiger would have to struggle hard with orthodoxy was, we are glad to say, not well grounded. Hence the few years still allotted him to live, were not embittered by unrelenting enemies. The circumstances in Berlin in 1870 were vastly different from those in Breslau in 1838.

Geiger entered upon his position in Berlin in February, 1870. His sermons and religious school were great favorites with the people. His sermons on the occasion of the celebration of the 200th anniversary of the Berlin Congregation† and on Kosch,‡ were published. He lectured alternately in both Synagogues of Berlin before inspired Congregations.

The Synod at Muenchen, 1870, could not be held on account of the German-French war, but two years later the second and last Synod was held at Augsburg, in which Geiger had taken great interest. This Synod pleased him better than the one at Leipzig, because a

---

*The Prussian government insisted on the change of the name "Hochschule" to that of "Lehranstalt" (Institute of Learning). We are informed by Prof. Lazarus, the founder of the Institution, that it is very prosperous, and that many students of the Breslau Seminary and Budapest "Rabbinats-Anstalt" come to Berlin to finish in the "Lehranstalt" their theological education. The students are called to positions before their studies are finished. See Geiger's letter to Prof. Lazarus, October 5th, 1869, also letter to the Directory of the Berlin Congregation, October 6th, 1869 (Posthumous Works, V, pp. 324, 325 and 326). To all those of my esteemed readers who enjoy this, my book, I can conscientiously say that without Geiger's acceptance of the Berlin Rabbinate, I would not have been so fortunate as to form Geiger's acquaintance and to become his enthusiastic disciple. For it was Geiger, who, by his sermons and writings, influenced me to leave the orthodox school of Dr. Hildesheimer in Berlin, and to espouse the cause of Reform. Geiger's removal from Frankfort to Berlin was therefore instrumental in the publication of this book.

†September 10th, 1871, Zeitschrift, IX, pp. 241-255.

‡At the coffin F J. L. Kosch, member of parliament.

more progressive spirit animated its members* and more important and radical resolutions were passed there.

Lazarus and Geiger published the transactions of the Augsburg Synod.† This was the last Synod which Geiger attended, and, alas, the last Jewish Synod in Germany.

Of Geiger's literary activity in Berlin we mention his pamphlet against the Prussian Ober-Kirchenrath on the "Conversion to Judaism." This great light of the Church had sent a Ukas to the pastors standing under his jurisdiction in which he ordered them in every case where a Christian embraced Judaism, to make known this "painful news" to their parishioners, to mention the name of the apostate, to give public expression to the feeling of mourning on account of this apostasy, and to admonish the Congregation "to pray that God may have mercy on the renegade and may let him recognize the error of his way." The Jewish Congregation of Berlin protested energetically against such a piece of mediaevalism and earned the applause of a number of enlightened Christians, who came out in a strong declaration against this intolerant act on the part of the church government. Geiger criticised in his brochure, not only the "Ukas" but the "general behavior of the church toward Judaism in modern times."

Aside from his "Zeitschrift "Geiger published the third volume of his: "Judaism and its History,"‡ which owed its existence to the lectures delivered in the winter-months of 1870 in Berlin.

---

*See Zeitschrift of W. U. L., VIII, 81-100. See also letter to Stern: "The retarding elements were absent, and a fresh, courageous spirit pervaded the Synod."

I refer to my resume of the resolutions of the Augsburg Synod in the Yearbook of the Central Conference of American Rabbis, pp. 111-117, (Cincinnati, 1891, Bloch Publishing Co.)

†Berlin, 1875, Louis Gerschel, 262 pages.

‡Judaism and its History, III vols. containing the history of the thirteenth to the sixteenth century, inclusive. Breslau, 1871, 200 pages.

But the crowning success of his Berlin career was the lectures from 1871 until his death, which he delivered before students, some of whom were Christian and some did not study theology. These lectures were first given in the Epraim-Veitel-Heine Institution of learning, together with D. D. Steinschneider, Lebrecht, Aub, and Haarbruecker. But since the establishment of the "Hochschule fuer die Wissenschaft des Juden-. thum's," they have been delivered there. The author of this book regards it as the greatest happiness of his life to have enjoyed the privilege of attending all these lectures in both Institutions. Only those who were so fortunate as to have this privilege* are capable of forming an idea of Geiger's power as a lecturer on Judaism. Those who only heard his sermons could not enter into the true being of the man. But in his lectures amidst enthusiastic students, who were inspired by the ideals of a science of Judaism, who had the ambition to labor in the cause of Reform-Judaism, to propagate his ideas, to continue his difficult, but sublime task, there he was in his element. Though sixty years old, he spoke like a man of twenty, his eye was aglow, the "Shekhina" seemed to rest on his face when he introduced us into the intricacies of Jewish history, literature, philosophy, and particularly of Biblical criticism. There we sat, spell-bound, listening, catching fire from his fire, and inspiration from his great mind. We made of course notes, but his lecture would become so interesting, his eloquence so magnetic that it was impossible to write, and when the bell rang admonishing us that the academic hour had passed, nobody was more sorry than we, his students, admirers and enthusiastic disciples. Other Professors of the "Hochschule" delivered also more or less instructive lectures, but from experience the author of this book can say, that it happened less often that one of the students missed a lecture of Geiger than one of the other Professors. The author of this book never

*There are only four in this country, Felix Adler, the author, of this book, Emil G. Hirsch and Sale.

appreciated better the full meaning of the words of Jeremiah: "My word is like the fire, and like a hammer, which splinters rocks," than after a lecture of Geiger. Alas for Judaism, that only such a short space of time was allotted to this great man for his work. With his death the "Hochschule" could exclaim: "My glory, my splendor, and my pride has departed." He himself considered these three years just on account of his activity in the "Hochschule" as the happiest of his life. No hour was too early, or too late, no weather was too hot or too cold for this work, for which he received no pay. In case of indisposition he requested his disciples to come to his house in order not to lose a lecture. He lectured at 6 o'clock in the morning and at 7 o'clock in the evening. He was always glad to hear the opinions of his students on different subjects, in connection with his lectures, no matter how erroneous these views were. He was free of the "Professorenduenkel" (conceit) so common among German Professors of Universities and among the Professors of the Breslau Seminary.*

We cannot even attempt to give here a synopsis of his lectures. The subjects of his lectures were: "The History of the Twelve Tribes," (1871), "Universal Introduction into the Science of Judaism," "Introduction into the Biblical Writings," "Pirke Abot"† and "Genesis." In a letter to Wechsler he speaks very enthusiastically about this work: "What is wanting in our days," he exclaims, "is able, young theologians with firm convictions. The 'Hochschule' aims to satisfy this want. We have a band of brave, enthusiastic students, and if material support could be given them, as they are recruited from the poorer classes, their number could be considerably increased. It is impossible for me to devote to this, my work, the

---

*Frankel and Graetz had the reputation of being proud and distant.

†"Ethics of the Fathers," philologically, historically and homiletically treated. All these lectures are published in the Posthumous Works, Vol. II, p. 1-216 and Vol. IV

time which I should like to devote to it. I lecture five
times during the week, * * and the preparation
for such scientific lectures demands a great deal of
time and labor. I would cheerfully give more lectures
but I cannot overtax myself."* "These lectures," he
writes to Stern, December 27th, 1872, "tax my time
to such an extent that I could hardly manage in the
last few months to answer a letter."† Whenever a
prominent man, particularly a good Reformer, died, he
felt keenly the los to the cause. So he writes to
Wechsler after the death of Dr. Mayer, of Stuttgart:
"He has accomplished much for his circle, and has
reached the goal of his life. But again I have to repeat with you the question, Where is the after-growth,
which will replace such men?" He deeply regretted
that the majority of the younger Rabbis were hostile,
or at least indifferent to the Reform-movement, because
they had no courage of their opinions.

After Luzatto's death he writes to M. A. Levy:‡
"Whenever a man dies in our day we stand perplexed,
because in the first place there are no men to replace
them, and secondly, because people want a man who,
however, should not be a man." It was for this reason
that he labored so hard for the "Hochschule," which
he thought would produce *men* for the Jewish pulpit.§
Now it must not be inferred from Geiger's enthusiastic
activity in the "Hochschule," that he favored the
method in which the Institution was conducted. Oh,
no. He objected in the first place to the management
of the "Hochschule" by a Curatorium (Board of Gov-
ernors). According to his idea of a Jewish theological
faculty, such Institute should be managed by the Professors only, and not by men standing outside. He
further did not consider mere lectures sufficient, but regarded seminary exercises of the students as a necessity.
He further objected to the principle of having Profes-

---

*Posthumous Works, V, p. 335, letter November 25th, 1872
†Ibidem, p. 256.
‡November 2d, 1865 Posthumous Works, V, p. 300.
§See also his letter to L. R. Bischoffsheim, ibid. pp. 346-353.

sors, representing opposite religious views, teach in one and the same institution. We can say from experience that this latter objection in particular was well justified. There was, for instance, the Professor of the Talmud, Dr. Loewy, a fanatic and zealot of the worst type, who spoke in the meanest, most ungentlemanly manner of Geiger to us, the students, and who went so far in his rudeness toward Geiger, that he never recognized him. Loewy is a disciple of Frankel and Graetz.

The following three mottoes of Geiger, which he wrote under his three pictures (Frankfort, 1839, Breslau, 1846 and 1857), give an insight into his ideals and aspiration.

1. "I have tried so far to harmonize the two different missions of author and Rabbi. I believe that I have not undertaken an unnatural union, and I patiently await the only authoritative verdict which the God of truth will render. To him my life and my aspiration remains consecrated."*

2. "Through knowledge of the past to the understanding of the present, through comprehension to belief."

3. "To draw from the past, to live for the present, to work for the future."

Geiger was an enthusiastic Rabbi, and prized this vocation higher than that of the author. Preaching was his favorite occupation, and the introduction of the least Reform in worship or practical life was a source of the greatest pleasure to him. The older he grew the greater became his love and enthusiasm for religion and Judaism, and therefore he labored so zealously and energetically for Reform as the only means to perpetuate the Jewish religion. But notwithstanding his very liberal ideas he practiced even those ceremonies which he most forcibly attacked in his writings.

He did so, because he did not want to give the enemies of Reform the satisfaction of saying that the Jewish Reform-movement is simply a question of con-

---

*Posthumous Works, I. p. 504.

venience.* He looked upon the movement from an idealistic point of view, and cheerfully offered sacrifices in its behalf so far as his convenience and pleasure were concerned. It was no doubt unpleasant for Geiger, who strongly opposed the dietary laws,† to take part in a social affair and to abstain from the food spread on the table, or travel long distances without the enjoyment of a decent meal. Still he lived up to the dietary laws, and had even to bear the sneers of his radical friends. He hated atheism and ridicule of religion, and was merciless in his criticism against scoffers. His mind was very pious and mild; he never missed saying a short German prayer after meals. His pen was very forcible in defense of what he considered right, but he was tolerant toward others who differed from him in their opinions. Envy and jealously he did not know. He was an optimist, who never despaired of the final victory of truth and justice over error and wrong. He always judged others favorably, and excused their shortcomings. He was charitable without making a show of it, knew how to touch the hearts, and moved even those who did not share his advanced views. His religious instruction in his school (Religions-Schule) was so animating that his pupils still speak of it.

His scientific and official activity, his intercourse with friends and his family-life, were the only pleasures for which he cared. Theater and amusements had little charm for him. He loved simplicity, comfort and the strictest regularity.

In the last few years of his life he felt really happy, occupying the most prominent Rabbinical position in the world, enjoying a scientific activity as Professor of a theological faculty, where he could mould the minds of future Rabbis, recognized and appreciated by the

---

*That orthodoxy did not learn much since that time, is proven by the fact that even to this day this argument is still its only weapon.

†See his letter to Zunz. "These dietary laws, so devoid of spirit and sense, and so hostile to sociability."

literary world,* and possessing love and strength to labor. Apart from this he was blessed with excellent health and good children, his sons being very prominent in their professions. Although sixty-four years old, Geiger had no gray hair, and could be seen at five o'clock every morning standing at his desk working. For he never sat down while studying. In a poem (of Aug. 7, Norderney 1871), Geiger prayed that he may never live to see the day when his mind and heart should cease to be active while his body is still unimpaired. His wish was fulfilled. October 22d he was as usually engaged in scientific labors, was in the best of humor, and went to bed cheerfuly. In the morning of Friday, October 23d, he was found dead in his bed. No trace of death-struggle was visible in his face; a paralytic stroke of the brain destroyed the labora'ory of the deep thinker. The heart which beat so warm for religion and science was still.†

The funeral took place October 26th, from the elegant new Berlin Synagogue at the Oranienburger Strasse. The Temple was illuminated, the pulpit draped in mourning, exotic plants filled every available nook. The mourning assembly made an impression not easily to be forgotten, not so much on account of its quantity, but of its quality. With a few exceptions,

---

*See Berthold Auerbach's description of Geiger's last birthday celebration, May 24th, 1874, in the "Gegenwart," 1874, p. 293, where Berthold Auerbach said in his toast, that the future historian would have to say that Abraham Geiger has done for judaism of the nineteenth century what Moses Mendelssohn has done for Judaism of the eighteenth century.

†The leading orthodox paper of Germany, "Israelit" Dr. of Lehman (Mainz), had the following announcement of Geiger's death: "An diesem Tage wurde ausgerottet die Person in Israel, die meinen Bund zerstoert hat" (On this day the person who has destroyed my covenant was cut off from Israel), to which Prof. Dernbourg, of Paris, in his necrologue on Geiger remarks as follows: " And thus they, the pious ones, have greeted his death with an exclamation of joy! A prince in Israel had fallen, and they clapped their hands and attempted to vilify the dead man, while they did not dare to look into the rigid face of the living. We turn away with disgust from this degrading spectacle, and with that contempt which he would have shown to such bacchanalias." (Jued. Zeitschrift, F. W. U. L. XI, p. 307).

the men who claimed literary distinction were present to show their last honor to the most distinguished Rabbi of the nineteenth century, to the man who has done more than any other man toward the work of denationalizing the Jews and toward creating a scientific Jewish Theology.

After the singing of a dirge by the choir, Dr. Aub, the life-long friend and colleague of Geiger, delivered the funeral oration, which moved the assembly to tears, and was considered the greatest effort of his life.* Rev. Dr. Goldsmidt of Leipzig spoke in the name of Geiger's disciples and followers, saying among other things, that while the number of his disciples who actually sat at his feet in Breslau, Frankfort and Berlin might not be very large, almost every modern Rabbi of this century belongs more or less to his pupils, as he has been by his epochal writings the teacher of teachers. Rev. Dr. Ungerleider, Rabbinats-Assessor, preached at the grave. The Congregations of Breslau, Wiesbaden and Frankfort were represented by delegations. Rev. Dr. N. Bruell, of Frankfort; Dr. Vogelstein, of Stettin, and the author of this book, then Professor at the "Samson-Realschule" at Wolfenbuettel, were among the Rabbis outside of Berlin who hastened to Geiger's funeral. In May, 1875, the Jewish Congregation at Berlin unveiled the monument erected to the memory of Geiger, the inscription of which reads as follows:

"*The Jewish Congregation of Berlin to its never-to-be-forgotten teacher and leader, Abraham Geiger.*"

Eighteen years have elapsed since Geiger's death, but the position of Geiger is not yet filled. The Congregation of Berlin has since that time elected several "Rabbinats-Assessors," but no—Rabbi.

Since that time in Germany the Jewish Reform-movement has gone backward rather than forward. No Rabbinical Conference or Synod in the interest of Reform-Judaism has been held there since Geiger's

---

*While Aub was a great theologian, he was not prominent as preacher.

death. With the exception of the Weekly published by the author of this book from 1876 to 1881, no periodical advocating Reform-Judaism has been published. Whenever Rabbis met in Conference, it was for insignificant material interests of the profession. Germany, the cradle of Reform-Judaism, has since Geiger's death lost its prestige. German Judaism of to-day presents to the impartial observer the sad spectacle of religious indifference, atheism, hypocrisy, Jesuitism and most absurd orthodoxy, in short, materialism of the worst type. There are now more cases of apostasy among the German Jews than ever before since the forties.

But Reform-Judaism is no longer dependent on Germany. America has entered upon the heritage of German Reform-Judaism. In fact Reform-Judaism in this country is nothing more and nothing less than German Reform-Judaism, "bone of its bone, and flesh of its flesh."

The future of Reform-Judaism in this country is most promising, and from the results already accomplished we may gather the cheering hope of still greater things yet to come.

INDEX.

ANALYTICAL INDEX.